D0322574

Music Therapy and Autism
Across the Lifespan

of related interest

**Early Childhood Music Therapy and Autism
Spectrum Disorder, Second Edition**
Supporting Children and Their Families
Edited by Petra Kern and Marcia Humpal
ISBN 978 1 78592 775 1
eISBN 978 1 78450 688 9

Collaborations Within and Between Dramatherapy and Music Therapy
Experiences, Challenges and Opportunities in Clinical and Training Contexts
Edited by Amelia Oldfield and Mandy Carr
Foreword by Rebecca Applin Warner
ISBN 978 1 78592 135 3
eISBN 978 1 78450 402 1

Tuning In Music Book
Sixty-Four Songs for Children with Complex Needs and Visual Impairment
to Promote Language, Social Interaction and Wider Development
Adam Ockelford
ISBN 978 1 78592 517 7
eISBN 978 1 78450 955 2

Tuning In Cards
Activities in Music and Sound for Children with Complex Needs and
Visual Impairment to Foster Learning, Communication and Wellbeing
Adam Ockelford
Illustrated by David O'Connell
ISBN 978 1 78592 518 4

Music, Language and Autism
Exceptional Strategies for Exceptional Minds
Adam Ockelford
ISBN 978 1 84905 197 2
eISBN 978 0 85700 428 4

Music Therapy and Autism Across the Lifespan

A SPECTRUM OF APPROACHES

Edited by Henry Dunn, Elizabeth Coombes,
Emma Maclean, Helen Mottram and Josie Nugent

Foreword by Professor Adam Ockelford,
University of Roehampton, United Kingdom

Jessica Kingsley *Publishers*
London and Philadelphia

First published in 2019
by Jessica Kingsley Publishers
73 Collier Street
London N1 9BE, UK
and
400 Market Street, Suite 400
Philadelphia, PA 19106, USA

www.jkp.com

Copyright © Jessica Kingsley Publishers 2019

All rights reserved. No part of this publication may be reproduced in any
material form (including photocopying, storing in any medium by electronic
means or transmitting) without the written permission of the copyright owner
except in accordance with the provisions of the law or under terms of a licence
issued in the UK by the Copyright Licensing Agency Ltd. www.cla.co.uk or in
overseas territories by the relevant reproduction rights organisation, for details
see www.ifrro.org. Applications for the copyright owner's written permission to
reproduce any part of this publication should be addressed to the publisher.

Warning: The doing of an unauthorised act in relation to a copyright work
may result in both a civil claim for damages and criminal prosecution.

Library of Congress Cataloging in Publication Data
A CIP catalog record for this book is available from the Library of Congress

British Library Cataloguing in Publication Data
A CIP catalogue record for this book is available from the British Library

ISBN 978 1 78592 311 1
eISBN 978 1 78450 622 3

Printed and bound in Great Britain

Accompanying video files can be downloaded from
www.jkp.com/voucher using the code MTLIFESPAN

Contents

Foreword 7
Adam Ockelford

Acknowledgements. 9

Introduction 11
Henry Dunn

Prelude: The Unanswered Question. 15
Auriel Warwick

Part 1: Improvisational Approaches

1. Clinical Trials: Are Music Therapists Deluding Themselves?. . . 35
   Amelia Oldfield, Laura Blauth, Johanna Finnemann and Órla Casey

2. Evolving a Contemporary Psychoanalytically Informed
   Relational Music Therapy with Children with High-Functioning
   Autism in Specialist School Placements 57
   Joy Gravestock

3. 'Fight It Jake! Fight It!' The Ethics of Encouragement with
   Clients with an Autistic Spectrum Condition 77
   Robin Bates

4. Musical Interaction Therapy (MIT) for Children with Autistic
   Spectrum Conditions (ASCs): Underlying Rationale, Clinical
   Practice and Research Evidence 97
   Dawn Wimpory and Elise Gwilym

5. Group Clinical Improvisation as a Practice of Ritual and
   Connection for Young People with Autistic Spectrum
   Conditions. 137
   Becky White

6. Shared Experience: Learning from Other Modalities in
   Therapeutic Work with an Adult with an Autistic Spectrum
   Condition 155
   Alastair Robertson

Part 2: Collaborative Approaches

7. Music Therapy with Children with Autistic Spectrum
    Conditions and Their Families 179
    Josie Nugent

8. How Do Music Therapists Share? Exploring Collaborative
    Approaches in Educational Settings for Children with Autistic
    Spectrum Conditions. 197
    Emma Maclean and Claire Tillotson

9. Finding a Place: Context-Based Music Therapy in a Transitional
    Centre for Children with Autistic Spectrum Conditions 227
    Kate Fawcett

10. A Team Approach to Supporting Mark's Journey to Increased
    Social Engagement: Music Therapy Work with a Young Man
    With Autism. 251
    Cindy-Jo Morison

Part 3: Music Therapy Approaches Connected with Autistic Identity and Culture

11. Voice and the Autistic Self: An Exploration into How Non-
    Verbal Voicework in Music Therapy Can Support Intersubjective
    Relatedness 271
    Tina Warnock

12. Valuing Neurodiversity: A Humanistic, Non-Normative Model
    of Music Therapy Exploring Rogers' Person-Centred Approach
    with Young Adults with Autism Spectrum Conditions 297
    Beth Pickard

13. Self-Realisation in Music Therapy: Developing Insight into the
    Young Autistic Person's Sense of Self in the Quest for Wholeness
    Through a Synthesis of Music Therapy, Psychosynthesis and a
    Developing Sense of Self 331
    Peter Whelan

    Postlude: Music Therapy and Autism Across the Lifespan 355
    Elizabeth Coombes and Emma Maclean

    *Appendix 1: An example of integrating ideas from music therapy
    into classroom music making* 373

    Contributors to the Book 377

    Subject Index. 385

    Author Index. 391

Foreword

With one or two notable exceptions, music has tended to be under-represented in the broad sweep of recent research pertaining to the wide range of interventions that are intended to support those who are on the autism spectrum. At the same time, a target-driven education system in the UK has led to an undue emphasis on cognitive outcomes for all children, including those with additional needs. Hence this fascinating new book is particularly welcome, tackling, as it does, issues that can affect people on the autism spectrum across the lifespan: emotional regulation, wellbeing, an anchored notion of self in relation to other, feelings of empathy and a sense of fulfilment through creative artistic expression.

How is it that music, which is no more than abstract patterns in sound, has the capacity to promote an awareness of self, to foster emotional literacy and to facilitate social interaction? It is because music is a language beyond words, whose sequences of notes are free to convey pure emotion, unfettered by the need for semantic understanding. The sense of music can be grasped through pure exposure: its meanings are self-evident to us all, including those on the autism spectrum. Hence, to those, like music therapists, who have open ears and a willingness to engage with others, music offers a means of reaching out beyond the prejudices and confines of neurotypicality to children and adults who exhibit different ways of thinking.

Beyond this, since many of the abilities required for musical understanding stem from more general cognitive attributes, music has the power to promote wider development. For example, beneath the recognition of music's universal self-imitating structures lies the notion of 'cause and effect' – an awareness that one thing can act on another to effect change. This line of thinking extends to people too: if I copy the sounds that you make, then I allow you to exert an influence on me. And I must in some respects *be like you*. The emotions that I experience as I make sounds like yours may be the same as the emotions that you experience. And the process is reciprocal. If you imitate me, then you are allowing me to affect what you do, and to a degree you must understand me, must know how I feel, must even have a sense what it is like to be me. So it is that the music that clients and their therapists bring to sessions is uniquely placed to bind them together across the spectrum of neurodiversity.

Professor Adam Ockelford,
University of Roehampton

Acknowledgements

We would like to thank the authors who contributed to this book for sharing their clinical approaches with us; Professor Adam Ockelford for his Foreword; Jessica Kingsley Publishers for supporting this project; and, most importantly, all the people on the autistic spectrum who, through their work with us, have taught us so much about themselves and ourselves.

Introduction

HENRY DUNN

In 2008 I set up the Autistic Spectrum Conditions Network for the British Association for Music Therapy. The network was formed to share knowledge and resources between music therapists who worked with people on the autistic spectrum, and to act as a contact point for people outside our profession who wanted to learn more about our work. We had meetings to which we invited a variety of speakers from within the music therapy profession, such as Amelia Oldfield, Jackie Robarts and the late Tony Wigram. We also invited speakers from other related fields, such as Adam Ockelford, Professor of Music and Education at the University of Roehampton, who kindly offered to write a Foreword for us, and Rita Jordan, Professor in Autism Studies at the School of Education, University of Birmingham. During the early years of the network I began to think about the possibility of a publication focusing on music therapy and autism in the United Kingdom, as there seemed to be a gap in the autism literature in terms of giving a voice to the wide diversity of practice happening across the lifespan. This formed the basis of a discussion at a network meeting at the University of Roehampton, at which Adam Ockelford also spoke. It therefore seemed very appropriate that he provide the Foreword when the book came to fruition.

The project continued to develop in my mind until 2016, when I took the step of approaching Jessica Kingsley Publishers to see if they would be interested in this potential publication. They were very enthusiastic, and asked me to submit a full proposal. Realising that it was not something I could work on alone, I put out a request for co-editors. I was keen to recruit editors from all four countries of the United Kingdom, given the focus of the book, and have been very fortunate to be able to do this. Josie Nugent is the co-editor based in Northern Ireland; Emma Maclean is based in Scotland; Elizabeth Coombes is based in Wales; and Helen Mottram, like me, is based in England. This then made it more likely that we would have chapter submissions from each country, as my co-editors could encourage potential contributors from their areas.

We then put out a request for abstracts, and put together a full proposal which, to our delight, was accepted by Jessica Kingsley Publishers. We focused on three themes that emerged in the abstracts, though there are overlaps between them. These are: Improvisational Approaches, Collaborative Approaches and Approaches Connected with Autistic Identity and Culture. In these sections the diversity of music therapy practice is shown and celebrated, matching the diversity of the autistic spectrum. The authors have a variety of experience, both in terms of their workplaces and the length of their careers.

Alongside continued efforts to increase our knowledge about autistic spectrum conditions from a medical and scientific perspective, there is a growing sense of an 'autistic community', where voices and experiences are shared. The internet has been a great help in this, as many people on the autistic spectrum can find face-to-face contact difficult, and because it opens the community up to a global audience. Websites such as Wrong Planet,[1] Ambitious About Autism[2] and the National Autistic Society's community pages[3] have sprung up to support this growing sense of shared identity. Within the arts, there is a website called Awe in Autism,[4] set up by violin virtuoso Laura Nadine, who is herself on the autistic spectrum. This celebrates the artistic talents of people on the autistic spectrum, with links to the performers' own websites and performances.

It has been important, we feel, to include the voices of the people we work with, and those around them, in this publication, describing the musical exchanges and participation in music therapy sessions alongside informal and formal feedback and some use of measurement tools and research processes. This lends greater authenticity to what is written, helping practitioners to ground theory in clinical practice and to tailor clinical practice to the needs of people with autistic spectrum conditions across the lifespan.

---

1   www.wrongplanet.net
2   www.ambitiousaboutautism.org.uk
3   www.community.autism.org.uk
4   www.aweinautism.org

We believe that this publication showcases the way that music therapy is able to respond to the uniqueness of the individual and the great diversity within the autistic spectrum, in a way that offers respect and value for each person as they are. As you read on, you will begin to experience the many ways authors demonstrate therapeutic and personal attitudes, sensitive musical and verbal responses that seek to engage with different communications, both musical and non-musical, and an overall desire to relate deeply to their clients in a way that helps them cope, participate and grow. We have chosen to use the term 'autistic spectrum conditions', as it reflects the diversity of conditions on the spectrum, and feels more respectful than 'disorder', with its implication that autism is something that should be cured and is innately wrong. Our hope is that this book will be informative, helpful and inspiring, whether you are a music therapist, health, education or social care professional, a person on the autistic spectrum, a family that contains one or more people on the spectrum, or someone with an interest in autistic spectrum conditions.

Prelude: The Unanswered Question

AURIEL WARWICK

Gentle merging and swirling patterns of sounds from the strings – atmospheric, mesmerising and unworldly. Suddenly, the mistiness is interrupted by a trumpet call – clear and penetrating, at once discordant yet somehow making sense. BBC Radio 3 was on as usual in our house and I had come into the sitting room without knowing what this music was. I was transfixed and had to wait to hear what it was. I had heard some of Charles Ives' (1874–1954) music before, with clashing bands and dissonances but nothing like this. The piece was called 'The Unanswered Question' (Ives 1908). As I reflected on the impact it had made, I felt an identity with it, relating it to the effect on me of working with children on the autistic spectrum: the sense of not knowing, together with the challenge of how to relate to the enigma of the condition.

At this time, I was very involved in clinical work, specialising with such children. When I was writing my first paper on work with a boy with an autistic spectrum condition to present to the World Congress for Music Therapy in Paris in 1983, I came across a quote which made a similar impression to the Charles Ives piece. This was from Henry Thoreau, a 19th-century American essayist, poet and philosopher, in his book, *Walden* (2016, p.175): 'If a man does not keep pace with his companions, perhaps it is because he hears a different drummer. Let him step to the music he hears, however measured or far away.' These words, to me, embody the essence of therapy with such children. The influences of both the words and the music have remained with me throughout a long career, beginning in 1972 when I was appointed as the first full-time music therapist for children with special needs in the UK by the Oxfordshire Education Authority. Prior to my training, I had worked for a short time as a music specialist in secondary education both in New Zealand, where I'd grown up and studied music, and in England.

In my initial naivety, I thought I was confident about working in the education setting: after all, I had been a teacher and had some understanding of how the education system worked. While that was true, I wasn't so prepared for the task of creating my own identity as a therapist rather than a teacher and my role in the school setting. This was shortly after the new Education Act (Handicapped Children) 1970, giving all children the right to education, and so the former junior training centres under the health sector became schools within the education sector. Inevitably, initial referrals were made on the assumption that Child D would benefit from music therapy because they liked music. I found I had to stick firmly to my premise that I was using music as a tool for communication, presenting an opportunity for the child to express himself and discover an identity through a medium which did not have to rely on words. Over the years, the understanding of who I was, as far as heads, teachers, assistants and other therapists were concerned, improved but needed constant reinforcement. The only support I had was from termly meetings with the county music advisor who had set up the post – a man who fervently believed in the power of music as a therapeutic tool. The pathologies of the children with whom I worked were varied at the outset, but, as time went on, more children referred had autistic spectrum conditions. I strongly suspect that the main reason was, although they appeared to respond positively to music, to have them out of the classroom for half an hour so that the teachers could give more time to other equally needy children who were not so demanding of time and attention.

With hindsight, at the time of my training, the practice of music therapy was much more prescriptive than it is now and there was a strong sense within the profession of trying to find an identity, with the frictions that inevitably come with that searching. Whose method was 'the right one'? It is a tribute to the profession that we have grown through those teething pains and can better acknowledge and accept differences, some of which depend on the client group – and the therapists working with them. Change and evolution is important for each and every therapist.

The remainder of this book will concentrate on the sharing of clinical practice and experience. As I have been retired for some years, I shall not be describing, as in case studies, the development of the unique relationships formed with children who cover the enormous range of the conditions – from the very disturbed non-verbal to those described as high-functioning or diagnosed with Asperger's syndrome who taught me so much about their world. What I want to share with the reader are reflections on how I developed as a therapist and the changes I had to make in attitude, approach and how I related to these complex people, covering an age range from early childhood through to young adults.

I shall never forget the first and vital change I had to make – and I'm thankful that it came during my first year of practice. It taught me the dangers of making assumptions, which may be based on others' perception of a particular child. This was a six-year-old girl, referred because 'No one knows what to do with her' (a staff member's comment). She was non-verbal and lived in a world of her own. It was very difficult for school staff to reach her but maybe music would. There was a strong emphasis in music therapy training on improvisation and so, true to that method, I had all the instruments at my disposal displayed for this little girl, whom I shall call Gillian, to choose from. However, she showed no interest in them at all but chose to stand at the window, gazing out, seemingly oblivious to any reaching out to her on my part. As the weeks went on, I felt more of a failure. Why wouldn't she respond and what was I doing wrong? I might also add: what effect was my increasing anxiety having on her in her self-absorbed state? After ten or so weeks, I went to the head teacher to share these anxieties with her and to question whether music therapy was right for this child. The head was sympathetic and agreed that I should end the therapy at Christmas. With an end in sight and thinking about how to include Gillian in the ending, four weeks away, I was able to let go of some of the frustration of working with someone who couldn't or wouldn't respond in any way. At the beginning of the third week before the end of the term, after the 'Hello' song, I strummed two E minor chords on the guitar and began to improvise in song my feelings of sadness that I couldn't reach her. This was spontaneous: I felt I had nothing to lose at this point. The remainder of the session continued as usual where the total input was from me, singing and playing on the instruments, matching her 'far away' mood. The turn-around happened the following week, the penultimate week of the therapy. The conscious part of me had forgotten the improvised release of my own feelings of the week before – but I found myself strumming two E minor chords again. Suddenly, a small, pure-sounding voice vocalised the melody I'd used the previous week. Gillian was in her usual place, gazing out through the window but there was the sense of a dramatic connection. For me, this was the sound of that trumpet call in 'The Unanswered Question'. I realised that I should never assume that just because someone wasn't responding by vocalising or playing in a conventional way, it meant that there was no response. It reminded me that music is experienced on many levels. It may be expressed through interaction with the therapist but it is also receptive. I reported what had happened to the head – and the music therapy continued for a further year. Gillian began to respond vocally, but always avoiding eye contact. She must have felt able to do this without pressure from me that she should be doing something along the lines of what I thought was conventional music therapy. I was beginning to learn how to be with her and to accept who she was. Later it was reported to me that following each successive session, she was put on the toilet – where she would sing. Message to all therapists: responses may happen when and where you least expect them!

Learning how to be with clients, whether on the autistic spectrum or not, must always be present for the therapist. It can be as simple as just being within the boundaries of the four walls of the therapy room. For the inexperienced, newly qualified therapist, this can be difficult. There is the danger of trying to do too much and sometimes putting unconscious expectations on the client which are too much to bear. People with autistic spectrum conditions can be very seductive and clever at manipulating others to the point of an unhealthy merging between client and therapist, beyond the point of making an initial connection. Throughout my career, I've found it necessary to be aware that therapy is about the building of a trusting relationship between four separate beings – or more in the case of group therapy.

During the final years of my time with the Education Authority, I was privileged to be part of the team known as the Chinnor Autistic Units, started by a forward-thinking head of a primary school in Chinnor and a returning-to-work teacher whom he called on to tutor a challenging child diagnosed as being on the autistic spectrum. The head teacher was concerned that the child should not be excluded from the mainstream school. The teacher he employed was Sheila Coates who made her mark in Oxfordshire and beyond as someone creative, who did not bow to the conventions of what education should be. She strongly believed in therapeutic education and was responsible for having Juliette Alvin, one of the pioneers of music therapy in Britain, as the first music therapist working in the unit. I heard Sheila and John Richer, clinical psychologist in the paediatrics department of the John Radcliffe Hospital in Oxford, present their work during an in-service training day, and was so impressed with their work in therapeutic education that I was determined to work with them, should the opportunity arise. A couple of years later, it did, and for me it opened the way towards working at a deeper psychotherapeutic level and being part of a team who shared similar philosophy and objectives. As time went on and the units expanded into other parts of the county, more of my time was taken up with children referred to the units, which eventually became a service, with highly trained staff also doing outreach work.

Learning how to be with someone with an autistic spectrum condition is as varied an exercise as the number of people the therapist is working with. I found myself reflecting more and more on what the autistic condition might feel like. How different was the sound of that other drummer? I began to think about how relevant society's current tendency to put people in convenient boxes is – which can so easily lose sight of the uniqueness of us all. To what extent was I guilty of this in my therapeutic approach and was I missing some aspect of the client's persona which I should be working *with*, rather than ignoring? For each one of us, there is a time when we may have been rigid with fear or shock, or highly anxious in a new or strange situation to the extent that we feel overwhelmed with sensory overload. Either we may withdraw to an inner place within us if unable to remove ourselves physically from that situation, or else lash out with inappropriate behaviour in the heat of the moment. How much more difficult it must be for many of our clients.

I also wonder whether we do our clients an injustice by being over-conscious of the condition itself. While we do need to understand the diagnostic criteria, as therapists we must never forget that we are dealing with a person rather than a condition. When newly qualified, I was more overwhelmed by the condition rather than recognising that the condition isn't the whole person. One of my more challenging clients was a nine-year-old boy who was referred to me a second time, following a break – I'd worked with him as a six-year-old during a research project for a psychologist's PhD. He was verbal but used his own form of communication via his favourite television programmes. It baffled the teaching staff until they began to understand that he was describing his own situations in his life story through particular media characters who represented those close to him. During this second course of therapy, he wouldn't interact with me through turn-taking, which he had done when he was younger. Instead, he used a tambour or tambourine to beat while he told his story. He didn't want me to be a passive listener but to improvise on the piano to illustrate the emotional content of what he was saying, particularly his anxieties. I had never been invited to participate in this way before and I was fascinated by it. However, I was also aware of the dangers of the merging I have already mentioned. It would be too comfortable to be drawn in rather than remaining as someone separate but with empathy. As soon as I felt the relationship was sufficiently stable, I took the plunge (that's what it felt like!) and began to sing my interpretations of what might be happening for him: to bring the fantasy into reality. I discovered that if I misinterpreted what he was declaiming, he was able to correct me in a very reasoned way, sometimes without needing the screen of the characters but referring to the actual people they represented. If I stopped, he demanded that I should continue at the piano. It felt as though he needed the continuity of my improvising as a foundation to his thought and speech processes, rather as someone with Parkinson's disease may be able to move more easily to music. In a similar way, a few years later, I was working with a teenage girl who liked to improvise with me in piano duet. As we played, she talked in a more natural way than without the music. Music is about feeling, and as an accompaniment, it seemed to be less of a problem for these young people to express something of themselves. Rhythm and structure within music is an important part of this. I often wished that I could understand what was happening to the neural pathways in the brain while this was happening. What might be significantly different from the neurotypical brain?

When the client has no expressive speech, the therapist is working in the unknown, and in the early stages of my work there was always the uneasy feeling of whether I'd got it right or not. Trusting the gut feeling is a huge learning curve for any therapist while being prepared to acknowledge that one might be wrong. At the same time, I found it important to take the time and opportunity to talk to teachers and key classroom assistants. It was a positive two-way process, each being able to inform the other while respecting the issue of confidentiality. Making appropriate boundaries was important when I was only in a particular setting once a week. I think my awareness of confidentiality issues was too rigid when I first started, until I realised that some sharing of ideas and questions about a child were an important part of being good enough at my job. I could gain important information from a teacher about how the child was in class and how they reacted in certain situations while, in turn, I could advise about how the child was in the music therapy room without being specific and why less challenging behaviour was demonstrated. There were some raised eyebrows when I showed, through video or audio clips, that a different aspect of the child's personality was revealed during the music therapy session. One example of this was when a very withdrawn girl, who was very passive in the classroom, sparked into life when drumming with me on bongo drums. Here was the discovery of a feisty young lady who had plenty to say for herself through her drumming and positive interaction, using a medium which didn't depend on speech. This was enjoyable for both of us.

Change in approach depends on the increase of understanding or an altering of perception. I found this often happened after attending a child's annual educational review. Sometimes this took place out of school hours, where all professionals from other services concerned with the child were invited to present a report where relevant. I needed to be proactive about this in some instances. I might be in a school only once a week; however, I was determined that a report from me should have its place in the overall context of the child's care while raising the profile of music therapy. As parents were also invited, here was an opportunity for me to meet them and to hear their side of the story – their anxieties, frustrations and hopes for the future of their child. Sometimes a parent wouldn't or couldn't come but those who did made the multi-disciplinary team feel more complete, where problems could be talked through with suggestions made for management as an example. Music therapists are trained to work with what the client presents. Therefore I was not constrained by specific aims and targets imposed by the education system. As my reports tended to emphasise what the child was able to do rather than what he couldn't, the feedback from parents was how much they appreciated a more positive assessment of their child. There was a gain for me, too. I often pondered at some length on the changes which took place during the sessions immediately following the review. I wasn't conscious of changing the way of working with that child. But the change in my perception of a broader picture beyond the school did seem to open up new pathways of communication with the child. Maybe the shared music revealed a greater depth of understanding. I would like to think so.

In 1986, I was invited by a clinical psychologist with a keen interest in music therapy to take part in research for her PhD. Pierrette Mueller wanted to study mother/child/therapist interaction, taking music therapy into the family home. I was happy to take part as this also interested me – but not without feeling apprehensive at the same time. This, without doubt, was the steepest learning curve of my career! To the best of my knowledge, such a project had never been done in the UK before. Each mother taking part in the programme was involved in an activity with her child for 15 minutes before music therapy and again for 15 minutes after so that the mother/child/therapist interaction could be measured. When she was with her child in music therapy, she was not there as an observer but as a participant. In some cases, the mums felt inadequate when improvisation took place. If I were to repeat the exercise in similar circumstances, I would have two to four sessions with each mother to give them some experience of playing and singing in a spontaneous way. Under the strictures of the research, I was not allowed to give any instruction, either before or during the period. I was not happy about this as there was the potential for making the mum feel at a loss. For my part, the challenge was how to involve mum so that she didn't feel this way – real empathy needed here in a way I hadn't experienced before. Initially, it needed to be fun. As the entire proceedings were filmed, the presence of the video camera was inhibiting for the adults and that included me. It did improve as time went on, but there were still a few mothers who said they found the camera intrusive. The children were more used to the video camera as it was often used in the classroom.

The research period was divided into two halves, where one group involved mother and child in the music session and the second group was the child with me alone. In the second half, the groups switched over so that in the second group the mothers were involved and in the first they were not. As time went on, I became more comfortable and accepting of the situation, and therefore more relaxed. However, there were two mothers for whom I felt concern as it became clear just how difficult they found their relationships with their children, not only in the therapy session. Both were in the first group. I was not only the therapist for the child but also had a responsibility towards mum, who needed caring for as well. I was constrained by the non-directive role I was asked to play during the research. I discussed this with Pierrette who took the problem to her supervisors. They agreed that at the end of the research, I should have one or two sessions with the two mothers again present with the children as they had been at the beginning. During the second phase, when they weren't present in the therapy session, these mothers were still in the house, so could hear the musical interaction. Both mothers agreed to the additional sessions. My apprehensions returned. However, we were very pleasantly surprised to find that only one session for each was necessary. Something had happened over the intervening time when mother wasn't in the music therapy session (but still involved in the 15-minute activity before and after, playing a game, reading to the child or drawing). Each mother found it much easier to relate to her child through playing and singing, which had been so difficult before. This was an unexpected and positive outcome. Increasing familiarity with the concept of the research which must have felt so alien at the outset, even though taking part was their choice, seemed to have helped. Perhaps the playfulness of the interaction, without a target in sight, was a factor as well as mother being in a situation, apart from the music therapy, where she was required to do an activity of choice with her child before and after music. What was significant for me was experiencing the dynamics within the family home and how to be accepted there. Pierrette, the camera and I were the intruders. I also found it difficult in the beginning to observe the times when the child responded more positively to me than to mum – I felt guilty. The joy was when the mothers developed enough confidence to take over some of my role. Maternal involvement in music therapy can have a positive outcome.

As a musician, I always had high expectations of myself. As a therapist, I could not project such high expectations on other people. Too often I have found that many professionals can have a high-handed approach to the problems of those they work with, whether in education, health or other disciplines. Working with families helped me to realise that where an outsider might consider the resolution of a problem to be a simple one, it may not be so for that family or individual. Learning to be non-judgmental is an important aspect in how to be with another person and how to be in tune with that person. There were times when I didn't find this easy in the early days. When I could let go, it was liberating, allowing me to be open to the client's experience at that time while keeping a sense of my own identity. People with autistic spectrum conditions, where the sense of self is so vulnerable, may try to become part of the therapist with whom they feel safe and contained. There is a danger of this becoming too comfortable for both, and there comes a point at stages of the therapy when the therapist must be strong and intuitive enough to challenge and encourage the client that they can take a step beyond that safety, particularly where therapy is concerned with the recognition and expression of difficult emotional states.

I spent three years working with a boy who was referred to me because of his high level of anxiety and problems with understanding emotions. He was verbal and enjoyed music lessons in the mainstream primary where the unit was situated. He was keen to have his individual sessions but during the first session I began to wonder whether music therapy would be appropriate. I found myself being lectured – a blow-by-blow account of what each instrument was called, what it was made of, how it was played and what it sounded like. I had to sit and listen. I felt totally controlled. It would be too easy for any therapy to move into an educational mode and it was very clear that this child was so anxious that he could not cope with scary concepts like feelings. I needed to begin where he was, while encouraging him to venture out from the safe place he'd put himself into. This was a time of waiting with intense listening on my part. After something like 15 minutes, gaps in the narrative appeared, giving me the opportunity to interject with chords on the piano. 'Michael' stopped, put down the instrument he was demonstrating and came over to stand beside me at the piano.

There was a short silence before I initiated a single atonal chord to which he responded with one of his own. Communication had begun. At the end of the session, he sang one 'Goodbye' and replied to my question that he would like to come next week. At the beginning of the second session, there was a short period after the exchange of 'Hello' when he reverted to lecturing mode, but he became more interested in coming to play improvised duets at the piano. He was more relaxed and was able to share his innate musicality which was a joy to work with. In time, he initiated playing other instruments, but was rather wary of the drum and cymbal. I was not allowed to play them until he felt safe enough with me. It didn't take Michael long to realise that these instruments were excellent vehicles for releasing powerful emotions even though he was not prepared to acknowledge them verbally. I thought in depth about this and took the questions to my clinical supervision with a child psychotherapist, also a musician. Sooner or later I would need to challenge Michael's fear of what he was feeling. A breakthrough came about a year into therapy when he stormed into his session and let rip on the drum and cymbal, supported by solid chords from me at the piano. He stopped and looked at me. I said, quietly, that that was angry music – and he was angry. He shouted at me, 'I'm not angry!' and beat furiously again. When he stopped, I repeated that he was angry. He seemed to crumple and, for me, the penny dropped. This child was equating being angry with being bad. I talked to him about this and tried to explain as simply as possible that anger in itself wasn't bad; it was how anger was coped with – and the drum and cymbal provided a good way for expressing such strong feelings. He looked puzzled at first but this was followed by relief. This was significant in that the therapy could move in the direction of why he was referred in the first place. This doesn't mean that the change was immediate – it certainly wasn't – but the music therapy session became a safer place for him to explore and own his feelings.

At the end of the second year, there was a three-month break in Michael's therapy when I spent time in New Zealand. It was essential to prepare him for the break while letting him know that we would continue when I was back. He wanted to know where New Zealand was and went and found it in an atlas when he got back to class. He didn't appear to be upset by the imminent break until the final session before I left. I could hear him stamping down the corridor to the music room. There was no greeting but furious beating on the drum and cymbal instead. I was shouted at – 'You're going to New Zealand and I don't like it when you go to New Zealand!' Gradually, he calmed until, just before the 'Goodbye' song, which was always improvised, he said, very quietly, that he was sad that I was going away. This was the first time that sadness was expressed verbally. It was an important shared moment but I also felt a rush of delight that he was able to tell me how he felt.

Having the opportunity of working with someone as responsive as Michael is always rewarding for a therapist. However, there are many days when the therapist feels as though they are floundering, particularly when working with a non-verbal client. There are many 'unanswered questions' and it takes experience to gain some insight into how it is for the client with an autistic spectrum condition. What has been most helpful in recent years is the amount published by people with the condition. To me, this has been far more valuable than any research paper: I need the individual, human aspect which I may then be able to relate to a particular client. One of the early writers and speakers in my clinical experience was Donna Williams. Here was a very intelligent woman who was prepared to explain what life was like for her during both childhood and adulthood. I found her first book, *Nobody Nowhere* (Williams 1992), revealing and helpful.

CASE STUDY: DAVID

David was five when he was referred – a highly anxious small boy who would prefer to curl into a ball like a hedgehog. Indeed, I was warned that he could do this when moving from one place to another. His classroom was at the other end of the school campus from the music therapy room. He was ready enough to hold my hand to walk but as soon as we crossed over to the path from his usual playground, he curled himself over my arm, making it very difficult to move at all. Instinctively, I began to sing an improvised song about where we were going and the music we might make to a nursery tune. Slowly, he unwound himself so that we could walk on. Until he felt safe and became aware of the weekly routine, David needed the impetus of this song to stimulate his freedom of movement. Once in the therapy room, he settled and enjoyed sitting at the piano with me. Exploring the keys in a similar way to that of an 18-month-old child, he was beside me but not with me. He chose to play in the bass which presented more of a challenge for me, improvising in the treble. I had to rethink how to provide enough structure to support his vulnerability. However, as he relaxed into the new situation over about ten weeks, there seemed to be a change from his random, repeated clusters to more cohesion in what he was playing. The 'flapping' style slowed in tempo and seemed more thoughtful. I had been supporting what he was doing with slow, containing chords but now could provide more melody within that structure. The most significant moment was when, after a long improvisation in duet, we ended together with a sustained chord. Then, for the first time, he turned and looked at me for about five seconds – an important acknowledgement for each of us, I felt. Through his playing, which extended to the drum and cymbal beside the piano, David showed that he could express playfulness, anger and stillness in a way that was more difficult outside the therapy room. Communication had become relationship. Teaching staff supported this when shown video clips during the termly feedback sessions I provided. Music therapy was important to him and his family. However, could generalisation into other areas of his life be proved? I don't know the answer, even though the benefits could be observed within the session itself. I was heartened by the opinion of Dr John Richer who said during a discussion that what developed during the course of a session was valid regardless of whether there was generalisation or not.

It's easy to present the obvious successes of our work, but more usually it can be very difficult to evaluate how it is for the non-verbal client except through their sounds and demeanour. The trumpet calls, as in the Ives piece, provide validation, but there can be a lot of hard graft with the not-knowing – where the client hears another, more remote drummer. Further insight came when, after I'd retired from the education authority, I was invited to work with young adults in a unit for those on the autistic spectrum in a college of further education. Most of the students were verbal: a few of them I remembered as young children in the Chinnor units which later became the service for autism (more name changes to the service followed). I feel very fortunate to have had this opportunity of insight into how many of these young people, aged from 16, had developed in the ensuing years. However, with that development, came the secondary problem of depression, possibly caused by the growing awareness of their condition in comparison with the neurotypical world. The staff had appraised what they were doing for and with the students and there was a consensus that therapeutic input was missing. An artist and I were appointed.

Apart from educational input, the staff worked with the students in life skills and socialisation. There was role play and discussion, with the students encouraged to talk about their difficulties experienced in a confusing and often frightening world, and how they should cope in a variety of social situations. Within this climate – before increased imposition of education initiatives – I felt free to support what the specialist tutors were aiming for – to give each student the opportunity to become more confident in neurotypical society, to feel secure enough to face individual problems through the medium of music and words. As a musician, music had been foremost in my work, but in this particular setting, music wasn't always the initial connection. Befriending was. Listening to these young people and just being with them in a comfortable and secure environment, where there was the opportunity to make music, affirmed the many years of work with children. A few found the concept of improvising strange and were frightened of 'getting it wrong'. It might be embarrassing to even try until feeling safe enough with me that they were not going to be judged. Early on in this chapter, I mentioned that I thought that improvisation *had* to be the basis of therapy as a result of the emphasis in training. However, I began to realise that there were many instances when using pre-composed or recorded music, especially songs familiar to the clients, provided the basis of the therapeutic relationship. During those five years, the students taught me a lot about pop music culture!

One 19-year-old man arrived at college on a part-time basis. He came with his mother to visit the unit one morning when I was working with another young man of about the same age. When 'Paul' walked through the front door, he could hear the pop-style improvisation on drums and keyboard from the music room which was by the main entrance. They were greeted by the coordinator and taken through to the large kitchen where one of the tutor groups was cooking. Evidently, Paul had made a comment about the music on the way. However, when he got into the kitchen, he found the size of the room, the whiteness of the units and the number of people too much to cope with. A few minutes later, I saw a note being pushed under the door – could Paul come into the music room to listen? I passed the decision over to the client who agreed, seeming to like the prospect of an audience. Paul was ushered in and introduced. His anxiety was evident in his hunched posture as he sat on a chair close to me at the keyboard. As the improvisation began, Paul began to relax a little, with his hands tapping on his knees from time to time. The client was quite confident in his social skills and when the improvisation ended, the two began to talk about favourite groups. From this experience, Paul asked if he could have music therapy and came to college on a day when I was there. This began a therapeutic relationship based more equally between music and talking. After his fourth session, he asked me about Asperger's syndrome and told me the diagnosis had been made when he was 13. However, he had no understanding of what it was and was distressed. I was bothered by this and, after consultation with the head of the unit, phoned his mother to say that, with her permission, I was prepared to talk to him about it. She agreed and seemed grateful for the offer. The following week, during a break, Paul and I met. He told me he felt relieved to have some insight as he thought he was going mad.

I had suggested to Paul that he was welcome to bring in a favourite CD each week if he wished. This was a successful way of connecting for some of the students. While he was happy to do this, most of the session time he spent on the drum kit with me at the keyboard. Although he presented himself as quiet and lacking in confidence, his playing could be powerful, lacking coherence. His favourite band was Nirvana and he began to talk at length about Kurt Cobain, his depression and his suicide. The sounds he particularly enjoyed were the distorted guitar sounds. I wondered what it was about the distortion which he seemed to relate to. I asked him if this was how he felt inside. He turned to me and agreed. There was a sense of connection with him. He seemed relieved that I had some insight into his feelings and that I wasn't making any judgment. Paul became very open about his feelings which extended into how he perceived the world about him. He was very aware of his own vulnerability which could sometimes overwhelm him. I shall never forget his thank-you card, given when therapy ended: a simple statement thanking me for helping him to understand himself.

The experience of working with young adults was an added challenge for both musical and personal skills. It was also immensely satisfying to have the opportunity to make relationships based on trust and respect. Looking back on changes in my own approach working with clients on the autistic spectrum, I would say that my approach has been in keeping with my training which was psychodynamic, relating the clinical use of music to establish a connection with each client, to present an opportunity for communication but going beyond that to enabling him or her to experience what relationship can mean within a secure environment. Boundaries are important. In my opinion, I think there can still be a tendency within the general public to believe that therapy is about 'letting it all hang out'. None of us can feel safe without the boundaries of knowing what can be accepted and what cannot. If our clients are to survive in the neurotypical world, they need support through what means are available to them in learning how to cope.

From my own experience of being a music therapist, my training was the time of beginning that step into the unknown. My more down-to-earth analogy is that of passing the driving test, then really learning what it means to drive. It has been those many remarkable young people who, through their own individuality and needs, have provoked any necessary changes in my approach. They had their own journeys – but so, too, had I. The journey may cause one to stumble. There are occasions when we, the therapists, need to forgive ourselves. When we work with integrity, the clients can forgive more than we often give them credit for. I'm thankful for those times when I have been able to be with the drummer each of them has heard. Sometimes all the therapist can do is be in the moment with the client. Little can be more. Much of the work can seem foggy and disconnected, but therapy is a waiting game, while becoming intuitively aware of when to challenge and when to let be. Then, maybe, those trumpet calls in 'The Unanswered Question' will be heard and have meaning.

References

Education Act (Handicapped Children) 1970. London: C.H.Baylis.

Ives, C. (1908) 'The Unanswered Question'. In Thomas, M.T. (2002) *The San Francisco Symphony: An American Journey.* San Francisco: Red Seal.

Muller, P. and Warwick, A. (1993) 'Autistic Children. The Effects of Maternal Involvement in Therapy.' In M. Heal and T. Wigram (eds) *Music Therapy in Health and Education.* London: Jessica Kingsley Publishers.

Thoreau, H. (2016) *Walden,* Sweden: Wisehouse Classics. (Original work published 1854.)

Williams, D. (1992) *Nobody Nowhere.* London: Doubleday.

PART 1

IMPROVISATIONAL APPROACHES

Clinical Trials: Are Music Therapists Deluding Themselves?

Amelia Oldfield, Laura Blauth,
Johanna Finnemann and Órla Casey

Introduction

Recent years have seen an increased demand for outcome measures in music therapy practice. This chapter will describe and reflect on a music therapy outcome study with children between the ages of four and seven with autistic spectrum conditions (ASC) in Cambridgeshire. This project was part of a large randomised controlled trial (RCT) entitled: 'Trial of Improvisational Music Therapy's Effectiveness for children with Autism' (TIME-A) (Geretsegger, Holck and Gold 2012) which involved children in ten different sites in nine different countries. There were two sites in the UK (one in Cambridgeshire and one mainly in London) and one each in Australia, Austria, Brazil, Israel, Italy, Norway, South Korea and USA. In total 364 children were included. Overall results of the project were reported back at a meeting in Bergen, Norway, in November 2016 and were published last year (Bieleninik *et al.* 2017a). The main reason we are writing specifically on work taking place at the Cambridgeshire site is that we thought that culture and other circumstances surrounding the work might explain the discrepancy in our part of the trial between the quantitative data obtained from the observational assessments and the qualitative reports. An example of cultural differences or variation in societal structures across the sites was that in the UK children between four and seven are mostly attending school, which is not the case in other countries. Another factor was the density of the population in South East England which meant that we had access to a relatively large number of children with a diagnosis of ASC, attending a number of special and mainstream schools in the area. In addition, the availability and sophistication of diagnostic services varied from site to site which had implications for how many children could be tested at specific times during the trial. The music therapists involved in our Cambridgeshire project, as well as the parents of the children receiving music therapy and the staff in the schools the children attended, all felt that music therapy had been helpful. However, the quantitative results of our trial did not show this. This led us to ask the question: are we all deluding ourselves?

Another reason why we wanted to investigate further was that we had access to both the qualitative and the quantitative data from our own site. We therefore wanted to explore our own data in more depth and report back on both quantitative and qualitative results.

Background

Amelia Oldfield first heard of the large TIME-A international music therapy trial when she was at a University Consortium meeting in Jyvaskyla, Finland, in 2012. She wondered then whether it might be possible to set up a trial site in Cambridge. She was encouraged by the fact that the Norwegian team who were organising the trial would provide half of the necessary funding, and also by the fact that it might be relatively easy to set up the intensive treatment required for the trial in schools which children with ASC between the ages of four and seven would be attending. However, she was uncertain whether the main tool that was being used to measure progress, the Autism Diagnostic Observation Schedule (ADOS), would be sensitive enough to pick up changes. Thoughts regarding the advantages and disadvantages of the ADOS from the authors' experience will be revisited and further explored in the second half of this chapter. A few months later, Amelia met up with Órla Casey, head of music therapy services for Cambridgeshire Music, the County Council schools service, who was very enthusiastic about going ahead with the project. Together they applied for, and were successful in receiving, funding from the local Evelyn Trust for the project. They both remained unsure about the usefulness of the ADOS in the trial but reasoned that it would be beneficial for music therapy in the area to set up this project which would finance further music therapy for children and possibly establish music therapy in schools that had previously not employed music therapists.

The TIME-A project

Half of the 364 children enrolled in the TIME-A study received music therapy treatment for five months and the other half of the children served as a control group. For those children allocated to music therapy treatment, half received weekly music therapy sessions and the other half received three music therapy sessions a week. All families, regardless of the randomisation result, were offered three parent counselling sessions, conducted either by the music therapist or by another professional. Change was evaluated through the ADOS (the primary outcome measure) and the Social Responsiveness Scale (SRS) which was a secondary outcome measure. Parents were also asked to rank their child's quality of life on a scale of 1 to 100.

The ADOS is a play-based observational assessment which aims to diagnose autistic spectrum condition. It is administered by a qualified clinician who scores the child's behaviours using a range of items relating to language and communication, reciprocal social interaction, stereotyped behaviours and restricted interests. Four different modules of the test are used depending on the child's verbal ability (Lord *et al.* 1999).

The SRS is a questionnaire designed to quantify autistic symptomology across a wide range of severity and takes approximately 15 minutes to complete. Parents respond to 65 items using a four-point Likert scale covering domains such as reciprocal social interaction and stereotypic interests (Constantino and Gruber 2005). Testing took place pre-treatment, after two months, after five months (which was at the end of treatment for those receiving music therapy) and, as a follow-up, after a year.

Specific characteristics of the Cambridgeshire site

There were many aspects of the trial which we had to comply with in order to conform with the research guidelines set out by the organisers of the project in Norway. For example, there were strict guidelines about when the ADOS and SRS tests should take place and how soon after these tests treatment might begin. The person carrying out the ADOS tests had to have received appropriate training and had to be 'blind' to which children were receiving music therapy treatment. Nevertheless, there were some aspects of the work which were different because of the way education and services for families with children with ASC are provided in the UK and because of the music therapy training in the UK. Finally, there were some aspects that we chose to do slightly differently in our Cambridgeshire site.

The most important difference between young children's lives in the UK and the other countries involved in this study is that children in the UK start school at four years old. Therefore, all the music therapy treatment for this project took place in schools. This was a huge advantage in some ways as it meant that the parents did not have to take their children to a music therapy treatment centre or hospital. This could have been particularly difficult for families allocated to receive music therapy three times a week. As a result it is not surprising that in the UK there were very high levels of music therapy attendance during the study. Most of the ADOS tests also took place in the schools which enabled our psychologist, Johanna Finnemann, to test 'batches' of children which might have been more difficult to arrange in an out-patient setting. In practice, the fact that the music therapy treatment had to occur in schools meant that Órla had to first liaise with the schools, often introducing staff to music therapy and explaining what the schools would have to provide in terms of rooming and equipment. The music therapists providing the treatment in the schools (Órla Casey and Laura Blauth) had to continue to liaise with teaching staff not only to arrange appointments but also to discuss the treatment the children were receiving and ensure that the children's needs were being met. All this work meant that we raised parents' and staff's expectations about music therapy and we therefore felt it would be important and ethical to provide some music therapy to those children allocated to the control group. In order not to interfere with the research protocol, we therefore budgeted to provide 12 weekly music therapy sessions 12 months after the control group children had been randomised to the study, and after all the necessary tests had been carried out on these children and their families.

A disadvantage of working in schools was the dependency on the school for the smooth running of the therapy sessions and assessments. The music therapists often had to spend time finding and preparing spaces for music therapy treatment and the psychologist sometimes struggled to find a room in which to test the children. Working as 'outsiders' in schools meant that the music therapists and the psychologist had to make sure they maintained contact with the frequently changing teaching staff, to ensure that children were available for sessions and supported by the classroom teams. Being involved in a research project within a school for a time-limited period meant that the music therapists and the psychologist were less involved in multi-disciplinary decisions than they might have been if they had been regular members of the team. It also wasn't always easy getting hold of parents to arrange parent counselling sessions or the filling in of the SRS questionnaires, something that would have been easier if parents had been bringing their children to an out-patient centre. Another difficulty we experienced was working around the school holidays and particularly the six-week summer break. Some schools arranged for the buildings to be open so that parents could bring their children to school during this time. However, in general, we tried to ensure that the children's five-month music therapy treatment did not overlap with the summer holidays.

The high density of the population in the East of England meant that we randomised 92 per cent of the number of children we had set out to recruit to the study. It also meant that when you added 'our' children to those recruited by the other site in the UK, the UK was the country that randomised most children to the project (118 children out of a total of 364, meaning that the UK randomised 32 per cent of all the subjects in the study).

Before embarking on this project, music therapy was already well established in a number of schools in Cambridgeshire, with clear guidelines in place on methods of working and music therapy practice (Tomlinson, Nall and Casey 2012). One characteristic of this approach is that music therapists liaise closely with parents, setting up meetings with parents at the end of each term to feed-back regarding their child's progress in music therapy. Video excerpts of music therapy sessions are frequently used to enhance this process. It therefore seemed logical for the music therapists providing the treatment in the trial also to provide the counselling sessions the TIME-A research protocol required for all the parents.

This counselling work has been explored in some depth by Laura and shown to be invaluable to the families of the children receiving music therapy treatment (Blauth 2017).

Music therapy in the UK with this client group

There is a relatively long history of music therapy with children with autism in the UK with pioneering music therapists such as Alvin (Alvin and Warwick 1991/1978) and Nordoff and Robbins (1971) writing early descriptive accounts of their work in this clinical area. In a more recent textbook about music therapy in schools (Tomlinson, Derrington and Oldfield 2012) one of the 13 chapters is specifically devoted to describing work in a special school for children with ASC (McTier 2012) but many other chapters also focus on case studies of children with ASC (Davies and Rosscornes 2012; Hall 2012; Tomlinson 2012).

While music therapists in the UK can have somewhat different approaches which may be based on different theoretical and philosophical perspectives, all music therapists working with children with ASC tend to use live and mainly improvised music making in their sessions, in addition to songs and some other pre-composed music. The building up of a relationship with the child and sometimes the family will be a central part of the process, as well as focusing on therapeutic goals to work towards. This general description fits in with the current definition of music therapy outlined by the British Association for Music Therapy (BAMT 2017).

Oldfield (2006, p.90) attempted to define the characteristics of her music therapy approach with children with ASC. Her approach is not radically different from that of other UK music therapists, but she tried to be specific about what defined the work and tease out important defining features. After some general observations about the layout of the room and the beginnings and the endings of the sessions, she described eight points which she felt were central to her work in this area. These were: the motivating aspect of music therapy sessions; the structure inherent in the music therapy sessions and in music making; the balance between following and initiating; the basic non-verbal exchanges; the fact that children can be in control in a constructive way; movement combined with music; playfulness and drama in music; and working jointly with parents.

Many of these points are covered by Geretsegger *et al.* (2015) when they describe the common characteristics of improvisational music therapy approaches used by music therapists in the TIME-A project. It is therefore perhaps not surprising that UK music therapists working on the TIME-A trial had no difficulties conforming with the 'Unique and Essential Principles' for Improvisational Therapy outlined in this article. However, as pointed out in Oldfield (2016) there may be 'Additional Features' (a category mentioned in the original Geretsegger *et al.* 2015 article) in music therapy work in the UK such as: 'providing varied and appropriate music material', 'using the geography of the room', 'the balance between following and initiating – shifting control' and 'working with parents to support the child, but also considering the parents' own needs' which characterise the work of music therapists working with children with ASC in the UK.

Description of the Cambridgeshire study

A total of 37 children (31 boys, 6 girls) with a mean baseline age of 5 years 8 months were randomised for the Cambridge arm of the TIME-A study. Of these children, ten were randomised to high-intensity music therapy (three sessions a week), nine to low-intensity music therapy (one session a week) and 18 to standard care (no music therapy until after the study was completed). Children in the high-frequency music therapy group received a mean of 41.2 music therapy sessions (range: 23–50) whereas children allocated to low-frequency treatment received an average of 15.6 (range 5–20) music therapy sessions. No child in the control group received any music therapy until after the study was completed. For the purposes of statistical analysis all the children receiving music therapy (low intensity and high intensity) were combined. This was because the number of children was quite low and it was very unlikely that we would get statistically significant results if the children were divided into three groups (high intensity, low intensity and control group). Even in the main paper (Bieleninik *et al.* 2017a), the primary outcome analysis did not differentiate between high- and low-intensity groups.

Quantitative results

ADOS data at baseline and five months was available for all the 19 children from the music therapy group and 14 children from the standard care group. SRS data at the same time points was available for 16 music therapy children and 11 children receiving standard care. Fifteen parents from the music therapy group completed quality-of-life ratings for their child and family, whereas only 11 child-related and ten family-related quality-of-life ratings are available for the children of the standard care group. The higher loss to follow-up in the standard care group likely reflects a lower engagement with the study and research team which is also echoed in the fact that parents of children in the standard care group attended fewer counselling sessions than parents of children in the music therapy group. This difference was calculated as being significant (p = 0.002).

Difference scores for each measure (ADOS, SRS, QoL) were calculated so that a higher score always reflects an improvement in symptom severity or quality of life. The following figures illustrate the change in ADOS scores, SRS scores and quality-of-life scores.

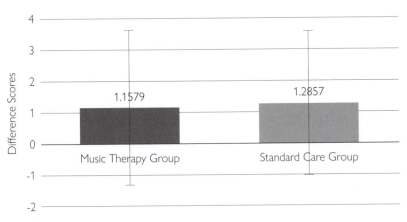

Figure 1.1: Change in ADOS scores

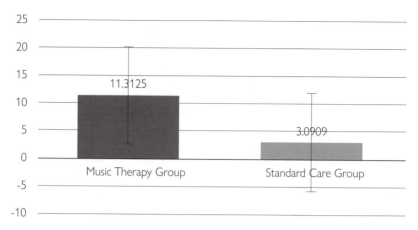

Figure 1.2: Change in SRS scores

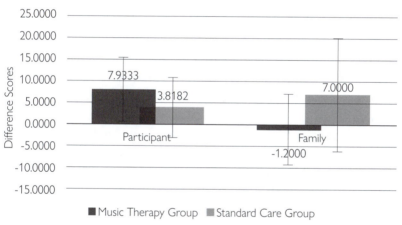

Figure 1.3: Quality-of-life ratings for the participant and the family

Although these graphs look very different from one another and Figure 1.2 in particular appears to show a difference between the two groups in favour of the music therapy group, the variation of improvement between the children was so great that the improvement shown was not big enough to be statistically significant.

Thus there was no significant difference between the treatment groups for the changes in ADOS scores ($p = 0.940$) or SRS scores ($p = 0.246$). Nor was there an observable change for the reported quality of life of the child ($p = 0.502$) or the family ($p = 0.316$).

Case studies

In her role as a music therapist and parent counsellor in the Cambridgeshire trial, Laura worked with 26 families enrolled in the trial. In the following, she will present two case studies in order to illustrate aspects that seem to be characteristic of the work in this project in the UK. In the first case, quantitative data obtained from the primary and the secondary outcome measures are in accordance with each other and with qualitative reports given by the therapist, the parent and the school. The second case gives an example of discrepancy not only between the quantitative data gathered from the primary outcome and the qualitative reports but also between the primary and the secondary outcome.

CASE STUDY: HARRY

Harry was four years old when Laura started the music therapy sessions with him. He had been randomised to the high-intensity treatment group. Over a period of five months, Harry received 50 individual sessions. Being an affectionate and smiley little boy, he was liked by the staff in his school. However, they struggled to include him in the classroom activities as he showed high levels of energy and had difficulties sitting or concentrating. It was unclear how much language he understood. Harry was the only non-verbal child in his classroom which concerned his mother greatly. Laura and Harry's mother therefore agreed that the music therapy intervention should aim to encourage Harry to use his voice, to vocalise and to sing, as well as to help him to focus on individual activities for longer.

In the first sessions, Harry was accompanied by a teaching assistant who was familiar to him and could provide emotional and physical support. In the beginning, Harry was constantly moving and pacing around the room and he did not show any prolonged interest or engagement in a musical activity. He discarded instruments quickly and often got distracted by his desire to climb on furniture and instruments. Laura only kept carefully selected instruments in the room and concentrated on vocalising, hand-clapping and movement games. This worked well in the beginning, and Harry made good progress in his ability to focus and engage. However, at around session 20, Laura felt that they had reached a plateau and for a while it seemed difficult to move on in a meaningful way.

Maybe Harry could not process any more and develop any further in this short amount of time? Maybe the high frequency of sessions proved to be tiring for both therapist and child? At this time, Harry developed a fascination with opening and closing the door and with switching the lights on and off repeatedly. The sessions felt more fragmented again. A positive change was made possible when Laura started to offer Harry equally interesting but more acceptable sensory experiences by, for example, removing his shoes and inviting him to play the tambourine with his feet. Laura also realised that as an effect of seeing Harry three times a week her music had become a bit repetitive and unimaginative. Becoming aware of that enabled her to include again more sudden and dramatic changes, playfulness and humour in the music which seemed to re-engage and motivate Harry. He delighted in dancing and showed his creativity and musicality when inventing movements for their music. Laura and Harry always spent time in the sessions to celebrate and enjoy his energy. This seemed to enable him to also concentrate on a given task and to control his impulses. As described by Harry's mum, this development translated into other settings as well:

> I've never really seen him play, sit down and play with his toys, but now he is on my rug, he is sitting there for ages, lying there with the train, playing with it for ages, like good 20 minutes. Even at dinner time he got a little bit better. The sitting for me has definitely got better.

Harry struggled to access some of the instruments because of his difficulties with fine motor control. However, he started using his voice from the first session, possibly as a response to Laura's singing and vocalising. Consequently, the sessions were often centred on mutual vocal improvisations. At first, Harry made short babbling sounds but soon the phrases became longer and often included melodic lines. The vocal dialogues incorporated imitative responses of Harry's sounds which aimed to reinforce his sense of identity and self-awareness. He seemed to be delighted when Laura copied and mirrored his sounds, and he responded with more singing. As he was encouraged to use his voice, he started exploring different facets of it and he incorporated a wider range of sounds, pitch and volume into his vocal repertoire. The high intensity of sessions three times a week allowed for quick progress regarding Harry's confidence and ability to use his voice in a playful, creative and interactive way. In addition, Laura continued to invite his teaching assistants and his teacher to the sessions regularly and discussed with them possible ways of implementing singing and music making in the classroom activities. A teaching assistant expressed her thoughts after having observed a session: 'I feel quite emotional because I haven't seen him like that before. I'm amazed to see how music is able to get through to him'. Meeting Harry's mum for the three parent counselling sessions enabled Laura to show her video excerpts of Harry's music therapy and to discuss as well as suggest musical ideas with her to use at home. Towards the end of therapy, Harry used words and word approximations confidently to communicate with Laura. He even developed his own number song and joined in singing familiar songs with her. His mother talked about this development in the last parent counselling session:

> He, actually, he sings so much! It's unbelievable. Even this morning he woke up at half six in the morning and he just sits there and sings. And he says all of it and it's just like, my baby can talk! He talks through that and that's amazing!

For TIME-A, Harry was assessed with ADOS Module 1 which is used with children with, at most, single words. At baseline, his social communication algorithm score was 23 (higher scores reflect more obvious autistic symptoms during the assessment). He obtained a score of 49 when adding up all 29 ADOS symptom items rather than only those related to the diagnostic algorithm. After five months, Harry's social communication algorithm score was 14 (9 points less than his original score). Similarly, his overall score composed of all 29 items reduced considerably to 28 (21 points less than his original score). The data obtained from the primary outcome measure suggests a reduction in autism symptom severity. This result accorded with the test results of the secondary outcome measure. In the SRS filled in by parents, Harry received a raw score of 113 at baseline, and of 93 after five months, indicating a change of symptom severity from the severe to moderate range. The results of both assessments reflect the development observed by the clinician, the child's mother and the teaching professionals. Harry's mum attributed the positive change to the music therapy intervention:

I think music therapy has opened his mind up if that makes sense. I really think it's done amazing for him. I think music makes him happy. I don't know, it just makes him active, it makes him happy, it makes him, I don't know, I can't explain it, it just… it really is amazing, absolutely amazing. If only he could have it all the time.

CASE STUDY: SIMON

Simon was almost five years old when he was enrolled in the trial. Having been allocated to the low-intensity treatment group, Simon attended 20 individual music therapy sessions in his school. He grew up bilingual and seemed to have good receptive language skills in both English and Polish. When Laura first met Simon, he used only a few words to communicate and tended to repeat them anxiously until an adult echoed his words back to him.

His general presentation in the early music therapy sessions was that of a child driven by a nervous inner energy. He ran around the room, touched every instrument briefly, pushed over chairs and instruments, grabbed beaters and hit everything he could reach with them, including guitars and the wall. Within seconds the room was in a state of chaos and Laura found herself constantly reacting to prevent harm to the child and damage to the objects. In order to help Simon release his energy and channel it in a more constructive way, Laura placed a large drum and cymbal in front of him. He immediately hit them loudly and frantically. When Laura supported his drumming with simple chord progressions, played loudly but steadily from the piano, he beamed at her. Even though Simon was only able to sustain the mutual playing for a few seconds, they had experienced a first meaningful musical connection.

It was obvious that Simon enjoyed music making and that he was fascinated by instruments, but that he needed lots of support to access them in a safe way. It proved helpful to reduce the amount of distractions in the room and to provide a clear beginning and ending to each activity. For example, Simon responded very well to the ritual of saying '1-2-3-Finish' to bring an activity to a close before moving on to the next instrument. Laura kept the sessions predictable with recurring elements such as a 'Hello' and a 'Goodbye' song. Simon was fond of this familiar structure and it seemed to help him to relax and concentrate.

In sessions five to 11, Simon appeared less fidgety but very emotional and often tearful. Simon's expressive language skills improved immensely during this time. However, what he said in the sessions was often quite concerning. He murmured, for example, 'We're not afraid of that' or 'We're not crying'. He sometimes repeated 'mummy later' more than 30 times in a session and he told Laura in all these seven sessions that he had a 'broken leg', a 'broken arm' or another broken body part. Simon clearly experienced strong feelings and seemed to struggle to make sense of them. Laura was encouraged that he now felt safe enough to express some of his emotions. She started to incorporate his statements into improvised songs, which Simon seemed curious about, and he added varied instrumental accompaniments. He also increasingly allowed Laura to calm him with soft music, nursery rhymes and 'young' musical games at times when he appeared unsettled and anxious.

From session 12 onwards, Simon started to sing to himself about his feelings and his daily routine. Laura felt that matching his verbal, instrumental, facial and physical expressions musically allowed Simon to listen to himself and to access feelings he had previously masked in constant activity. Singing and music making seemed to help him to understand and communicate his emotions and to feel heard. Simon's increased ability to express himself verbally was also reflected by his more varied use of musical parameters. His instrumental playing now had a stronger feeling of pulse, and he experimented freely with rhythms and dynamics. When showing video excerpts from the sessions to his mother, she commented on this development: 'Yeah, he's definitely different than before where he was like drumming and just making lots of noise. Now he's like exploring different instruments and sounds.' Towards the end of therapy, Simon seemed more at ease with himself and the people around him. Consequently, he became more able to try to tolerate new activities and experiences. In their last parent counselling session his mother told Laura:

> Before when we were singing at home very often he was like 'No, no, stop it' so we had to stop but now he don't mind when

we're singing. Yeah, he's happy, a very happy boy now! We're doing lots of new things now. He's open for new things now.

Even though Simon used words to communicate when he was enrolled in the project, he did not consistently use phrase speech and was therefore assessed with ADOS Module 1. At baseline, his score on the social communication algorithm for Social Affect was 14. All 29 item scores together added up to 26. At five months, the overall score amounted to 30 (increased by 4 compared with the baseline). Similarly, the social-communication algorithm score worsened significantly and Simon received a score of 19 (an increase of 5 points) at this time point. This result is very disconcerting. The change in ADOS scores does not match the clinical observations of Simon's development over the course of the music therapy intervention. Furthermore, the ADOS scores stand in stark contrast to the results of the parent-rated SRS. In the SRS, Simon obtained a raw score of 103 at baseline, and a raw score of 66 after five months. Whereas the score at baseline falls into the category severe range, the score after five months corresponds with the mild range. That means that, according to the SRS, we can see significant improvement in symptom severity after five months. The discrepancy between the results of the primary and the secondary outcome is striking.

In addition to the change picked up by the SRS, Simon's mum described in their second parent counselling session what she observed at home: 'I see progress, but it's like big progress right now, on his concentration, on his focus. His speech is–, oh, it's incredible now. It's like, you know, just opened for talking.' Simon's progress that was notable in the music therapy sessions seemed to have generalised across different settings, including home and school. One of his teachers commented at five months that Simon 'seems to be happier and more settled after the sessions' and described his overall development as being 'really positive. He's doing really well.'

One of the most encouraging developments Laura could observe in the music therapy sessions was that, as Simon became more able to express himself, he also became more interested in interacting with her. He seemed less isolated and more able to engage in mutual improvisations and reciprocal communication.

This change was also noticed by his mum and it seemed to be an important aspect determining quality of life of the family:

> Before was like, he was always on his own, then we catch a moment when he's, you know, when he's with us but now it's different: He's always with us, then sometimes he's forgetting about us and he is on his own. It's amazing.

Discussion/reflections

In both cases, Laura's clinical observation, feedback from parents and teachers, and the secondary outcome measure SRS describe a positive development of the child. However, the primary outcome measure used in the trial, the ADOS, only indicates improvement for one child (Harry) and even suggests a significant worsening of symptom severity for the other child (Simon). In order to understand and evaluate this, it is helpful to look at the differences between the two cases. Even though both children are male, are of a similar age and have a diagnosis of childhood autism, their verbal abilities differ significantly. At the beginning of treatment, Harry had no expressive verbal language and his receptive language skills seemed well below his developmental age. Simon, on the other hand, had good receptive language skills and used words to communicate. Whereas Harry had been assessed as having an IQ < 70, Simon had been assessed as being of average intelligence. It might be worth investigating whether music therapy is more effective with children who have a low IQ or whether the improvement in children with a low IQ is captured more effectively by the ADOS. We can approach this question by thinking about the type of change that occurred in the two described cases. Harry's progress was easily quantifiable and measurable: he was able to sit and focus for longer, he displayed less sensory-stimulating or attention-seeking behaviour, he vocalised more often, he started to use words. The changes in Simon's behaviour were maybe more difficult to capture: he appeared happier and less stressed, he became more able to express and manage strong feelings, he became more able to tolerate new experiences and he seemed more interested in interacting with other people. Similarly, even though the changes in ADOS attempt to measure changes in social interaction, the ADOS doesn't always capture the effects that hyperactivity or overall anxiety, for example, could have on all the behaviours displayed in the test.

The ADOS was administered by a 'blind' assessor. The SRS was rated by the parents who were not blinded about the group allocation of their child and who might have been biased. One could say that this makes the results of the secondary outcome measure less meaningful. However, it could be argued that, on the contrary, this makes the SRS an especially valuable measurement. ASC is likely to have an impact on the whole family and not only the child diagnosed (Greef and Van der Walt 2010). Studies have shown that caregivers of children with ASC suffer more often with depression and anxiety (Khanna *et al.* 2011) and that they experience higher levels of stress and aggravation than the general population (Dabrowska and Pisula 2010; Estes *et al.* 2009). If parents feel that their child develops well and that their autism symptom severity improves, they are more likely to feel less stressed themselves. This will not only affect their own mental health but also affect their interaction patterns with their child in a positive way. The perception and opinion of parents is essential when working with young children and when investigating the suitability of interventions.

An important difference between the qualitative reports and the SRS compared with the ADOS is the amount of time the child's life is being examined. Whereas the SRS and the observations of therapist and teacher consider the behaviour of the child on different days over several months, the ADOS is a snapshot of the child's behaviour during 30 minutes on one particular day. With children such as Simon, who have intense anxiety on certain days, the ADOS is more likely to capture results inconsistent with the overall presentation of the child compared with children whose mood is more stable. These different factors might explain why, in Simon's case, the data obtained from his follow-up ADOS assessment at 12 months seem to be conflicting with the results from the ADOS administered at five months. At 12 months, Simon received a social communication score of 9 (Baseline: 14; 5 months: 19). Adding all 29 item scores together amounted to 14 (Baseline: 26; 5 months: 30).

Thinking about another child enrolled in the trial, one might even question the suitability of any of the applied quantitative measures. Joshua, a bright and verbal child, was allocated to the high-intensity treatment. His ADOS social communication scores were 14 at baseline, 9 at two months, 17 at five months, and 13 at 12 months. These very diverse results make it difficult to determine a definite development in any direction. The secondary outcome measure rated by parents indicates a slight worsening of symptom severity after five months: the SRS total score increased from 107 at baseline to 116 at five months. At the same time, however, Joshua's parents emphasised in the parent counselling sessions and towards teaching staff how much he had progressed during the last months. They wrote to Laura: 'We cannot thank you enough for the wonderful work. We know he has enjoyed every session with you and it has made a HUGE difference to him and to us.' Similarly, feedback from teachers and Laura's observations indicated a positive development regarding Joshua's social communication skills as well as his emotional wellbeing over the course of music therapy.

How can we interpret these discrepancies between the quantitative and the qualitative results? One possible explanation takes into account the situation of families with children with ASC and how setting up a research project that offers a previously not provided treatment may influence data. Joshua's parents were desperately looking for support. It is conceivable that they tried to paint the worst possible picture of their situation to the research team. They might have hoped that filling in the questionnaires in a certain way could lead to more treatment provision. Towards the professionals working with their child, however, they expressed their appreciation of the intervention.

Overall, then, we are suggesting that for a variety of reasons the measures that were used in this study were not giving us the information we needed. The ADOS was originally designed as a diagnostic tool rather than as a way of measuring changes in symptom severity and thus might not have been able to pick up some of the smaller changes. A recent study by Bieleninik et al. (2017b) confirms that the ADOS is not an effective way to measure changes over time. It could also have been influenced by factors such as the overall levels of anxiety or arousal of the child. As mentioned earlier, this was something both Amelia and Órla were aware of before starting the trial, but they still went ahead with the investigation as it was felt that any increased knowledge or interest in the field could only be beneficial. They were also aware that there was no other suitable standardised measuring tool available. The SRS was providing somewhat more reliable information, but because all the families in the Cambridgeshire trial were 'new' to music therapy, many parents were anxious about losing this provision and therefore at times consciously or unconsciously exaggerated the severity of symptoms in order not to lose out on possible future services. A couple of parents expressed concern about whether positive assessment scores would mean their child would no longer have access to music therapy treatment. Also it should be noted that this data was collected in different ways: sometimes the SRS was filled in while the music therapist was in the room with the parent, and sometimes it was sent to parents to fill in at home. With the therapist in the room, parents were able to clarify items that were unclear and the therapist was able to reassure parents that their responses would not affect treatment allocation. After a positive counselling session with the music therapist, parents might have been more favourably disposed to their child than if they were struggling on their own with difficult behaviours at home.

Nevertheless, despite our disappointment with the quantitative results of this trial, we all feel pleased and grateful that we have been involved in this research.

This project has inspired several of the music therapists providing the treatment to investigate aspects of the work in more depth and start PhD studies. Providing clinical supervision for a group of music therapists all working with the same client group has enabled Amelia and the therapists involved to think more about the specific characteristics of the UK music therapy approach in this area. The trial also forced us all to reflect on the effects of intensive (three times a week) music therapy interventions which would be difficult to examine in ordinary contexts because most music therapists are not employed long enough in any one institution to easily provide therapy sessions three times a week (Oldfield *et al.* 2016).

From a pragmatic point of view, over 700 music therapy sessions were provided to 37 families who would otherwise not have had access to these music therapy sessions or the counselling sessions. Four schools who previously had not had music therapists working with them have been introduced to this work and three of them have decided to provide the funding for the service to continue after the trial ended. The general profile of music therapy in schools in the area has been raised, with an increasing interest in music therapy interventions. Many staff and parents will be awaiting the results of our trial with interest. Having become interested and enthused by music therapy, will they now be discouraged by our quantitative results and no longer seek this intervention? We hope not. We trust that they will remember the excitement and enthusiasm they have previously felt and expressed.

Does this mean that some results are more or less 'true' than others? Do the figures mean that the parents, the children, the staff and the music therapists are all deluding themselves? Rather than opting in favour of one type of information, the message we would like to give is that it is important to look at the whole picture and consider different types of data and information. The case descriptions and the variety of the information provided by different data sources remind us that it might be misleading to look at quantitative results in isolation.

References

Alvin, J. and Warwick, A. (1991) *Music Therapy for the Autistic Child*. Oxford: Oxford University Press. (First published 1978.)

BAMT (2017) *What is Music Therapy?* London: BAMT. Accessed on 30 July 2017 at https://www.bamt.org/music-therapy/what-is-music-therapy.html.

Bieleninik, Ł., Geretsegger, M., Mössler, K., Assmus, J. *et al.* (2017a) 'Effectiveness of improvisational music therapy versus enhanced standard care for children with autism spectrum disorder: The TIME-A randomized controlled trial.' *JAMA 318*, 6, 525–535.

Bieleninik, Ł., Maj-Britt Posserud, M.-B., Geretsegger, M., Thompson, G., Elefant, C. and Gold, C. (2017b) 'Tracing the temporal stability of autism spectrum diagnosis and severity as measured by the Autism Diagnostic Observation Schedule: A systematic review and meta-analysis.' *PLoS ONE 12*, 9, e0183160.

Blauth, L. (2017) 'Improving mental health in families with autistic children: Benefits of using video feedback and parent counselling sessions offered alongside music therapy.' *Health Psychology Report 5*, 2, 138–150.

Blauth, L., Georgaki, A., Grant, C., Papadopoulu, P. and Sandford, S. (2016) 'Intensive music therapy for young children with autistic spectrum disorder – A viable alternative?' Roundtable at the British Association for Music Therapy Conference (BAMT) Glasgow.

Constantino, J.N. and Gruber, C.P. (2005) *Social Responsiveness Scale: Manual*. Los Angeles, CA: Western Psychological Services.

Dabrowska, A. and Pisula, E. (2010) 'Parenting stress and coping styles in mothers and fathers of pre-school children with autism and Down syndrome.' *Journal of Intellectual Disability Research 54*, 3, 266–280.

Davies, E. and Rosscornes, C. (2012) 'Setting up and Developing Music Therapy at a Children's Centre and Croft Unit for Child and Family Psychiatry.' In J. Tomlinson, P. Derrington and A. Oldfield (eds) *Music Therapy in Schools: Working with Children of All Ages in Mainstream and Special Education*. London: Jessica Kingsley Publishers.

Estes, A., Munson, J., Dawson, G., Koehler, E., Zhou, X.H. and Abbott, R. (2009) 'Parenting stress and psychological functioning among mothers of pre-school children with autism and developmental delay.' *Autism, 13*, 4, 375–387.

Geretsegger, M., Holck, U. and Gold, C. (2012) 'Randomised controlled trial of music therapy's effectiveness for children with autism spectrum disorders (TIME-A): Study protocol,' *BMC Pediatrics, 12*, 2 doi:10.1186/1471-2431-12-2.

Geretsegger, M., Holck, U., Carpente, J.A., Elefant, C., Kim, J. and Gold, C. (2015) 'Common characteristics of improvisational approaches in music therapy for children with autism spectrum disorder: Developing treatment guidelines.' *Journal of Music Therapy 52*, 2, 258–81.

Greeff, A.P and Van der Walt, K. (2010) 'Resilience in families with an autistic child.' *Education and Training in Autism and Developmental Disabilities 45*, 3, 347–355.

Hall, J. (2012) 'The School Challenge: Combining the Roles of Music Therapist and Music Teacher.' In Tomlinson, J., Derrington, P. and Oldfield, A. (eds) *Music Therapy in Schools: Working with Children of All Ages in Mainstream and Special Education*. London: Jessica Kingsley Publishers.

Khanna, R., Madhavan, S.S., Smith, M.J., Patrick, J.H., Tworek, C. and Becker-Cottrill, B. (2011) 'Assessment of health-related quality of life among primary care-givers of children with autism spectrum disorders.' *Journal of Autism and Developmental Disorders 41*, 9, 1214–1227.

Lord, C. *et al.* (1999) *Autism Diagnostic Observation Schedule: Manual*. Los Angeles, CA: Western Psychological Services.

McTier, I. (2012) 'Music Therapy in a Special School for Children with Autistic Spectrum Disorder, Focusing Particularly on the Use of the Double Bass.' In J. Tomlinson, P. Derrington and A. Oldfield (eds) *Music Therapy in Schools: Working with Children of All Ages in Mainstream and Special Education*. London: Jessica Kingsley Publishers.

Nordoff, P. and Robbins, C. (1971) *Therapy in Music for Handicapped Children*. London: Victor Gollancz.

Oldfield, A. (chair), Sandford, S., Grant, C., Blauth, L. *et al.* (2016) 'Intensive Music Therapy for Young Children with Autistic Spectrum Disorder – A Viable Alternative?' [Conference Roundtable] In U. Aravinth, M. Pavlicevic and G. Watts (eds) *Revisioning Our Voice: Resourcing Music Therapy for Contemporary Needs*. London: British Association for Music Therapy.

Oldfield, A. (2006) *Interactive Music Therapy – A Positive Approach: Music Therapy at a Child Development Centre*. London and Philadelphia: Jessica Kingsley Publishers.

Oldfield, A. (2016) 'The Future of Music Therapy with Persons with Autistic Spectrum Disorder.' In C. Dileo (ed.) *Envisioning the Future of Music Therapy*. Philadelphia, PA: Temple University's Arts and Quality of Life Research Center.

Tomlinson, J. (2012) 'Music Therapy in a Special School: Investigating the Role of Imitation and Reflection in the Interaction between Music Therapist and Child.' In J. Tomlinson, P. Derrington and A. Oldfield (eds) *Music Therapy in Schools: Working with Children of All Ages in Mainstream and Special Education*. London: Jessica Kingsley Publishers.

Tomlinson, J., Derrington, P. and Oldfield, A. (2012) *Music Therapy in Schools: Working with Children of All Ages in Mainstream and Special Education*. London: Jessica Kingsley Publishers.

Tomlinson, J., Nall, K. and Casey, O. (2012) 'Looking Back on the Development of a Service.' In J. Tomlinson, P. Derrington and A. Oldfield (eds) *Music Therapy in Schools: Working with Children of All Ages in Mainstream and Special Education*. London: Jessica Kingsley Publishers.

Evolving a Contemporary Psychoanalytically Informed Relational Music Therapy with Children with High-Functioning Autism in Specialist School Placements

Joy Gravestock

Introduction

This chapter is first and foremost a story: the narrative of my journey within music therapy attempting to grapple with the complexities and multiplicities that are the real experiences of children underlying their diagnostic description of 'high-functioning autism'. My work has been in situations where there has often been a lack of coherence, where not all the ends can be made to tie up, and not everything is easily delineated and quantified. I do not present a critique of music therapy's engagement with psychoanalytic ideas in this context (as there already exists such description) but instead intend, as Marks-Tarlow (2008, p.xviiii) suggests, 'not to supersede previous clinical theories so much as to contextualise them', by describing how psychoanalytic thinking helped me make sense of music therapy as an alive, evolving process emerging out of unique interpersonal moments of meeting. Each moment is original when working with material as rich as the human mind, brain, self and soul, constructed in a myriad of bio-psycho-social ways. I follow Daniel Stern's (2004) emphasis of first giving significance to the 'now' moments of therapy before later theorising about their meaning.

This story describes creating a music therapy space for each child where they could simply 'be' with another person, without expectation, and explore ways of being together. It will describe how such deceptively simple being revealed aspects of children's inner world experience. Initially thought about in classically psychoanalytic ways, further training also led to draw upon contemporary ideas emerging from relational and attachment theories (Trondalen 2016; Wilkinson 2006).

I am not proposing here a 'model' but simply describing how a music therapy approach evolved that privileged 'being' over 'doing'. There was no directive placed upon the therapy other than that the time and the space were there, as were the instruments and therapist. What happened then was open to exploration, causing me to draw upon all that was available in order to make sense of shared emergent experience. Though we remain rooted in theoretical ideas of work, developing a thoughtful eclectic practice means adapting theories if the lived experience of clients does not fit with our preconceptions. 'Lived experience', as it is understood in qualitative research, defines a representation and understanding of the clients' human experiences, and how these influence the therapist's perception of knowledge. The work then is always evolving.

The approach

The theoretical understandings I utilise here were honed first through my clinical experiences in the therapy room, which then led the way to writing and thinking. Trained in a psychoanalytic model of music therapy (Priestley 1994), I have undertaken much additional training, especially in the fields of psychoanalysis, relational therapy, trauma and attachment. A synthesis of these ideas and positions informs a theoretical base for sense-making (Stone 2017) about the work.

Sense-making describes how we understand ambiguous situations and is the process of creating situational awareness and understanding in situations of high complexity or uncertainty. It is an effort towards understanding connections between people, in order to understand their trajectories and act effectively with them. This, alongside my clinical supervision, shaped and developed understanding and hypotheses about what emerged in music therapy sessions. Sense-making values first lived experience of both client and therapist, allowing for openness to new understandings which may come from the client, as well as from other sources, before making theoretical sense of interactions and communications. Often children who received diagnosis commented that they felt no agency in the process. I hoped music therapy might simply offer a place where exploring meaning for these children and young people's lived experiences could increase their agency as we engaged together in sense-making.

I was fortunately able to step away from diagnostic process (as the children had ongoing links to their psychiatrist/psychologist), and from a linear focus on improving symptomatic presentations, or externalised objectives. Rather, descriptions of diagnosis and symptoms were viewed as a source of communication which could be thought about within an empathic space. This approach privileges client processes of being and becoming (Sills 2008), occurring in the presence of a therapist who listens for the implicit, whilst witnessing and holding difficulties and dilemmas. What is shown time and time again in research about therapy is that it is the quality of the therapeutic relationship that makes a difference to people's lives (Gordon 2009), and I trusted that this held true also for these children described as presenting with features of high-functioning autism.

The children

The age range of the children I worked with was wide, from seven to 19. Although 'high-functioning autism' isn't an official diagnostic term, it is often used to refer to people who have a higher level of cognitive, social and verbal ability than some others on the spectrum. All of the children I worked with had, despite their difficulties, managed to remain in mainstream education for many years prior to exclusion. Under phenomenal yet unrecognised stress, these children were high achievers but at great emotional cost to themselves. Much was expected of them, which they were unable to sustain. This was especially apparent whilst transitioning to secondary education, when there were more people to encounter, larger, noisier areas, and all this whilst puberty was occurring. All children had exhausted intensive support resources in mainstream education but it seemed that families had to be perceived as struggling or even failing at accessing support before being considered for a very expensive and contested place in a specialist school.[1]

Exclusion, however, had also often been an oblique route to gaining diagnosis. Some children spent up to four years outside of any formal education, during which time they may also have been finally diagnosed. Excluded ostensibly because they were described as demonstrating unmanageable behavioural issues for mainstream schooling, their behaviours were later constructed as symptomatic of their diagnosis. This exacerbated children's sense of being viewed by the world as naughty or delinquent or dangerous, particularly if they came into contact with the police and legal system.

Whilst the diagnostic process itself could be experienced as highly variable, the complicating factors around this, including the accrual of support and funding and social circumstances, could also inform the narratives of children and families. The complex journeys, as described in the case studies below, can require exploring without blame or judgment as we encounter each child in music therapy.

CASE STUDY: ROSIE

Rosie's parents, hearing on the grapevine which psychiatrist was 'good' or 'bad', requested to go to one likely to give the diagnosis they preferred. One psychiatrist was seen as 'expert' and likely to give a high-functioning autism diagnosis, whereas another was more likely to construct the symptoms as either attention deficit disorder or family problems.

This demonstrates how lived reality for families can be that diagnoses accrue particular funding and support, including educational resources. Families may make choices on behalf of the child or young person about how to navigate this process. On other

---

1   It is my experience that a number of special schools now are run by large 'chains', and the slow process of privatisation means local authorities have less control over education. Whilst the state is obliged to provide for this population, it is difficult in a climate of austerity, and complex funding. Arrangements can sometimes appear to affect how diagnosis is made, and who gets placed where.

occasions, as shown in the following case study, diagnoses may be part of complex social circumstances.

CASE STUDY: BRIAN

Brian seemed to have barely any clinical symptoms, and those he did present with were equally well described as attention deficit or attachment issues. For his family (who were involved in child protection procedures) it felt better to have an autism diagnosis rather than anything else. Psychologically, this meant pathology could reside entirely within him, meaning there was no requirement for systemic change.

The settings

This work took place across multiple settings including those where any child with an identified special educational need might be placed (and so were being schooled alongside other children with very different diagnoses), and specialist places in schools ring-fenced for high-functioning autistic spectrum disorder. In these highly specialised settings, children might be formally educated about their diagnosis. The curriculum would have a large focus on enabling them to cognitively understand the difficulties they had, in the belief that this cognitive awareness would enable them to manage aspects of their expressed behaviour.

None of the children were in a residential placement, so school formed only part of their daily life as they returned to homes and communities. Thinking in therapy inevitably included a focus on school life; equally, issues around family and social life would be brought into sessions. Working as a freelance therapist enabled me to hold a relatively neutral space for children, as I could think with them about any issues they brought regarding the way they experienced school, as they saw me as separate to the school system. Some children welcomed and embraced their diagnosis and felt that it had improved life. Others disbelieved diagnosis (one child telling me, 'I'm not a stupid autistic like the people here!') and resented attending a special school which often meant they had to leave home early in the morning to travel many miles. One teenager reported being singled out in his community as 'going to the *spastic's* school'. Unsurprisingly, then, relationship to diagnosis and to special education were large features in the work.

Each child in each context could have massively different plans, some coming from a social work referral, others from health, and involving team care from a variety of professionals, most of whom were located outside of the school context, such as psychiatrists and psychologists. Ultimately, I was exploring if there was room for contemporary psychoanalytic thinking, and, if so, what an emergent approach might look like.

Sessions were always designated as 45 minutes of direct contact in the room in music therapy focused on free improvisation. Additional time was given to my writing up, reflecting alone and consulting with staff. Some children could not initially tolerate this length of contact, and others would attempt to gain more. Both challenges to the time boundary enhanced my thinking about their specific needs and gave further insights into their internal worlds.

The work occurred in school time only, which meant children would have frequent, regular, planned breaks from music therapy. The rhythm of the school year, though presenting this difficulty of multiple protracted breaks, did at least provide a frame of regularity. As work continued over years with each child, they experienced the rupture of breaks, but also repair when we consistently came back to sessions.

From the outset, I advocated for long-term work. This is not always easy to argue for; however, within this setting it became apparent to the staff that once a child was engaged in the work, it was imperative that they continued their therapy until both child and therapist agreed it would be right to end. There was some pressure on resources at times, and occasional demands to work differently – for example, to offer time-limited blocks of therapy so more children might be seen – but given the severity of the need of children being presented, it was agreed that work should endure for as long as it was needed. Staff came to value the longevity, and the insights music therapy provided for the whole team into children's worlds beyond their diagnosis. Long-term work was especially important where children had multiple experiences of workers engaging for a brief period with them before being allocated elsewhere, thus often replicating earlier separations, losses and rejections which had already gained dominance of their inner world experience.

Theoretical frame

A psychoanalytic framework of thinking (Priestley 1994) was enhanced by further trainings in relational music therapy (Trondalen 2016), trauma (Van der Kolk 2014), attachment (Wilkinson 2006) and embodiment (Totton 2015). This emerging, evolving, eclectic thinking equipped me to consider a diverse range of comorbid diagnoses and labels given to children. I used freely improvised music, as well as valuing silences, with all children. With some I included toys and art materials, where, for example, a particular theme may have emerged, and its expression might be aided by additional modes for expressive and symbolic play.

I made sense of musical communications through a combination of lenses which could embrace all the muddles, ambivalence, multiplicity and ambiguity that was often presenting in the room. There can be similarities between symptoms diagnosed as an autistic spectrum condition and other disabilities (Wigram 1992), including an apparent attachment disorder, which is described in the case study below.

CASE STUDY: FRANCESCA

Francesca was referred to music therapy because the multi-disciplinary team struggled to agree about diagnosis. Some felt elements of the child's presentation were possibly more about attachment and had recently discovered she was an adopted child. In her music therapy, it became increasingly apparent that she lacked definite diagnostic autistic spectrum condition features, but certainly had issues with relating, which we felt made more sense thought about in the context of her history of disrupted early attachments.

This approach has therefore enabled my own process of thinking about diagnoses beyond its apparent parameters.

Referral and consultation processes

In all of the settings, from the offset children would be referred by a member of the teaching staff, often as they felt they were either showing musical ability or enjoyed music. To encourage more appropriate referrals, I began to root the work within a broader model of training and consultation to staff. Teachers and unqualified teaching assistants were encouraged to think about complex and difficult presentations they struggled to manage and give meaning to these in the classroom in annual training sessions. On a weekly basis, I also held open consultation slots in my various rooms, which teachers could book into at any point. This created a boundaried system for discussion and meant that we were able to avoid the sort of conversations a staff member might risk starting in a less confidential space, such as the classroom, staff room or corridor, or without a time limit. Consultation would not detail the content of any particular child's therapy, but rather would help staff to think broadly about the many issues presenting, and how our joint thinking might help the child. Because the work was school-based, parents did not refer their children, but would be consulted about their child's proposed attendance and welcomed to discuss this with school and myself. I devised referral and consent forms and procedures, which over time the children I worked with helped to evolve further themselves, including what, in their view, they felt mattered and their own expectations of therapeutic processes.

Consultations proved diverse, ranging from staff talking about specific issues with a child, to revealing their own personal issues influencing the way they reacted to the child. I felt listening to staff was necessary and discussed this in my own supervision. Is it our role to ameliorate such issues and to fluidly support staff, or not? Sometimes doing so has opened out a space which has led to the child's experience being improved. 'Sense-making' extended then within the school, and also with how I thought about parallel processes in my own supervision.

Evolving the approach

Relational music therapy is a term used to address 'lived experiences, specifically, relational lived experiences in a jointly improvised musicianship between client(s) and a music therapist, exemplified through professional music therapy practice' (Trondalen 2016, p.ix). Music therapists who adopt this approach for practice draw largely on the work of Daniel Stern who described significant moments in therapy as 'hot present moments' (1996), later termed 'moments of meeting' (1998). Stern suggests that 'major change is the result of a series of microscopic changes that result from therapeutic involvement processes within a given time span, be it a moment or a microsecond' (Stern cited in Trondalen, 2016, p.ix).

Stern interweaves theoretical and clinical phenomena, and this was how my own approach emerged. I engaged first with each child or young person in the room, and from the clinical phenomena that arose in our lived experiences, such as transference and counter-transference,[2] I tried to draw theoretical hypotheses. Resisting the imposition of a method of working with clinician-led aims and objectives, I desired to offer a free space for these children to literally come and play in. I hoped that in the space offered by non-directive free improvisation, clients might be able to reveal unconscious embodied aspects of their own lived experience.

Improvisational music therapy is an individualised intervention that can facilitate moment-by-moment motivational and interpersonal responses in children with autistic spectrum conditions. Compared with other therapeutic interventions utilising music as a background or contingent stimulus, a psychoanalytic music therapy approach involves the interactive relational use of live, improvised music to engage children in a process which endeavours to shine light on unconscious experience. Improvisation through music gives room for spontaneous self-expression, emotional communication and social engagement. Within a non-directive space with a responsive therapist, moments of communicative emotion, relational synchronicity and embodied relating might arise. Children who were reported to have struggled to relate with other professionals in school seemed more able to express themselves when given space where diagnosis was not always entirely foregrounded. Without directions to respond to, children became willing to initiate play and engage further. Improvised music making with these children and young people enabled a child-led focus of attention.

---

2   Transference is understood to be when the client projects unwanted psychic material, including earlier experiences in relationship, on to the therapist who in turn receives and holds the material until such a time as it can be given back and owned by the client. Countertransference is understood as the reactions that the therapist will experience in relation to the clients' transference. These are understood not to be the therapist's own feelings but generated by the client's material.

Relational music therapy also seeks to privilege an intersubjective perspective. Drawing on Stern's ideas (1985, 1998, 2004), therapeutic change is understood as coming about through non-verbal processes at the micro level. To consider patterns of relating in depth, I placed importance on considering the transference and countertransference experienced in the room with children. In this way psychoanalytic thinking helped to underpin the meaning I ascribed to both music and relationship. Through this a sense could be gained of the child's internal world, the way in which this was peopled, and the ways in which it influenced actions and behaviour in the child's life and relationships. By encountering the child in the space and bringing my reflections and 'sense-making' back to the music-making relationship, we could together begin to make meaning from our experiences.

Musically, I drew on both expressive and receptive methods. Often children would, for whatever reason, need to be silent in the room, sometimes for many weeks, and come gradually to music making. I would listen, not just to sounds but to the entire sounding of a child's embodied presence (Sletvold 2014). There is tremendous value contained in such non-verbal implicit communication at a micro level. This can also be thought of in Winicottian terms (1958) as a necessary state of being preceding playing. One 11-year-old boy stated, 'If we look, we might see each other', and proceeded to sit gazing at me for weeks, before being able to move to playing music. Looking in this way felt like a very primitive and early mode of being.

The core value of music therapy was thus that it offered the children and young people a place to be met as they were and to experience playing together with another and explore different patterns of relating. Within both the space and the music, difficult feelings and thoughts could be revealed, known, shared and made more manageable.

Music in relationship

Musical language, or communicative musicality, has been shown to precede the development of verbal language as a pre-verbal embodied experience of intrinsic pulse and gesture (Daniel and Trevarthen 2017). Babies have been shown to communicate through embodied rhythm and repetition, which clearly relate to elements of musical language. The emotional tone of the mother's voice is first heard in the womb and responded to non-verbally and across different modalities long before verbal language is acquired. This knowledge can be used to form a basis for advocating that children who struggle to relate through verbal language could benefit from a non-verbal modality, such as music therapy, to experience therapeutic relationship and experiment with new ways of relating. Music therapy may help children with an autistic spectrum condition feel more connected internally with a sense of self. It might also offer a way of 'speaking without words', relating with someone who carefully attunes to establish and development a therapeutic relationship. This can often constitute an emotional and relational experience that has not previously been available.

Some children and young people with autistic spectrum conditions can be seen to possess innate musical abilities, which music therapist Karen Gold (2016) suggested could mean music might helpfully be thought of as their first language. Two children I worked with had what is often called savant ability – extraordinary skills not exhibited by most people. When the predominant language for a therapeutic setting is music, it can invite these children and young people into relationship on their terms, using the language of music. Relationship is what I aimed for, in contrast to the isolation felt by children excluded from mainstream education and struggling with family and social relating, and shared language is vital to relationship. Todres (2007, p.80) states that sharing language is part of 'feeling more connected with one's self and with an other who validates that self. The experience of isolation is reduced and greater intimacy with oneself and the other is enhanced.'

Conversely, for other children with high levels of musical skill, music itself could be a problematic language when it served to function as a psychological defence against feelings and intimacy. I often encountered children who could play sophisticated, complex music, but the emotional tone would lack any vitality. Musical elements such as high volume and continuous repetition seemed to constitute something like a sensory skin that could effectively shut out me and my playing. I became aware that repetition was a constant feature of the music of many children I was working with. This included music repeated within the session itself, but also music that was repeated week to week as sessions progressed. Another constant feature in the music was a very loud, and excluding, dynamic, the playing of certain children even causing pain because of its high volume. Children could lock into their own world and exclude others in this music, and it would often reveal how much they struggled to connect with others.

As music therapists, we might feel pleased that a child immediately or continually plays music in our sessions. We can believe the child is communicative and relationship-seeking. However, not all music making is relational, and at times music itself can be a strategy to defend against real intimacy. I would find with many children that if I were allowed to play at all, I would only be allowed to play as the child dictated, and in the way they wanted. I would feel merged into the child's music, in an experience neither shared nor relational as it held no sense of separate identities, no separation of self and other, and tended to leave me feeling objectified. At such times, it seemed important to hold my own feeling experience, as well as attending to the client's experience, without detracting from it or turning it into something else. If I could not stay with difficult material, then I understood that a meta-message may be discouraging permissive exploration of that area.

However, merging like this can, for some children, offer a positive experience when it constitutes a necessary enactment of a primitive state that may have been missed. For example, one child was able to later verbally describe how he felt intrinsically heard and understood. My 'sense-making' of his experience was that it seemed that his unconscious might be able to speak to my unconscious in improvised music making. My own feelings about the music, insights gained about transference and countertransference experienced and explored in supervision helped to consider each individual experience of merging.

Other music would initially seem very alive and as if it were asking to be joined in with. However, there would again be a sense that life and vitality were missing, and if I was allowed to join at all, I would rapidly find myself feeling sleepy or even bored. I might consider both of these emotions as transferential feelings experienced when encountering sublimated anger. However, I could make different interpretations of what might be the functions of such music. Defensive music might serve to protect the child's self against risk or could meet a child's need to keep a protective and defensive psychological skin around the self. The child might be seeking out a sensorial experience where they can feel totally sufficient in their own body, and volume and repetition might provide this. Fast, loud, repetitive music with an emphasis on beat can provide what Martin Lawes (2010) described as a sensory floor or ground or what Jos De Backer (2004) described as an acoustic containing skin between us. For some children this music, instead of providing a psychological barrier, might provide a safe, embodied base from which to relate to the therapist. It is interesting that many children in therapy stated that their favourite genre of music to listen to was dub-step, and the repetition and pulse of dub-step seemed also to provide this function.

Being and presence

Free musical improvisation thus forms the foundations of an approach that seeks to neither label the child or young person further nor to change them within interactions, but rather hopes to reach out, and make contact, with the hope that they might then reach back in relationship. The philosopher Levinas (1969) describes an ethics of encounter with a presence which allows the other to be who they are and to leave behind their false self. This describes to me what potentially becomes available in music therapy.

Levinas's notion of shared presence feels close to Winnicott's (1958) writing about a baby being enabled to play freely in the presence of the mother without being impinged upon, nor feeling abandoned. In a relational model of therapy, an attentive being-with therapeutic presence (Eberhart and Atkins 2014) describes a position where the child or young person is simply enabled to present their communications as they are, existing without need for interpretation or intervention. Stern (2004) similarly describes the state of 'moving along' where mother and infant play together just for the sake of it. There is no goal, but rather the experience of improvised relating in the moment is enjoyed for its own sake. Children can be themselves in a supportive presence where the unexpected is given room, and possibility exists for pivotal moments to emerge.

The value of psychoanalytic thinking

I worked with staff to clearly articulate what is understood by psychoanalytic thinking, to assure them that there was value in what was an unfamiliar approach. In time, it enabled collaborative sense-making of the inner worlds of children, whilst also recognising that any context for internal worlds arose within a complex interplay of bio-psycho-social factors. For the children I saw, there were certainly difficulties experienced in sharing the stage of the world with others. Using a psychoanalytic approach enabled me to consider this beyond the diagnosis of an autistic spectrum condition and retain an openness towards dynamics such as sibling rivalry and competition in families, which might also underlie a need to shut out the world. As such, work was located around the relationship with me, as an other who might gradually become tolerated, as well as being competed for within school.

I found myself needing to think about representations children enacted, and worked to bring these out more by including some art and play materials in some sessions. Symbolic play offers children a chance to experiment with the world in representations that they create themselves, and music can provide a safe container for symbolic enactments. Many children and young people used musical instruments to represent people or situations, and to enact family life and dynamics, sharing parts of their inner world. Children varied in their degree of capacity for imaginary play, but for those able to use it, this provided another way of using space to explore. The room could begin to become populated with characters from the child's inner world, held within the music and the therapy frameworks.

Music as holding

The holding facility within music can be provided by musical elements such as pulse, beat and repetition, which may contribute to a felt sense of stability and self-containment. It is then, within these structures, that the very nature of free improvisation allows children to feel empowered, offering space for them to know and experience themselves in different ways.

Musical holding links, again in a Winnicottian sense (1958), to the early facilitating environment provided by the good-enough mother, where states of what differentiates me and not-me are not yet clear. To encounter a sense of self (the me) in relationship with an other who is a different self (not me) means to let go of rigidity of self. This invokes the potential for overwhelm and fragmentation, especially for children and young people with an autistic spectrum condition. Perseverative or merged play might be necessary for children to first feel grounded and merged with the therapist. Out of this holding space might then come risk and experimentation with other ways of relating.

The value of the approach: a place to be autistic

Working with children with autistic spectrum conditions has shed light for me on what remarkably differing lived experiences exist. Sometimes children described as high-functioning are able to articulate aspects of their experience of having an autistic spectrum condition, and my work with these children has certainly informed my work with non-verbal children too. As music therapists, we perhaps listen differently to the phenomenological world of the child and young person. Todres (2007 p.34) writes that, 'although the therapist is willing to experientially participate in the client's world, (s)he does not necessarily react in the same way as the client to this world'. Each level of recoil from encounter that children and young people express can only be released by themselves when they realise their concerns are truly listened to and cared for by a witnessing therapist.

The children and young people I worked with sometimes appeared to demonstrate more severe autistic spectrum condition features than had first been recognised within the multi-disciplinary team. Often, I felt that these children and young people were dealing with what Gold (2016) movingly described to me as the 'agony of insight' into their diagnosis. Children and young people need to know that their therapist can survive the emotional impact of their situation and self. Such an ability to experientially witness the reality of the child's world, participate within it and survive it improves the therapist's ability to let-be (Todres 2007). In such a state of attentive being-with, as music therapists we must willingly be absorbed into the child or young person's world.

Musical play may provide a less threatening experience of being two people relating together, where even emotions such as hate can be expressed and tolerated. The attentional and acoustic space surrounding both me as therapist and the child or young person exists as a phenomenon in its own right. Within this space, music made together can become a 'third object' (Ogden 2012) present between us within the room. Music exists as transient temporal form, yet can become almost tangible, literally vibrating in the molecules of air between us, and within the ear drums of us both, as well as resonating in other parts of the body, hence being a total embodied experience (Totton 2015). Music becomes then, I suggest, a place where the immediacy of what happens between the child and me can sometimes be addressed, then survived, and even serve eventually to deepen the child's faith in the value of human contact.

Reflections and conclusions

The psychoanalyst Daniel Siegel (2007) writes that clinical experience is enriched when we can embrace the reality of uncertainty. He advocates that therapists develop the art of 'not knowing' and relinquish our grasp on prior preconceptions or expectations. This leaves us open and receptive to experience things as they are, and not as we wish they would be. I learned to approach my work in such an exploratory manner, embracing this 'not knowing' position in order to learn from relationship. Marks-Tarlow (2008, p.297) writes that our work is 'like life itself, open-ended, ever in flux, and too complex to ever fully grasp'. I believe my work has helped me to understand and engage with how cut off these children and young people can feel from relationships, whilst being desirous of connection. This became emergent via the long slow process of entering individual worlds, and remaining there for a long while, before starting to engage in shared 'sense-making'. This is the very process of relational work; we make it as we do it. Much contemporary thinking in psychoanalysis increasingly recognises the value of joining the client, attending, witnessing and being present in a relational sense in the given moment, or the 'now' moment as Stern would have it.

Starting this journey working within the psychoanalytically framed music therapy approach that I trained in, I found myself developing an eclectic approach to meet the variety of needs presented. I hoped to offer a space wherein children could express and explore their feelings and fantasies about the interpersonal therapy relationship, without fear of the implications that such acknowledgement would have in other everyday school contexts. When, as therapist, I was neither swallowed up within nor destroyed by the experience, I could become humanly present, without loss of access to a meta-perspective. I discovered that by working within an intersubjective relational therapeutic approach both the child or young person and therapist might experiment with closeness and distance. This, in turn, led me to consider my own development as a therapist, regarding intimacy and separation issues, and the central role of supervision (Kuchuck 2014).

This chapter offers only a snapshot of my experiences of working in this way, at this time. The work is not straightforward simply because all the children share, or appear to share, a diagnosis. There is much more to encounter as I continue to engage with muddles, ambivalence, multiplicity and ambiguity. Psychoanalytic thought has underpinned the meaning given to both the music and behaviours that these children have shared. Free improvisation, sometimes with the addition of talking and playing with toys and art materials, has provided a basis for shaping relational space in long-term work. Within this approach of working through each year, and over many years in special schools, a rhythm has been able to develop for each child and young person which offers experiences of being close enough to another, yet within which they might also have space to be able to create distance. Non-directed free clinical improvisation can perhaps open a space for relating in which unanticipated experience might emerge. The narratives that have formed and shaped children and young people can be explored, and opportunities offered for developing new ways of relating. Spaces can be created where change is possible, and children and young people might engage in 'sense-making' themselves.

To engage in the ways I have discussed depends upon a music therapist developing and possessing a quality of presence which can enable authentic connections with often difficult-to-reach children. Such connections, however small and tentative, form the foundations of a facilitative relationship in which the medium of music provides an aesthetic shaping of unconscious material. As music therapists, we experience musical relationship by participating in creating it. We become aware of potential musical connections, respond to them, hold them and continue to reflect on them. Longer-term work gives room and permission to watch, wait and wonder, which can sit alongside processes of diagnosing and treating. Imagination provides a bridge between children's sensory experiences and the unconscious worlds these might represent. For the children and young people I worked with, the inner sense of feeling cut off from experiencing life-giving relating had become external reality when they were excluded from mainstream education and defined as different.

To close, then, some final words from Todres (2007, p.118) which seem to define for me what being a music therapist working with this model of music therapy provided: 'We enter a land of many colours, of rage and hope, and we are asked to be resilient…to wait, and to grant the gifts of both aloneness and sharing.'

References

Daniel, S. and Trevarthen, C. (2017) *Rhythms of Relating in Children's Therapies. Connecting Creatively with Vulnerable Children*. London: Jessica Kingsley Publishers.

De Backer, J. (2004) *The Transition from Sensorial Play to Musical Form by Psychotic Patients in a Music Therapeutic Process*. Dissertation submitted for the degree of Doctor of Philosophy. Aalborg: Aalborg University, Institute of Music and Music Therapy.

Eberhart, H. and Atkins, S. (2014) *Presence and Process in Expressive Arts Work: At the Edge of Wonder*. London and Philadelphia: Jessica Kingsley Publishers.

Gold, K. (2016) Personal Communication. Cambridge.

Gordon, P. (2009) *The Hope of Therapy*. Ross-On-Wye: PCCS Books.

Kuchuck, S. (2014) *Clinical Implications of the Psychoanalyst's Life Experience: When the Personal Becomes Professional*. East Sussex: Routledge.

Lawes, M. (2010) Personal Communication. Cambridge.

Levinas, E. (1969) *Totality and Infinity: An Essay on Exteriority*. Pittsburgh, PA: Duquesne University Press.

Marks-Tarlow, T. (2008) *Psyche's Veil: Psychotherapy, Fractals and Complexity*. East Sussex: Routledge.

Ogden, T. (2012) 'The analytic third: Implications for psychoanalytic theory and technique.' *The Psychoanalytic Quarterly 73*, 1, 167–195.

Priestley, M. (1994). *Essays on Analytical Music Therapy*. Gilsum, NH: Barcelona Publishers

Siegel, D. (2007) *The Mindful Brain*. New York, NY: Norton.

Sills, F. (2008) *Being and Becoming: Psychodynamics, Buddhism and the Origins of Selfhood*. Berkeley, CA: North Atlantic Books.

Sletvold, J. (2014) *The Embodied Analyst: From Freud and Reich to Relationality*. East Sussex: Routledge.

Stern, D. (1985) *The Interpersonal World of the Infant: A View from Psychoanalysis and Developmental Psychology*. London: Karnac.

Stern, D. (1996) 'How do People Change in Psychotherapy Through Non-Verbal Means?' Paper presented at the Nordisk Forskernettverk i musikkterapi, NorFa, Gml. Vraa Slot. November, 15.

Stern, D. (1998) *The Motherhood Constellation: A Unified View of Parent-Infant Psychotherapy*. London: Karnac.

Stern, D. (2004) *The Present Moment in Psychotherapy and Everyday Life*. London: W.W. Norton & Company.

Stone, B. (2017) Personal Communication. Sheffield.

Todres, L. (2007) *Embodied Enquiry: Phenomenological Touchstones for Research, Psychotherapy and Spirituality*. Hampshire: Palgrave Macmillan.

Totton, N. (2015) *Embodied Relating: The Ground of Psychotherapy*. London: Karnac.

Trondalen, G. (2016) *Relational Music Therapy*. Gilsum, NH: Barcelona Publishers.

Van Der Kolk, B. (2014) *The Body Keeps the Score*. London: Penguin.

Wigram, T. (1992) 'Differential Diagnosis of Autism and other types of Disability. Keynote paper to the 1991 Annual Congress of AMTA, Sydney, Australia.' *Australian Journal of Music Therapy*, 3, 16–26.

Wilkinson, M. (2006) *Coming into Mind. The Mind-Brain Relationship: A Jungian Clinical Perspective*. East Sussex: Routledge

Winnicott, D. (1958) 'The capacity to be alone.' *International Journal of Psychoanalysis* 39, 5, 416–420.

CHAPTER 3

'Fight It Jake! Fight It!' The Ethics of Encouragement with Clients with an Autistic Spectrum Condition

Robin Bates

Introduction

This chapter has as its fulcrum a single eight-second incident which occurred during a music therapy session with Jake (a pseudonym), a non-verbal adolescent client with an autistic spectrum condition. From a focus on this incident, the chapter pans out to view the therapeutic landscape of working with autistic spectrum conditions, studies its ethical topography and concludes with a useable paradigm for working with this client group. Rather than looking at the aetiology of autism, it instead looks at the phenomenological experience of being with a client with an autistic spectrum condition in the here and now, what feelings and unconscious processes are at work – what it's like to be together in the room. It also looks at the therapeutic trajectory behind this momentous incident and whether I was right to do what I did. Whilst we, as therapists, may feel that doing right and good is implicit in our role, sometimes this sense of beneficence can be the most important – and only – thing to hold on to.

On the outside of the door to my room where the incident occurred is a *Do Not Disturb* notice bearing my name and my HCPC registration number; I am a professional music therapist registered in the UK with the Health and Care Professions Council (HCPC). When a client enters my room, both of us are guided and protected by the Council's *Standards of Conduct, Performance and Ethics* (2016). This sets out a strict, professional code covering confidentiality, consent, safety, discrimination, record-keeping and boundaries. Adhering to this code, therapists have a professionally robust frame in which to work. Within that frame, however, when the door of the therapy room is closed to the outside world, in the interaction and therapeutic thinking which occur between therapist and client, the HCPC ventures only so far as to say: 'You will need to use your judgment so that you make informed and reasonable decisions and meet the standards. You must always be prepared to justify your decisions and actions' (HCPC 2016, p.4). It is under the charge of this last sentence, specifically when applied to music therapy sessions with clients with an autistic spectrum condition, that this chapter examines how such justifications can be reached. When in sessions with such clients, particularly those who are non-verbal, music therapists have to make decisions based on their observations and feelings: when to play music and when not, what manner of music to play, when to direct, when to lead, when to challenge. If the client seems reluctant or is resistant to playing, how far should the therapist encourage? Should such encouragement include hand-over-hand playing?

It is significant that in the index of two of the world's major texts on health care ethics, *Principles of Health Care Ethics* (1994) edited by Raanan Gillon, and *Principles of Biomedical Ethics* by Beauchamp and Childress (1989/1979), there is no entry for autism. There is no mention of autism in the more recent *Mental Health Ethics – The Human Context* by P. Barker (2011) and, surprisingly, no mention of autism in *Ethical Thinking in Music Therapy* by Cheryl Dileo (2000). This in itself suggests the difficulty in charting a passage through the rocky channels of ethics connected with autistic spectrum conditions. So, music therapists have to find their own way and can lean neither on the above texts nor the HCPC codes to help in precise ethical decisions. This chapter is intended to reveal and unravel the complexities of ethics in working with clients with an autistic spectrum condition and finally to illuminate an ethical path.

The incident

The music therapy room where the incident happened is about 4.5 metres long by 3 metres wide. It has a good upright piano, a few large djembe drums, a guitar, various percussion and, on a small central table, a set of table tubes – a construction of metal tubes suspended by a crisscrossed elastic cord over a hardwood frame. Pentatonically tuned, these produce a gentle room-filling sound when tapped with a rubber-ended beater.

I had been working at the special school for eight years and had been having a weekly 50-minute session with Jake for almost a year; the incident happened in our 28th session. His initial referral carried two main objectives: to make a connection with Jake and to develop and improve interaction. Prior to beginning sessions, I had met with his parents, who both said how much Jake loved music at home, how he was 'happy in his own little world' and how they had heard wonderful things about music therapy. They were anxious and sad that they couldn't have 'normal interactions' with their son – such as cuddling up on the sofa – and feared that, despite seeming happy, Jake might have been a lonely boy in his 'cut-off' world. Jake had been on my waiting list for over a year and they were overjoyed that it was now his turn.

Jake had been at the school for 11 years after being diagnosed with an autistic spectrum condition at the age of four. Completely non-verbal, he expressed himself vocally with hisses and grunts, walked always on tiptoe and was in a mixed class of six adolescents with autistic spectrum conditions. Before starting work with Jake and when happening to walk past his classroom, I would see him sitting on the floor in the corner amidst a messy scatter of Lego bricks. He would be scooping up handfuls of these bricks and pouring them over his own head, an activity referred to by his teacher as 'having a Lego shower'. He often repeated this all the school day, apart from meal times and playground time. His teacher agreed with Jake's parents that Jake was 'happy in his own world' and added that Jake seemed uninterested in joining class activities. Although Jake could not tolerate being touched by anyone, classroom staff physically helped him to sit on a chair for group activities during which Jake hissed throughout, immediately returning to his 'Lego shower' at the end.

On the day of the incident I had collected Jake from his classroom as I always did, at precisely 10:15am. He was rocking from toe to toe at the door anticipating my arrival. We had walked along the corridor to my room and Jake had gone inside, hissing. I closed the door. He went straight to the table tubes, picked up a beater and began rocking to and fro, his eyes focused on the tubes. As usual I went to the piano and began the 'Hello' song which I had used since our very first session. This was a simple 'Hello Jake', repeated twice, with the *Hello* on middle D and the *Jake* on the A above – a perfect fifth. Jake remained in his rocking mode alongside the table tubes, a beater clutched in his right hand and poised six inches above the tubes as if shaping up to play. After the 'Hello' song I joined him, standing on the other side of the instrument; I tapped two of the tubes lightly, playing a perfect fifth. His facial expression was that of intense determination to play.

Jake had never touched an instrument in a session apart from in our 16th meeting when he had accidentally brushed a hand against the strings of the guitar and scampered into the corner hissing, shielding his eyes and ears. But he had attended every session, always came eagerly and stayed until the end – which the school saw as remarkable for someone who rarely left his Lego shower corner. We had never had eye contact and he had never directly responded to anything I played or vocalised. In all the sessions prior to the incident, Jake had been non-interactive, initially playing iteratively with a drumstick on the floor in a corner, sometimes sitting passively, sometimes rocking on one spot.

For several sessions before the incident I had noticed a change: an intentionality had emerged. Jake had a number of times seemed to be just about to play one of the djembes but then something seemed to restrain him, his muscles seemed to go into spasm and he recoiled. It looked as if an invisible heavy hand was stopping him. In my mind, this was the heavy hand of autism, frustrating and irremovable.

Facing Jake over the table tubes in this 28th session, each of us brandishing a beater and shaped up to play, I felt the force of this intentionality. Something was revving up and it needed release; one foot was on the accelerator and the other on the brake. This was the fervour in which the incident occurred: Etna was rumbling. I quietly but audibly mouthed 'Fight it Jake, fight it!' between clenched teeth. I was willing him to take the risk, to play. Then I took a risk: with my free hand I took his hand which was holding the beater; his arm muscles relaxed, he yielded. I then moved his hand to the tubes, helping Jake to tap one note. In the sound of that one note, his whole body seemed to relax as if an enormous tension had been released.

He dropped the flats of his feet to the ground and looked at me. Although fleeting, this look seemed to be that of grateful relief.

A few seconds after the incident, Jake, unaided by me, drew the beater across the tubes and grinned widely, playing a confident *glissando*. Then he played each tube slowly one by one, pausing to allow me to tap the tubes too. It was a duet, a turn-take on a pentatonic scale. Jake had interacted willingly with another human being, listening, waiting and responding. At the end of the session, I took Jake back to his class, feeling that here was the breakthrough, here was the transformative point.

The session had indeed been pivotal. It transformed our relationship and what consequently happened in the room from that day until I stopped work with Jake one year later as a result of waiting-list pressure. Standing at his classroom door that day, I watched as Jake went straight to his corner, tipped out the box of Lego bricks and resumed his showering; he seemed blithely to continue where he had left off as if nothing had happened. But something had happened; it seemed a roadblock had been removed. In subsequent sessions Jake made forays into the world of interaction: more eye contact, more listening and responding, exploration of other instruments. Usually gravitating to the table tubes, these interactions, albeit tentative and fleeting, had increased both in number and duration when sessions came to an end.

The ethics of encouragement

I returned to the music therapy room, closed the door and for half an hour wrestled with and tried to process my own Lego shower of feelings and thoughts. If his teacher's and his parents' assumption that Jake was 'happy in his own world' was true, why was I using music as a way of encouraging him to leave his world and join mine? Was I using music as a weapon in order to achieve this? As John Hamilton hauntingly suggests: 'Music tracks down everyone within its range, rudely and without regard. Unlike the eyes, the ears have no lids' (Hamilton 2008, p.112).

Why did I feel compelled literally to manipulate Jake into taking a risk? Why did my 'Fight it Jake, fight it!' seem inappropriately pushy? What did I know about the 'heavy hand of autism'? Who was I to encourage Jake to take the risk of interaction? Was I the coercive agent who removed Jake's autonomy and what right did I have to do that? What was the experience like for Jake? Did it help him to feel better in the world? These questions were to seep into all of my work with clients with autistic spectrum conditions: was it right to use music to encourage these people to leave their comfort zone and enter the unpredictable, scary world of human interaction? Music is a powerful therapeutic tool and can affect clients profoundly, leading to change. Gary Ansdell (1995, p.87) describes this potential of music as 'musical quickening':

> Quickening is more than just stimulation, it is more than the effect of sound and physiology. Its real gift is the unexplainable power to animate not just the flesh but also the spirit – to give an impulse which makes someone want to act, want to respond.

How could I be sure of the beneficence in all of this? As a music therapist, was using music to entice Jake into a social world the right thing to be doing? I seemed to be caught in a thorny thicket of ethical doubts and assumptions. Hacking my way out of this thicket involved a profound test of my own ethical stance, my own assumptions, my own emotional responses to Jake's anxiety. I put under ethical scrutiny my own being as a music therapist, my position as a member of a caring profession and what it was for me to be a responsible human being working with people with all the unknowns in our understanding of autistic spectrum conditions. After a long reflective process, I realised that this struggle was, of itself, critical to my practice and I eventually arrived at a useable paradigm which offers resolution to all of these questions.

In the world of not-knowing which surrounds autism, and particularly working with those clients for whom the realm of words is not available, it is important to hold on to things we do know or have utter faith in. It is important, through all the unanswerables and unmeasurables connected to autistic spectrum conditions, to have an ethical rudder. I needed some serious help to find a rudder I could rely on, so I turned to the writings on ethics, particularly health care ethics, by its foremost thinkers.

One of the major concerns of health care ethics is autonomy, a human right clearly stated here by the liberal philosopher Isaiah Berlin: 'I wish my life and decisions to depend on myself, and not on external forces of any kind. I wish to be the instrument of my own, not of other men's acts of will' (Berlin 1969, p.131).

And a more imperative statement is declaimed in one of the weightiest tomes of health care ethics (Holmes and Lindley 1994, p.672):

> Therapists, like medical practitioners, are enjoined to do nothing which might compromise a patient's autonomy: they should, for example, avoid attempts to coerce, control or cajole them into courses of action, even when motivated by a benevolent desire to prevent patients from acting against their best interest.

I had fallen at the first ethical fence, then; I had taken Jake's hand and used it to play a musical instrument. My will had prevailed. I had robbed him of his autonomy; the act was coercive. Furthermore, I had no idea what Jake's best interest was; perhaps it was just to stay in his comfort zone under his Lego shower. Was it in Jake's best interest for me to encourage him to quit his insulated world and enter the world of interaction, to join the social world? Perhaps Jake's will was indeed to join the social world – but his autistic spectrum condition was a resistive barrier preventing it. The concepts of will and resistiveness were a core element in the therapeutic approach of Paul Nordoff and Clive Robbins, two pioneers of music therapy in the UK. Described by Kenneth Aigen (1998), their approach considered 'the channelling of the will [as] an appropriate and essential part of therapy processes' (p.31). He later observes that the Nordoff–Robbins approach uses 'the power of music to bring resistiveness into its equivalent level of participation' (p.274) and that 'it is a basic assumption of this work that the benefits of doing so are self-evident.'

In Albert Camus' *La Peste* (2000/1947) there is a character, an asthmatic patient of the protagonist Dr Rieux, whose sole activity between meals every day is to count peas from one pot to another. Twelve pots and it's time for lunch, fifteen and it's dinner time, ten more and it's time for bed. Camus, an existentialist philosopher, challenges the reader with the implied question – is this man's life less meaningful than ours? The parallel with the image of Jake spending his days at school under his Lego shower is clear. Attempting to make a moral judgment on this is deeply unsettling. Why do Jake's school, his teacher, his parents, his educational psychologist and me, his music therapist, think that we have the right to change his behaviour if Jake's way of being in the world seems to be working for him and is doing no harm to others?

Recent writings on autism have focused on whether society should view autistic spectrum conditions as deficit or difference. Charlotte Brownlow examines therapeutic approaches to autistic spectrum conditions which have normalisation as their guiding principle – aimed at changing the behaviour of those with an autistic spectrum condition in order to fit in with 'normal' (neurotypical) people, which, in other words, say to those with an autistic spectrum condition: learn these behaviours to conceal your deficit. 'The clear implication of such interventions is that people must change in order to accommodate the neurotypical world' (Brownlow 2010, p.17).

Brownlow goes on to quote views from people with Asperger's syndrome which reveal bitter resistance to this view: 'I don't want to pretend to be normal. I want to be me' (p.18). This leads me, as a music therapist, to a very uncomfortable thought; it forces me to face the unpalatable possibility that my manipulation of Jake's hand was the opposite of what he wanted me to do.

It is tempting to fall into a defensive logic here, an avoidance of ethical spikes. It goes like this: Jake is non-verbal, has an autistic spectrum condition, has a Statement of Special Education Needs, is in a special school. The school, as the agent of beneficence, has commissioned me as a professional to deliver music therapy with the objectives written on his referral form. The school pays me for this and I would be dodging my professional responsibility if I didn't follow their brief. Therefore, as a commissioned professional, it is my duty to follow their objectives and encourage Jake through the use of music into the world of interaction. Fine – but when I am in the room with Jake, it's just me and him, I am the agent of beneficence. I am left to rely on two inner resources to guide me. First, the experiential information I receive from being with Jake in the room: how does it feel and what might my feelings tell me about how he is feeling? Second, my ethical rudder, my credo – which is this: that the only purpose of therapy is to help people better enjoy life or better endure it. Wrestling with my own doubts after Jake's 28th session revealed something of a paradigm: I would hold a clear ethical direction and I would be guided by Jake who would let me know incrementally how he felt about it. These two elements offered a steady course for us both; here was my useable, ethical and reliable paradigm.

A graduated approach – building on what you know

Much has been written about the importance of a solid therapeutic frame and I repeat and affirm that here. A safe, protected, uninterrupted space with consistent boundaries is the critical portal for a graduated music therapy approach. Jake's session, for example, was always on a Tuesday from 10:15 to 11:05 in the same room. This allows the creation of what Winnicott referred to as 'the potential space' (Winnicott 2005, p.135) – a held space where creatively transformative things can happen. Shakespeare's image of the 'wooden O' (*Henry V*) – referring to the circular wooden building of the Globe Theatre in Elizabethan London – carries the same metaphorical power of a space in which a story can unfold. Better still is the image of the French poet Mallarmé (2008/1897) who wrote of 'A place where nothing takes place but the place'. Much has been written about the therapeutic concept of the holding environment – and a graduated approach to music therapy uses the concept as a starting point. Structure and consistent routine help a client with an autistic spectrum condition to feel safe, help filter out excessively stimulating occurrences and allow a therapeutic relationship to grow. Musical input from the therapist, with its potential of musical quickening (Ansdell 1995) needs to be clear, simple and introduced gradually. Too much too soon and the quickening may be too much for the client with an autistic spectrum condition to process. The graduated approach to music therapy is essentially governed by close observations of the client's reactions and monitoring the phenomenological temperature in the room – what it *feels* like. Increasingly complex rhythms, melodies, vocalisations, harmonies, timbres are introduced carefully, each element evaluated under this therapeutic scrutiny.

The things I knew – and could prove – about my work with Jake were simply that he came every week, demonstrated eagerness in anticipation of the session, and stayed to the end. These hard facts seemed to offer a clue. Perhaps Jake's compulsion to come to music therapy came from a basic human drive to connect with others – an idea which forms the main thrust of the Object Relations school which holds that from birth, human beings have an instinctual impulse to connect with the object or the other: 'the human being is essentially social: our need for contact with others is primary and cannot be explained in terms of other needs or reduced to something more basic' (Gomez 1997, p.2).

I found this theory appealing and I fell into its arms. It was shouldered by heavyweight thinkers (Melanie Klein, Donald Winnicott, John Bowlby) whose writings had for me resonated on a deep level. And it offered a way of assuaging my own feelings of uselessness, rejection, doubt and despair which I experienced in the first eight sessions with Jake when with a drumstick he spent the whole of almost every session playing iteratively a loud ostinato on the floor in the corner with his back to me. The quality of this was forbidding, loud and anxious – and there seemed no way for me to join him in it. It felt as if he was telling me to leave him alone: back off. Like it or not, this was the feeling in the room at that time with Jake: *leave me alone.* Throughout, I held on to the idea that beneath all this, there was a human who wanted to relate. Jake was coming to the sessions, he was with me in the room, it seemed that he wanted to be there. This felt significant and I allowed the Object Relations idea of the human instinctual impulse for interaction to underpin my thinking. Jake was human, he wanted to interact, I was helping him through the medium of music, and by following this way of thinking I felt insulated against ethical doubt. My ethical rudder was steering us in the right direction and it felt that we both had a hand on the tiller.

Jake's barrage of sound which he created during our first eight sessions forced me to be silent. If I had attempted to join in with him, I would have needed to play very loudly and the thought of that felt both competitive and intrusive – as if I was elbowing my way in. Moreover, I would not have been hearing what Jake's music was telling me, not hearing the subtext of the music: *let me just be here, I'm anxious and need time and space to process this new experience.*

In feeling pushed out and rejected, perhaps I was experiencing how Jake felt in the social world. If I had played and cranked up my volume to match Jake's, wouldn't I have been displaying an inability to stay with these feelings, acting them out rather than processing them as a way of trying to understand how Jake was? I would have been guilty, as my supervisor used to say, of giving my client a blank canvas and covering it with my own paint; in other words, making the therapeutic space more about me than for Jake.

Reflecting on how my relatively inactive silence seemed necessary for Jake enabled me to formulate a graduated approach to working with clients with an autistic spectrum condition, both verbal and non-verbal. Often initially presenting with behaviour similar to Jake's, verbal clients with an autistic spectrum condition can flood the session with their words, whilst non-verbal clients with an autistic spectrum condition can fill the session with iterative activity such as playing with a transitional object, flat-palming a keyboard, tooting a mouth organ, tapping a drum, etc. There is at the outset of a course of sessions always anxiety – and this is not only felt by the client; it is also felt by the therapist. As Bion famously pointed out: 'In every consulting room, there ought to be two rather frightened people' (Bion 1990, p.5). At the outset of sessions with Jake we were both feeling anxiety; the difference was that I was able to contain my anxiety whilst Jake expressed his through loud and iterative play. Sandra Brown noted this quality of iterative play in her work with a 12-year-old girl with an autistic spectrum condition, saying it felt it was 'her way of holding on to some kind of order and coherence and of shutting out anxieties and fear, both in terms of her own little understood emotions, and also in dealing with the demands inherent in social relationships' (Brown 1994, p.19).

An unintrusive silence during initial sessions with all therapeutic antennae switched on serves two functions. With Jake, this first respected his need freely to express how he felt being in the room with me – and this may have also included shutting me out, keeping at bay any interaction from me which might have de-railed or curtailed him. Second, it demonstrated to Jake that I was able and robust enough to allow uninterrupted safe space for him to express his anxiety. It was the beginning of a developing trust which was essential in the trajectory to the momentous incident in session 28 and, importantly, it allowed me to experience and process Jake's projected feelings.

Complete therapeutic inaction and marmoreal silence is not what I am advocating here. The hues of silence are many. When you're alone, silence can offer a comfortable space for reflection – as in silent prayer – and it can offer sweet respite from the clamorous world of sound. On the other hand, when in the company of one or more people, silence can lead to the persecutory feeling that you are required to interact and to reveal something of yourself. This is perceived as external social pressure – such as may arise from being in a room with a therapist, for example. For those with an autistic spectrum condition, this is likely to exacerbate what is already intolerable: on top of being frustrated by external forces, they are already frustrated by themselves, their condition.

Harmony – handle with care

Being with Jake, although it felt important that our 'place' for music therapy should be safe and uncluttered by me, there was something else. This was the feeling, compelled by the Object Relations idea of the instinctual impulse to connect, that Jake *wanted* me there and that he wanted to interact; my presence was necessary. Moreover, I felt the need to offer Jake gentle reminders that I was there: alive, present and available. I was a music therapist cohabiting this space with a client with an autistic spectrum condition and I had at my disposal a medium unequalled in its precision for the expression of feeling: music. I chose an unadorned, perfect fifth as my precise message to Jake, reminding him that I was there: two notes, a D and an A, played slowly one after the other on either the piano or the table tubes. As well as being the twin pillars of my 'Hello' song, they served as a wordless reminder, sparingly and gently played throughout Jake's iterative play, his rocking or his silence. Helpfully, it may have also had a familiar resonance for Jake – in that it features in many popular songs and as the first notes of some children's songs he had probably heard a thousand times in classrooms and at home throughout his childhood.

Phenomenologically, the perfect fifth carries a feeling of boundaried space, rock steadiness, potentiality – expectancy for something to happen within it, like Shakespeare's 'wooden O'. Beethoven used the perfect fifth to open his ninth symphony: where hushed strings create a feeling of anticipatory, boundaried space. The feeling is invitational: something is being called, something is going to happen.

So, the perfect fifth, with its simple, open and beckoning quality, offered Jake and me a way of beginning a graduated approach to music therapy. Each relationship between a music therapist and a client with an autistic spectrum condition is, of course, different and each therapist will be alert to the specific harmonic/melodic/rhythmic formulations which appeal to their individual clients. Physiotherapists and professional masseurs also employ a graduated approach when working on tired or damaged muscle groups. They begin massage with a technique called *effleurage* – a soothing, gentle, stroking movement which helps prepare the muscles for deeper tissue work called *petrissage*. This musically unobtrusive but emotionally present way of being with Jake was our *effleurage*, without which I wonder whether we would have reached the plateau of possibility which enabled our later momentous incident, the gateway to what felt to be our deeper work – our *petrissage*.

There is more to harmony than the perfect fifth, of course, and I here need to step back to take in the view of the kaleidoscopic variables of harmony and the range of affect that different harmonic formulations carry. Every music therapy training in the UK would endorse Mendelssohn's words, that 'music expresses emotions that are too precise for words'. If we accept this as true and that each subtle variation of harmony can communicate a different emotion, then maybe each of these emotional shades can be felt by a client with an autistic spectrum condition. Bisect the perfect fifth with an F sharp and the resulting D major triad sounds wholesome, solid and positive with its connected feelings of satisfaction and security. Bisect it with an F natural and the emotional climate changes altogether; you're in the dour realm of the minor mode with its melancholy and tragic shades. And that's just for starters. Add another note, another two – or a whole flat-palmed cluster and you're in different emotional regions. Even more emotionally potent than the tonic-to-dominant perfect fifth is a harmonic device which ought to come with the warning *handle with care*: the dominant seventh. For me, the sound of the dominant seventh tightens my stomach muscles. It's a chord which badly needs to be resolved, a chord which creates a tension that cries out for relief. When deployed, it casts a musical spell, bestowing an almost irresistible gravity to the tonic. It is a chord which wants to go home.

A 'Goodbye' song is the dominant seventh's natural habitat – that of preparing an ending, a cadence. I use a dominant seventh in all of my 'Goodbye' songs with clients with an autistic spectrum condition, holding the chord on either piano or guitar beneath the words *'I'll see you again next...'* letting the tension build before resolving with *'...week'* on the tonic. In the second year of weekly sessions with Jake, three sessions after session 28, when I had felt and observed an increase in his will to interact, I began to hold the chord a little longer each time, allowing the tension to build – with Jake transfixed in anticipation – before releasing it on the tonic *'...week'*. In our 37th session, unable to contain the suspense, Jake supplied the word *'week...'* – the first recognisable word I had ever heard him utter. Of course, there can never be an off-the-shelf prescription of harmonic levers for clients with an autistic spectrum condition (*'play this chord to begin with, play this chord when you get stuck, play this chord at the end, etc.'*); each client will come with their own likes, dislikes, fears and secrets. Nevertheless, a graduated music therapy approach, navigated by a therapist who is aware of his or her musical resources and who is governed by an ethical rudder, may gently encourage clients to connect in new and different ways.

The ancient Greeks used two words for describing time. One was *Chronos* – sequential tick-tock, *chronological* time; the other was *Kairos* – which describes the propitious moment, the moment of something coming into being, the moment of change. Daniel Stern refers to this, describing such moments as 'Moments of meaning …in which two parties achieve an intersubjective meeting' (Stern 2004, p.151). And I wonder whether this is the experience of time felt by a person with an autistic spectrum condition. The incident in session 28 seemed to be a Kairos moment for Jake; there were others too, not least when he first uttered the word *week* at the end of our 'Goodbye' song. With clients with an autistic spectrum condition, it may be that the only way to create such moments of positive change is through a patient and graduated path.

Countertransference and biological template

Some changes in harmony, some leaps in melody, some shifts of gear in rhythmic pulse can produce a precise emotional response, as described above. Sudden harmonic wrenches, *accelerandi* and *rallentandi* are amongst the stock tools of trade for composers and performers who seek musically to alter the emotional climate. Some music therapy clients adopt a monotonous, repetitive style of play: tapping a drum, finger-poking a single key on a keyboard, for example, or playing iteratively a drumstick on the floor as Jake did in his first few sessions. Such clients seem 'stuck' in such a mode of play. For a client with an autistic spectrum condition stuck in this way of playing during an improvisation, musical changes instigated by the therapist may offer the client a way of easing into a new mode of self-expression, a new way of being. And the therapeutic use of such change will be influenced by how the therapist is feeling in the session with the client: countertransference phenomena. Mary Priestley (1994) explains such phenomena succinctly as 'all of the unconscious reactions that a therapist has towards a patient, and especially to the patient's transference' (p.74).

In sessions with Carlos, a non-verbal seven-year-old boy with an autistic spectrum condition, we had established a regular episode of calm and pleasant improvisation, he on a pentatonic metallophone, me on piano, noodling around on an F major chord, supporting him. It all felt very holding, safe and cosy. After three sessions almost dominated by this, I began to feel bored and frustrated; the music felt soporific, almost anaesthetic. I felt an urge to wrench the music up into the subdominant, the B flat major, a fresh elevating experience. Although we had found a way of just being with each other, it felt like we weren't going anywhere, there was a stasis. If my antennae were working properly, perhaps that's what Carlos was feeling too: 'Come on, Robin, lead me on, I'm ready.' Processing these feelings after the session led to some questions which sent me scurrying to my supervisor. What did it mean for Carlos that his therapist (me) was a man and not a woman? For my clients with an autistic spectrum condition, how might their engagement with music therapy be affected by my being a man? Is the therapeutic light refracted by the biological template of the therapist?

Kenneth Bruscia (1995) acknowledges such refraction and stresses the importance of examining the issue of therapist gender: 'it helps therapists to acknowledge the unavoidable biases that gender brings to their theories, research projects, and clinical practices, either unconsciously or unintentionally' (p.195). Bunt and Hoskyns (2002) speak of 'the containing and holding energies of female therapists and the penetrating and invasive energies of the male therapists' (p.313). Together with my supervisor we explored how, for Carlos, I may have provided the father-figure object of his transference. Indeed, being a man – with my male voice and physicality – I was unavoidably attracting these transferences of my clients. We considered the Winnicottian concept of the good-enough mother (Winnicott 1991/1964) and also the role of the father. Whilst the good-enough mother's business is in holding and containing her child, the father's role is often that of extending the child's experience, encouraging and watching over them whilst they take risks. Perhaps this was the feeling I was registering with Carlos – and perhaps this was the feeling which compelled my hand to take Jake's hand in session 28. Perhaps I was acting out this instinct which was embedded in my own biological template of being a man. Was this a bad thing? I didn't think so – but would a female therapist have felt the same?

I was once on the receiving end of this predominantly male compulsion. During my first – and only – mountaineering experience on a university trip to Snowdonia, I found myself 200 feet up a sheer rock face, clinging on ten feet from the top, spreadeagled in the letter X with sweat on my back, terrified to move. Leaning over the top and shouting down at me were our two experienced male climbing instructors: 'Come on, Robin, you can do it! Move your left foot NOW! You're not going to fall!' After ten minutes their high-octane macho cajoling prevailed: I made the move. The resultant feelings of euphoria after achieving the move were unforgettable and I nearly danced a jig at the top, so proud and relieved was I of my achievement. I did it!

Did Jake experience similar feelings when I took hold of his hand in session 28? Did I lead Jake to a better enjoyment of life by taking him out of what Michael Blastland, in his moving account of life with his son, Joe (with an autistic spectrum condition), calls the 'poverty of experience, an excessive selectivity which means he neither can, nor cares to, dip into the rest of life's data' (Blastland 2007, p.17)? Certainly, the look of grateful relief on Jake's face after I had helped him to play seemed to express an enjoyable experience. Perhaps Carlos too was asking me in the transference to do something which triggered my fatherly *let's take a risk* impulse. When, at our first meeting, Carlos's parents, like Jake's, had said,

'He's happy in his own little world', the word '*little*' may have been heard as a challenge by this embedded instinct. Such instincts come from a level deeper than countertransference, operating beneath its radar. In a graduated approach to working with clients with an autistic spectrum condition, such impulses in the therapist must be identified, acknowledged, perhaps restrained.

Conclusion – and a workable paradigm

Some years ago, I was concerned that a conference I was organising would not attract enough participants. I happened to mention this to one of the senior paediatricians in my area. 'Just put the word "autism" in the conference title', she said, 'and they'll come flocking.' I didn't, but the implication was clear: the 'A' word was a magnet and people are attracted because they are hoping to get answers, revelations which will dispel the despair of not knowing. I have been to many conferences, workshops and seminars with the 'A' word in the title and have always left feeling stimulated but still wearing a blindfold. The world of autism has yet to yield its secret; for us music therapists and other professionals, it still beguiles. Nevertheless, when you step as a professional music therapist into a room with a client with an autistic spectrum condition, you need clearance from all doubt, assumption and preconception. First, and most importantly, identify your ethics: does what you are doing feel *right*? Trust your feelings of just being with your client and trust your client to let you know whether they find the experience tolerable or not. This is the paradigm. Consider that autism does not nullify the basic human impulse to interact but may render interactions less straightforward, sometimes intolerable. Follow your ethical rudder and know that your client's hand is on the tiller as well as your own. Allow the space and the silence to do their work and gently ease yourself into the space using simple, sparing musical statements. Be aware of your own impulses. Allow the power of simple harmonic formulations to wield their musical quickening. Wait for the moments of connection – the Kairos moments – and monitor their frequency. When they swarm, change is happening.

I happened to see Jake in a supermarket a year after he had left school, walking on tip-toe down the biscuit aisle with his parents. Smiling, swinging his arms and looking quite genial, he seemed oblivious to the teeming traffic of people and trolleys around him. I saw him at the checkout, screening his eyes with one hand, rocking to and fro, giggling when his dad said something. Insouciant and calm, he seemed perfectly at ease in the world. I have to confess that, considering Jake and his way of being on that day in the supermarket, the breezy way he looked to be engaging with life, aloof from the mendacious, tricksy world of the rest of us, I found I had something to expiate: an envy. In my final report on my work with Jake, I lamented that I had had to end our music therapy sessions together as a result of waiting-list pressure in the school. I noted that his interactions had increased and that I would be delighted to resume sessions with Jake if an appropriate slot became available. It never did. I have no doubt that had sessions been allowed to continue, so would have the increase in Jake's interactions, both non-verbal and verbal.

Was I right to take Jake's arm and make him play that note back in session 28? If the end result was that Jake learned how better to enjoy his life or better endure it, then yes, I was. And here in the supermarket, in society, four years on from our music therapy time together, it looked as if he was having a good day.

References

Aigen, K. (1998) *Paths of Development in Nordoff-Robbins Music Therapy*. Gilsum, NH: Barcelona Publishers.

Ansdell, G. (1995) *Music for Life: Aspects of Creative Music Therapy with Adult Clients*. London: Jessica Kingsley Publishers.

Barker, P. (2011) *Mental Health Ethics: The Human Context*. London: Routledge.

Beauchamp, T.L. and Childress, J.F. (1989) *Principles of Biomedical Ethics* (3rd edition). New York, NY: Oxford University Press. (first edition published 1979.)

Berlin, I. (1969) *Four Essays on Liberty*. London: Oxford University Press.

Bion, W. R. (1990). *Brazilian Lectures: 1973 São Paulo; 1974 Rio de Janeiro/São Paulo*. London: Karnac Books.

Blastland, M. (2007) *Joe: The Only Boy in the World*. London: Profile Books.

Brown, S. (1994) 'Autism and music therapy – is change possible, and why music?' *Journal of British Music Therapy* 8, 1, 15–25.

Brownlow, C. (2010) 'Presenting the self: Negotiating a label of autism.' *Journal of Intellectual and Developmental Disability* 35, 1, 14–21.

Bruscia, K. (1995) 'Modes of Consciousness in Guided Imagery and Music (GIM): A Therapist's Experience of the Guiding Process.' In C.B. Kenny (ed.) *Listening, Playing, Creating: Essays on the Power of Sound*. New York, NY: Albany.

Bunt, L. and Hoskyns, S. (2002) *The Handbook of Music Therapy*. London: Routledge.

Camus, A. (2000) *The Plague (La Peste)*. London: Penguin Classics. (Original work published 1947.)

Dileo, C. (2000) *Ethical Thinking in Music Therapy*. New York, NY: Jeffrey Books.

Gillon, R. (1994) *Principles of Health Care Ethics*. Chichester: Wiley.

Gomez, L. (1997) *An Introduction to Object Relations*. London: Free Association Books.

Hamilton, J.T. (2008) *Music, Madness and the Unworking of Language*. New York, NY: Columbia University Press.

Health and Care Professions Council (2016) *Standards of Conduct, Performance and Ethics*. London: HCPC. Accessed on 30 March 2018 at: http://www.hcpc-uk.co.uk/assets/documents/10004EDFStandardsofconduct,performanceandethics.pdf.

Holmes, J. and Lindley, R. (1994) 'Ethics and Psychotherapy.' In R. Gillon (ed.) *Principles of Health Care Ethics*. Chichester: John Riley & Sons.

Klein, M. (1959) 'Our Adult World and its Roots in Infancy.' In M. Klein (1988) *Envy and Gratitude and Other Works*. London: Virago.

Mallarmé, S. (2008) 'Un coup de dès jamais n'abolira le hazard.' In S. Mallarmé (translations by E.H. and A.M. Blackmore) *Collected Poems and Other Verse*. London: Oxford World's Classics. (Original work published 1897.)

Priestley, M. (1994) *Essays on Analytical Music Therapy*. Barcelona: Phoenixville.

Stern, D. (2004) *The Present Moment in Psychotherapy and Everyday Life*. New York, NY: W.W. Norton & Co.

Winnicott, D.W. (1991) *The Child, The Family and the Outside World*. London: Penguin. (First published 1964.)

Winnicott, D.W. (2005) *Playing and Reality*. London: Routledge.

CHAPTER 4

Musical Interaction Therapy (MIT) for Children with Autistic Spectrum Conditions (ASCs): Underlying Rationale, Clinical Practice and Research Evidence

Dawn Wimpory and Elise Gwilym

Introduction

Employing a timing-based model of autistic spectrum conditions to explain the practice and outcomes of MIT

This chapter presents a social timing-based model of autistic spectrum conditions (Wimpory, Nicholas and Nash 2002; Nicholas *et al.* 2007) to justify the use of Musical Interaction Therapy (MIT). MIT aims to facilitate interactive synchrony for young children with autistic spectrum conditions whilst their caregiver (e.g. a parent or teaching assistant) engages them in one-to-one interaction. The music therapist gives live timing support through improvised music that facilitates and emphasises the interaction between carer and child. MIT functions therapeutically as an exaggerated and prolonged experience of preverbal interaction. MIT has been practised with pre- and primary school aged children for three decades in North Wales, where it represents a cross-agency clinical and research collaboration between the NHS, Local Authority Social Services/Education and the School of Psychology at Bangor University.

Autistic deficits may be explained by a timing-dependent model (Newson 1984; Nicholas *et al.* 2007; Wimpory 2015; Wimpory and

Nash 1999b; Wimpory *et al.* 2002) informed by the social and symbolic development of typical infants (Newson and Newson 1975; Trevarthen and Aitken 2001). In this chapter, Dr Dawn Wimpory (Consultant Clinical Psychologist – Lead for ASDs and Lecturer) outlines the characteristics and importance of early interactive social timing (or temporal synchrony), and its likely developmental consequences, in both typical and autistic development, in order to clarify the need for MIT. Dawn Wimpory presents methodological considerations concerning MIT, then five introduces the perspective of Elise Gwilym, one of the current MIT music therapists. This section considers how MIT has some similarities with the joint work of Paul Nordoff and Clive Robbins and is compatible with Pavlicevic's (2002) descriptions and interpretations of parent–infant interaction. Elise Gwilym then focuses, through a short case study, on how she uses improvised music in MIT to facilitate transactional development in child and caregiver interaction skills.

In the final sections of this chapter, Dawn Wimpory considers research evidence that indicates positive changes in social communicative development in children with autistic spectrum conditions who are receiving/have received MIT. These include the emergence of teasing and symbolic play, retained at two years follow-up (Wimpory, Chadwick and Nash 1995). The significance of these developments is explained by early aspects of the chapter that clarify their role within the developmental trajectory of typical children, in contrast to that of those with autistic spectrum conditions. MIT is now the subject of a larger-scale service-based study in the NHS along with other linked studies exploring broader timing difficulties in autistic spectrum conditions, ranging from genotyping to gait analysis (Nicholas *et al.* 2007; Wimpory, Nicholas and Foster 2018; Wimpory *et al.* in progress).

Background evidence from research into typical development
Timing in preverbal interaction and implications for children with autistic spectrum conditions
Video recordings of the preverbal interactions of typically developing babies highlight how the interactive timing, between

themselves and their parents, is crucial (Trevarthen and Aitken 2001). Trevarthen and Malloch (2009, p.3) write that 'an inborn musicality is clearly uncovered in acoustic analyses of parent/infant vocal interactions, where, independent of verbal communication, a shared sense of time and the shaping of jointly-created pitch contours describe phrases and narrative cycles of feeling'.

Such interactions are characterised by flexible cross-modal monitoring of impulses that are actively generated by both infant and adult (Trevarthen 1986; Trevarthen, Kokkinaki and Fiamenghi 1999). Even newborns, through vocalizing or movement, can synchronise precisely with particular salient moments in an adult's communication (Malloch 1999). These early exchanges or proto-conversations, between a young infant and an adult, are characterised by very sensitively timed conversational turn-taking (Trevarthen and Aitken 2001). At six weeks of age, a slow turn-taking rhythm becomes established (paced at 1 in 900 ms). Within another month or so, the beat of shared vocal play speeds up within parent–infant social games (paced from 1 in 700 or 1 in 500 ms).

Within typically developing children's patterns of conversation, there is congruent pattern matching between the conversing children. Specifically, pause lengths vary together, towards a match in mean pause-duration between conversational partners. This synchrony of pause-duration in verbal conversations includes those of young typically developing children (Welkowitz, Cariffe, and Feldstein 1976). Preverbal use of switching pauses typically develops from around nine months (Jasnow and Feldstein 1986). In temporal synchrony, the duration of each partner's switching pauses become increasingly statistically similar to the mean over time. Temporal synchrony has been repeatedly validated as an aspect of typically developing preverbal interaction (Feldman 2007). Feldman identifies three types of interactive temporal synchrony within preverbal interaction: matching (with perfect synchrony of partner contributions), sequential (where one partner leads another) and organised synchrony. The two former can occur alone or as components of organised synchrony. The ongoing patterned format of temporally organised synchrony is revealed through time series analysis, after any individual periodicities have been removed; it is also known as mutual or temporal synchrony and becomes well established from about nine months (Stern 1985).

Where interactive video links are employed to desynchronise maternal contributions during interaction with typically developing five-month-olds, the infants show avoidance such as looking away, as well as distress (Murray and Trevarthen 1985; Nadel *et al.* 1999). Within the timing-based model of autistic spectrum conditions, outlined within this chapter, such a scenario could be regarded as a crude simulation of the experience of infants later with autistic spectrum conditions where biologically based timing impairments may affect both their perception of social interaction and their contributions to it.

Transitioning from preverbal timing to symbolic functioning and implications for children with autistic spectrum conditions

Interpersonal synchrony is initially dependent on an infant's experience of that infant's own rhythmic functions, and then on the relation of these to the communication of a familiar person. Even the heart rates of infants and their mothers become attuned during interactive synchrony (Moshe and Feldman 2006). Experience of preverbal interaction, at the pre-symbolic stage, appears to support the development of tacit interactive knowledge (Jaffe *et al.* 2001; Stern 1974, 1985, 1995).

A preverbal interactive context, where the synchronicity of active communicative turn-taking and affective experience can play a crucial role, includes creating and acquiring an increasingly sophisticated shared understanding. This hosts the emergence of symbols at around the first birthday (Feldman 2007; Newson and Newson 1975; Wimpory *et al.* 2000). These early joint action formats include, for example, playing 'Peek-a-boo!' in different moods, speeds and contexts, etc. The fact that such playful encounters or scenarios are often familiar, yet varied, means that they can readily come to stand as symbolic representations themselves. Indeed, infants' earliest mental representations often characterise their significant others.

Over time, physical objects become incorporated into an interaction. This transition from primary to secondary inter-subjectivity, involves the interactive focus progressing from a person-to-person focus to a more inclusive focus on person–object–person. Playful teasing, by parents and infants, is common in preverbal interaction (Reddy 1991, 2001, 2008) and often facilitated through issues of timing during non-verbal play. For example, the words, 'S-l-o-w-l-y, s—l—o—w—l-y, quickly!' might typically involve exaggerated speech and rotating hand movements coordinated with the verbal content. This example, demonstrates how teasing involves playfully sabotaging another person's expectations which often depend on patterns of timing.

Playful teasing by an infant both involves some mental representation of parental expectations on the part of that infant, and precedes other manifestations of symbolic functioning that may involve physical objects (Hoika and Gattis 2008; Reddy 1991, 2001, 2008; Trevarthen and Logotheti 1987). Such insights, gleaned from typical development, can be informative in developing appropriate strategies for helping children with autistic spectrum conditions to move towards teasing, empathy and symbolising/pretending.

Later consequences or correlates of temporal synchrony in preverbal interaction

As indicated above, the experience of differing attitudes, including teasing, during preverbal interactive play with and without objects, may enable appreciation of the 'double meanings' required for symbolic play (Hobson 1993; Reddy 1991; Trevarthen and Logotheti 1987; Wimpory 1995; Wimpory et al. 2000). Parent–infant proto-conversations also provide the opportunity for acquisition of social use of language (Bates, Camaioni and Volterra 1975; Ninio and Snow 1988, 1996). These, and other developments that correlate with the temporal synchrony of preverbal interaction, match important areas of difficulty in autistic spectrum conditions, such as attachment, symbolic play, empathy and Theory of Mind (ToM). ToM involves the essential social skill of being able to take others' perspectives; it is typically tested through assessing a child's understanding of one character hiding something from another.

Levels of temporal organisation in the social attention of three month olds, predict infant–mother synchrony at six months and at two years of age (Feldman et al. 1996). Mid-range levels of vocal synchrony in four-month-olds predict the security of infant attachment by their first birthday (Jaffe *et al.* 2001). Mother–infant synchrony at nine months predicts self-control/regulatory skills and cognition at two years (Feldman, Greenbaum and Yirmiya 1999).

Typically developing three-month-olds' regulation of their own emotional states is characterised by non-random distribution of irregular cycles. Assessments of video recordings of these, through 250 ms time-frame analysis, have been found to predict those infants' symbolic functioning abilities at two years (Feldman and Greenbaum 1997). Such abilities include pretend play and use of words relating to internal states that, in turn, are considered to be precursors of social perspective taking or Theory of Mind (Feldman and Greenbaum 1997). Face-to-face synchrony in the infant's first year has been found to predict Theory of Mind at five years and empathy at 13 years (Feldman 2005, 2007).

Background evidence from research into autistic spectrum conditions

Social timing difficulties: from preverbal interaction onwards

Few research studies have considered interactive synchrony in autistic infancy. Kubicek (1980) found a lack of interactive turn-taking in a four-month-old, in contrast to his typically developing (TD) twin brother, through continuous analysis of interactions to an accuracy of 1/24 of a second (0.042 seconds). The autistic infant's responses (distress and avoidance, such as looking away) resembled those of some typically developing infants who, for the purposes of later research, were subjected to a time-delayed video link in interacting with their mothers (Murray and Trevarthen 1985; Nadel *et al.* 1999).

Suvini, Apicella and Muratori (2016) detected inter-subjectivity difficulties in video recordings of parent infant interaction involving a three-month-old later diagnosed with an autistic spectrum condition. This paper reflected the interests of its authors in that it employed a method of music therapy microanalysis whereby musical transcription methodology was used in analysing just the musicality/sound qualities of the interaction. This contrasts with conventional microanalytic research studies of early interaction that employ more objectively derived temporal measurements of visual, as well as auditory, aspects. Although a temporal synchrony approach wasn't used by Hedenbro and Tjus (2007) either, the most striking differences between a child with an autistic spectrum condition and a typically developing cohort, studied from three months old, became apparent in their interactive synchrony measures at age nine months. Genuine mutual temporal synchrony typically emerges at this age.

Measures of temporal synchrony focus specifically on, and more objectively measure, the flow of interaction within a parent–child dyad. Such measures were employed by Trevarthen and Daniel (2005) with a pair of 11-month-old twins (regarded by their parents as identical), during one-to-one parent–infant interaction. The twin who was later diagnosed with an autistic spectrum condition (and Retts disorder) showed no well-timed co-regulation. In contrast, the typically developing twin showed synchrony as well as cyclic reciprocation of expressions. Trevarthen and Daniel's approach was particularly fine-grained, in that the video-recorded parent–infant interactions were coded at resolution of 0.04 seconds and analysed at 0.16 seconds.

Analysis of mother–infant free play, using larger time windows (of one and five seconds), failed to distinguish six-month-olds who were later diagnosed with an autistic spectrum condition from those who were later undiagnosed. The authors (Rozga et al. 2011) acknowledge that a microanalytic approach (e.g. involving, higher temporal resolution) may have proved more productive. Preliminary findings from current research by Dawn Wimpory's team at Bangor University, based on video recordings analysed at 0.086 of a second, confirm temporal synchrony difficulties for children with autistic spectrum conditions from two years old to primary school aged, even when these children appear to want to interact. In this respect, they contrast with the typically developing infants analysed so far in this research.

Retrospective parental interviewing reveals differences between children with autistic spectrum conditions, on the basis of their interactive turn-taking in infancy (Wimpory et al. 2000). Pre-schoolers with autistic spectrum conditions, in contrast to those with typical development, are disinterested in Motherese – the higher-pitched, flowing maternal speech that is usually facilitative of preverbal interaction (Kuhl *et al.* 2005) and are less likely to pick out their mother's voices when others' voices are superimposed (Klin 1992). Given that pitch tone perception, in individuals with autistic spectrum conditions, has been recorded as being unimpaired (Heaton *et al.* 2007; Mottron *et al.* 1999), these pre-schooler findings could more likely reflect how the difficulties in autistic spectrum conditions are primarily social (Fein *et al.* 1986; Hobson 1993).

However, there may be some more specific autistic spectrum condition impairment(s) pertaining to the social timing of communication (Amos 2013; Fitzpatrick *et al.* 2016; Marsh *et al.* 2013; Newson 1984; Wimpory 2015; Wimpory and Nash 1999b; Wimpory *et al.* 2002). Timing is an inherent part of social interaction, particularly preverbal interaction (Trevarthen and Aitken 2001) where participation carries important consequences and has associated developmental correlates (Feldman 2007).

Social reciprocity difficulties have long been central to the diagnosis of autistic spectrum conditions (American Psychiatric Association 2013) and broader timing theories of autism encompass circadian, neurological and/or communicative aspects of timing (Allman 2011; Boucher 2000, 2001; Brock *et al.* 2002; Courchesne *et al.* 1994; Grossberg and Seidman 2006; Newson 1984; Nicholas *et al.* 2007; Richdale and Prior 1995; Segawa 1985; Szelag *et al.* 2004; Tordjman *et al.* 2015; Welsh, Ahn, and Placantonakis 2005; Wimpory *et al.* 2002). Timing and/or other difficulties in the responsiveness or repertoire of infants and young children, with autistic spectrum conditions may make temporal synchrony harder for parents to achieve with them (Wimpory 2015; Wimpory and Nash 1999b). An important goal for MIT is to establish preverbal interaction and thereby facilitate its associated developmental benefits in social and symbolic functioning.

Timing-related difficulties with gesture and speech

Young children with autistic spectrum conditions have been found to be specifically insensitive to disturbed temporal linguistic synchrony (Bebko *et al.* 2006). In contrast, many children with autistic spectrum conditions are reported to be without difficulty in experiencing, or in some cases reproducing, music. It may therefore be that timing difficulties in autistic spectrum conditions specifically pertain to social communication.

Even able young people with autistic spectrum conditions have been found to have speech–gestural synchrony difficulties when telling a narrative. The timing of their gestures, in relation to their spoken language, has a negative impact on the quality of their story-telling (De Marchena and Eigsti 2010).

Prosody is the intonation and spoken rhythm that conveys emotional nuances and meaning. Difficulties in expression and perception persist in children with autistic spectrum conditions even when they are intellectually able (Hesling *et al.* 2010; Peppe *et al.* 2007; Peppe *et al.* 2011). Their difficulties are linked with respect to emphasis, emotional affect and rhythm (Hesling *et al.* 2010). They also prefer voices that are synthesised and without prosodic intonation (Burack *et al.* 2001).

Early chronographic analysis found that the interactions of adolescents with autistic spectrum conditions with their parents were characterised by longer switching pauses. These verbal high-functioning participants, with autistic spectrum conditions, never achieved temporal synchrony in their interactions (Feldstein *et al.* 1982). This contrasts with the temporal synchrony findings, presented above, that are a regular feature of even preverbal typically developing infants.

Developmental correlates of preverbal interaction and the core deficits of autistic spectrum conditions

In summary, it seems that many deficits of autistic spectrum conditions could be directly linked to impairments in the skills required for early preverbal interaction (facial expression, gesture, prosody, turn-taking, etc.). However, research findings from typical development indicate an apparent developmental role for temporal synchrony within preverbal interaction. The lack of temporal synchrony development in autistic spectrum conditions could precipitate important symbolic functioning deficits in affected individuals. There are autistic deficits in each of the following areas and each of these has been shown to correlate developmentally with temporal synchrony in typical infancies: symbolic functioning/ social pretence, social-emotional adaptation (Feldman and Eidelman 2004; Harrist *et al.* 1994), empathy, ToM, and attachment (Jaffe *et al.* 2001). Therefore it seems appropriate to consider the therapeutic value of an approach aiming to foster social timing and temporal synchrony in the interactions of those receiving MIT.

Description of Music Interaction Therapy
Outline of the approach
This section examines MIT and the communicative approach within which it is embedded (Christie *et al.* 1992; Prevezer 1998; Wimpory and Nash 1999a, 1999b). MIT is specifically based around interactive play between a child with an autistic spectrum condition and their familiar carer; it parallels those parent–infant interactions in typically developing children, where interactive games predominate (Reddy *et al.* 1997), which lead to developments including language in typically developing children (Christie *et al.* 1992). Although parents try to communicate with their infants who have autistic spectrum conditions, these babies often cannot make sense of these early dialogues (at least partly due to the social timing difficulties outlined above) and so cannot participate in the way that typically developing children find enjoyable and beneficial. MIT can offer an enhanced and prolonged experience of preverbal interaction play patterns within the carer–child dyad, supported by a music therapist.

During MIT, a familiar carer attempts to engage a child with an autistic spectrum condition through playful one-to-one interactive experiences without toys. Through the support of live and often improvisational music, the therapy aims to facilitate and build on any sociability the child might have, offering generous playful opportunities for the familiar carer and child to tune into each other and experience a shared focus through creating a musically supported dialogue. The music therapist provides a scaffolding support (Bruner 1983) to enhance either partner's role to enable the creation and growth of preverbal discourse.

The music therapist and carer jointly endeavour to create a giving-and-taking experience of communication between the carer and the child with an autistic spectrum condition. These experiences may enable such a child to communicate even before they intentionally and actively contribute (i.e. even whilst the child is still at the pre-intentional stage of communication). As within the preverbal interaction patterns of typically developing children with their carers, the carer within MIT aims to balance the timing and amount of his or her interactive contributions to the level that the child can tolerate. The carer does this by being sensitive to the child's expressive movements and non-verbal cues.

MIT is based on an understanding that social timing difficulties significantly undermine the ability of children with autistic spectrum conditions to benefit from the ordinary preverbal interaction opportunities that they are offered. MIT is not designed as a form of psychodynamic remediation of the parental–child relationship or to facilitate emotional or broader behavioural regression in the child. Instead it focuses on facilitating the appropriate developmental level of the child's social communication; it is used alongside more advanced expectations of self-help or cognitive skills together with age-appropriate demands in other areas of (e.g. physical) development. Within MIT, the child is largely given communicative control. The contributions of both carer and child, whether or not they are intentionally communicative, receive scaffolding support (Bruner 1983) from the music therapist that decreases over time according to the child's need. There is therefore an inverse correlation between the richness of the developing child–carer interaction and the necessity for music therapist support.

Strategies employed within MIT (e.g. action rhymes, tension-expectancy games, vocalising, (situation) songs, running commentary, pausing, following the child, imitation, scaffolding and shared attention)

- Action rhymes, lap games, familiar and spontaneous social routines can all be used to scaffold communication. These play routines are part of early social play between adults and typically developing young children. Established 'tension-expectancy games' (Nind and Hewett 1994) such as 'peek-a-boo' and 'I'm coming to get you' (Prevezer 1998) and spontaneously created social games (e.g. through repeating a child's action) often involve simple speech or chanting, with exaggerated playful intonation often matching the timing of the actions, and can be enhanced by playful physical contact. Within MIT, extensions of what are essentially increasingly sophisticated forms of lap play, through action rhymes and chanting, create a platform for developing more appropriately integrated intonation and social timing that remain important when the child develops more formal spoken language and gesture. An example of a simple lap game involving 'peek-a-boo' would be where a parent places a child on their lap whilst covering their own face with their own hands. The parent then uncovers their face whilst exclaiming 'peek-a-boo! I see you!' and the game can be repeated with variations including the child's own eyes and/or hands whilst the dyad may be in a variety of different positions.

- Vocalising provides enjoyable experiences in its own right, whilst co-vocalising and singing with another can support feelings of bonding. This is also a significant part of the carer's relationship with the music therapist as well as with the child with an autistic spectrum condition; it can therefore enhance the motivation of all participants within MIT.

- Songs, both familiar and spontaneous, offer a predictable and familiar framework for children and are used frequently within typically developing child–parent interaction. Songs are often accompanied by movements which support the meanings of the lyrics and offer a predictable and familiar framework for children. Their volume, tempo, wording or pausing can be varied in response to the context and the child's needs. The language of set songs tends to be clear, with repetitive formats and can enable a child to gain experience in communicative timing and sequencing. A carer's familiar sequential actions maybe imitated by a child, or that child may initiate a song, even non-verbally, by using its familiar actions.

- Situation songs (Kolar-Borsky and Holck 2014), in particular, can employ a simple running commentary; they help give salience to the child's activity, enhance their sense of self and provide a narrative thread. With this comes the potential for communication. Within MIT, the child's or carer's actions or mood, or the interaction itself, can all provide topics for comment. For example, if a child might jump, the carer makes an identical action and sings, together with the music therapist: 'jump, jump, jump away' with appropriate timing.

- Pausing, by adults, during singing and action rhymes, can be employed in a way that is less intimidating than when used within spoken language. Unlike speech, singing enables adults to enunciate exaggeratedly, take longer over words (to help a child keep pace) and to pause and wait for any response. Pauses can be subtle or clearly marked for dramatic effect and give different degrees of support in helping a child to anticipate points within play routines or interactive songs. Such processes facilitate the occurrence of shared experience, which enables children with autistic spectrum conditions to benefit from the social games that are readily enjoyable and helpful to typically developing infants.

- Imitating or following the actions of the child by performing actions (e.g. patting, swinging) such as offering a cooperative action (e.g. a 'high-five') can assist in realising their potential communicative influence on others. Within typical development, this facilitative element has been identified as the illusion of control (Urwin 1984).

- Scaffolding: Within preverbal interaction, parents select, then imitate and comment on the most socially poignant of typically developing infants' behaviours. This both affords particular significance to certain aspects of any infant's behaviour and provides a ready launch pad for turn-taking. Such strategies enable the social scaffolding (Bruner 1983) that provides a child with the experience of social agency and effective communication that is required for facilitating meaningful language development. Within MIT, both the carer and music therapist's combined or complementary use of strategies, such as running commentary and imitation, assist the child in acting intentionally to influence how the adult participants will proceed.

- Shared attention is a primary goal within MIT and 'needs to become a habit in order for quality relationships to develop' (Prevezer 1998, p.11). For example, imitation of the child's actions or vocalisations can help confirm that sense of self and other that enables a shared focus, leading on to reciprocity.

- Mood sensitivity is a characteristic of both MIT and music therapy (Grocke and Wigram 2007). The child's movement is followed by sensitive use of musical and singing pauses in anticipation of the child's subsequent act. The music quietens if the child avoids the carer, and becomes more exciting if the child approaches them, gradually reaching a crescendo with the highpoint of dramatic games (such as 'Tickle under there!'). Moments of connection arise from the carer's and music therapist's constant responsiveness to the child.

The role of music in MIT

Whilst music has yet to be empirically proven as an essential element of MIT, preliminary evidence indicates that it facilitates development in children with autistic spectrum conditions in this context. Imitation, playful repetition and social routines are all integrated elements of MIT that have been found to facilitate sociability by pre-schoolers with autistic spectrum conditions even when employed without live music (Wimpory 1995). However, further preliminary findings from current ongoing research, contrasting interaction with and without MIT support, suggest that the live use of improvisational and/or spontaneous supportive music in MIT makes these strategies more effective (Wimpory et al. in progress).

As a timing-based medium, the music of MIT has a unique potential role in supporting the timing of reciprocal interactions (Newson 1984; Wimpory 1995). Social timing difficulties within the child are manageable within MIT, partly because the carer's role, and the music therapist's accompaniment, can enable the child to enjoy participating. Musical support, for timing in particular, may make social experiences more accessible and predictable to a child with an autistic spectrum condition. Autistic spectrum conditions may be characterised by specific impairment in relation to the social timing of ordinary communication but not in the perception of musical timing; some individuals with autistic spectrum conditions who show exceptional musical ability indicate that this can be a relatively unimpaired area in autistic spectrum conditions (Heaton 2013). On a practical level, the music within MIT can be supportive emotionally and, through enabling overlapping turns, or smoothing over missed turns, interaction can be experienced without a feeling of disjointedness.

Appropriately timed play by the carer with the child, and the music therapist's skilful manipulation of timing in responses to the dyad, may help develop competence in a child with an autistic spectrum condition in timing their contributions to an interaction (Prevezer 1998). Within MIT, sensitive musical accompaniment can enhance the child's perceptions of the carer's behaviour. For example, a child with an autistic spectrum condition may find it difficult to join or tune in with the tempo or mood of a spontaneous social playful behaviour, but the live accompanying music can make it more predictable, as well as more enticing and rewarding.

The music therapist will sometimes use music or speak briefly during sessions to suggest how the carer might play with the child. A strong supportive relationship between the music therapist and carer is essential to enable the latter to risk trying out their own or suggested playful strategies that may not yet be part of their usual repertoire with the child. MIT's live music may simultaneously assist both parent and child in becoming more relaxed. Whilst broader social timing is the focus of this chapter, this concept may well incorporate more specific timing-dependent issues, such as timbre, rhythm, etc. that may also be addressed through MIT, as they would through other forms of music therapy.

The perspective of Elise Gwilym, one of the current MIT Music Therapists

How MIT relates to MT: a similarity in approach to Nordoff-Robbins; vitality affects and use of dynamic form in MIT

Following Trevarthen and Malloch's (2009) acoustic analysis of preverbal interaction in typically developing infants, I propose that MIT's aim is to help create 'a shared sense of time and the shaping of jointly-created pitch contours' that 'describe phrases and narrative cycles of feeling' in play, facilitated by synchronous musical improvisation (Trevarthen and Malloch 2009, p.9). The set-up is different to usual music therapy in that I am playing keyboards or guitar in an unobtrusive corner of the room, facilitating the participating adult and child to interact with each other, without using objects or instruments. In using the term, 'participating adult' throughout this section, I'm referring to a participating parent or carer, or to a participating teaching assistant, as I work with any of these at home or in community or school settings.

My own training in Bristol had a music-centred philosophy but also an underlying humanistic emphasis. An introduction to the use of a co-therapist in the Nordoff–Robbins approach prepared me for working in a trio, including a parent or teaching assistant not trained as a music therapist. Paul Nordoff's background as an eminent American composer and pianist, and Clive Robbins's, as a special needs teacher, served as an example of how a combination of skills and knowledge could work together. Stern's vitality affects (1985, p.54) have been influential in my thinking – 'elusive qualities [that] are best captured by dynamic, kinetic terms, such as "surging," "fading away," "fleeting," "explosive," "crescendo," "decrescendo," "bursting," "drawn out," and so on'. I feel an intuitive affinity for Pavlicevic's dynamic form that 'corresponds to Daniel Stern's vitality affects but is explicitly musical in character' (Pavlicevic 1997, p.121). Dynamic form can explain the nature of the interpersonal events between the participating adult and child that can be facilitated by therapeutic musical improvisation in MIT.

Pavlicevic (2002) writes about the way a mother attunes to her child: '[T]he mother apprehends the dynamic form of the movement i.e. its tempo, irregular rhythm and unexpected lengths of phrases, and expresses these qualities in her vocalization which accompanies the infant's movement.' MIT can be thought of as the natural extension of this as the main focus is to support the participating adult through synchronous musical improvisation to explore different ways of attuning to a child with an autistic spectrum condition. Compton Dickinson (2018) states that 'it's universal in therapies now that we need to do embodied work'. MIT includes both embodied work and stimulation of the auditory sense (Berger 2002) as it works across modalities, while the level of support from me is carefully attuned to their relationship. This means that the music that I use may mirror, reflect, support and enhance vitality affects evident in movements, sounds and perceived emotions, as the parent/teaching assistant and child interact. The music is reduced in the early observational stages, in verbal suggestions during therapy and as the therapeutic intervention comes to a close. At the end point it is hoped that the participating adult will have gained new confidence in interacting with their child in different ways.

In order to consider the triad of music therapist, co-therapist and child in Nordoff–Robbins' music therapy practice in more depth, I revisited some early film (Nordoff and Robbins 1972). This highlighted that Paul Nordoff (playing piano and sometimes singing) receives very little eye contact with the child. In contrast, when Clive Robbins holds an instrument for a child, he is the one at whom the child glances whilst he beams and responds to her, seemingly sharing her emotions and facilitating her to express herself. I realised that, in MIT, the music can facilitate three aspects: the child (as Nordoff did); the participating adult who facilitates the child (as Robbins did); and the temporal synchrony/social timing between the participating adult and child.

I do not try to introduce any 'basic beat' (Nordoff and Robbins 1971) but, in congruence with the developmental model that underlies MIT, I apply Stern's idea of vitality affects to match the different timings of these three aspects. This is how I help to support the synchrony within the dyad. The interaction can also be considered within Winnicott's (1971) concept of 'potential space' that I aim to support and facilitate between the participating adult and child, rather than between myself and the child. As the dyad shares their play, they realise that the music also carries the same idea or emotional state (as a potential parallel to Theory of Mind) and this helps to scaffold and bond adult and child. In the early stages, where the child needs to develop their sense of social timing in relation to the parent, who may also need to adapt their timing in relation to the child, I always work towards facilitating the dyad's adaptation and timing through my music.

Aims as developed in practice

Throughout all phases and aspects of MIT, my greatest challenge is to support the temporal synchrony/social timing between the participating adult and child, as closely as possible, through improvisation. When a child can sustain a level of engagement for approximately three-quarters of the session where music is played, they may be ready to be challenged further. Because the synchronous improvisation in the music gives the child's actions communicative and emotional intent, we see dynamic form, patterning and sequencing develop naturally within the play. The section below examines each aspect of the developing relationship as it occurs with the additional support of music therapy in practice.

Establishing shared attention

'The infant recognises the form of her vocalisation [his mother's] as being related to his arm movement. (He knows that she has a sense of how he feels.)' (Pavlicevic 2002).

The child and parent may have already-established play routines but I ask the parent initially to allow their child to lead, and for the parent to follow – all this is accompanied by synchronous improvised music from me. I help the participating adult to recognise different cues, to watch, wait and follow these with the aim of the child recognising that they are leading and can intentionally influence the music and their parent's response. Any vocalisation that the child makes is responded to by their parent (with similar pitch and rhythm) and play-events develop. Play-events are formed out of the child and parent/teaching assistant responding to one another and serve as proto-conversations and lead on to more embellished conversational topics and exchanges. As these play-events increase in richness of creativity and communication, play-events that start life individually can lead into one another or even become intertwined, and then form narrative cycles of play that are continuously creative.

For example, one child would run around the keyboard with his mum commenting 'run, run, run' as he did this. Then he would sit in a chair to wait for her to approach dramatically (cue 'Teddy Bears' picnic' as a basis for improvisation from me) and this would lead into a 'fingers walking up the body' game (which already existed in their repertoire but now was added on here). After several repeats of this, they then lay down on the floor as they were tired and his mum initiated fingers walking on the floor as symbolising a train (cue 'Chattanooga Choo Choo' song as improvisation), the child imitated with his fingers which led to a game of going round and stopping (using interpersonal synchrony in both timing of facial glances and use of fingers). Over time, a game of walking 'slowly slowly…run' was added at the beginning and, as the body parts were now known to the child from the walking fingers game, they could be requested to be held out to the parent for the parent to play with, leading on to another cycle of play-events involving free play movement of feet.

One notable event was where the child had noticed that the parent had moved slowly to slow music and fast to fast music, to accompany the child. This child began to command the parent with 'fast' or 'slow', using the vocabulary the parent had used as commenting, thus leading to another extension of the cycle. Meanwhile, I was improvising music to support their temporal synchrony/social timing while the tunes that I chose to improvise upon reflected the play-events. This is similar to a *leitmotif* – an associated melodic phrase or figure that accompanies the reappearance of an idea, person or situation, and supports the organic growth of communicative and emotional intent, patterning and sequencing that develop naturally within these narrative cycles of play. In this way the improvisation of the interlinked music and play, within MIT, corresponds to Pavlicevic's 'dynamic form' (1997, pp.130–131), except that the dyad is supported by the music therapist,

> Thus the musical interaction displays the communicative quality of the interaction and, conversely, non-musical acts such as gestures, movements, vocalisations reveal musical, interactive features…

If we return once more to concepts from the literature on the intimate, intersubjective interaction between a mother and her infant, we can describe this fluid engagement as a 'dance'.

The aim of my music in MIT is to facilitate a relationship between parent/teaching assistant and child that becomes synchronous 'in that they meet, match and reflect aspects of one another, attuning to one another through spontaneous music-making of great fluidity and flexibility' (Pavlicevic 1997, p.132).

The way that I find myself using music to support the child–parent/teaching assistant dyad allows me to assess different aspects of interaction. I watch out for the child's 'capacity for organizing dynamic form' (Pavlicevic 2002), noting how many play-events are instigated by the child, or taken over from the parent/teaching assistant, and observing whether they are new or repeated, as well as registering their level of variety and creativity. This might include: how the child changes what they usually do, or how they do it; whether they use any sequencing; and the length of their contributions. Finally, I note if there is an unusually animated response to a particular leitmotif or improvisation. From the very beginning, the improvised synchronous music seems to stimulate new ideas, the connections between ideas and the formation of patterns and sequences in the play, because this is the very nature of music itself.

Selective attunement and negotiated timing

'The parents' intersubjective responsivity acts as a template to shape and create corresponding intrapsychic experiences in the child' (Stern 1985, p.208).

In this phase of selective attunement, the parent/teaching assistant is supported through the music to enhance their synchrony and sensitivity to their child, and so I encourage face-to-face relating in particular. Most importantly, I encourage the parent/teaching assistant to do so in the role of facilitator, encouraging them to hold the child's gaze and use facial expression to give the message that they are continually checking in with them as to what might happen next and when – and then responding as soon as possible when the child initiates. This 'holding' of engagement, which can only be used effectively when the child is already engaged with the person (and might otherwise be counter-productive), serves to facilitate negotiated timing without interfering with the flow of communication. The lead can still flow imperceptibly between them, so even if it is the participating adult who initiates (and in this phase it would be within the overall idea being used, not a new one), this continual negotiation of timing enables the child to practise timing themselves, in relation to the participating adult, on an ongoing basis. My synchronous improvised music aims to support their negotiated timing and facilitate their temporal synchrony/social timing.

Depending on the child's level, if a participating adult uses language during MIT, I suggest a one-word level, usually verbs, used in a commenting capacity so as not to place excessive demands on the child. The participating adult is encouraged to match the pitch, rhythm and vowel sounds of any vocalisations. I note the ratio of who initiates what, within the play-events. I also reflect on the quality of the play-events, noting both where repeated patterns are developing and how the frequency of these may be increasing. I note any changes in eye contact, such as increased regularity, sustained length and its quality, in terms of timing and intention. Referential looking almost never occurs in autistic spectrum conditions. It involves looking to an object and back to see if another person is also noticing that object. This and whether the length of gaze is indicative of the child to 'read' the face is paramount in social development. If I feel, at any time, that there is a disconnection between the improvised music and the therapeutic relationship, I may ask the participating adult what they think might be happening, or I may make suggestions to them during the session. During the discussion afterwards, I use probing questions to help the adult realise for themselves what was going on and what they were doing that facilitated the child to interact.

Pausing and pacing

The important quality of a sensitive caregiver's mis-matching is that it is not far beyond the infant's capabilities and that it offers an expanded and more complicated social environment for the infant. (Tronick, Als and Adamson 1979, p.367)

This quote describes the structure of early face-to-face communicative interactions in typical development. Pausing may be employed as a deliberate strategy to challenge the child to adapt their social timing in MIT. The participating adult may be given verbal support to reflect on how they pause or how to vary the pace of their response sensitively enough to ensure that their child does not disengage; this is supported musically by my following the participating adult's timing. I aim to match the timing of the music to this slowing down and pausing, in order to support the child to adapt their timing responses and to help create anticipation and resolution. The child's capacity to be flexible within the dynamic form shows their 'emotional profile' (Pavlicevic 2002) but also their level of autistic impairment. During early MIT sessions, I often guide the participating adult away from familiar structures, such as a nursery rhyme or a shared familiar interaction. If they can use structures flexibly, this may serve to both cue the child and give the child time to respond to the participating adult; this can become very useful in creating negotiated timing and practising interpersonal synchrony. However, I prefer to encourage free play initially and to let this develop its own dynamic form, as free play has spontaneity. The unpredictability of this spontaneity can reflect the flexibility and responsiveness of pre-verbal communication and may enhance development of skills that the child needs.

Negotiating the lead

> It is all too easy to suppose that a patient is being resistive when in fact it is the therapist's lack of attunement which limits the development of a mutual relationship. (Pavlicevic 2002, p.5)

When negotiating the lead, a participating adult can respond to or build on an established event within the dyad's repertoire or they can initiate or respond to an entirely new event. If the child seems unresponsive to an ongoing negotiation, we return to previous successful strategies, such as facilitating shared attention in order for the child to experience their autonomy again before being reintroduced to negotiation. If the participating adult is stuck on doing or leading, rather than play and negotiation, we may return to selective attunement and temporal synchrony in order for the participating adult to 'be' with the child more, rather than to continue 'doing' or leading.

I assist the participating adult in language mapping and modelling language if appropriate. I also aim to assess the quality of play. For example, I ask myself: are both the participating adult and child initiating, leading, following and negotiating their timing within the flow of play? How varied and creative is the play? Is facial expression developing in the child in combination with the expected increase in communication skills, such as body language, gesture and vocalisation?

Conversational temporal synchrony

> When the therapist and patient come to a place of sharing the shape of the improvisation, they jointly define the structure and fluctuation of the music and jointly explore its musical possibilities. (Pavlicevic 2002)

A 'mature' session of MIT is when the music therapist, participating adult and child come to jointly define the structure and fluctuation of the improvised music, and to jointly explore all play possibilities. All parties are influencing one another within this jointly created musical improvisation (Nordoff and Robbins 1977) and jointly created activity improvisation. Within MIT, I am primarily a facilitator. However, as the participating adult and child are 'attuned' not only to each other (Stern 1985) but also to the improvisation accompanying their play at this stage, we therefore inevitably all influence each other and the lead flows imperceptibly between us as we co-create. Nordoff and Robbins (1971, p.143) describe how they would encourage an activity such as, 'a combination of song and story…depicting characters or it may be a dramatic experience with incidental music'. A comparison may be made here, with the roles taken on by the participating adult and child within their play. Certainly, in MIT, I strive to 'enter into the scope and meaning of the child's activity, supporting the experience it carries', as described by Nordoff and Robbins (1971, p.144).

Apart from creating *leitmotifs* for certain interactions or movements to reflect their shared meaning in the music, my main challenge in MIT is to time my improvisation to support the temporal synchrony of the dyad. The fluctuations of their temporal synchrony can be so quick, so fleeting, so unpredictable, that sometimes I feel my music is like a ribbon fluttering, bending and dancing in the wind to their interpersonal synchrony. In supporting the parent, my challenge is to work out how each parent learns best. Is it, for example, through video feedback with facilitative questioning, and/or verbally with written feedback? I thereby adapt my support to their preferred learning style.

Working without instruments and including the participating adult

The model of MIT is explicit that neither the child nor participating adult should have an instrument. However, in my early experiences of MIT (in 2003), I used to bring a gathering drum, as it felt so exposed to be without an instrument. I stopped doing this after a while as I found that playing an instrument, or using any object in MIT, distracted the child, not only from looking at a person but also from being highly engaged with that person. This is especially true for pre-school children with autistic spectrum conditions.

Oldfield (2006, p.187) set up an investigation to study ten pre-school children with autistic spectrum conditions, each receiving weekly music therapy sessions at a Child Development Centre over a period of two school terms. (MIT sometimes occurs in schools, though also happens at home or at a local community venue where there are no distractions in the room or where there is more space.) She writes that one result was unexpected: '[T]he video analysis showed that, for a number of children, as their levels of engagement increased, the amount they actually played the instruments decreased.' The same is true for MIT: that without instruments or any objects, the relationship of child and participating adult is enhanced, as eye contact is much more frequent. As no instruments or objects are needed for interaction within MIT, this encourages the participating adult to carry on working therapeutically during the week, using strategies developed in the MIT session.

By including the participating adults in MIT, I see effective development in temporal synchrony/social timing as the child begins to develop and to enjoy working with their familiar adult. I also encourage parents to incorporate MIT strategies into their daily routine, especially popular at bedtime, and teaching assistants to incorporate MIT strategies into their timetable to ensure it happens daily. So, instead of one hour a week, the child may receive therapy for several hours a week. However, outside the MIT sessions, everyone reports that the interaction doesn't last as long and that it's harder to keep the child focused without the music. Informal feedback suggests that the participating adults find MIT an intense and stimulating therapy of shared meaning that can facilitate effective development in social timing, symbolic play, attachment and empathy. Most parents comment, by the eighth session, that they can see significant progression in their child that is generalising into their broader life. Teaching assistants have commented to me about how they believe that the bond created in MIT has helped the child to trust them in the classroom and so has facilitated their cooperation and learning there.

Allowing these children to have the support of a familiar adult and freeing them from playing an instrument, releases them in their self-expression. It also enables them to experience temporal space through the music, to order their play within an event, and then to place them in cyclical sequences (but not necessarily the same order). Having the parent to work with them, the person they know best, is an advantage as well as a motivation. I believe that this is because having to process both the interaction with the participating adult and the sound/meaning of the music stimulates the child's brain even more than therapeutic music alone.

I believe that the typical aims associated with music therapy for this population are enhanced even more when working with a significant other. Such aims include:

> sensory integration issues, attention and extended eye contact, rhythm internalisation for organising body movements and muscular control, auditory tracking, auditory integration and figure-ground focus, eye-tracking, information processing, behaviour, independence, self-awareness and self-knowledge, organization of self and environment, awareness of others, and a variety of cognitive issues. (Berger 2002, p.136)

Within MIT, the child becomes engaged at a conversational level of interaction (the richest form of interaction) for longer periods than is usual without the music. MIT sessions can each last for up to an hour as, over time, the child becomes engaged in processing the physical, the socio-emotional and improvised synchronous music with their significant other.

Case study by Elise Gwilym, one of the current MIT Music Therapists
Introduction to James
This case study shows MIT work with James and his mother. As a Consultant Clinical Psychologist – Lead for ASD, Dr Dawn Wimpory actively contributed to James's clinical assessment within her NHS role. Dr Wimpory and other multi-disciplinary colleagues observed an experienced clinical psychology colleague administering the Toddler Modules of the Autism Diagnostic Observation Schedule (ADOS-2; Lord et al. 2012a, 2012b). The results of James's ADOS assessment were considered along with Dr Wimpory's clinical observations and additional findings from her diagnostic interviewing. The interviewing employed the Detection of Autism by Infant Sociability Interview (DAISI; Wimpory 2013). This assessment process led to a diagnosis of autism for James when he was aged two years and eight months.

The NHS Clinical Psychology Child Disability service, in North West Wales, uses 'autism' as the diagnostic term for those children with autistic spectrum conditions whose social communication and associated behaviour is more seriously affected. Like most children who share his diagnosis, James also has a learning disability. Speech and Language Therapy assessment conclusions were congruent with those from Clinical Psychology and he later attended a school for children with special needs.

Although, at the time of diagnosis, James might occasionally have glanced in his mother's direction, his mother felt this was the best that he could offer her in terms of eye contact. He was preverbal and was very interested in objects that could spin, becoming fixated on them for long periods at a time. Professionals often commented positively on the accuracy of James's mother's observations of James and the value of her contributions to MIT. From the start, she quickly used the skills that she learned in MIT, beyond the sessions throughout each day with James and this helped preverbal conversations to become established over time. James's mother herself was extremely pleased with his response to the MIT sessions that began shortly after his diagnosis.

JAMES AND HIS MOTHER – A DETAILED ANALYSIS, WITH TIMINGS, OF APPROXIMATELY TWO MINUTES OF INTERACTION IN MIT

James's MIT video recorded session, described below, was one of those facilitated through grant funding from Jessie's Fund, provided in addition to his NHS-supported MIT programme. The recording can be downloaded from www.jkp.com/voucher using the code MTLIFESPAN. Any MIT video recordings, made publicly available through this chapter, demonstrate my freelance MIT, funded by Jessie's Fund, and are therefore independent of my NHS collaboration with Dr Dawn Wimpory.

This clip shows James at age three and a quarter after he has had a term of MIT followed by a gap of four weeks due to non-clinical reasons. James is non-verbal and began to vocalise during early sessions of MIT. This is his fourth ever session to be held at home and it provides an example of a 'proto-conversation' where his mother responds to James's vocalisations as though they are all intentionally communicative. She imitates pitch and rhythm at a fast pace and sometimes makes remarks to me during the interaction (this is helpful to me to know what is going on as I am not always aware of eye contact, etc.).

Although James's mother's pace is naturally fast, MIT allowed her to tune in to James's pace; this support enabled James to slow down and even to start communicating. Within MIT, their communication grew within the context of their relationship. At 2 seconds (s.) James's mother says 'ready', enhanced by vigorous cadence in the music, and plays 'Peek-a-boo' with James's feet. Then James makes the same vowel noise, 'egh' followed by 'by-by' (at 7s.) that his mother reiterates. In this way, James seems to be saying that he wants the Peek-a-boo game again, as he offers his feet, and laughs happily when his mother says 'A-ha'.

At 15s., James's mother instigates by tapping on James's chest and he starts vocalising at once. His mother joins in, mutters something to me whereupon James stops vocalising but then recommences. Then his mother joins in with James's vocalising, with a long 'ugh' vocalisation again (which has vibrato due to her tapping). My music is dominated by long high notes in anticipation of tapping, alternating with slow trills as I'm not sure when the tapping will begin so I choose to do supportive music for it (5s., 12s.) that doesn't require detailed timing. I have a little repeated leitmotif for the tapping (16s.) with a held Ab above to match James's pitch (24s.).

At 31s., James sings a semitone higher and I move up to the A. James is also singing on E and D which I also try to match below the A. James's mother is making low-pitched held notes that encourage and affirm James, saying to me at 35s., 'What is that?' as if to say she's not quite sure what's going on but carries on anyway. At 43s., and at 47s., she stops, but James places her hands back on his chest. It seems to be stopping and I'm not sure what is going on so I offer a semitone higher as an invitation to James to carry on (48s.), but meanwhile James's mother starts singing 'ba-ba-ba-ba' to a slower tempo so I slowly arpeggiate a dominant 7th in case we are changing tack (49s.).

James sings clearly pitched high notes (51s.) and there follows 'conversational' singing that I could describe as a 'conversation without words' between James and his mother – She says 'Hell of a story!' (1m. 12s.), accompanied by gentle lilting music. I pause the music abruptly at 1m. 17s. to reflect James's movement with his foot but on reflection I could have initiated more gentle music, providing Winnicott's 'arms'. For a child that is hardly ever still, this is a protracted time of eye contact and vocal engagement. At 1m. 21s. James's mother asks, 'Is it finished?' and I ask, 'Is he looking?' to check this and, if it is the case, to encourage his mother to continue (she replies, 'All the time then'). But this is one of those moments where we are not quick enough and we 'lose' the child (perhaps because we talked to each other).

At 1m. 26s., James utters a high note – it could be to start singing again or the start of a protest. I have the feeling that his mother isn't sure either about what James wants, and initiates a tickle at 1m. 27s. that he doesn't seem to like and he fidgets. I start the gentle music straight after the tickle in the hope of getting it back on track and James's mother placates him by tapping his thighs (1m. 35s.). James relaxes and assumes eye contact, to which she says 'Hi Babe' (1m. 42s.) and 'Hi' (1m. 45s.; she told me afterwards that she felt 'in contact' with him in a closer way than ever before) and James places his thumb in his mouth, waving his arm languidly, vocalising low sounds and smiles (1m. 55s.) – a rare thing for him at this age – until he coughs.

James's mother imitates the cough and James makes a high long sound (2m. 3s.) that both his mother and my piano imitate, and James sings four high notes and two low notes, showing some control over pitch and rhythm. James finally pushes away to become more energetic again as the highly engaged interaction ends.

When I later began working with James again, a couple of years later, with his one-to-one teaching assistant in his special needs school, his teacher reported that since restarting MIT, James became more alert and much more communicative in class, giving more eye contact. In those school MIT sessions, he became able to maintain 40m. of engaged social interaction with lots of sustained eye contact (with, on average, three 'breaks' of 3m. of dancing in front of the keyboard).

Conclusion of the music therapist's perspective

Such free flow of communication, supported by improvisation, can produce a rich level of conversational engagement full of shared meaning. Given the approach of MIT, which has a focus on timing, it is my role to pay careful attention to the social timing between the parent and child and to introduce musical play that allows them to improve their awareness of social timing and to develop reciprocity. This can involve different improvisational techniques, which may begin with matching and develop with increased shared musical understandings or *leitmotifs* developing over time. Increasing the frequency and length of these shared moments can have an observable enhancing effect on relationships and communication between each participating adult and child.

Research evidence for Musical Interaction Therapy

Research analysis of at least 25 children with autistic spectrum conditions, undergoing MIT, is currently in progress (Wimpory *et al.* in progress). Preliminary findings indicate that MIT for autistic spectrum conditions is associated with both emergence and increase of temporal synchrony in parent–child interaction, in contrast to the same dyads' interactions filmed during one to one natural interactive toy-free play, on the same day. This research employs a temporal synchrony analysis at a resolution of 86 milliseconds (0.086 seconds). Other broader analyses, such as the Dyadic Communication Measure for Autism (DCMA; Aldred *et al.* 2012), are also being simultaneously explored to determine whether non-temporally measured aspects of interpersonal synchrony generalise beyond the MIT sessions and over time. This is part of a programme in North West Wales, where children with autistic spectrum conditions are offered MIT and/or another form of therapy called PACT (Pre-school Autism Communication Trial; Green *et al.* 2010). Randomised clinical trial (RCT) research analysis of PACT has previously established that parental synchrony with their child with an autistic spectrum condition, during one-to-one interaction, is a mediating factor for positive change (Pickles *et al.* 2015).

Like MIT, PACT is modelled on the established strengths of typically developing child–parent interaction, but PACT does not involve music. Both MIT and PACT are currently offered in North West Wales through a programme known as Interactive Music and PACT (IM-PACT). Within IM-PACT, MIT and PACT are each geared towards increasing parent–child synchrony; the MIT component is specifically offered to those with more marked levels of autistic spectrum conditions and associated social timing difficulties.

Completed research case studies, of children originally showing classic presentations of autism (as well as learning disability), include findings confirming that MIT is associated with positive change when compared with previously established baseline developmental measures and/or trajectories (Wimpory 1995; Wimpory and Nash 1999a). Research-recorded positive changes include the frequency of Episodes of Social Engagement (ESE), involving active sociability by a child with autism looking towards their mother's face whilst simultaneously exhibiting an additional positive communicative behaviour.

ESE-based findings from combined video recordings of play with and without toys, in a published case study showed, for example, how full MIT contrasted favourably with four phases of MIT's component elements. These phases that showed statistically significant differences from full MIT were: (i) baseline; (ii) passive exposure to audio recordings of pre-recorded MIT sessions during a period whilst the music therapist provided the mother with social support, but no MIT; (iii) continuation of this social support combined with MIT-training for the dyad (rather than the pre-recordings); and (iv) post-MIT where only the social support from the music therapist was maintained.

Interestingly, ESEs were statistically significantly higher during passive exposure to pre-recorded MIT sessions than during baseline, and a positive significant difference was found for this initial passive exposure compared with its later combination with the music therapist social support. However, in statistical terms, the phase of passive exposure to pre-recorded MIT did *not* compare favourably with full MIT or with any other of the cumulatively introduced phases of MITs component parts (Wimpory 1995 *et al.* 1999a).

Another seriously affected child showed improvements in social communication (specifically: eye-contact, social acknowledgement, initiation of four turns of interactive involvement) in association with seven months of MIT, published as a peer-reviewed evaluated case study. Her progress significantly exceeded the baseline developmental trajectories that were established over four months before the MIT began. More importantly, these improvements were recorded as still in evidence during analysis two years later (the total period of MIT having been 12 months). These gains, made during MIT, appeared to carry over into interactive play with the child's mother outside of MIT and to be retained as part of the child's development despite her otherwise classic presentation of autism and learning disability (Wimpory 1995; Wimpory *et al.* 1995).

There were other developments, made by this child, such as teasing and symbolic play, that weren't present in the initial baseline months and that more usually represent very significant and persistent areas of difficulty in autism (Baron-Cohen 1987;

Heerey *et al.* 2005). These behaviours are interesting because they spontaneously developed during the MIT period, once the practice of rich preverbal interaction had become well established. Rather than having been the focus of any specific or predetermined training, they appear to reflect the facilitative nature of such interaction. These spontaneous developments resemble patterns more characteristically seen in typical development, where conditions for the onset of teasing (proto-symbolic) and pretend play more naturally arise during natural interaction patterns (as outlined previously in 'Background evidence from research into typical development'). These broader developments were also maintained at two years' follow-up, where research analysis of video recordings showed that child social attentiveness was generally continuous (Wimpory 1995; Wimpory *et al.* 1995).

The developments in this last evaluated case study support the social timing developmental model of social and symbolic development, as presented in this chapter. The MIT findings, in this entire section, are particularly encouraging because work by other researchers has found that where parents achieve greater one-to-one interactional synchrony with their children with autistic spectrum conditions and learning disability (through parent-mediated non-musical intervention), this predicts their children's communication outcomes for up to 16 years later (Siller and Sigman 2002, 2008).

Discussion

In conclusion, an essential element of MIT appears to be the music therapist's temporally sensitive improvised music as they scaffold an interactive experience between the carer and child with an autistic spectrum condition. It is also important that, within MIT, the child with an autistic spectrum condition is given the illusion of communicative control; this has been previously identified as so important in typical language development (Urwin 1984). The MIT music helps repair any loss of synchrony, so the child is able to move from being given communicative control, to sharing and negotiating that control with the participating carer.

Dawn Wimpory, and her research colleagues' theory, of the developmental cascade of autism is that social timing difficulties (inherent in the child) disable the development of preverbal social interaction, thereby inhibiting the development of social and other developmentally related skills. These skills include teasing, symbolising/pretend play, empathy and more sophisticated manifestations of attachment. MIT is associated with emergence and increases in temporal synchrony. This chapter has outlined an account of how MIT may also be associated with the developmental sequelae of temporal synchrony, such as teasing and pretending (Wimpory 1995), that more typically remain significant areas of impairment in autism.

Both MIT research and the clinical practice of MIT are compatible with the interaction-based theoretical perspective outlined within this chapter (Fein *et al.* 1986; Hobson 1994; Newson 1984; Wimpory 1995, 2015) which suggests that 'a minimum level of reciprocity may be necessary as a basis for a shared meaning and communicative intent, and social disinterest in autistic children may thus contribute to delays and failures in language and pretend play' (Fein *et al.* 1986, p. 208).

This chapter is based on the understanding of a concurrent and a developmental role for social timing in the social, communicative and symbolic deficits of children with autistic spectrum conditions (Courchesne *et al.* 1994; Newson 1984; Wimpory 1995; Wimpory and Nash 1999). Both the clinical and research evidence presented above indicate how MIT might impact on the development of social timing to enable the development of temporal synchrony and then other associated developments, more typically problematic in autistic spectrum conditions, such as teasing and pretending. MIT has an important role in addressing the temporal synchrony difficulties that are now beginning to be recognised in the broader research context of autism. Relevant research includes anomalies in timing genes that influence both body clock and communicative timing across different species (Nicholas *et al.* 2007; Wimpory *et al.* 2002).

MIT originally evolved in the context of applied developmental psychologists, and their education and drama therapy colleagues, responding with musical support to the clinical needs of children with autism (Wimpory 1986; Wimpory and Christie 1986). Since then, it has been readily adopted by music therapists, who bring particularly finely timed musical and other sensitive skills in working with children with autistic spectrum conditions. MIT complements other communicative non-musical approaches to ameliorate communication using developmental models, such as Intensive Interaction (Nind 2000) or PACT (Green *et al.* 2010). This chapter highlights how MIT is in some ways compatible with many forms of music therapy, in addressing the social communication needs of children with autistic spectrum conditions. However, a recent international multi-centre RCT indicated a general lack of measured effect for one-to-one improvisational music therapy in reduction of autistic spectrum condition symptomatology (Crawford *et al.* 2017). In the light of this, Bangor University's ongoing research analysis of music therapists' contribution to autistic spectrum conditions, specifically through MIT (with measures derived from a social timing/interactive synchrony perspective), may now be particularly appropriate (Wimpory *et al.* in progress).

With acknowledgements to Psychology Assistants, Dr Dawn Adele Owen and Judit Elias Masiques (of Betsi Cadwaladr and Bangor University Health Board, BCUHB) as well as to the parents and children, especially to James and his mother, for their contribution to this chapter and for participating in BCUHB's and Bangor University's research analysis of MIT.

References

Aldred, C., Green, J., Emsley, R. and McConachie, H. (2012) 'Brief report: Mediation of treatment effect in a communication intervention for pre-school children with autism.' *Journal of Autism and Developmental Disorders 42*, 3, 447–454.

Allman, M.J. (2011) 'Deficits in temporal processing associated with autistic disorder.' *Frontiers in Integrative Neuroscience 5*, 2, 1–2.

American Psychiatric Association (2013) *Diagnostic and Statistical Manual of Mental Disorders* (5th ed.). Washington, DC: APA.

Amos, P. (2013) 'Rhythm and timing in autism: Learning to dance.' *Frontiers in Integrative Neuroscience 7*, 21, 1–15.

Baron-Cohen, S. (1987) 'Autism and symbolic play.' *British Journal of Developmental Psychology 5*, 2, 139–148.

Bates, E., Camaioni, L. and Volterra, V. (1975) 'The acquisition of performatives prior to speech.' *Merrill Palmer Quarterly 21*, 3, 205–226.

Bebko, J.M., Weiss, J.A., Demark, J.J. and Gomez, P. (2006) 'Discrimination of temporal synchrony in intermodal events by children with autism and children with developmental disabilities without autism.' *Journal of Child Psychology and Psychiatry 47*, 1, 88–98.

Berger, D.S. (2002) *Music Therapy, Sensory Integration and the Autistic Child*. London and Philadelphia: Jessica Kingsley Publishers.

Boucher, J. (2000) 'Time Parsing, Normal Language Acquisition, and Language-Related Developmental Disorders.' In M. Howard and S. Perkins (eds) *New Direction in Language Development*. USA: Springer.

Boucher, J. (2001) 'Lost in a Sea of Time: Time Parsing and Autism.' In C. Hoerl and T. Cormack (eds) *Time and Memory*. Oxford: Clarendon.

Brock, J., Brown, C.C., Bucher, J. and Rippon, G. (2002) 'The temporal binding deficit hypothesis of autism.' *Development and Psychopathology 14*, 2, 209–224.

Bruner, J.S. (1983) *Child's Talk: Learning to Use Language*. Oxford: Oxford University Press.

Burack, J.A., Charman, T., Yirmiya, N. and Zelazo, P.R. (2001) *Development and Autism: Messages from Developmental Psychopathology*. Mahwah, NJ: Lawrence Erlbaum Associates.

Christie, P., Newson, E., Newson, J. and Prevezer, W. (1992) 'An Interactive Approach to Language and Communication for Non-Speaking Children.' In D.A. Lane and A. Miller (eds) *Child and Adolescent Therapy: A Handbook*. Buckingham: Open University Press.

Compton Dickinson, S. (2018) London: BAMT podcast: Music Therapy Conversations, Episode 10. Accessed on 20 May 2018 at www.bamt.org/british-association-for-music-therapy-resources/podcasts.html

Courchesne, E., Townsend, J., Akshoomoff, N.A. and Saitoh, O. (1994) 'Impairment in shifting attention in autistic and cerebellar patients.' *Behavioural Neuroscience 108*, 5, 848–865.

Crawford, M.J., Gold, C., Odell-Miller, H., Thana, L., Faber, S. and Assmus, J. (2017) 'International multicentre randomised controlled trial of improvisational music therapy for children with autism spectrum disorder: Time-A study.' *Health Technology Assessment 21*, 59, 1–40.

DeMarchena, A. and Eigsti, I. (2010) 'Conversational gestures in autism spectrum disorders: Asynchrony but not decreased frequency.' *Autism Research 3*, 6, 311–322.

Fein, D., Pennington, B., Markowitz, P., Braverman, M. and Waterhouse, L. (1986) 'Toward a neuropsychological model of infantile autism: Are the social deficits primary?' *Journal of the American Academy of Child and Adolescent Psychiatry 25*, 2, 198–212.

Feldman, R. (2005) 'Mother–Infant Synchrony and the Development of Moral Orientation in Childhood and Adolescence: Direct and Indirect Mechanisms of Developmental Continuity.' Paper presented in the Biennial Meeting of the Society for Research in Child Development, Atlanta, GA.

Feldman, R. (2007) 'Parent–infant synchrony and the construction of shared timing, physiological precursors, developmental outcomes, and risk conditions.' *Journal of Child Psychology and Psychiatry 48*, 3–4, 329–354.

Feldman, R. and Eidelman, A.I. (2004) 'Parent–infant synchrony and the social-emotional development of triplets.' *Developmental Psychology 40*, 6, 1133–1147.

Feldman, R. and Greenbaum, C.W. (1997) 'Affect regulation and synchrony in mother-infant play as precursors to the development of symbolic competence.' *Infant Mental Health Journal 18*, 1, 4–23.

Feldman, R., Greenbaum, C.W. and Yirmiya, N. (1999) 'Mother–infant affect synchrony as an antecedent of the emergence of self-control.' *Developmental Psychology 35*, 1, 223–231.

Feldman, R., Greenbaum, C.W., Yirmiya, N. and Mayes, L.C. (1996) 'Relations between cyclicity and regulation in mother–infant interaction at 3 and 9 months and cognition at 2 years.' *Journal of Applied Developmental Psychology 17,* 3, 347–365.

Feldstein, S., Konstantareas, M., Oxman, J. and Webster, C.D. (1982) 'The chronography of interactions with autistic speakers – An initial report.' *Journal of Communication Disorders 15,* 6, 451–460.

Fitzpatrick, P., Frazier, J., Cochran, D.M. and Mitchell, T. (2016). 'Impairments of social motor synchrony evident in autism spectrum disorder.' *Frontiers in Psychology, 7,* 1323.

Green, J., Charman, T., McConachie, H. and Aldred, C. (2010) 'Parent-mediated communication-focused treatment in children with autism (PACT): A randomised controlled trial.' *The Lancet, 375,* 9732, 2152–2160.

Grocke, D. and Wigram, T. (2007) *Receptive Methods in Music Therapy: Techniques and Clinical Applications for Music Therapy Clinicians, Educators and Students.* London and Philadelphia: Jessica Kingsley Publishers.

Grossberg, S. and Seidman, D. (2006) 'Neural dynamics of autistic behaviours: Cognitive, emotional, and timing substrates.' *Psychological Review 113,* 3, 483–525.

Harrist, A.W., Pettit, G.S., Dodge, K.A. and Bates, J.E. (1994) 'Dyadic synchrony in mother–child interaction – relation with children's subsequent kindergarten adjustment.' *Family Relations 43,* 4, 417–424.

Heaton, P. (2013) 'Autistic Savants.' In F.R. Volkmar (ed.) *Encyclopedia of Autism Spectrum Disorders.* New York, NY: Springer.

Heaton, P., Williams, K., Cummins, O. and Happe, F.G.E. (2007) 'Beyond perception: Musical representation and on-line processing in autism.' *Journal of Autism and Developmental Disorders 37,* 1, 355–360.

Hedenbro, M. and Tjus, T. (2007) 'A case study of parent–child interactions of a child with autistic spectrum disorder (3–48 months) and comparison with typically developing peers.' *Child Language Teaching and Therapy 23,* 2, 201–222.

Heerey, E., Capps, L.M., Keltner, D. and Bring, A.M. (2005) 'Understanding teasing: Lessons from children with autism.' *Journal of Abnormal Psychology 33,* 1, 55–68.

Hesling, I., Dilharreguy, B., Peppe, S., Amirault, M., Bouvard, M. and Allard, M. (2010) 'The integration of prosodic speech in high functioning autism: A preliminary fMRI study.' *PLoS One 5,* 7.

Hobson, R.P. (1993) *Autism and the Development of Mind.* Hillsdale, NJ: Lawrence Erlbaum Associates.

Hobson, R.P. (1994) 'Perceiving Attitudes, Conceiving Minds.' In C.M. Lewis and P. Mitchell (eds) *Origins of an Understanding of Mind.* Hillsdale, NJ: Lawrence Erlbaum Associates.

Hoicka, E. and Gattis, M. (2008) 'Do the wrong thing: How toddlers tell a joke from a mistake.' *Cognitive Development 23,* 1, 180–190.

Jaffe, J., Beebe, B., Feldstein, S., Crown, C.L. and Jasnow, M.D. (2001) 'Rhythms of dialogue in infancy: Coordinated timing in development.' *Monographs of the Society for Research in Child Development 66,* 2, 1–132.

Jasnow, M. and Feldstein, S. (1986) 'Adult-like temporal characteristics of mother–infant vocal interactions.' *Child Development 57,* 3, 754–761.

Klin, A. (1992) 'Listening preferences in regard to speech in 4 children with developmental disabilities.' *Journal of Child Psychology and Psychiatry and Allied Disciplines 33,* 4, 763–769.

Kolar-Borsky, A. and Holck, U. (2014) 'Situational songs – therapeutic intentions and use in music therapy with children.' *Voices: A World Forum for Music Therapy* 14, 2.

Kubicek, L.F. (1980) 'Organisation in Two Mother–Infant Interactions Involving a Normal Infant and His Fraternal Twin Brother Who Was Later Diagnosed as Autistic.' In T. Field, S. Goldberg, D. Stem and A. Sostek (eds) *High-Risk Infants and Children: Adult and Peer Interactions.* New York, NY: Academic.

Kuhl, P.K., Coffey-Corina, S., Padden, D. and Dawson, G. (2005) 'Links between social and linguistic processing of speech in preschool children with autism: Behavioural and electrophysiological measures.' *Developmental Science 8*, 1, 9–20.

Lord, C., Luyster, R.J., Gotham, K. and Guthrie, W. (2012a) *Autism Diagnostic Observation Schedule, Second Edition (ADOS-2) Manual (Part II).* Toddler Module. Torrance, CA: Western Psychological Services.

Lord, C., Rutter, M., DiLavore, P. C., Risi, S., Gotham, K. and Bishop, S. (2012b) *Autism Diagnostic Observation Schedule* (second Edition). Torrance, CA: Western Psychological Services.

Malloch, S. (1999). 'Mother and Infants and Communicative Musicality.' In I. Deliège (ed.) *Rhythms, Musical Narrative, and the Origins of Human Communication. Musicae Scientiae, Special Issue, 1999–2000.* Liège, Belgium: European Society for the Cognitive Sciences of Music.

Marsh, K., Isenhower, R.W., Richardson, M.J. and Helt, M. (2013). 'Autism and social disconnection in interpersonal rocking.' *Frontiers in Integrative Neuroscience 7*, 4, 1–8.

Moshe, M. and Feldman, R. (2006) 'Maternal and Infant Heart Rhythms and Mother–Infant Synchrony.' Paper presented at the Biennial Conference of the World Association for Infant Mental Health, Paris, France.

Mottron, L., Peretz, I., Belleville, S. and Rouleau, N. (1999) 'Absolute pitch in autism: A case study.' *Neurocase 5*, 6, 485–501.

Murray, L. and Trevarthen, C. (1985). 'Emotional Regulation of Interactions between Two-Month-Olds and Their Mothers.' In T.M. Field and N.A. Fox (eds) *Social Perception in Infants.* Norwood, NJ: Ablex.

Nadel, J., Carchon, I., Kervella, C., Marcelli, D. and Reserbat-Plantey, D. (1999) 'Expectancies for social contingency in 2-month-olds.' *Developmental Science 2*, 2, 164–173.

Newson, E. (1984) 'The Social Development of the Young Autistic Child.' Paper presented at the National Autistic Society Conference, Bath, England.

Newson, J. and Newson, E. (1975). 'Inter-subjectivity and transmission of culture – social origins of symbolic functioning.' *Bulletin of the British Psychological Society 28*, 437–446.

Nicholas, B., Rudrasingham, V., Nash, S., Kirov, G., Owen, M.J. and Wimpory, D. (2007) 'Association of *Per1* and *Npas2* with autistic disorder: Support for the clock genes/social timing hypothesis.' *Molecular Psychiatry 12*, 6, 581–592.

Nind, M. (2000) 'Intensive Interaction and Children with Autism.' In S. Powell (ed.) *Helping Children with Autism to Learn.* London: David Fulton.

Nind, M. and Hewett, D. (1994) *Access to Communication: Developing the Basics of Communication with People with Severe Learning Difficulties through Intensive Interaction.* London: David Fulton.

Ninio, A. and Snow, C.E. (1988) 'Language Acquisition through Language Use: The Functional Sources of Children's Early Utterances, in Categories and Processes.' In Y. Levi, I. Schlesinger and M. Braine (eds) *Language Acquisition.* Hillsdale, NJ: Lawrence Erlbaum Associates.

Ninio, A. and Snow, C.E. (1996) *Pragmatic Development.* Boulder, CO: Westview Press.

Nordoff, P. and Robbins, C. (1971) *Therapy in Music for Handicapped Children.* London: Victor Gollancz.

Nordoff, P. and Robbins, C. (1972). *Irvin Can Beat The Drum, Part 3.* Accessed on 20 April 2018 at www.youtube.com/watch?v=iOiWn08vZw0.

Nordoff, P. and Robbins, C. (1977) *Creative Music Therapy.* New York, NY: John Day.

Oldfield, A. (2006) *Interactive Music Therapy – A Positive Approach: Music Therapy at a Child Development Centre.* London: Jessica Kingsley Publishers.

Pavlicevic, M. (1997) *Music Therapy in Context: Music, Meaning and Relationship.* London and Philadelphia: Jessica Kingsley Publishers.

Pavlicevic, M. (2002) 'Dynamic interplay in clinical improvisation.' *Voices: A World Forum for Music Therapy.* Accessed on 20 April 2018 at www.voices.no/mainissues/Voices2(2)pavlicevic.html.

Peppe, S., McCann, J., Gibbon, F.E., O'Hare, A. and Rutherford, M. (2007) 'Receptive and expressive prosodic ability in children with high-functioning autism.' *Journal of Speech Language and Hearing Research 50,* 4, 1015–1028.

Peppe, S., Cleland, J., Gibbon, F., O'Hare, A. and Castilla, P.M. (2011) 'Expressive prosody in children with autism spectrum conditions.' *Journal of Neurolinguistics 24,* 1, 41–53.

Pickles, A., Harris, V., Green, J. and Aldred, C. (2015) 'Treatment mechanism in the MRC preschool autism communication trial: Implications for study design and parent-focused therapy for children.' *Journal of Child Psychology and Psychiatry 56,* 2, 162–170.

Prevezer, W. (1998) 'Entering into interaction: Some facts, thoughts and theories about autism, with a focus on practical strategies for enabling communication.' Report published at the Elizabeth Newson Centre.

Reddy, V. (1991) 'Playing with Others' Expectations: Teasing and Mucking About in the First Year.' In A. Whiten (ed.) *Natural Theories of Mind,* Oxford, England: Blackwell.

Reddy, V. (2001) 'Infant clowns: The interpersonal creation of humour in infancy.' *Enfance 53,* 3, 247–256.

Reddy, V., Hay, D., Murray, L. and Trevarthen, C. (1997) 'Communication in Infancy: Mutual Regulation of Affect and Attention.' In G. Bremner, A. Slater and G. Butterworth (eds) *Infant Development: Recent Advances.* Hove: Psychology Press.

Reddy, V. (2008) *How Infants Know Minds.* Cambridge, MA: Harvard University Press.

Richdale, A.L. and Prior, M.R. (1995) 'The sleep-wake rhythm in children with autism.' *European Child and Adolescent Psychiatry 4,* 3, 175–186.

Rozga, A., Hutman, T., Young, G.S. and Rogers, S.J. (2011) 'Behavioral profiles of affected and unaffected siblings of children with autism: Contribution of measures of mother[]infant interaction and nonverbal communication.' *Journal of Autism and Developmental Disorders 41,* 3, 287–301.

Segawa, M. (1985) 'Circadian rhythm in early infantile autism.' *Shinke Kenya No Shinpo 29,* 140–153.

Siller, M. and Sigman, M. (2002) 'The behaviors of parents of children with autism predict the subsequent development of their children's communication.' *Journal of Autism and Developmental Disorders 32,* 2, 77–89.

Siller, M. and Sigman, M. (2008) 'Modeling longitudinal change in their language abilities of children with autism: Parent behaviors and child characteristics as predictors of change.' *Developmental Psychology 44,* 6, 1691–1704.

Stern, D. (1974) 'Mother and Infant at Play: The Dyadic Interaction Involving Facial, Vocal and Gaze Behaviors.' In M. Lewis and L. Rosenblum (eds) *The Effect of the Infant on Its Caregiver.* New York, NY: Wiley.

Stern, D. (1985) *The Interpersonal World of the Infant: A View from Psycho-Analysis and Developmental Psychology.* New York, NY: Basic Books.

Stern, D. (1995) *The Motherhood Constellation.* New York, NY: Basic Books.

Suvini, F., Apicella, F. and Muratori, F. (2016) 'Music therapy microanalysis of parent–infant interaction in a three-month-old infant later diagnosed with autism.' *Health Psychology Report 5,* 2, 151–161.

Szelag, E., Kowalska, J., Galkowski, T. and Poppel, E. (2004) 'Temporal processing deficits in high-functioning children with autism.' *British Journal of Psychology 95,* 269–82.

Tordjman, S., Davlantis, K.S., Georgieff, N. and Geoffray, M. (2015) 'Autism as a disorder of biological and behavioral rhythms: Toward new therapeutic perspectives.' *Frontiers in Pediatrics 3,* 1.

Trevarthen, C. (1986) 'Development of Intersubjective Motor Control in Infants.' In M.G. Wade and H.T.A. Whiting (eds) *Motor Development in Children: Aspects of Coordination and Control.* Dordrecht, Martinus Nijhoff.

Trevarthen, C. and Logotheti, K. (1987) 'First Symbols and the Nature of Human Knowledge.' In J. Montangero, A. Tryphon and S. Dionnet (eds) *Symbolism and Knowledge,* Cahier No. 8, Geneva: Jean Piaget Archives Foundation.

Trevarthen, C. and Aitken, K.J. (2001) 'Infant inter-subjectivity: Research, theory and clinical applications.' *Journal of Child Psychology and Psychiatry 42,* 1, 3–48.

Trevarthen, C. and Daniel, S. (2005) 'Disorganized rhythm and synchrony: Early signs of autism and Rett syndrome.' *Brain and Development 27,* Suppl. 1, 25–43.

Trevarthen, C. and Malloch, S.N. (2009) 'The dance of wellbeing: Defining the musical therapeutic effect.' *Nordic Journal of Music Therapy 9,* 2, 3–17.

Trevarthen C., Kokkinaki, T. and Fiamenghi, G.A. (1999) 'What Infants' Imitation Communicates: With Mothers, with Fathers and with Peers.' In J. Nadel and G. Butterworth (eds) *Imitation in Infancy.* Cambridge: Cambridge University Press.

Tronick, E., Als, H. and Adamson, L. (1979) 'Structure of Early Face-To-Face Communicative Interactions.' In M. Bullowa (ed.) *Before Speech: The Beginning of Interpersonal Communication.* Cambridge: Cambridge University Press.

Urwin, C. (1984) 'Language for absent things: Learning from visually handicapped children.' *Topics in Language Disorders 4,* 4, 24–37.

Welkowitz, J., Cariffe, G. and Feldstein, S. (1976) 'Conversational congruence as a criterion for socialisation in children.' *Child Development 47,* 1, 269–272.

Welsh, J.P., Ahn, E.S., and Placantonakis, D.G. (2005) 'Is autism due to brain desynchronization?' *International Journal of Developmental Neuroscience 23,* 2–3, 253–263.

Wimpory, D. (1986) 'Developing sociability in preverbal children with learning-disability (autism).' *Bulletin of the British Psychological Society 39,* 1086, A147–147.

Wimpory, D. (1995) *Social Engagement in Pre-school Children with Autism.* PhD Dissertation, University of Wales, Bangor, Gwynedd, UK: PhD Dissertation.

Wimpory, D. (2013). 'Detection of Autism by Infant Sociability Interview (DAISI).' In F. R. Volkmar (ed.) *Encyclopedia of Autism Spectrum Disorders.* New York, NY: Springer Reference.

Wimpory, D. (2015) 'A Social Timing Model of Autism, Informed by Typical Development.' In A. Vatakis and M.J. Allman (eds) *Time Distortions in Mind: Temporal Processing in Clinical Populations*. Leiden: Brill Publications.

Wimpory, D. and Christie, P. (1986) 'Recent research into the development of communicative competence and its implications for the teaching of autistic children.' *Communication 20*, 1, 4–7.

Wimpory, D. and Nash, S. (1999a) 'Musical Interaction Therapy for Children with Autism.' In C. Schaeffer (ed.) *Innovative Psychotherapy Techniques in Child and Adolescent Therapy* (2nd edition) New York, NY: Wiley.

Wimpory, D. and Nash, S. (1999b) 'Musical interaction therapy: Therapeutic play for children with autism.' *Child Language Teaching and Therapy 15*, 1, 17–28.

Wimpory, D., Chadwick, P. and Nash, S. (1995). 'Musical interaction therapy for children with autism – an evaluative case-study with 2-year follow-up – brief report.' *Journal of Autism and Developmental Disorders 25*, 5, 541–552.

Wimpory, D., Nicholas, B. and Nash, S. (2002) 'Social timing, clock genes and autism: A new hypothesis.' *Journal of Intellectual Disability Research 46*, 4, 352–358.

Wimpory, D., Nicholas, B. and Foster. (2018). *High Resolution Temporal Analysis of Gait in ASD* (manuscript in preparation).

Wimpory, D., Hobson, R.P., Williams J.M.G. and Nash, S. (2000) 'Are infants with autism socially engaged? A study of recent retrospective parental reports.' *Journal of Autism and Developmental Disorders 30*, 6, 525–536.

Wimpory, D., Nicholas, B., Masiques, J.E., Powell, A. and Muth, A. (in progress) *Social Timing Analysis of Musical Interaction Therapy and Free Play Interaction without Toys in Young Children with Autistic Spectrum Disorders*.

Winnicott, D.W. (1971) *Playing and Reality*. London: Tavistock Publications.

CHAPTER 5

Group Clinical Improvisation as a Practice of Ritual and Connection for Young People with Autistic Spectrum Conditions

BECKY WHITE

Introduction

This chapter will focus on music therapy groups for adolescents with autistic spectrum conditions, exploring groups as opportunities for social interaction and communication. Through the example of a short hypothetical case study, I will examine how music therapy groups can be understood as social rituals (Collins 2004). Within this context, the role of the therapist's music will be considered, exploring the improvisational processes of grounding, single-line melodic improvisation and matching (Wigram 2004).

My approach to working with this client group is situated in the borders between psychoanalytically, developmentally informed and music-centred music therapy. I have drawn on the early relationship theories of Trevarthan and Malloch (2000), who consider mother–infant communication to be inherently musical. I have been predominantly influenced by the concepts of Winnicott (1971), focusing on the importance of play and creativity for health and wellbeing in childhood and adulthood. In addition, I have been influenced by music-centred dialogues (Lee 2003; Ansdell 2014) in which music is considered the important locus of change, as the therapy takes place first through the musical processes, which in turn creates a beneficial therapeutic relationship.

Personal experiences of adolescent music groups

I would like to briefly contextualise my interest in groups and music. I first became absorbed in small music groups and improvisation at secondary school, putting together a brass ensemble with friends for an exam. My trombone teacher made an arrangement of 'When the Saints Go Marching In' including 12 bars of solo improvised trombone. This was a highlight of my school days, and a formative experience of building peer relationships through music. It was a moment of close bonding between friends, and a chance to explore self-development.

Since youth, my interest has continued and taken various forms: becoming a member of small rock, pop and jazz bands, and listening to live chamber music, jazz groups or small ensembles.

As a music therapist, I am interested in small group work, enjoying the complexity of interactions, communication and inter-subjective behaviours. When studying for a Masters degree, I realised that my interest in music therapy group work was simply an extension of my original interest in small groups. With this personal background in mind, I would now like to explore adolescent behaviours, music making in this developmental period and the challenge adolescence poses for young people with autistic spectrum conditions.

Adolescence and autistic spectrum conditions

Adolescence is a time of transition from childhood to adulthood, encompassing early to late teens, potentially continuing through to the twenties. Typically, during adolescence there is self-development and evaluation, often in relation to academic and athletic abilities, appearance, social relations and moral conduct, which can affect self-esteem and relationships. As a young person moves away from family influence, integrating social interaction and attitudes of peers, groups of friends take on a significant importance. Young people begin to strongly identify with crowds or large groups of peers with similar tastes, styles of dress or musical interests; simultaneously, they usually form small cliques or peer groups of mixed gender, which can provide social, emotional or self-esteem reinforcement (Brown, Mory and Kinney 1994; Cross and Fletcher 2009).

Psychologists and sociologists have typically studied teenage years as a troubled, difficult period of life; however, there is evidence to suggest that this is only one aspect of the picture, and adolescence encompasses a wide range of behaviours and types of development (Steinberg and Morris 2001). With the onset of puberty, the adolescent must manage physical, hormonal and emotional changes, as well as negotiating social status and interactions. It is therefore a period when there are many factors to manage for the individual, and the support of peer groups can be crucial. The use of music by adolescents to create peer bonding has been well documented by both ethnomusicologists and psychologists who have studied identities in music (Finnegan 2007/1989; MacDonald, Hargreaves and Miell 2002, 2017). It is typical for the young adult to join a group, aligning themselves with a specific type of music and displaying this through clothes, music and behaviour. Engagement with music and musical activities can benefit the development of self-identity and esteem. Tarrant (2002) discusses the behaviour of teenagers forming strong musical allegiances to specific types of music. In addition, the educationalist Green (2008) has examined how teenage boys (and some girls) typically form rock and pop bands to explore self-identity and the transition from childhood to adulthood. The music ethnographer Finnegan (2007/1989), in a study of music making in an English town, explored small and large groups of music fans and amateur musicians. She noted the groups had similar musical interests, dressed the same, had regular times and places to meet and functioned to build social relationships with peer bonding. An interesting example of this is the UK youth Northern Soul scene, in which fans wore wide-bottomed trousers, blouses, shirts and jackets covered in special badges; the music was unique and rare, consisting of 1960s and 1970s American B-side Motown music (Constantine 2014). During the 1970s, youth culture in the north of England became saturated in this music, adolescents formed a new tribe (MacDonald *et al.* 2002), creating an identity and sense of belonging. In this way, it is common for typically developing teenagers to access music in groups, form specialised musical tribes and utilise music to engage and help build self-development, esteem and understanding of relationships.

In contrast, the challenge of teenage years can be enormous for young people with autistic spectrum conditions. It can be very hard to form the necessary sense of belonging and development of identity and engage in music with peer groups. They are faced with developmental transitions, as well as living with a disability, making it doubly difficult to connect in typical adolescent social interaction and communication activities (Carter *et al.* 2014).

Young people with autistic spectrum conditions can have significant difficulties with sensory processing differences (National Autistic Society 2017). In addition, some adolescents have severe problems with language and communication processing, on both a verbal and non-verbal level. As a result, individuals may often rely on familiar routines, contexts and augmented communication systems to understand what is being conveyed, such as PECS – Picture Exchange Communication System (Pyramid Educational Consultants 2018) – or specifically structured educational programmes such as TEACCH – Treatment and Education of Autistic and Related Communication Handicapped Children (UNC School of Medicine 2010). Sensory processing differences, being hyper- or hyposensitive to touch, sound or light, and reduced functioning in vestibular (balance) and proprioceptive (body awareness) systems, can radically affect an individual's ability to engage in social interaction and communication and alter the perception of an environment. These sorts of disabilities for young people with autistic spectrum conditions can result in specific behaviours such as frequent repetitive movements, hand flapping, pacing, self-harm, absconding or difficulties with transitions (moving from one place to another). This can result in a lack of direct relationships or contact with others, leading to loneliness, low emotional states or depression (Test, Smith and Carter 2014).

Music therapy, group work and autistic spectrum conditions

I would now like to ask the question: can music therapy groups provide or replace the usual musical tribes that form in adolescence? In partial answer to this, research has shown that music therapy can provide benefit and support for development in communication skills, social interaction, sensory integration and emotional awareness, as well as aid in the reduction of challenging behaviours (Warwick 1984, 1995). Randomised controlled studies have demonstrated the potential for increased social engagement, attention span and development of cognitive and communication skills (Kim, Wigram and Gold 2008; Gattino *et al.* 2011; Geretsegger *et al.* 2014).

In the literature there are a few studies which focus on music therapy groups for children and young people with autistic spectrum conditions. One of the earliest examples was demonstrated by Nordoff and Robbins (1971, 2007) who utilised the dramatic play 'Pif-Paf-Poltrie', in which groups of children with alternative learning needs worked on the forming of relationships and exploration of emotions. Other early examples include Bryan (1989) who ran a music therapy group, employing improvised music to encourage social interaction, and Alvin and Warwick (1991/1978) who worked with two boys with autistic spectrum conditions and two with typical development, integrating and building up peer relationships. Later, Walsh-Stewart (2002) describes running a group for children developing social-emotional communication, combining the TEACCH program with psychodynamic music therapy. Finally, McTier (2012) describes the use of the double bass in a group for two 13-year-old boys, encouraging engagement and providing emotional support. Elsewhere I have written about the running of a group for adolescents similar to that of Walsh-Stewart (2002), combining a psychodynamic music therapy approach with a visual communication system (White 2015). There are some additional case group examples, although not focused on autistic spectrum conditions. Nicholls (2002) describes a group she ran for adolescents with severe emotional and behavioural difficulties using vocalisations to frame improvised music and build relationships. Derrington (2012), in a mainstream school with adolescents with learning disabilities and emotional and behavioural difficulties, writes about music therapy interventions as a way to increase peer bonding and the quality of relationships. More recently, Strange, Odell-Miller and Richards (2017) describe a group for adolescents with severe and alternative learning needs, using improvised piano to encourage relaxation, enliven and then diminish challenging behaviours. This literature demonstrates the possibilities for adolescents with autistic spectrum conditions to benefit from group music therapy, especially in terms of communication and social interaction. To explore this further, I would now like to present a brief 'hypothetical' case study describing a typical music therapy group session. This will serve to illustrate the discussion that follows.

The music therapy group

The case study below describes a music therapy group, in a state alternative learning needs school, for three middle-period (aged 14–16) adolescents with autistic spectrum conditions. Let's suppose the young people, whom I shall call Max, Sally and James, were referred to music therapy because they had been observed making initial peer interaction attempts in the playground, such as standing parallel to each other, holding on to the same play activity equipment (balls and skipping ropes) and running together. All of the adolescents had very early abilities of expressive communication, at a two- to three-word level, using PECS as augmented communication aids. In addition, James had severe sensory processing difficulties, often finding bright lights and noise overwhelming. Both Max and Sally had some behaviours which prevented them from accessing the full school timetable. Sally had difficulties with transitions from one room to another. She often sat beside a door and would stay in the same position for long periods of time, which seemed to be due to a mixture of sensory processing difficulties and emotional anxiety. Max also had some transitioning problems, but was encouraged to move between classes by use of an electronic tablet playing his favourite pop songs. Thus, Max was able to utilise recorded music to motivate him and to structure his transitions throughout the day. All of the young people had communication and social interaction needs. The session case study is taken from three months into the therapy, at session 12.

CASE STUDY: MAX, SALLY AND JAMES

Three young people, a teacher and teaching assistant enter the music therapy space. In the room there is a piano, a bass amp, an electric bass guitar, an acoustic guitar, a bag of percussion instruments and a circle of chairs. The session begins with the therapist singing 'Hello' to the group members and playing on the piano, whilst a large drum is passed around by the teacher. The group members quietly vocalise in response and slowly and gently touch the drum with outstretched hands. The therapist considers how each group member is getting used to being in the room once again, and notices how they are haltingly touching the drum. The bag of percussion is opened and instruments carefully laid out on the floor. The therapist plays a few bars of a simple melody on the bass and then waits, giving space for the young people to initiate. Over the course of ten minutes, very slowly Max and Sally reach out and start to pick up the instruments. Sally selects the thunder drum (a plastic tube with a spring), an instrument she has a preference for, and places it on her lap. Max picks the maraca and shakes it vigorously. James continues to sit quietly and listen, gently rocking in his seat. The therapist plays a simple, slow, repetitive melody on the bass. Sally spontaneously vocalises, making lyrical melodic sounds which rise and fall in pitch. This seems to incite Max into vocalising; his sounds are guttural and repetitive. Together with the vocalising, the therapist expands the melodic bass line, weaving new musical ideas and fragments of melody, all the while reflecting the quality and pitch of the group's music. The teacher and teaching assistants also pick up instruments and play them quietly, accompanying the young people's sounds. James suddenly jumps up from his chair as if agitated, pushes it over and vocalises short, loud vowel sounds, pacing the room. One of the teaching assistants places the chair back and offers James ear defenders, which he wears. He continues to pace the room but appears calmer and is less vocal. At the same moment, Sally vocalises loudly and frequently, and the therapist plays intensely and fast, in response to the increased movement and sounds of the group. The improvisation lasts for up to 30 minutes. When the session comes to an end, the group members each help to pack away the instruments into the bag, and the therapist gently sings 'Goodbye'. As the group leave, the therapist reflects that the young people seemed to have been both simultaneously relaxed and excited. After the session, in a meeting with the teacher and teaching assistant, they all comment that there was a feeling of being together.

Discussion

This illustration of a music therapy group in this case study can be compared to a musical ritual or adolescent musical clique (Brown *et al.* 1994). I have experienced in my practice that music therapy groups for adolescents with autistic spectrum conditions have resonance with the musical cliques of rock and pop bands of typically developing adolescents. Feelings of togetherness, high levels of connection, relating and building of peer relationships all contribute to the musical garage experience of the young autistic person (Green 2008). The very basis of the group as a gathering together of people, in which music therapy provides a differing space to that of the classroom, with increased flexibility of choice, individual freedom, consistency, space and allowing crucial time to engage at their own pace, implies that music therapy groups for young people with autistic spectrum conditions have a unique and important role. This type of music therapy group has the potential to support these young people to initiate communicable and social responses through improvised sounds.

The sense of togetherness (commented on by the school staff) is crucial to thinking about the group as a musical ritual (Brown *et al.* 1994). Musical ritual can be intangible, but nonetheless present, as a group forms an identity or takes responsibility for musical and social processes. The psychotherapist Yalom (1995) describes this phenomenon, group members taking ownership of group processes, as an important aim and focus of therapeutic work. He asserts that through a group choosing ownership, they are able to grow in self-awareness and development. In this case example, there was potential for a sense of belonging and group identity, evidenced through the young people's responses to each other, the vocalisations of Sally and Max, or room-pacing of James.

In order for a group to come together, to function as a unit, there need to be several components in place to bring about the processes latent in the music and social interaction. A first element to be considered is the passage of time. If a group consistently takes place over a long period (months or even years), this can facilitate a strong familiarity with routine and room. A group at its most rudimentary can be a gathering of bodies, creating a potential experience of shared emotion and joint attention. In terms of viewing ritual as interaction-focused, this can be thought about as an assembly of people or the first essential element of ritual (Collins 2004). Second, music therapy can provide a diverse space in which individuals can have some measure of influence and freedom of choice. In this case example, the framework provided a combination of a loose structure and opportunity for spontaneity as follows:

- 'Hello' section – a drum was passed round the group; therapist supported with voice and piano.

- Bag of percussion instruments was opened; group members were encouraged to make any free choice; therapist supported on electric bass guitar.

- Therapist sang 'Goodbye'.

With this base there could be room for spontaneous changes initiated by the young people, such as the sudden opening of a cupboard, introducing new instruments, and thus changing the musical timbre of the session. Third, the nature of the music, in being fluid, supportive and flexible and not confined to the bounds of the pre-prepared material, could have an impact on the creation of togetherness. Through this musical approach, Sally, Max or James could be given an experience of flexibility or perhaps an understanding that this was a time when they could make their own choices (e.g. either to take part or to withdraw). In this context the therapist's musical intervention could be to attempt to match individual vocalisations with voice or through instrumental tonality, pitch and rhythm, encouraging and drawing out the young people into musical explorations. Fourth, the coming together of the group can be encouraged by the teacher and teaching assistants, who can assist practically, but also support emotionally, in being familiar adults accompanying the young people on their musical journeys.

It is not unusual for some ritual-like groups in music therapy to conjure up strong levels of effervescence and emotional energy (Collins 2004). I have previously experienced something similar when working with a group of adolescents with alternative learning needs, who brought robust levels of enthusiasm to music therapy group work (White 2005). In addition, in many contexts, such as in performance, informal and formal music making and music therapy, improvised music groups have the potential to be highly intense and social experiences, involving great levels of trust, risk and relationship (Cooper 2016). They can promote interpersonal relationships and inclusivity, creating situations where there is potential for everyone's participation to be valued (Monson 1996). In work with young people with autistic spectrum conditions, this kind of connection can take relatively long periods of time to become established. For example, it is possible to imagine that some of the group had difficulty with moving from class to music therapy. In these cases, the aid of an instrument as both a communication prompt and sensory hard object, to give a sense of physical security and to help with the transition, could have assisted in the journey from class to music therapy space. Tustin (2013/1992) portrays the child's need to hold on to hard objects, such as cars or stones, in order to feel a sense of bodily presence and emotional containment. In this case an instrument, such as a tambourine, could have a triple role: it could be a communication tool, a hard and physical sensory object to press into hands or a transitional object. The Winnicottian 'transitional objects' (1971, p.2) are objects commonly used by developing infants to defend against anxiety and facilitate the transition from being attached to the mother to becoming an individual. For some of this group, whilst it may have been a challenge to walk down the corridor to begin with, using instruments in this way could support the transition to become quicker and potentially less anxiety-provoking.

The heart of the music therapy work is the music itself; without this, the group (and ritual) would simply be a gathering of people. I would now like to consider the role of the therapist's music in creating opportunities for musical rituals in groups.

The role of the therapist's music

In this section I shall discuss the role of the therapist's music, describing the use of the bass guitar and voice, examining the techniques of grounding, single-line melodic improvisation and matching (Wigram 2004).

The bass guitar

The bass has seldom been written about in music therapy literature. McTier (2012) considers the use of the double bass (a relative of the bass guitar) with children and young people with autistic spectrum conditions, describing its therapeutic potential to provide rhythmic and harmonic frameworks and emotional containment. Further to this, Piccinnini, Pizziolo and Preston (2015) discuss the double bass and the bass guitar as useful instruments for creating groove, ostinatos, pulse and rhythmic cues.

Being primarily a bass guitarist, I have frequently used the electric or acoustic bass guitars in music therapy groups. I consider it important for a music therapist to take advantage of, but not be confined to, their main instrument. As Oldfield, Tomlinson and Loombe (2015) convey, it is an advantage for therapists to use their first instrument, since in this they will have high levels of flexibility, skill and proficiency.

In addition to delivering traditional bass lines, the bass can be used melodically, harmonically or percussively, with the potential to be employed in the following ways:

- playing repetitive ostinatos

- bass lines which provide a groove or beat

- altering the sound, adding percussion instruments, hanging bells off the fret board, inserting shakers under the strings

- hitting the body of the instrument with hands or beaters

- playing it upright, horizontal or laid on knees

- playing on the bridge, or up and down the neck

- adding electronic effects and pedals

- utilizing finger picking or strumming

- playing double stops

- playing single-line melodies.

In the group case study example, the bass functioned as a grounding and melodic instrument. The music was intended to be predictable, whilst simultaneously encouraging exploration of sounds with social interaction. I will now briefly discuss the three clinical improvisation techniques of grounding, single-line melodic improvisation and matching (Wigram 2004) in relation to the events in the group example.

Grounding

Grounding can be tonal, harmonic or rhythmic. Wigram (2004, p.91) defines it as stable music which acts as an 'anchor' and suggests using open chords, a steady pulse, establishing a tonality, predictable harmonies or repetitive motifs. The therapist's music in the group work is an example of providing an anchoring function, through low repetitive sounds with wide harmonic frequencies. This is a platform created by establishing a melody on the bass, with a tonal centre drawn from the pitches of the individual vocalisations, having the effect of sonically underpinning the group's music.

I find the bass guitar is an ideal instrument to create grounding due to the timbre, the low register and wide vibrations. For Max, Sally and James, it may have had a sensory, calming and physically relaxing effect and may have enabled the group to regulate sensory, vestibular and proprioceptive systems, which are related to bodily presence, balance, movement and touch (Berger 2002). In psychoanalytic literature these systems have been understood as awareness of sensory shapes or continual flow of bodily presence, rather like feeling the shape of a chair against your legs (Tustin 2013/1992). It is possible that a young person with an autistic spectrum condition can become stuck on one shape, or the making sense of it on the skin, which becomes blocked in some way. The psychotherapist Alvarez (1992) describes this idea in her case study of Robbie, a severely withdrawn child. She portrays how Robbie seemed to have no firmness to his body, and an ethereal quality to his presence. Alvarez's intervention was to employ a strong timbre in her voice, trying to bring alive the child into realisation of the sensory shapes he was experiencing. It is as if, through the timbre of her voice, she was seeking to give Robbie the energy and robust presence of another person, something which he could push against, and in turn discover his own sense of self. Similarly, using the solid timbre of the bass may have helped Max, Sally and James to become increasingly aware of their physical and emotional selves and following this facilitate moments of social interaction and communication.

The principles of tonal grounding can equally be applied to rhythmic or harmonic grounding, through the use of repetitive rhythms and familiar harmonic threads to create structure and form. If music has some recognisable organisation, this can provide a foundational hold for the more chaotic or random sounds made by a group. Preson (Piccinnini *et al.* 2015) demonstrates that a key function of the bass guitar in music therapy can be to hold a steady pulse in chaotic sound, or join together disorganised noise, rather like a sort of musical glue. My personal process is to listen to the overall soundscape of the group, as a whole piece of music, and create musical grounding which brings the disparate noises together. Grounding can literally hold a young person in sound; it can provide aural structure which potentially offers a musical context for the group to operate within.

Single-line melodic improvisation

In the case study, melody was used as a method of aural structure. Wigram (2004) asserts the usefulness of frameworking melodies in music therapy, which he states can be 'inspiring and encouraging … stabilizing and containing' (p.118). In the case example the therapist began by playing the simple melody on the bass and pausing, waiting and allowing enough time for Max, Sally and James to create sounds. She noticed there was a strong sense that they were waiting for directions so she aimed to provide a little prompting, but simultaneously ensuring there was sufficient space for spontaneous acts to occur. The result of this was that for the initial ten minutes the group sat in relative silence, only slowly reaching out to touch the instruments.

The waiting space was important. It was leaving time for the play to happen, for the young people to make their own choices, to choose instruments, vocalise and perhaps interact socially. This could be understood as facilitating the creation of a potential space. Winnicott (1971, p.47) describes the psychological space that can transpire between people, where play, creativity and connections can occur, as such a 'potential place'.

As Max, Sally and James slowly began to make sounds, the therapist typically played a simple melody on the bass, providing a familiar structured musical cue. The melody was designed to act as a guide and encourager, communicating 'here we are again' and 'it is okay to explore the instruments'. As this happened, she instigated improvising and developed the melodic line. Some useful melodic improvisation techniques are as follows:

- repeating the melody with one or two notes altered

- playing slightly behind the beat and adding syncopation

- taking the first two bars, and using them as a basis for improvisation

- playing the whole melody in a different key

- playing the melody back to front

- playing in the same key but a different register (higher or lower)

- using a different time signature such as three-four (waltz time).

Through these techniques and the repetitive nature of the line, the music in the case study could provide a consistent secure structure which simultaneously encouraged spontaneous play, social interaction and emotional containment.

Matching

There are several definitions of matching: Wigram (2004, p.84) describes it as playing music which is 'compatible' with but different to the clients sounds; Pavlicevic (1997, p.126) outlines it as 'partial mirroring', imitating some of the client's music but changing other aspects. Wilson and MacDonald (2015) have charted a model of cognitive decisions musicians make when working in improvised music groups. They identify matching (not using the term directly) as the moment when a musician makes a choice between changing another musician's music or maintaining it. Applied in a music therapy context, this could suggest that the therapist makes a choice to join the client in their sounds. Another way to think about matching is that the musicians have separate identities (Wigram 2004) but their music complements each other. It is like understanding the different musical contributions as part of a set, a matching hat and coat, or a matching teapot and cup. Essentially, matching communicates 'I am with you and hear you, but I am different from you'.

In summary, the role of the therapist's music was to underpin the clients' sounds as a whole, and to concurrently listen to and match individual contributions. This was parallel to holding a musical adjustable lens, constantly switching between a macro and micro view. Grounding can be considered the wide lens and matching the smaller. In the case study the therapist used the bass in a grounding role and her voice as the matching instrument. The matching consisted of singing about what the young people were doing, drawing on the tonal and rhythmic content of their vocalising, and reflecting back individual contributions.

In improvised music in music therapy the techniques of grounding, matching and single-line melodic improvisation can be key (Wigram 2004). Grounding can facilitate security of form, regulate sensory processing and create a sense of emotional well-being; the use of matching communicates close listening and inter-relationship with the young person; and the employment of single-line melodic improvisation simultaneously provides structure and flexibility.

Conclusion

Adolescents often use music to address issues of identity, peer bonding and social interaction (MacDonald *et al.* 2002, 2017). Young people with autistic spectrum conditions can find it difficult to access informal music making opportunities and initiate for themselves (Carter *et al.* 2014). Group music therapy can potentially provide an alternative, in which peer social interactions and self-esteem can be explored. In this chapter I have briefly discussed a hypothetical music therapy group for three young people with autistic spectrum conditions, considering the social interaction and role of the therapist's music. The music therapy group was simultaneously similar and different to that of a teenage music ritual or clique, often experienced by typically developing adolescents (Brown *et al.* 1994; Cross and Fletcher 2009). It provided an opportunity to build peer relationships through music, but unlike a clique was not peer-instigated, but framed and facilitated by a therapist, within a formal school setting. For this population of adolescents, it can be difficult to initiate musical activities, relying on adults or carers to do so. Thus, at its fundamental level, it was a chance to experience togetherness, which may have been both exhilarating and anxiety-provoking. The shared interaction was facilitated by the outer framework: the secure room; consistent time, routine and place; the inner framework: the musical activities; the same instruments; support staff; and flexible, specific, improvisational musical techniques. This combination in music therapy can create opportunities for social interaction, sense of connection, emotional effervescence, togetherness and group ownership. At its core, a music therapy group such as this can provide adolescents with the experience not only of relating through music and sounds, but of taking ownership, making it their time, place and crucially their own music. As the therapist observes the togetherness that can occur between the group members, she can only continue to wonder and be curious about each individual's phenomenological lived experience of the music, the place and the therapy. A group such as this has the potential to become a music therapy garage band, a unique musical tribe, or a way of being in music addressing the social, communicative, interactional and peer-bonding needs of young people with autistic spectrum conditions.

References

Alvarez, A. (1992) *Live Company: Psychoanalytic, Psychotherapy with Autistic Borderline, Deprived and Abused Children.* London: Routledge.

Alvin, J. and Warwick, A. (1991) *Music Therapy for the Autistic Child.* Oxford: Oxford University Press. (First published 1978.)

Ansdell, G. (2014) *How Music Helps in Music Therapy and Everyday Life.* Abingdon: Ashgate Publishing.

Berger, D.S. (2002) *Music Therapy, Sensory Integration and the Autistic Child.* London: Jessica Kingsley Publishers.

Brown, B.B., Mory, M.S. and Kinney, D. (1994) 'Casting Adolescent Crowds in a Relational Perspective: Caricature, Channel and Context.' In R. Montemayor, G.R. Adams and T.P. Gulotta (eds) *Personal Relationships During Adolescence.* Thousand Oaks, CA: SAGE.

Bryan, A. (1989) 'Autistic group case study.' *British Journal of Music Therapy 3,* 1, 16–21.

Carter, E.W., Common, E.A., Sreckovic, A., Huber, H.B. *et al.* (2014) 'Promoting social competence and peer relationships for adolescents with autistic spectrum disorder.' *Remedial and Special Education 35,* 2, 91–101.

Collins, R. (2004) *Interaction Ritual Chains.* Princeton, NY: Princeton Universal Press.

Constantine, E. (2014) *Northern Soul: Dance Hall,* Universal Pictures (UK). Accessed on 21 January 2018 at www.bbc.co.uk/programmes/p02jfx6c.

Cooper, C.M. (2016) 'Collective improvisation.' *Journal of Multidisciplinary International Studies 13,* 2, 1–6.

Cross, J. and Fletcher, K.L. (2009) 'The challenge of adolescent crowd research: Defining the crowd.' *Journal of Youth and Adolescence 38,* 2, 747–764.

Derrington, P. (2012) *Music Therapy for Youth at Risk: An Exploration of Clinical Practice through Research.* PhD. Cambridge: Anglia Ruskin University.

Finnegan, R. (2007) *The Hidden Musicians: Music-Making in an English Town* (2nd edition) Middletown, CT: Wesleyan University Press. (First published 1989.)

Gattino, G.S., Riesgo, R.D.S., Longo, D., César, J.C., Leite, L. and Faccini, L.S. (2011) 'Effects of relational music therapy on communication of children with autism: A randomized controlled study.' *Nordic Journal of Music Therapy 20,* 2, 142–154.

Geretsegger, M., Elefant, C., Mossler, K.A. and Gold, C. (2014) 'Music therapy for people with autism spectrum disorder.' *Cochrane Database of Systematic Reviews* 6, CD004381. DOI: 10.1002/14651858.CD004381.pub3.

Green, L. (2008) *Music, Informal Learning and the School: A New Classroom Pedagogy.* Hampshire: Ashgate Publishing.

Kim, J., Wigram. T. and Gold, C. (2008) 'The effects of improvisational music therapy on joint attention behaviours in autistic children: A randomized controlled study.' *Journal of Autism and Developmental Disorders 38,* 1758–1766.

Lee, C. (2003) *The Architecture of Aesthetic Music Therapy.* Gilsum, NH: Barcelona Publishers.

MacDonald, R.A.R., Hargreaves, D.J. and Miell, D. (eds) (2002) *Musical Identities.* Oxford: Oxford University Press.

MacDonald, R.A.R., Hargreaves, D.J. and Miell, D. (eds) (2017) *Handbook of Musical Identities.* Oxford: Oxford University Press.

McTier, I.S. (2012) 'Music Therapy in a Special School for Children with Autistic Spectrum Disorders, Focusing Particularly on the Use of the Double Bass.' In J. Tomlinson., P. Derrington and A. Oldfield (eds) *Music Therapy in Schools: Working with Children of All Ages in Mainstream and Special Education.* London: Jessica Kingsley Publishers.

Monson, I. (1996) *Saying Something: Jazz Improvisation and Interaction.* Chicago, IL: University of Chicago Press.

Nicholls, T. (2002) 'Could I Play a Different Role? Group Music Therapy with Severely Learning Disabled Adolescents.' In A. Davies and T. Richards (eds) *Music Therapy and Group Work: Sound Company.* London: Jessica Kingsley Publishers.

Nordoff, P. and Robbins, C. (1971) *Therapy in Music for Handicapped Children.* London: Victor Gollancz.

Nordoff, P. and Robbins, C. (2007) *Creative Music Therapy: A Guide to Fostering Clinical Musicianship* (Second Edition: Revised and Expanded). Gilsum, NH: Barcelona Publishers.

Oldfield, A., Tomlinson, J. and Loombe, D. (2015) *Flute, Accordion or Clarinet? Using the Characteristics of Our Instruments in Music Therapy.* London: Jessica Kingsley Publishers.

Pavlicevic, M. (1997) *Music Therapy in Context: Music, Meaning and Relationship.* London: Jessica Kingsley Publishers.

Piccicnni, J., Pizziolo, P. and Preston, J. (2015) 'The Bass (the Double Bass and the Bass Guitar).' In A. Oldfield., J. Tomlinson and D. Loombe (eds) *Flute, Accordion or Clarinet? Using the Characteristics of Our Instruments in Music Therapy.* London: Jessica Kingsley Publishers.

Pyramid Educational Consultants (2018) Picture Exchange Communication System (PECS), Pyramid Educational Consultants. Accessed on 21 January 2018 at https://pecs-unitedkingdom.com/pecs.

Steinberg, L. and Morris, A.S. (2001) 'Adolescent development.' *Annual Review of Psychology 52,* 83–110.

Strange, J., Odell-Miller, H. and Richards, H. (eds) (2017) *Collaboration and Assistance in Music Therapy Practice: Rules, Relationships and Challenges.* London: Jessica Kingsley Publishers.

Tarrant, M. (2002) 'Adolescent peer groups and social identity.' *Social Development 11,* 1, 110–123.

Test, D.W., Smith, L.E. and Carter, E.K. (2014) 'Equipping youth with autism spectrum disorders for adulthood: Promoting rigour, relevance and relationships.' *Remedial and Special Education 38,* 2, 80–90.

National Autistic Society (2017) *Sensory Differences.* London: The National Autistic Society. Accessed on 21 January 2018 at www.autism.org.uk/about/behaviour/sensory-world.aspx.

Trevarthan, C. and Malloch. S.N. (2000) 'The Dance of wellbeing: Defining the musical therapeutic effect.' *Nordic Journal of Music Therapy 9,* 2, 3–17.

Tustin, F. (2013) *Autistic States in Children* (revised edition). London: Routledge. (first edition published 1992.)

UNC School of Medicine (2010) TEACCH Autism Program. UNC School of Medicine. Accessed on 21 January 2018 at www.teacch.com.

Walsh-Stewart, R. (2002) 'Combined Efforts: Increasing Social-Emotional Communication with Children with Autistic Spectrum Disorder Using Psychodynamic Music Therapy and Division TEACCH Communication Programme.' In A. Davies and E. Richards (eds) *Music Therapy and Group Work: Sound Company.* London: Jessica Kingsley Publishers.

Warwick, A. (1984) 'The autistic child.' *British Society of Music Therapy Monograph for Autistic Disability,* 11–15.

Warwick, A. (1995) 'Music Therapy in the Education Service: Research with Autistic Children and their Mothers.' In T. Wigram, B. Saperston and R. West (eds) *The Art and Science of Music Therapy: A Handbook.* Chur: Harwood Academic Publishers.

White, B. (2005) 'The whirlwind group, a group for young people with disabilities moving into adulthood, and the working relationships that supported the clinical work in a special needs school.' No Man is an Island, Groups, Partnerships and Teams in Music Therapy: British Society of Music Therapy and Association of Professional Music Therapists Conference, London.

White, B. (2015) 'What sound can you make? A case study of a music therapy group for children with autism, learning disabilities and challenging behaviours.' *Approaches: An Interdisciplinary Journal of Music Therapy 7,* 2, 197–206.

Wigram, T. (2004) *Improvisation: Methods and Techniques for Music Therapy Clinicians, Educators and Students.* London: Jessica Kingsley Publishers.

Wilson, G.B. and MacDonald, A.R. (2015). 'Musical choices during group free improvisation: A qualitative psychological investigation.' *Psychology of Music 44,* 5, 1029–1043.

Winnicott, D.W. (1971) *Playing and Reality.* London: Routledge.

Yalom, I.D. (1995) *The Theory and Practice of Group Psychotherapy.* New York, NY: Basic Books.

CHAPTER 6

Shared Experience: Learning from Other Modalities in Therapeutic Work with an Adult with an Autistic Spectrum Condition

ALASTAIR ROBERTSON

Introduction

Over recent years I have learned to listen for the many subtle languages which can unfold in the therapy room. The movement which inevitably comes with music, the quiet gestures which can be seen on the periphery, the suppressed excitement and fear of unfilled spaces – all of these have opened up new possibilities. This chapter will detail a therapeutic journey with a man I shall call Donald, not his real name. It will outline twists and turns that led me towards integrating ideas from other arts therapists, occupational therapists and psychologists and helped Donald and me to give shape to our work as we navigated the journey together.

I first became interested in music therapy during the late 1970s, while training as a nurse in learning disabilities at one of the many large National Health Service (NHS) institutions of the time. I chose to do the Nordoff Robbins postgraduate diploma in music therapy. The Nordoff Robbins approach emphasises that music in itself provides the key to therapeutic change. Nordoff Robbins practitioners in the UK have since developed a Community Music Therapy model (Ansdell and Pavlicevic 2004) – now a registered training course. Over the years, this model has greatly influenced my work with people with an autistic spectrum condition.

Autistic spectrum conditions and the arts therapies

The story of autistic spectrum conditions over the last five decades has unfolded in parallel with the development of the arts therapies and other disciplines. In the 1970s Meltzer *et al.* (2008, first published 1975), Tustin (1992/1981) and others working in psychotherapy began to develop theories around the broader picture of autistic spectrum conditions. Although a psychotherapist, and using talking therapies, Tustin also used play and art materials in her work. In the same decade, Nordoff and Robbins (1971) and Alvin (Alvin and Warwick 1991/1978) were developing music therapy with children and adults. With the influence of the psychoanalyst Winnicott (2002), Trevarthen, Aitken, Papoudi and Robarts (1996) and other psychologists, the playful and interactive nature of therapy using the arts began to be increasingly explored.

The different arts therapies have cast light on various aspects of autistic spectrum conditions. Both music therapy and dance/movement therapy work in an interactive manner creating a transient playful space between client and therapist. In contrast, art therapy has tended to use the client's artwork for interpretation, rather than the art therapist engaging in artwork themselves – although Bragge and Fenner (2009) refer to this shifting in recent years. The co-improvised nature of music therapy and dance/movement therapy draws the client with an autistic spectrum condition into a dynamic relationship during the session. To engage in a creative medium, be it music, movement or art, is an expression of self. To engage in this with other people adds the dimension of human interaction, where sparks of creativity ignite in the space between participants. How much the agent of change in this process resides in the medium and how much in the relationship between therapist and client is the subject of much research and debate.

Care in the community and new music therapy approaches

In the early 1990s, there was a move towards providing care in the community which led to the closure of many NHS institutions for people with a learning disability. The subsequent increase in community care settings resulted in a growth of arts activities and therapies provided by a range of third-sector organisations. As people left their places in hospital, boundaries were being shaken up. For some, this had unintended consequences of isolation. For many with an autistic spectrum condition, accommodation was set up based on the view that they would find the unpredictability of people in the community too demanding. In this situation the dangers of vicious cycles of insularity are high. I have many clients whose difficulties appear to have arisen from increasing self-stimulatory patterns of behaviour which have developed to replace the lack of social interaction and fill a void.

Ansdell (2002) looked at this fast-changing picture and realised that music therapy was being provided in these new community settings using alternative formats with much more permeable boundaries. This led him to question whether the existing models of music therapy were still fit for purpose. As Ansdell (2002, p.30) says in relation to this newly developing concept of Community Music Therapy (CoMT), 'it is not seen as possible to work with an isolated individual, or to locate problems entirely *within* an individual, or to see problems as solely biological, psychological or social'. This statement feels particularly relevant in the context of autistic spectrum conditions, where individuals are so often seen and treated in isolation.

Barriers

Although autistic spectrum condition is the term used in this book, over time the words used to describe this condition have evolved and shifted. They have included the words autism, autistic spectrum disorder, autistic spectrum condition and other variations, as society seeks the definition which will most accurately reflect the current understanding. Changes in diagnostic criteria have resulted in a wider frame of reference and increasing numbers of people being diagnosed. An awareness of the possibility of autistic traits within ourselves and others may help us all in recognising some of the barriers at work in this area. Wilson (2014, p.63) contends that we all have areas of mild autism. Tustin (1992/1981) makes numerous references to autism in us all and refers to the black hole she recognised in herself, which Sinason (2010/1992, p.71) notes in paying tribute to Tustin's contribution to the understanding of learning disabilities. I choose to highlight this because it seems that many internal and external barriers can be erected in the therapeutic context by the therapist. Language, physical objects or even a dogmatic approach can all be used by the therapist for defensive purposes. The recognition of the therapist's feelings as part of the dynamic process puts the therapist's inner condition more in the spotlight. This may be one reason that the professional bodies insist on monthly supervision for all working therapists and why personal therapy is part of all of the arts therapies training courses.

Urwin (2011) points to the importance of keeping communication open with the carers of people who have an autistic spectrum condition. I use the word carer to encompass everyone with any responsibility of care towards the client, be it in professional capacity such as nurse or support worker, or personal capacity such as family or friend. Throughout my work as a therapist I have experienced interaction with carers to be a constant source of insight and learning. I have observed many care organisations struggling not to become trapped in set trends and patterns when working with this client group, reflecting a stuck quality which belongs to the condition itself. Thinking about these organisational trends and patterns has also influenced my work, and helped me to shine light on the stuck qualities within myself and my own therapeutic practice.

CASE STUDY: DONALD

The following case study took place in the music therapy room in an inpatient NHS treatment and assessment unit for adults with a learning disability.

I have now been working with Donald for more than eight years. Initially, he had individual sessions and then later joined a group co-facilitated by various professionals including nursing, occupational therapy and psychology. I received supervision in various formats during this time with art, dance/movement and music therapists. My lasting image of Donald, a large man in his 50s, is of him standing, rocking back and forward at the windows of the ward and clutching the books he always holds in his hands. Donald was referred to music therapy because of his difficulties in managing or talking about his emotions. His fluctuating mental health made him unpredictable, with periods of paranoia and hallucinations. Often his anger was directed at other patients, blaming them for the slightest transgression. Donald had reasonable use of language but it was limited to very passive and functional interactions. He had difficulties around changes in routine and a fear of letting go of his books. He had limited engagement with others, choosing to be on his own or distant from others in the ward. Nursing staff felt that because of his interest in music, music therapy might be something that could engage him in a more expressive interaction and create an outlet for some of his frustrations. Prior to this he had limited therapeutic input due to his challenging and erratic outbursts of physical aggression. However, he was in a relatively settled period at the time of referral.

Meeting in the music

Initially, in the individual sessions Donald could not sit, pacing around the room looking out of the windows as if to check that his ward was still there. Early sessions were filled with his loud bass voice and occasional bursts on the drum when he could briefly let go of his books with one hand to pick up a beater. It was as though the books brought him protection from the need to engage with others too directly. The sessions were weekly, often fraught with huge anxiety. Donald would retreat to the toilet where I could hear him berating himself for 'not doing things properly'. It was as though he felt safe enough in the toilet to express an angry part of himself, whereas in the therapy room he was still testing out me and the space. The large bass drum seemed to be the best instrument to match the energy and anxiety that he brought with him in those early days. Slowly, after many sessions, he began to realise that it was safe to strike the drum as hard as he wanted and that I would respond from the piano, an instrument which could match the size and volume of the drum but also have the potential to reflect a different experience. He would occasionally move away from the wall during the session, pick up a beater and jab at the drum when I was playing the piano, tentatively trying something out.

This was Donald's first experience of sharing something from within himself. He may have been expressing paranoia, anger, anxiety or fear of his own size and power. What exactly I could not be sure, but the emotion was being channelled into a potentially shared creative and contained act. It did begin to occur to me that, to some extent, I might be using the piano as security in much the same way as Donald used his books. This limited contact was an honest reflection of how far he was prepared to engage at this time, and acceptance of this brought an integrity to the sessions, as seen in the quote made below from my session notes:

> The short bursts of drumming feel like a message of wishing to connect as well as a warning that he is not ready for more than a very brief explosive communication. We start community songs together but they quickly turn into an anxious and garbled hurtle towards the end.

One of the first songs we were to sing was 'It's a long way to…' using his hometown in place of Tipperary. He would often introduce himself using an abbreviation of his Scottish surname as though proudly holding a sense of himself and his heritage. Despite the strong feelings being expressed, I guessed that most of the songs he chose would have been sung in the hospital in the past as part of community events – he had been in hospital for about 30 years. Although anxiety came through in his rush to end the songs, I felt they were an indicator of him having internalised a sense of his part in a community and wondered how many times he had stood on the edge of events, joining in the singing.

It was the growing bursts of improvised drumming that felt like a sharing of something new. As the bursts of drumming slowly extended, we began to build brief musical phrases between us. I introduced march-like riffs at the piano, and the music we then produced together, while not exactly playful or relaxed, was nonetheless born of something within Donald which was finding expression. Later I introduced pipe band marches and again wondered how often he had stood and watched pipe bands. We were establishing basic building blocks for a shared space around these marches. Donald's frantic and emotional bursts on the drum were beginning to be transformed as together we integrated these into our co-produced marches and songs. I often joked about being envious of his deep bass voice and expressed my enjoyment of his occasional large warm smiles. These brief interactions provided a glimpse into another kind of contact and, looking back, I wonder how important these moments were for him.

The books

It was to be a long time before Donald could put the books down to engage fully in a joint creative process. The books could be seen as something like the 'autistic object' that Tustin (1992/1981, p.95) describes. These objects, which can be physical things, behaviours, gestures or vocalisations are used in a way that completely or partially blocks interaction with other people. The books were one of the most obvious manifestations of Donald's autistic defences. I realised through speaking to the nurses who knew him well that he did not always hold on to the books when he was in other settings. He did not seem to wish to show them to anybody or to share them in any way. There were also occasions when he did not have his books with him when he arrived for our sessions and at these times he was often more agitated. I did wonder if the real way forward would be through working with the object – the books – which seemed to be creating the barrier.

Tustin (1992/1981, p.116) describes a sensitive teacher drawing a child with an autistic spectrum condition into a playful engagement using the very piece of cloth the child played with constantly in her isolated world. On the other hand, would it be better not to engage directly with Donald's need for his books, as they clearly brought him security? The image arose of choir singers holding on to and hiding behind music sheets for their own security. Whilst one might consider this as limiting their true engagement in the group experience of singing and making music together, it may also be essential to create a safe space to begin with.

The three years of individual work were not a smooth path, with gaps in Donald's attendance. Despite this, his visits to the toilet reduced, the internal voice seemed less persecutory and he seemed to have internalised a positive weekly experience of shared musical activity. Hope began to grow in me. The nurses talked about Donald's eagerness to attend and he often asked about the next session when we came to sing 'Goodbye'. I could see from observations outside the sessions that Donald did not choose to spend all of his time on his own. When I looked in more detail and spoke to his nurses, it became clear that he would engage with others at a distance, often on the periphery of groups. From his preference for community songs and Scottish marches, I recognised a wish to be a part of something bigger. Most of his shared experiences with others were from a safe distance. It was at this time that I also observed Donald as part of a carol-singing event at the assessment unit. Watching him sway with his books in hand, I could hear him sporadically joining in with the others as they sang 'Silent Night'. I could hear that his march-like rhythm did not quite fit the almost waltz-like rhythm of the style the others were singing in. However, he clearly wanted to be there and to join in, despite this apparent clash.

This raised a question for me about individual work and the merits and limitations of this in relation to autistic spectrum conditions specifically. Donald, not unlike many others with this condition I have observed, was clearly drawn to other people despite the tension between this and the need for his own space. He always seemed happy to return to the ward with familiar people there providing security, but he was also clearly drawn to the music therapy session, despite the challenges for him. Despite this positive progress, I believed that moving Donald to group sessions where he would know some individuals already would offer him security whilst at the same time removing some of the intensity of individual work.

Group work

The group Donald was to join had been running for about a year and we had used various formats in response to requests from members of the group. At that time there were six people attending once a week for 45 minutes and interaction was mostly verbal. The group started with an activity using a variety of illustrated cards and postcards which I had collected over a period of time. Each member would choose a card from an assortment provided. The use of such cards had been suggested by an art therapy colleague and provided an activity less exposing than drawing or the drumming. The subjects on the cards were limited by myself and my co-therapist and depicted a range of scenes, mostly people in various groupings. The cards, being physical objects, acted as reminders of topics from week to week. Donald would pick a card and move back to the wall as others commented on his choice. This appeared to be a safe early encounter with the group. However, although he acknowledged the comments, he could not make any himself.

We also used songs as part of this group, especially to end sessions. Donald could take part in choosing these, singing them from his place on the periphery of the group, bringing something new to them with his deep voice. As the group brought stability and balance to Donald's need to rush towards the end of songs, by holding their steady singing pace, I sensed a slight tension arising but one which was manageable. There was also a powerful, cohesive quality to the singing. Many people did not know all of the words, but collectively we could usually reach the end together and this achievement created a bond. Songs were also used by the group when events became too challenging. Anyone could spontaneously request a song at any time which gave those making the choice a powerful ownership in the process.

On the periphery

Although he still held his books, it was the process of group discussion and acceptance around Donald's wish to stand at the wall that became the authentic link between him and the others in the early sessions of the group. Maybe, as Alvarez and Reid (1999, p.7) say, 'gradually, patients may begin to get interested, not yet in us, but in our interest in them'.

Donald's position on the periphery became a major focus for discussion in the group. This focus empowered the group and created a power shift away from the therapists. Holding the card along with his books, standing at his usual distance, Donald seemed to be increasingly comfortable with the questions and comments. In the playful joking and general interest in Donald's need for periphery, were there similarities with the teacher who used the autistic object (the cloth) to draw her pupil into engagement? Were we able to play together with the idea of group engagement? Donald's issue around sitting with us, or not sitting with us, was the object around which we all met at this time and it was important that this could be negotiated in a safe way.

Although the group was already established prior to his arrival, Donald did know the others outside the sessions and it was beginning to take on aspects of a 'secure base' (Bowlby 2010/1979, p.103). I felt this offered a form of stability to Donald that had been more difficult to provide for him in the individual sessions. The continuity provided when the group sang some of the same songs Donald knew so well from his individual sessions also contributed to his growing sense of comfort and engagement. In turn, Donald's engagement in the songs, even though still offered from the periphery, allowed the whole group to feel more secure and cohesive. At the end of one of these songs a round of applause broke out. This spontaneously developed into a game between Donald and the group as claps were thrown back and forward, accompanied by laughing and smiling – explicit acknowledgement of an important shared experience.

Whatever need Donald had for standing at the wall, there was also a clear, if quiet, message that deep down he wished to join us. Captured presenting at a conference in Paris in the film, *Life, Animated* (Ross Williams 2016), Owen Suskind, who has an autistic spectrum condition, says, 'the way people see those with autism is that they don't want to be around other people… That's wrong! …the truth about autistic people is that we want what everyone else wants, but we are sometimes misguided and don't know how to connect with others.' The issue of where we stand in relation to a group is one that resonates with us all at some level. There had been an agreement within the group that members could take some time out if they were upset at any point, and some of them occasionally did so. This helped to normalise the need to stand in a different relationship to the group at times of difficulties.

Drawing together

In time the group began to make decisions about other activities they might like to engage in. Donald, like the others, made his wishes known. One suggestion was to pull the chairs into a smaller, more intimate circle around a coffee table where we would each have a sheet of paper and coloured crayons for drawing. Donald could not directly engage in the drawing himself at this point, but would direct others to draw on his sheet, often shouting at them in his frustration when they were not clearly drawing exactly what he wanted. There was gradual relaxation as we tentatively talked about his difficulty in not managing to draw, and the anxiety of others in response to his shouts. Over many months Donald began to accept this and manage his own emotions. Although still unable to pick up a crayon, he was making clear choices of colour and content in the artwork and also making occasional comments on the work of others. This was clearly safer for him than comments at and about people made directly to their faces. Later still he began to dip his hand into the box as though looking for a specific colour but unable to find it. The anxious dipping into the box reminded me of his engagement in singing and my frustration that he could not sustain the encounter for long, rushing to draw it to a close. However, the natural lack of a time signature in drawing, which is inherent in music and inevitably drives the pace, meant there was more space and opportunity for negotiation. Despite my anxieties about losing the structure provided by the musical framework, I realised that this medium was proving to be less pressured for the group. A new dynamic was developing.

After some initial sharing at the beginning of sessions, everyone was keen to get the paper out, including Donald, even though he was still not drawing at this point. Once we had settled down with our individual sheets of paper and negotiated the sharing out of crayons, a collective feeling of focus settled on the work in hand. I was struck by the different dynamic of this compared with my individual music therapy sessions with Donald. Within the group drawing activity he had more chance to contribute in his own time. Now spending much more time sitting with the group in close proximity, Donald would occasionally join in with brief spontaneous comments on his own. Even though at times this appeared to mimic what was started by others, there was a real sense of him making an effort to join in. Spontaneous verbal interactions, arising between group members as they drew, contributed to a more measured flow of communication and group cohesion.

Donald began asking for the others to draw him not only cars and trucks, but other themes as well. There came a point when he asked for a drawing of himself. Unlike the anxious bursts of engagement on the drum in individual sessions, he seemed to have more control in this process which was unfolding within the group through the artwork, starting with inanimate objects and ending with a picture of himself on the page. Although Donald still sat clutching his books, he was opening up to the group using art made at the hand of others.

Finding himself

There was clearly a parallel journey happening in which Donald used language to facilitate more than mere responses or very concrete requests and observations. He said 'wonderful' in response to a question about how everybody felt in the group one week. It was as though he had discovered something in the word 'wonderful' and was filling it with his own wonderfulness. He repeated the word a number of times as though trying it out, clearly expressing a newly found part of himself.

When words are delivered with no emotion, they are flat. When delivered with feeling and invested with meaning, they are filled with melody. Donald's use of this word had an improvised musicality that expressed his coming to life in the group, a freedom and playfulness that felt very new for him. Ogden (2004/1989, p.80) describes the word 'napkin' deconstructing before him one evening, as he repeated it over and over again. When we repeat a word in this way, we can experience it fall apart from the original meaning. An internal splitting takes place within our mind, which can feel disturbing and cause a separation from our trust in the symbolism of language. However, for Donald, the symbolism of language seemed to be coming alive as he began to use it to integrate and express the feelings being experienced as he engaged more and more in the group. This was no longer mimicking.

Release of colour
In the next series of sessions, after a break of a few weeks, we decided to share a flip chart between the group, at first sharing a single sheet and taking turns to make our contribution. After everyone else had drawn, Donald stood up, slowly went over to the filing cabinet and with great care and anxiety put his books down and seemed suddenly released from a huge burden. He walked over, picked up a felt marker, casually removed the lid and began to draw lines around the edge of the paper, framing everyone else's drawings. He then returned, put the lid back on the marker and proceeded to choose another and continue the process. This was repeated with all four markers before he returned to pick up his books and sit down. This was his contribution to a shared portrait of the group. As far as we were aware he had never made any drawings before.

After four years we had reached a tipping point where Donald's wish to share in the drawing experience had outweighed his need for the security of his books. This had the feeling of a quiet solo performance in colour, something he could not manage in music. The modelling by others in the group had supported him to this point, giving him confidence to follow. I noted that I, as the therapist, was less comfortable in the activity of drawing whereas Donald seemed to be freed up. This felt like a point of significant change.

In the following weeks Donald became increasingly comfortable. Often he took the initiative to draw first, not waiting for the others to begin. We also decided that everyone should have their own sheet of paper. Donald's drawings were expansive and abstract. Framing the edge became a more fluid, sweeping action, reaching into the centre of the page, and his feeling for colour became apparent as he carefully chose from the box to produce vibrant, abstract pictures. This seemed to reflect the change of Donald's position from the periphery of the group to sitting with the others. The release of colour in his drawing, combined with his large free arm gestures, bore witness to an internal change taking place.

Shifting boundaries

The group I have described in this case study changed through time from a closed group with a change in one facilitator, to one where the boundaries gradually became more permeable. Psychotherapy groups, which heavily influenced group work in the arts therapies, have typically ranged across three broad styles:

- closed stranger groups – a fixed number of clients who do not have a connection outside the group

- slow open groups – where the membership may change over a period of time

- open groups – open to anyone, although usually within a defined group of people or setting.

In practice there is flexibility in how these groups are run and in working with Donald I had to recognise both the importance of Bowlby's (2010/1979, p.103) 'secure base' as well as the loosening of external boundaries. During the group sessions Donald would often look out of the window to his neighbouring ward which seemed to give him comfort. He already knew several of the group members when he joined the group and this also offered him some familiarity and security. Perhaps on reflection when setting up this group, I had been too keen to use a well-recognised model – the closed stranger group. In doing so I risked losing sight of the importance of what Ansdell (2014, p.42) says about the need to use a model that fits the context: 'one size emphatically does not fit all'.

The group took place within a care setting for people with learning disabilities which created another larger boundary around the group. The high incidence of mental health illness in people with learning disabilities adds to the challenges around keeping strict boundaries for this client group. As is often the case in working with people who have learning disabilities, the boundaries around a group are blurred by the need for the therapist to communicate with carers. Many writers talk about the advantages of supportive links beyond the immediate group (DesNoyers et al. 1998; Hackett and Bourne 2014; Urwin 2011) and it felt as if these links had some specific benefits in my work with Donald. Despite appearing to be trapped by his own anxiety at times, Donald always seemed to want to be on the move, whether this was into the circle from the periphery, out again when he started drawing, or choosing to draw elsewhere. Eventually, he clearly experienced a wish to express himself more and to use language in a more emotionally expressive way, not only within the group but in his residential setting as well.

Around the time Donald was becoming more settled in the group, he chose for the first time to do a drawing in a different setting, with an occupational therapist who was part of his team. From there he had taken the drawing back to his ward. The presence of his drawing in the ward created a tangible link to the group and served to witness his creative self in time and space in a way that would have been less possible with other media.

My communication with the nurses provided enlightening glimpses into patterns of Donald's behaviour. It transpired that in the past they had tried in various ways to wean him from his books. When I spoke to them about this, they said that he held on to his books much of the time. It felt that their negotiation with him around this had brought a shared recognition of what the books meant for him. They were seen by the nurses as providing Donald with a form of protection and were recognised as very important to him. The books and his drawings were turning out to be links both within and outside the group. Having been anxious as a therapist about keeping tight boundaries, I began to acknowledge the value of softening these boundaries as part of Donald's journey.

Meeting points with support workers: some observations

As many people with a learning disability living in the community need to be accompanied to therapy, the brief meeting points with support workers at the beginning and end of sessions are potential spaces of boundary crossover witnessed by the client. These moments in time at the beginning and end of sessions can be emotionally charged for any number of reasons, and care needs to be taken around what is observed by the client. However, these brief exchanges can also sometimes lead to other opportunities for sharing struggles and experiences in this field of work.

After sessions, on returning with Donald to his nurses, I increasingly took care not to report that 'Donald was good today' – the statement that is often sought following a session. I try not to talk about clients at this point, but use the opportunity to engage support workers and clients together, especially when a client is non-verbal. Modelling communication in this way is an important message about the approach of the work and often reveals insights into how support workers relate to their clients.

One of the clearest manifestations of support workers becoming caught up in the patterns of a client's behaviour is when they speak about themselves or the client in the third person (as a parent might when speaking to a young toddler), as this is a characteristic of some people with an autistic spectrum condition. For example I might say to Mary, 'Is Mary feeling happy today?' There are arguments for using the third person for the sake of clarity or indeed to forge an alliance. However, when this is adopted without clear intention and simply becomes a habit, there is a danger of an unhealthy dynamic being triggered where carer and cared-for risk losing their identities in the moment. After all, learning correct use of the pronoun is an important part of human development, and sense of self and individuality are part of this journey. When I heard a new support worker say to the client she was supporting, 'You like Jane singing to you', I was confused, until later in the conversation I realised that Jane was in fact the support worker herself. In thinking about this later, I felt that the confusion in me very likely reflected general confusion in the communication. When we talked about this, the support worker said she did not even realise she was doing it.

At times this dynamic feels endemic in organisations and it is difficult to know if the roots are with clients or carers. Sinason (2010/1992), points to the importance of language, as changes over the years in the words to describe people with a learning disability suggest a subtle manoeuvring in society around this area. She reminds us of derogatory words used in the past such as idiot, imbecile, subnormal and others – a painful reminder, but one which gives a glimpse of hidden, unspoken feelings within our society about those with a learning disability. Being more conscious around our use of pronouns and indeed all our language in relation to people with an autistic spectrum condition will raise awareness and improve the quality of our interaction.

Organisational needs for structure and routine can easily turn into a mantra. Support workers working with people who have an autistic spectrum condition can unconsciously create restrictive and stultifying routines which never change for anyone involved. This is often compounded when support workers copy their client's spoken words or actions to placate their anxieties (echolalia – mirroring of speech, and echopraxia – mirroring of actions, both often present in people with an autistic spectrum condition). Continual mirroring – whether through anxiety or merely through habit – creates cycles of autonomic activity, with support worker and client repeating patterns of activity over and over, avoiding the need for direct engagement and negotiation over change. Careful two-way dialogue between therapist and support workers can support creative work in this area. The discussion around Donald's books with the nurses was initiated by me as I tried to understand what the books meant for him. As mentioned earlier, this communication turned out to reveal helpful information about the past but also fostered wider interest around the books and how they might be worked with. Urwin (2011, p.1) writes that 'it is important that professionals find ways of sharing information in order to establish a communication-enhancing environment around the non-communicating child'. Later on, Donald was helped to make a label with his name and stick this on to a sheet of paper which I saw him carrying around with his books. Taking one of his drawings back to the ward also created a link which provided the chance to share in the excitement of his development.

Supervision

Hawkins and Shohet (2012/1989) in their book, *Supervision in the Helping Professions*, highlight the importance of creating a space for carers in supervision, to think about the feelings that arise in them when caring for clients. Many authors write about these feelings, in particular as they arise in the therapeutic professions. The British Association for Music Therapy stipulates that music therapists receive clinical supervision at least monthly. It is recognised that traits associated with autistic spectrum conditions can trigger particular feelings and resistances in therapists and carers. If these feelings and resistances are openly explored in supervision, light can be shed on entrenched work patterns and attitudes.

Groups run in care homes that involve both support workers and clients have proven to be very effective in exploring some of the issues raised above. Through modelling responses to clients in the musical activity, it's possible to highlight the difference between copying and responding in a playful way. This can be done very simply using percussion instruments to play rhythmic patterns back and forth. There are central themes shared by all those involved in therapeutic work with autistic spectrum condition. As Ansdell (2002, p.28) says in relation to community music therapy:

> Musical relationships link up, connecting people and spaces: clients, staff, families, communities. The work can be closed-door work where a protected space is needed for the client. But more commonly there is an open door approach, with a natural yet safe permeability to the therapeutic frame, the safety residing as much with the therapist as the space.

The arts therapies offer different languages to clients with an autistic spectrum condition. When support workers are involved directly in group work dialogue, they are often witness for the first time to their clients' spontaneity and creativity. Increasingly, I find working with support workers brings new insights for all involved, enlivening the space through shared exploration both in the session and in follow-up discussions. This supervisory aspect to the work needs careful management but feels increasingly important for all carers of this client group.

Conclusion

Anxious bursts of shared music making were the beginnings of a creative encounter with Donald in my individual sessions with him. However, it was when Donald drew a frame around the drawings on the flip chart in the group setting that he took first steps towards individual creative expression. When he started to fill his own sheet of paper with subtle shades reflecting the colour of his clothes, we began to appreciate the extent of his frustration in earlier sessions when we could not supply the colour he was searching for. Clearly Donald has great sensitivity in this area. The swaying movements of his body as he drew seemed to arise instinctively from his satisfaction in the process. The movement was another expression of his growing spontaneity and enjoyment. Latterly, he began to hum as he drew, as well as sway from side to side, bringing together art, music and movement. By this time he was no longer waiting until everyone else had drawn before getting started himself.

Many referrals to music therapy are made out of a general frustration and inability to understand an individual with an autistic spectrum condition. What is usually clear is that the individual likes or responds to music. We need to bear in mind, however, that the lure of music can blind us to the reality of how powerful and threatening it can be for some people. The intense excitement of sharing music in early sessions can lead to over-stimulation and agitation, even fear, causing a defensive shutdown. A measured response from the therapist in the first sessions is important. Also important – to go back to the very opening words of this chapter – is an intense listening and alertness to unspoken communications unfolding in the therapy room. Donald brought with him a strong internalised sense of his family heritage and a connection with his co-residents, both of which clearly influenced his actions in the individual and group sessions. In the group, facilitated by changing co-therapists exploring different approaches and modalities, it was perhaps this heritage and these friendships, along with a creative kernel, which started to grow. Supervision from other arts therapies increased my awareness of potential barriers and allowed the work to develop in different directions. This enabled an unfolding of Donald's individuality to begin in the sessions and ultimately spread to enrich many aspects of his life.

Over the years I have learned a great deal from my efforts to communicate beyond the groups, and to open up discussion with carers. I have heard many well-worn assumptions expressed in relation to people with an autistic spectrum condition. I also hear most carers voicing perceptions which indicate qualities of warmth, intuition and understanding. Having said this, there is no denying the pervasive sense of an underlying institutional response permeating the language, actions and structures of the professional care and support offered to this group of people.

Organisations dependent on systems that lose sight of the individuals within them are in danger of cutting off one of their most creative sources. The therapeutic space must always acknowledge the needs of an individual or group. Donald had the freedom to influence the group development and in doing so helped me and my colleagues from nursing, occupational therapy and psychology make discoveries about him and ourselves. For myself, I became less afraid of letting go of musical structures and more interested in what other modalities could offer.

There is a great deal of confusion and misunderstanding around autistic spectrum conditions. This confusion is often exacerbated by the fact that many people who have this diagnosis also have a learning disability. To complicate matters further, people with a learning disability have a much higher likelihood of having a mental health illness than the rest of the population (Brown *et al.* 2011; Mental Health Foundation 2018). Therefore, autistic spectrum conditions are often entangled with other diagnoses and complex presentations. I believe every person has a healthy nascent spark. In my work with Donald there were many glimmers of this, including his first challenging striking of the drum, his enjoyment and surprise in using the word 'wonderful', and in the moment of his stepping up alone to the flip chart to draw. Identifying and engaging this healthy nascent spark, no matter how deeply buried, brings about the greatest optimism and hope – essential in keeping the therapeutic processes alive, unfolding and always focused.

References

Alvarez, A. and Reid, S. (eds) (1999) *Autism and Personality: Findings from the Tavistock Autism Workshop.* London: Routledge.

Alvin, J. and Warwick, A. (1991) *Music Therapy for the Autistic Child.* Oxford: Oxford University Press. (First published 1978.)

Ansdell, G. (2002) 'Community music therapy and the winds of change.' *Voices: A World Forum for Music Therapy 2,* 2, http://dx.doi.org/10.15845/voices.v2i2.

Ansdell, G (2014) 'Revisiting "Community music therapy and the winds of change" (2002): An original article and a retrospective evaluation.' *International Journal of Community Music 7,* 1, 11–45.

Ansdell, G. and Pavlicevic, M. (2004) *Community Music Therapy.* London: Jessica Kingsley Publishers.

Bowlby, J. (2010) *The Making and Breaking of Affectional Bonds.* London: Routledge. (First published 1979.)

Bragge, A. and Fenner, P. (2009) 'The emergence of the "Interactive Square" as an approach to art therapy with children on the autistic spectrum.' *International Journal of Art Therapy 14,* 1, 17–28.

Brown, M., Duff, H., Karatzias, T. and Horsburgh, D. (2011) 'A review of the literature relating to psychological interventions and people with intellectual disabilities: Issues for research, policy, education and clinical practice.' *Journal of Intellectual Disabilities 15,* 1, 31–45.

Davies, A. Richards, E. and Barwick, N. (2015) *Group Music Therapy: A Group Analytic Approach.* London: Routledge.

DesNoyers Hurley, A., Tomasulo, D.J., and Pfadt, A.G. (1998) 'Individual and group psychotherapy approaches for persons with mental retardation and developmental disabilities.' *Journal of Developmental and Physical Disabilities 10,* 4, 365–386.

Hackett, S. and Bourne, J. (2014) 'The Get Going Group: Dramatherapy with adults who have learning disabilities and mental health difficulties.' *Dramatherapy 36,* 1, 43–50.

Hawkins, P. and Shohet, R. (2012) *Supervision in the Helping Professions.* Maidenhead: Open University Press. (First published 1989.)

Meltzer, D., Bremner, J., Hoxter, S., Weddel, D. and Wittenberg, I. (2008) *Explorations in Autism: A Psychoanalytic Study.* Strath Tay: Clunie Press.

Mental Health Foundation (2018) *Learning Disability Statistics: Mental Health Problems.* Scotland: Mental Health Foundation. Accessed on 26 June 2018 at www.mentalhealth.org.uk/learning-disabilities/help-information/learning-disability-statistics-/187699.

Nordoff, P. and Robbins, C. (1971) *Music Therapy in Special Education.* New York, NY: John Day Company.

Ogden, T.H. (2004) *The Primitive Edge of Experience.* London: Karnac. (First published 1989.)

Ross Williams, Roger (2016) (director) *Life, Animated.* USA: A & E Indie Films, Motto Pictures, Roger Ross Williams Productions.

Sinason, V. (2010) *Mental Handicap and the Human Condition: New Approaches from the Tavistock.* London: Free Association Books. (First published 1992.)

Trevarthen, C., Aitken, K., Papoudi, D. and Robarts, J. (1996) *Children with Autism: Diagnosis and Interventions to Meet Their Needs.* London and Bristol, PA: Jessica Kingsley Publishers.

Tustin, F. (1992) *Autistic States in Children*. London: Routledge & Kegan Paul. (Original work published 1981.)

Urwin, C. (2011) 'Emotional life of autistic spectrum children: What do we want from child psychotherapy treatment?' *Psychoanalytic Psychotherapy 25*, 3, 245–261.

Wilson, P. (2014) 'A Group of Five Autistic Young Adults.' In M. Dolphin, A. Byers, A. Goldsmith and R.E. Jones (eds) *Psychodynamic Art Therapy Practice with People on the Autistic Spectrum*. London: Routledge.

Winnicott, D.W. (2002) *Playing and Reality*. London: Routledge. (First published 1971.)

PART 2

COLLABORATIVE APPROACHES

CHAPTER 7

Music Therapy with Children with Autistic Spectrum Conditions and Their Families

JOSIE NUGENT

Introduction

In this chapter I will discuss two contrasting collaborative engagements between the child, therapist and family members from my private practice in Northern Ireland and in the context of home-based working. There is a growing trend towards family-centred practice in many areas of healthcare (Deek *et al.* 2016; Saleeba 2008; Franck and Callery 2004) and music therapy is no exception to this. Family-based music therapy interventions include interventions for children and their carers and families in child development centres (Flower 2014; Oldfield 2006b, 2016), special education centres (Kaenampornpan 2017), community-based group music therapy and individual family-centred therapy in the homeplace (Jacobsen and Thompson 2017; Oldfield 2016; Warren and Nugent 2010). An international network has also been created for music therapists working with families to create informal learning opportunities for music therapists working in these contexts and opportunities to enrich practice (Thompson 2017b).

Family-based music therapy work was pioneered by Amelia Oldfield in child development centres (Oldfield 2006a, 2006b). She developed a method called Interactive Music Therapy at the Croft Unit for Child and Family Psychiatry, Cambridge, UK. It uses live, spontaneous, mostly improvised music making to achieve non-musical objectives. This approach focuses on offering children and families a positive experience and supports both the skill development of the child and the quality of the parent–child relationship. Here families can gain new insights into this relationship through the medium of music. The outcomes of a long-term music therapy intervention with a child and his family at this centre have also been documented, where positive effects could be seen both in the therapy room and in many other areas of the child's family life (Loombe 2017). Claire Flower's work in another child development centre focuses on the child/parent/therapist trio, looking closely at the relational processes between these three people. Pilot studies have shown that music therapy is experienced by the mother and therapist as a fluid active web of musical and interpersonal relationships: as individuals, various pairings and all three participating as a trio (Flower 2014).

Various kinds of family-based group music therapy have also been explored over time. Allgood (2005) describes a seven-week community group music therapy intervention for four families with a focus on the parents' perceptions. The parents felt it created a mutual platform, 'a place to be yourself for once', where all were able to participate at their own level (Allgood 2005, p.97). Sharing connections with other families in a safe environment was important and, for some, music therapy became part of their family time together. Parents also learnt about their child's limitations and abilities and about creating structure, pulling back a little and giving the child a chance to keep going.

A music therapy model documented by Bull (2008), delivered by a therapist and co-therapist, has some similarities with home-based music therapy. The mother–child dyad was placed in a larger group of mother–child dyads and this helped to resonate with a family setting. It was shown to support a mother–child relationship and by giving opportunities for chatting, it helped the mums to 'feel heard as an individual connecting with others experiencing similar difficulties' (Bull 2008, p.81). The setting also provided a space where a mum could find new ways to relate to her child and develop 'resources within to keep approaching her child in new ways' (Bull 2008, p.81).

Music therapy in the family home with children with autistic spectrum conditions and their parents was trialled by Alvin and Warwick in 1984, as it was seen as a consistent environment for both mother and child (Alvin and Warwick 1991/1978). A later study by Müller and Warwick (1993) showed that maternal involvement in music therapy in the home resulted in an increase in turn-taking and musical activity. Mothers also saw their child in a more realistic light following music therapy. It opened a door for a mother to interact with her child on equal musical terms and suggested that a child would be more prepared to interact if the mother was prepared to wait rather than 'goading the child into interaction' (Müller and Warwick 1993, p.229).

There have been a considerable number of studies on family-centred music therapy for individual children with autistic spectrum conditions. Studies by Thompson (2012) created a model for family-centred practice with pre-school children which focused on attunement to the child's mood and behaviour, and following the child's lead while also assessing the need for structure, choice and control. In this approach the therapist entices the child with motivating activities and works positively with the aim of keeping the child's anxiety levels low. A home-based randomised controlled trial study on social engagement abilities of children aged three to five addressed five different aspects of social communication, namely 'shared attention, focus on faces, turn-taking, response in joint interaction and initiation in joint attention' (Thompson, McFerran and Gold 2013, p.843). This study showed that family-centred music therapy improved social interactions in home and community environments and the parent–child relationship, but showed no improvement in language skills or general social responsiveness. Further qualitative analysis of the parent–child relationship with children aged three to six, using semi-structured video recorded interviews of parents who had attended family-centred music therapy, identified three aspects of positive change, namely the quality of the parent–child relationship, the parent's response to the child and the parent's perception of the child (Thompson and McFerran 2013).

Music therapy in a home setting can be challenging for both the therapist and family members (Mitchell 2017). The therapist can feel very vulnerable while adjusting to the dynamics of a family home. To be accepted into the environment one has to focus on building a strong, trusting and respectful relationship with each family member (Alvin and Warwick 1991/1978). The therapist has to adopt flexibility in their practice to be able to integrate oneself with family members and offer a rewarding service for all (Mitchell 2017). One also cannot forget that it is a privilege to be able to work in this environment as this gives the therapist a chance to work with a child and the family at a more intimate level (Mitchell 2017; Müller and Warwick 1993).

The environment where music therapy happens plays an important part in a child's freedom to be and interact. This freedom 'should include not only freedom to behave in a certain way and to organise the self but freedom from fear or obsessions which create emotional, intellectual, and social blockages' (Alvin and Warwick 1991/1978, p.8). The therapist's holding process (Levinge 1993) is central to meeting the needs of the child, who is faced with trying to find new sense of freedom and relational self in a familiar environment that has now changed. The therapist also needs freedom in the sense of a space in her mind where she can think of ideas and allow them to change and develop in the moment to be able to offer an environment where therapeutic relationships can grow between all participants. She also needs to be conscious and clear about the roles she takes on during a session (Jacobsen 2017; Thompson 2017a). These can include being an individual, dyadic and/or triadic therapist, and roles that are directive, person-centred and supportive. It is important that the therapist can consciously and fluidly shift between roles to meet the changing needs of each participant in the session.

When planning to work in home-based environments, one has also to ascertain whether it is best to address the child's needs only or the relationship between the child and family members. I have found that this will depend on each family's specific circumstances and expectations from a music therapy intervention. In this chapter, I will explore this and other ideas in two contrasting music therapy approaches from my private practice.

Collaborative music therapy in the family home

When I work in the homeplace,[1] I work in a sensitive and empathetic manner, listening to needs of both the child and family members, and pace the collaborative process accordingly.

---

1   I have used the word 'homeplace' as it is redolent and evocative for those of an Irish background as epitomised in Brian Friel's play *The Home Place* (Friel 2005).

My approach is music-centred with an underlying psychoanalytical thinking guided by the writings of Frances Tustin, Anne Alvarez and Donald W. Winnicott. Alvarez (1992), writes that we are all born as 'object-seeking' and 'object-related' (p.190) where the inner mind is 'full of living objects, memories and thoughts' which have their 'own power of existence' and are controlled by us (p.193). A child with an autistic spectrum condition can struggle with sensory perceptions and awareness, and this may result in them not being able to make emotional contact with a caring object. Psychoanalytic thinking suggests that to deal with this arrest in self-development, the child withdraws and shuts out the world around them and finds security in a self-created world. Tustin used the image of an autistic shell to portray this place of refuge and protection for a child (Spensley 1995). This inhibition in development is not seen as a regression and is instead seen as a deficit having both an emotional and cognitive aspects to it (Alvarez 1992), where the absence of imaginary and symbolic play is replaced by frequent use of repetitive rituals, such as hand flapping, rocking or obsessional interests.

All kinds of play have meaning, and imaginative play 'enlarges the internal mind of a child' (Alvarez 1992, p.165). For Winnicott, play happens in an intermediate area of experience between the mother and child, which is experienced as being neither inside nor outside but in-between. He introduced the concept of 'transitional phenomena', later calling it 'transitional or potential space' (Winnicott 1971). In this intermediate area of human experience, the individual's inner reality and external life are both present. The word 'transition' signifies the attributes of movement and a set of processes in the infant's psyche (Caldwell and Joyce 2011). Winnicott coined the terms 'transitional objects' to describe the first 'not me' possessions of the infant. These can be any object such as a teddy or a piece of cloth whose meaning and value becomes vitally important to the infant's personal experience of life (Winnicott 1971). With time, the object loses meaning and is replaced by another object. Winnicott was of the understanding that continued use of transitional objects can help a person resolve anxieties throughout life and lead to a healthy normal adulthood (Winnicott 1971). Winnicott extended the theme of transitional phenomena to study play and believed that an important feature of playing was the freedom to be creative, saying: 'it is in playing, and only playing that the individual child or adult is able to be creative and to use the whole personality and it is only in being creative that the individual discovers the self' (Winnicott 1971, p.63).

He saw play as 'a feature of life and total living' (p.64), where this intermediate area of imaginary play, belonging to both an inner and external reality, can be retained throughout life, making it possible for a person to live creatively. For children and adults with autistic spectrum conditions, there can often be an absence of this level of imaginary play (Bergmann *et al.* 2016; Music 2011). Music therapy can help stimulate the creative mind of the child or adult towards this kind of playfulness (O'Kelly and Koffmann 2007; Robarts 1996). It can create pathways of receptivity in the child's internal world and the creative musical processes of play and improvisation can encourage new forms of self-expression. Robarts (1996) suggests that this may help a child with autism regulate emotions and physiological responses, thereby bringing about a more real and united sense of self and new ways of connecting with others in their external reality. This psychoanalytic understanding of play as a creative way of living and engaging with others informs my daily practice as a music therapist.

I use play in music-centred ways through the medium of musical interactions, creatively driven in the moment. These include techniques such as modelling, turn-taking, following and initiating, improvised music making and in-the-moment musical stories, in addition to the use of songs and pre-composed music. I have found that creative musical play can assist the development of therapeutic relationships, the means by which I connect and engage with child and family members over time. It can effect beneficial changes in their social and emotional wellbeing by creating possibilities for new or alternative ways of socially connecting and interacting with each other. I have found this approach encourages a child to find new ways to self-express, emotionally regulate and grow in their interpersonal ways of relating with others.

Case studies
Setting and participants

Two contrasting interventions will be outlined to explore collaborative approaches to music therapy in the homeplace. They will describe my reflections of the evolving therapeutic relationships between the therapist and family members, through the process of creative musical play. Pseudonyms will be used to preserve anonymity and discussions will include illustrative case studies to give brief descriptions of the music therapy processes used.

Both children were aged five and had completed one year at school. Each intervention was preceded by a visit to the family home to discuss the child's needs, the family's hopes and realistic options and goals for the intervention, thereby establishing stepping stones towards the collaborative process of working in each family setting. This also gave me a chance to meet everybody and get a feel for the setting, the space being provided and time being allocated for music therapy. In both cases it was agreed to have a weekly 30-minute session in a designated room of the household where every effort was made to ensure the setting was safe and distraction-free. Detailed session notes were kept along with a reflective journal, which served as a means of looking at both studies from many different angles.

CASE STUDY: EWAN

This intervention was held over a period of 21 weeks preceded by a three-week assessment period. Sessions 2, 7, 14 and 21 were video-recorded over the course of the intervention. I worked individually with Ewan for the greater part in each session, with family members joining for group interactive play towards the end every week. It seemed important to first develop a therapeutic relationship with Ewan on his own and over time encourage development of his social interactive skills with family members.

Individual work

Ewan appeared to have an inherent wish to communicate and used words, short phrases and sang parts of songs and nursery rhymes to interact with others. For example, we had a conversation about the animals in McDonald's Farm and he initiated another conversation naming people and objects in pictures on the wall during the third assessment session. This communication appeared to be logically driven rather than having a creative imaginative input. He also enjoyed being a solitary performer, looking at himself in the mirror while singing and/or playing an instrument. This ability to perform, while appearing solitary in nature, served as an opening, which I could begin to attune to, helping him to play creatively and find more social, less solitary ways to interact with others.

It was also clear during the assessment period that Ewan's mind became easily overloaded. When this happened, he seemed to have a need to run away and leave the space, but always came back with a little verbal persuasion. There did not appear to be particular triggers for his need to leave the space, such as a type of activity, duration of an activity or sounds used. I therefore considered this behaviour to be suggestive of a fragmented mind struggling to process all aspects of an activity, where the mental links to forge integration may not have been formed early in life due to an arrest in self-development (Alvarez 1992). I also became mindful and observant that this inhibition in self-development could be related to sensory processing difficulties when an activity incorporated a mixture of audio, visual and tactile processing (Grandin and Panek 2013; Jao Keehn et al. 2016).

During the initial sessions, I focused on building a therapeutic relationship with Ewan using the processes of call and response, modelling and turn-taking, improvised music making and the use of songs. It was clear that he was immediately drawn to sonorous resonant sounds and these sounds appeared to hold his attention.

Ewan always immediately engaged with the pentatonic table tubular bells. He played in dialogue with me, always waiting for my reply. He appeared to need reassurance for his musical input and would look in my direction, making eye contact to see if I was ready to reply. This activity facilitated a gentle flow of non-verbal communication which grew from session to session and helped to develop Ewan's attention span to engage in new conversational ways with me for increasing periods of time, while also laying foundations for Ewan to develop his imagination and creative play skills in collaborative musical play. For example, he liked to explore the dynamics of the instrument using various kinds of mallets in conversation with my replies.

As the sessions progressed, Ewan appeared to have less of a need to engage in solitary performances and was happy to engage in creative play. Using instruments in imaginative ways greatly helped in this regard. For example, Ewan very much enjoyed using the djembe symbolically as a megaphone where we both spoke to each other through the instrument in humorous ways during many of the latter sessions. I similarly used my first instrument, the violin, innovatively with Ewan, to create unusual sounds and glissandi which he thoroughly enjoyed and indicated this by smiling and laughing lots while waiting for his turn to copy them.

As mentioned in my initial observations of Ewan, he could become easily overloaded and I soon realised that activities created with a simple song structure appealed to and connected with Ewan and provided a framework for extending our turn-taking activities. Use of such songs appeared to help Ewan become more restful in himself and more engaged. For example, Ewan gradually learnt to sing a song titled 'Fun for Drums' (Nordoff and Robbins 1968). He attained a level of focus to be able to engage in singing this song, taking his turn to hit a lollipop drum in dramatic fun ways for up to ten verses in latter sessions.

Visually and aurally stimulating sensory instruments, such as the ocean drum, took on a new meaning for Ewan in the latter sessions. He would engage with this instrument to self-regulate with my presence acting as a 'container' in a 'container–contained' therapist–child relationship, rather than running out of the room when feeling overloaded (Schuttleworth 1997, pp.28–29).

Ewan chose the ocean drum and brought it to the play area in the penultimate session. He swirled it whilst looking at me and vocalised 'ah' sounds that closely mimicked the swirling tones from the drum. When the drum rolled away from his reach, I took control of it, rolling it back so that we could begin to play with it interactively. We had a short turn-taking conversation, hitting the drum with mallets, but it was clear from both his vocal and musical replies that this was not what Ewan needed at this point in time. He confirmed this by re-possessing the drum, saying, 'I just sleep', whereby he placed his head on the drum to rest. I sang an occasional soft soothing pentatonic modal melody in reply to his request with the words, 'Ewan sleeps'. Ewan then proceeded to find his own way to self-regulate using the ocean drum to sleep on, occasionally rolling it and/or hitting it whilst vocalising, 'I just sleep' from time to time. I held a presence for Ewan during this period by sometimes singing variations of an original pentatonic melody created very softly in reply to his vocalisations.

The symbolic use of the ocean drum as transitional object of self-immersion and regulation (Winnicott 1971) appeared to bring Ewan to a more settled resting place within which he was ready to interact with family members for the latter part of the session.

Family work

Activities with Ewan and his family were of a structured nature to begin with – for example, passing a beat on a percussive instrument to a song created for the activity and accompaniment of familiar songs. In the initial sessions, while showing a wish and readiness to engage in musical play with family members, Ewan also appeared restless, and seemed to have a need to run away from the space, possibly indicating sensory overload. I therefore developed a different approach towards family-centred group play, gradually adding more fun-like, imaginative activities with reduced levels of audio/visual content.

I introduced a basket game in session 14. This activity was adapted for my music therapy practice from a Gina Davies (2013) Attention Autism activity where participants watch the facilitator model the use of objects taken from a white bucket. In the adapted version of this activity, each participant got a chance to play with an object/instrument from a basket after I had demonstrated how one could play with it. I created a song for the activity, which provided a fixed structure with an in-the-moment commentary for each person's actions with an object from the basket. This activity excited Ewan each week and led to new playful ways to interact with his brother, Mum and Dad, where each had a turn to take part in creative imaginative play with objects from the basket and to also lead the activity.

Having successfully introduced a basket game, I felt Ewan was now ready for an additional family-centred activity and I chose a different strategy. I created a series of visually orientated activities with coloured rhythm sticks as the visual modality can be easier for a child with autism who struggles with sensory overload. Additional reasoning for this strategy comes from the writings of Grassi (2014, p.64), who explains that sight operates 'according to a linear (two dimensional) and sequential mode' unlike hearing which is a multidimensional sensorial experience due to a person's sensitivity to vibration of sound. The visual activities included turn-taking, leadership games and the creation of letters and shapes. In the penultimate session with Mum, Dad and his brother, Ewan engaged to follow each person's leadership in a non-verbal turn-taking game with the rhythm sticks. This showed an advancement in Ewan's willingness to interact with family members where he remained for the duration of the activity, accepting the leadership of other family members during a group activity. In the final session, where only his mum was free to join for group play, I ceased to be the facilitator and let Mum take over to play with her son.

I used the rhythm sticks to create letters which Ewan and his mum copied. When Ewan recognised a letter, he vocalised what it was. When he saw 'L' , he saw it as a stepping stone toward making a triangle. I immediately chose to step back and let Mum facilitate interactivity with Ewan to complete this shape. I silently nodded and gesturally encouraged her to continue and together they created a square and rectangle.

CASE STUDY: PETER

This intervention took place with Peter's mum present as there appeared to be a very strong bond between Peter and his mum. It was agreed to have music therapy for a period of ten weeks and I adopted the role of a triadic therapist (Flower 2014), focusing on evolving relationships between Peter, Mum and myself. In the first session I, at times, felt and saw myself as an intrusion in the family's personal space.

Peter found it difficult to listen and be receptive to the greeting song and left the room. Each time he returned, I played a different instrument for him to listen to and respond. Only one instrument captured his attention on the first day – the ocean drum. He looked at it, placed his hands on it to briefly touch it.

I felt vulnerable during these initial sessions and adopted a flexible approach to integrate myself with the home setting and find ways to offer a rewarding service for all (Mitchell 2017). I also needed freedom in the sense of a space in my mind to be able to think in the moment and offer ideas and suggestions that could help build therapeutic relationships between all participants.

Peter rarely made visual contact with me during the initial sessions and preferred to connect with his own toys in play with Mum. This gave me an insight into the playful activities he enjoyed which included a collection of nursery rhymes with actions. For example, he loved the rhyme 'Hickory Dickory Dock' using Mum's self-created clock. He participated in a receptive way, watching Mum excitedly as she helped a mouse to run up the clock to strike a different hour, saying the hour struck each time. He also liked to be swayed over and back to the nursery rhyme 'Row, Row, Row Your Boat'.

My initial role centred around finding creative, playful ways to extend Peter's social interactive skills to include my new ideas in these familiar nursery rhymes. I also wanted to introduce percussive instruments as play tools for Peter and his mum, realising that I first had to focus on building a therapeutic relationship with both before this goal could be facilitated. I also had to take time to process what was going on in my own mind during these sessions. I needed to acknowledge my uncertainties about my therapeutic presence and my wish for control of the session. In reflecting on my need for control, I also needed to be 'open to change and development' in this triangular relational setting (Richards 2017, p.308). I realised I could learn from Mum's active presence in the session, instead of seeing it as a competitive intrusion. Mum worked in an enthusiastic, energised way with her son and this invigorated and excited Peter to take part in receptive ways with her. I therefore collaborated with his mum about the session content/activities at the end of each session, where we both made suggestions for the forthcoming session. This helped to establish a way of working with Mum and opened doors towards finding new ways to collaborate more closely with her and Peter during the session. For example, I exchanged 'Six Bottles on the Wall' for 'Five Fruits on the Wall', opening a pathway for Peter and me to connect in one of his favourite activities, while also enabling Peter to adapt to a small change in a well-known activity.

As the sessions progressed, I created new playful ideas in each activity which enabled my involvement. This meant that Peter had a chance to get to know me through the process of creative play, and a therapeutic relationship gradually evolved between Peter and me. This was noted in Peter making a lot more visual contact with me during the session and accepting the presence of a 'Hello' song where he vocalised each of our names.

Having an accepted greater presence in the active processes of the session led me to be able to subtly guide the direction of the session when I felt a need to do so. For example, I noticed that the session operated at a frantic pace and that Mum and I partly entertained Peter using nursery rhymes with actions. I addressed this observation and in collaboration with Mum set about slowing the pace of the session to create time and space to encourage Peter to take a more active role both vocally and physically in each activity. This was achieved vocally by leaving out words in a song and giving Peter time and a chance to say them. This process helped Peter to mentally coordinate what he wanted to say with the actions of an activity. He worked hard to achieve this and by the end of the intervention he vocalised words and part phrases in the songs such as 'Row your Boat' and 'Humpty Dumpty', making immediate eye contact with a joyful expressive face towards Mum and me.

This intervention initially focused on enhancement of the child–parent social interactive relationship with the therapist providing a holding environment (Levinge 1993). The holding process helped to reduce Peter's fear of change and through the imaginative process of play, familiar songs and nursery rhymes were adapted to create new avenues for Peter to interact playfully with the therapist and his mum. With time, Peter moved spontaneously from being an excited observer to an active participant.

I continued to adapt activities creatively, working with a greater individual presence in the trio with Peter and Mum as I wanted to create opportunities for him to take a more active part. For example, I used the five fruits in a new activity with tube-like spiral wire where Peter initially watched me doing all the actions for the song, naming each fruit as it was dropped down a spiral tube. In the penultimate session, to my surprise and joy, Peter spontaneously moved from being an excited observer to an active participant where he took possession of the spiral tube and said each fruit before he personally dropped it down the tube using the pentatonic melody I had created for it.

I also introduced activities for three-person participation, such as an initial greeting song and goodbye song, in which Peter enthusiastically participated, saying each person's name. Towards the end of the intervention, I felt that Peter was now ready to play with percussive musical instruments and I introduced a gong into a familiar activity with a self-created pentatonic song titled 'Over and Back' in the penultimate session.

I replaced scarves with a gong and interacted with Mum to hit the gong with a mallet as it swayed it over and back. We shared play of the gong while Peter eagerly watched, waiting in anticipation for a short while. On giving a mallet to Peter, he willingly hit the gong, counting as he hit it ten times: his first time to play a musical percussive instrument during these sessions.

A stepping stone had been reached through the process of creative imaginative play over a ten-week period. Peter's mum could now interact with her son in new ways using live percussive instruments, including tambourine, cymbal and gong, during play time together in the family home.

Reflections

This chapter discusses two contrasting family interventions for young children with autistic spectrum conditions from my private practice in the home place. It is mainly explored from the viewpoint of the therapist and focuses on growth in interpersonal relationships through the process of creative imaginary play. This contrasts with some previously published articles on family-centred interventions for young children with autistic spectrum conditions. These studies have created an approach for family-centred practice that have been measured and quantified with feedback from parent participation (Müller and Warwick 1993; Oldfield 2006b; Thompson *et al.* 2013; Thompson and McFerran 2013) and/or focused on the parent–child–therapist relationship from the view point of both therapist and parent (Flower 2014).

Considering the evidence base alongside my own practice-based experiences, I can nevertheless see many correlations. Studies by the Thompson group identified three aspects of positive change from their interviews with parents and one of these resonates with my personal findings, namely the parent–child relationship. The quality of 'the parent–child relationship' became more 'interactive' and 'interconnected' (Thompson and McFerran 2013, p.17) in both case studies described. Ewan's family members found new ways to interact with Ewan during group activities and Ewan enthusiastically looked forward to playing the basket game and games with rhythm sticks with his family. Peter's mum, through an evolving process of creative play, became more interconnected with her son, something she mentioned in our conversation at the end of the penultimate session.

My approach was guided by the psychoanalytic writing of Tustin, Alvarez and Winnicott, and I very much realised that I needed to create time and space to allow therapeutic relationships to grow whereby each child and adult were able to find new ways to interrelate with others. In the first case study, this approach very much appeared to help Ewan deal with a mind that often became overloaded and find new ways to self-regulate and interrelate with others. In the second case study, I adapted my approach from an inner wish to lead and be in control to a more flexible approach where I was willing to learn from the mother–child relationship. Mitchell (2017) also emphasised the need to be flexible in one's practice in the home setting. This resulted in a deepening in my connectivity with Mum, and, over time, acceptance by Peter, which gradually led to the development of an interactive relationship with him. While Flower (2014) writes about a fluid shifting of focus between individual, possible pairings and trios in such settings, my personal experience during the second intervention resulted in a deeper reflection into my presence as a therapist in the home setting. Issues of power, competition and control in my need to form a therapeutic relationship with Peter came to the fore and I had to find space within my psyche to reflect and be open to learning and adopting a holding position (Levinge 1993) where both Peter and his mum were given time to get used to my presence in their home.

The process of creative imaginative play is central in my approach towards growth in interpersonal relationships inspired by the psychodynamic writing of Winnicott (1971) and the music therapist Robarts (1996, 2014). The first case study highlighted a need to create novel, imaginative activities which were anticipation-focused and/or visually stimulating and tailored to connect with the fragmented mind of a child with an autistic spectrum condition that can become easily overloaded (Alvarez 1992). In the second case study, the play skills used in nursery rhyme activities were adapted imaginatively in a step-by-step manner from week to week. This led to the inclusion of live percussive instruments in play activities, therefore enlarging the internal mind of a child through creative imaginative play and helping Peter relate to his mum in new ways.

Conclusions

This chapter reflects on two collaborative music therapy interventions from my private practice with children with autistic spectrum conditions. It highlights the need for the therapist to be innovative, flexible and open to change and development in evolving relational processes between a child and family members. It also emphasises the importance of finding imaginative ways to let the child be free to be oneself and interact through the creative process of play. By reflecting on my work and relating my experiences to both psychodynamic and music-centred therapy practices, I hope that it will be helpful to other music therapists working with families in private practice.

References

Allgood, N. (2005) 'Parents' perceptions of family-based group music therapy for children with autism spectrum disorders.' *Music Therapy Perspectives 23*, 2, 92–99.

Alvarez, A. (1992) *Live Company: Psychoanalytic Psychotherapy with Autistic, Borderline, Deprived and Abused Children.* London: Routledge.

Alvin, J. and Warwick, A. (1991) *Music Therapy for the Autistic Child.* Oxford: Oxford University Press. (First published 1978.)

Bergmann, T., Sappok, T., Diefenbacher, A. and Dziobek, I. (2016) 'Music in diagnostics: Using musical interactional settings for diagnosing autism in adults with intellectual developmental disabilities.' *Nordic Journal of Music Therapy 25*, 4, 319–351.

Bull, R. (2008) 'Autism and the Family: Groups Music Therapy with Mothers and Children.' In A. Oldfield and C. Flower (eds) *Music Therapy with Children and their Families.* London: Jessica Kingsley Publishers.

Caldwell, L. and Joyce, A. (2011) *Reading Winnicott.* London: Routledge.

Davies, G. (2013). *Attention Autism.* Surrey: Gina Davies. Accessed on 15 October 2014 at http://ginadavies.co.uk/parents-services/professional-shop.

Deek, H., Hamilton, S., Brown, N., Inglis, S.C., Digiacomo, M. and Newton, P.J. (2016) 'Family-centred approaches to healthcare interventions in chronic diseases in adults: A quantitative systematic review.' *Journal of Advanced Nursing 72*, 5 968–979.

Flower, C. (2014) 'Music therapy trios with child, parent and therapist: A preliminary qualitative single case study.' *Psychology of Music 42*, 6, 839–845.

Franck, L.S. and Callery, P. (2004) 'Re-thinking family-centred care across the continuum of children's healthcare.' *Child: Care, Health and Development 30*, 3, 265–277.

Friel, B. (2005) *The Home Place*. London: The Gallery Press.

Grassi, L. (2014) 'The dimension of sound and rhythm in psychic structuring and analytic work.' *The Italian Psychoanalytic Annual 8*, 63–82.

Grandin, T. and Panek, R. (2013) *The Autistic Brain*. United Kingdom: Riderbooks.

Jacobsen, S. L. and Thompson, G. (2017) *Music Therapy with Families*. London: Jessica Kingsley Publishers.

Jacobsen, S.L. (2107) 'A Meaningful Journey – Including Parents in Interactive Music Therapy.' In S. Daniel and C. Trevarthen (eds) *Rhythms of Relating in Children's Therapies: Connecting Creatively with Vulnerable Children*. London: Jessica Kingsley Publishers.

Jao Keehn, R.J., Sanchez, S.R., Stewart, C.R. and Zhao, W. (2016). 'Impaired downregulation of visual cortex during auditory processing is associated with autism symptomatology in children and adolescents with autism spectrum disorder.' *Autism Research 10*, 130–143.

Kaenampornpan, P. (2017) 'Involving Family Members Who are Primary Carers in Music Therapy Sessions with Children with Special Needs.' In J. Strange, H. Odell-Miller and E. Richards (eds) *Collaboration and Assistance in Music Therapy Practice*. London: Jessica Kingsley Publishers.

Levinge, A. (1993) 'Permission to Play – The Search for Self through Music Therapy Research with Children Presenting with Communication Difficulties.' In H. Payne (ed.) *Handbook of Inquiry in the Arts Therapies: One River Many Currents*. London: Jessica Kingsley Publishers.

Loombe, D. (2017) 'Long-term music therapy at a child development centre: Changing and growing with Harry and his family: A case study.' *British Journal of Music Therapy 31*, 1, 32–88.

Mitchell, E. (2017) 'Music therapy for the child or the family? The flexible and varied role of the music therapist within the home setting.' *British Journal of Music Therapy 31*, 1, 39–42.

Müller, P. and Warwick, A. (1993) 'Autistic Children and Music Therapy: The Effects of Maternal Involvement in Therapy.' In M. Heal and T. Wigram (eds) *Music Therapy in Health and Education*. London: Jessica Kingsley Publishers.

Music, G. (2011) *Nurturing Natures*. Hove: Psychology Press.

Nordoff, P. and Robbins, C. (1968) *Fun for Four Drums: A Rhythmic Game for Children with Four Drums, Piano and a Song*. Pennsylvania: Theodore Presser Company.

O'Kelly, L. and Koffmann, J. (2007) 'Multidisciplinary perspectives of music therapy in adult palliative care.' *Palliative Medicine 21*, 235–241.

Oldfield, A. (2006a) *Interactive Music Therapy – A Positive Approach: Music Therapy at a Child Development Centre*. London: Jessica Kingsley Publishers

Oldfield, A. (2006b) *Interactive Music Therapy in Child and Family Psychiatry*. London: Jessica Kingsley Publishers.

Oldfield, A. (2016). 'Family Approaches in Music Therapy Practice with Young Children.' In J. Edwards (ed.) *The Oxford Handbook of Music Therapy*. Oxford: Oxford University Press.

Richards, E. (2017) 'Someone Else in the Room: Welcome or Unwelcome? An Attachment Perspective.' In J. Strange, H. Odell-Miller and E. Richards (eds) *Collaboration and Assistance in Music Therapy Practice.* London: Jessica Kingsley Publishers.

Robarts, J.Z. (2014) 'Music Therapy with Children with Developmental Trauma Disorder.' In C.A. Malchiodi and D.A. Crenshaw (eds) *Creative Arts and Play Therapy for Attachment Problems.* London: Guilford Press.

Robarts, J.Z. (1996) 'Music Therapy for Children with Autism.' In C. Trevarthen, K. Aitken, D. Papoudi, and J. Robarts (eds) *Children with Autism: Diagnosis and Interventions to Meet Their Needs.* London: Jessica Kingsley Publishers.

Saleeba, A. (2008) 'The importance of family-centered care in pediatric nursing.' *School of Nursing Scholarly Works 48.* https://opencommons.uconn.edu/son_articles/48/

Schuttleworth, J. (1997) 'Closely Observed Psychoanalytic Theory and Infant Development.' In L. Miller (ed.) *Closely Observed Infants.* London: Duckworth Overlook.

Spensley, S. (1995) *Frances Tustin.* London: Routledge.

Thompson, G. (2012) 'Family-centred music therapy in the home environment: Promoting interpersonal engagement between children with autism spectrum disorder and their parents.' *Music Therapy Perspectives 30,* 2, 109–116.

Thompson, G.A. (2017a). 'Families with Preschool-Aged Children with Autism Spectrum Disorder.' In L. Jacobenson and G. Thompson (eds) *Music Therapy with Families.* London: Jessica Kingsley Publishers.

Thompson, G.A. (2017b) 'The 'music therapy with families network': Creating a community of practice via social media.' *British Journal of Music Therapy 31,* 1, 50–52.

Thompson, G. and McFerran, K. (2013) '"We've got a special connection": Qualitative analysis of descriptions of change in the parent–child relationship by mothers of young children with autism spectrum disorder.' *Nordic Journal of Music Therapy 24,* 1, 3–26.

Thompson, G.A., McFerran, K.S. and Gold, C. (2013) 'Family-centred music therapy to promote social engagement in young children with severe autism spectrum disorder: A randomized controlled study.' *Child: Care, Health and Development 40,* 6, 840–852.

Warren, P. and Nugent, N. (2010) 'The music connections programme: Parents' perceptions of their children's involvement in music therapy.' *New Zealand Journal of Music Therapy 8,* 8–33.

Winnicott, D.W. (1971) *Playing and Reality.* London: Tavistock/Routledge.

CHAPTER 8

How Do Music Therapists Share? Exploring Collaborative Approaches in Educational Settings for Children with Autistic Spectrum Conditions

EMMA MACLEAN AND CLAIRE TILLOTSON

Introduction

This chapter draws on the experiences of two music therapists working with children on the autistic spectrum in educational settings. Claire is based in a school for children with autism four days a week and shares an office with other therapists employed by the school, including the Speech and Language Therapist, Occupational Therapist and Clinical Psychologist. Emma visits a number of different schools, some with specialist provisions attached, and has an office which is separate from other therapists working in the schools. Both authors originally trained in the Nordoff Robbins approach to music therapy and continue to keep music as a central part of their work whilst using elements of humanistic or client-centred (Nordoff and Robbins 2007; Rogers 2003/1951), interactive (Oldfield 2006a, 2006b) and developmental approaches (Schumacher and Calvet 2007; Stern 2010).

The chapter will use case studies to illustrate music therapy with children on the autistic spectrum and collaboration with other professionals across health and education. It will consider how music therapists share aims, progress and outcomes with their teams, other staff and parents/carers, with a specific focus on multi-disciplinary and transdisciplinary approaches. It will also discuss the unique approaches of music therapy, how these can become integrated within the wider team and how opportunities for targeted or indirect work can be created in collaborations.

Music therapy and autistic spectrum conditions

Music therapists usually receive referrals to work in schools when a child has difficulty communicating, interacting or expressing him or herself. Music therapy has been shown to help children with autistic spectrum conditions to improve social interaction, verbal communication, initiating behaviour and social-emotional reciprocity (Geretsegger et al. 2014; Gold, Wigram and Elefant 2006). Music is often described as a powerful tool which, when used therapeutically, can connect with a person's inner world and draw him or her into a shared musical relationship. The right amount of spontaneity and flexibility within structured musical improvisation can be seen to enable children to respond and engage in new and different ways when they realise that the therapist's music is reflecting something to do with them (Gold et al. 2006). Tustin (1990, p.32) writes that 'effective work with these children depends on their being "held" (psychologically) by a therapist who has some inkling of the peculiar world in which they "live and move" and their precarious sense of being'. Schumacher and Calvet (2007) look towards the developmental theories of Daniel Stern (2001) to capture ways in which inter-subjectivity can develop in a musical relationship. Stern (2010) outlines the central role of vitality forms in establishing meaningful connections and building dynamic flow in relationships. This role of musical and emotional attunement is recognised as a common characteristic of improvisational approaches and an integral way of working with children with autistic spectrum conditions (Geretsegger et al. 2015). In everyday practice, however, how can practitioners ensure that everyone is aware of why and how music can be used in communicatively meaningful ways and when a music therapist is required? What does this look like within the bigger picture, in the classroom, school and when linking in with families and carers?

Collaborative approaches

In a busy school environment, it can often be a challenge to plan and deliver collaborative approaches, to tailor support to each individual and to ensure that bringing unique approaches together creates collaborative advantage.

Whilst Claire is able to meet with the multi-disciplinary team on a weekly basis, it is often more difficult for teams to meet regularly owing to practicalities such as part-time working, timetabling or sharing facilities. Multi-disciplinary working can therefore often mean that individuals work independently with the child, meeting only to discuss progress with the team. Vaac and Ritter (1995) liken this level of collaboration to the medical model whereas Twyford and Watson (2008, p.25) describe it as 'communicative'. Communication may include face-to-face discussions in the corridor, on the telephone or in a formal meeting. It may also involve sharing of video and/or audio recordings to illustrate a particular observation or development and written documentation,[1] which can bring aims together from education, health and social care professionals alongside parent observations.

Music therapists can also advise, train others and work in partnership with families and other professionals. Working in partnership can often lead to further sharing in the design and delivery of therapeutic support in what are often described as transdisciplinary approaches (Twyford and Watson 2008, p.26). Sharing skills and bringing theories together may require the presence of all professionals involved to observe, discuss and evaluate the child simultaneously (Vaac and Ritter 1995; Wilson and Smith 2000). Twyford and Watson (2008, p.25) describe this level, according to practice in the UK, as including aspects of 'facilitative or observational' alongside 'fully integrated' work, suggesting an educational as well as a more equal partnership role.

Participation in experiential opportunities can be one of the most successful ways to educate other professionals, parents and families, or provide the opportunity to 'witness a change' (Hsu 2017).

---

1   Examples of multi-disciplinary documentation includes an EHC (Education, Health and Care) plan in England and Wales (UK Government 2014) and CSP (Coordinated Support Plan) in Scotland (Scottish Government 2010a). Both are for children and young people who require additional support form external agencies, including health and social care, to meet their additional needs.

Watson (2017, p.182) suggests that 'staff are encouraged to adopt the attitudes and approaches they see the therapists using, to develop their own relationships with group members'. Munro (2017, p.43) suggests the advantages, as well as learning about different approaches, are that staff can see 'hidden abilities' emerging in children.

Collaboration also has the potential to integrate music therapy within the wider team. As Vicky Karkou (2010, p.278) writes:

> Collaborations that 'work' have the potential to contribute to cultural shifts that question the tradition of the sole practitioner who works on his or her own in the back room, the basement or the kitchen area, forgotten and disconnected from the rest of the school.

Collaboration may bring greater benefits in the form of joint aims, shared planning and delivery with a range of different professionals and, as Sandall *et al.* (2005) suggest, with the family as well. Twyford (2008, p.86) writes that when all involved are open to sharing, being open and adapting, fully integrated approaches can give different perspectives and increase awareness of needs.

Educational staff members often take a leading role in coordinating the multi-disciplinary team in school settings. Karkou (2010, pp.13–14) writes that 'addressing emotional or social needs is seen as a way of supporting learning', suggesting that the expectations of psychological therapies in educational settings are predominantly linked to cognitive outcomes. This opinion is reflected in promotional music therapy literature: 'emotional and cognitive difficulties can affect a person's motivation to learn and may make it difficult for them to participate in class-based educational activities' (BAMT 2017). However, in collaborative work that includes families, aims may be linked to psychological or relational needs experienced in the family as much as in school. Some strategic documents outlining partnership working (Scottish Government 2010b) acknowledge that children may have individual or additional support needs beyond the curriculum and that Allied Health Professionals work in collaboration with education, families and social care to meet these. Nevertheless, with educational colleagues in the driving seat, aims may often need to be described in a common language.

Multi-disciplinary working: who is in the team, what do we communicate and how?

The team working with or around the child with an autistic spectrum condition will often include professionals from health, education and social care alongside families and/or carers. Good communication between all members of the team, including the child when appropriate, is essential to facilitate the best outcomes for each child. The following case study describes how Claire works in the team within the school.

CASE STUDY: THE 'THERAPY THINK TANK'

Claire is working with an in-house therapy team, sharing an office with other health professionals involved in supporting the additional needs of children with autistic spectrum conditions in the school. Weekly, the team meets to discuss issues around therapy services such as referrals, reports and annual reviews. The 'Therapy Think Tank' also involves the class teacher and invited parent/carers to discuss specific children. At these meetings it might be decided when individual music therapy would be appropriate or if joint therapy sessions with another professional, such as the clinical psychologist, would be more beneficial. Potentially, the team has the whole school on its caseload, so meetings are essential for prioritising who needs which mode of therapy and when.

The advantage of regular team meetings is that a range of professionals working with the same children are given the opportunity to share thinking and discuss expectations for therapeutic support. Using video and audio in multi-disciplinary meetings can be particularly useful in illustrating responses to music therapy. Focusing on key moments in a session may also facilitate a different type of discussion between professionals. These discussions and sharing can be essential in generating appropriate referrals and managing a caseload. In the example below, discussions with the team were pivotal in realigning the therapeutic journey for David.

CASE STUDY: DAVID

David was initially referred for music therapy by his mother and subsequently had both group music therapy and individual music therapy with Claire. During an initial term of group music therapy, David was very controlling. The sessions tended to centre around David as he would verbally demand attention and show almost no awareness of others in the group. It was decided between Claire, the class teacher and David's mother that he would gain more from individual music therapy sessions.

It had often been difficult to engage David in making music in the group. He presented as fragmented and would often flit from one instrument to another or from one tempo, or key, to another. It felt to Claire as if he did not want to form a musical relationship and was almost scared of doing so. During musical improvisations, if Claire found that she was matching David in tempo, dynamics or pitch, he would immediately move away. Ongoing communication with the class teacher confirmed that this also happened in the classroom.

Claire felt that if she could offer David a more focused experience of relating musically in the therapy sessions, then this experience could be transferred over to other aspects of his life. She communicated with the team her hopes that through musical improvisation in individual work she might be able to attune his fragmented presentation and find a different way of building a relationship. This would be with the hope that individual music therapy could support David in developing more reciprocal relationships.

Communication within the multi-disciplinary team can play an important part in ensuring that the roles of each person in the team are understood by others. In turn, this can provide opportunities for skill sharing in relation to specific children. In the next case study, Claire demonstrates the importance of understanding and sharing all of the therapeutic approaches contributing to educational aims.

CASE STUDY: BRIAN

Brian is responding very well to improvisational music therapy with Claire, particularly in the moments of attunement and mis-attunement, developing and building on reciprocal exchanges. Speech and Language Therapy, at the same time, are supporting the use of Intensive Interaction (Nind and Hewett 2001) approaches in the classroom, working towards similar aims of improving communication and reducing anxiety and self-harming behaviours. A meeting is arranged to share video from both therapies with staff in the school classroom and communicate the aims beyond the written reports. It is hoped that school staff will also learn from observing the videos more about the child's profile and contribute towards the multi-disciplinary aims.

Generating music therapy aims

Communication with the team can provide a more holistic picture of a child who is waiting for or continuing to receive music therapy input. Reports from Occupational Therapy may shed light on a child's sensory profile. The classroom teacher's reports may indicate areas of strength alongside unmet needs. Parents/carers may also contribute a lot of information about patterns of relating and communicating in the home setting, as well as significant changes or events which may have occurred in that child's life. An important part of describing music therapy aims to the multi-disciplinary team is therefore ensuring that it is clear how information has been collated alongside the music therapist's own observations during the assessment period.

The next case study introduces Bryony. Bryony was selected to participate in a short project investigating outcome measures for children with severe and complex needs. This case study shows how information about Bryony was collated for the project, from family and other professionals, as well as in the first music therapy sessions with Emma, to establish the aims for her music therapy.

CASE STUDY: BRYONY

At the time of the project Bryony was a ten-year-old girl with an autistic spectrum condition and global developmental delay as well as complex partial seizures, which were difficult to control with medication. According to Mum, Bryony always[2] *avoided contact with others at home, showing preoccupation with body parts/objects and*

---

2   The categories in italics were generated from a behaviour checklist sent to the family before the block of music therapy began.

using repeated sounds or movements. She would only occasionally *initiate play or extend play with others.* She often *cried, screamed, wailed, rocked, swayed or twirled, showing little awareness of others* and sometimes *made fleeting responses to others when stimulated.* In school Bryony was responding well in one-to-one intensive interaction situations.

In the music therapy room Bryony's chair, which had a strap as advised by Occupational Therapy, was positioned beside the piano on the right-hand side of the therapist. A drum and cymbal were positioned on the right-hand side of the chair. In the first week Bryony tolerated Emma's presence. She occasionally moved Emma's hand although often she made no response, which could have been seen as resistive. Bryony often used repetitive vocalisations and sought out sensory contact, such as putting out her hands or feet to be stroked or exploring tactile properties of instruments in her mouth. She engaged briefly with some instruments presented to her and clearly rejected those that she did not want to play. She could express a number of different mood states, which appeared to be dependent on seizure activity. She often chose to engage in child-led vocal dialogues when her short non-verbal vocalisations were mirrored, imitated or copied or when gaps were left in play songs.

Aims for Bryony in music therapy were described as supporting her to:

- continue to develop her interactions with an adult

- maintain shared attention for longer periods

- begin to copy an adult's actions or vocalisations

- develop turn-taking skills within structured interactions.

Emma was also expected to contribute, as part of the multi-disciplinary team, to other educational objectives, which included developing Bryony's emotional regulation and ability to manage her behaviour towards others.

Teachers, who often have to compile Individualised Educational Plans and other such documents, may ask music therapists for more measurable aims (Pethybridge 2013) or for more data which will demonstrate clearly measurable progress (Lawes 2012). Other professionals in the multi-disciplinary team will often incorporate measurement tools or assessment models that look at behaviours that are easy to observe and count, such as 'can you hold a pencil?' Whilst there may be elements of these multi-disciplinary tools, which can be assessed by music therapy, they do not always capture the unique information from music therapy relationships.

Making aims more measurable: rating scales

The collection of quantitative data in everyday practice can be time-consuming and often not cost-effective. However, there is great value in exploring how different rating scales categorise descriptive data into more numerical formats. Continued curiosity into what others are measuring, why and how, may further ground clinicians in generating aims that provide the clarity that other educational or health professionals are seeking. It may also ensure that practitioners continue to be informed by research. Whilst the rigour of some scales may appear beyond the everyday clinician, an understanding of the descriptions in each scale may support thinking and frame narratives of therapeutic progress. The next section looks at some rating scales and other measurements and considers how they can help to make aims more measurable.

Nordoff Robbins rating scales I and II (Nordoff and Robbins 2007)

First published in 1977 and later revised, these scales are based on humanistic values. Developed through observations in practice with reference to a behavioural checklist for children with autism, they are completed by the therapist. They provide two frameworks for representing both the child's engagement in the musical relationship and his or her communication with the therapist.

Scale I considers the musical relationship. It is interesting to note that the level of 'not relating' or *resistiveness* is rated concurrently with *participation*, recognising that there is a wide difference between a lack of awareness of others (level one) and a defensive avoidance (level three). This is particularly interesting when considering how music therapists describe aims and the relationship to contemporary psychodynamic thinking regarding the reduction in defences to 'resist regressive tendencies' on reaching level seven (Nordoff and Robbins 2007, pp.375–381).

Scale II measures the outcomes of communication through three different activities: instrumental improvisation, vocal responses and body movements. It rates seven levels from 'no musical communicative responsiveness' (level one) through 'sustaining of directed responses', where some give and take, musical organisation and phrases of songs may start to appear (level five) to 'enthusiastic and creative musical competence,' (level seven). Nordoff and Robbins (2007 pp.401–407) explain that the responses can been noticeable in all three activities, or in any one or two, acknowledging that communication develops across modalities.

Results for Bryony's engagement in a musical relationship (Scale I) recorded in detail over five weeks as part of a short study (Pethybridge 2010) can be seen in Table 8.1. In Bryony's first session, Emma's marking at level two shows wary ambivalence or tentative acceptance, which is exemplified in musical activities by the sense of being 'evoked', 'intermittent' and participating in something that 'cannot be sustained' whilst it also captures her tendency to resist with perseverative use of instruments voice or body.

Table 8.1: Nordoff Robbins Scale I: ratings over five weeks for Bryony

Week (Wk)		Wk 1	Wk 2	Wk 3	Wk 4	Wk 5
Scale I: Child–Therapist Relationship in Coactive Musical Experience	(4) Activity relationship developing					4
	(3) Limited responsive activity		2	2	2/2	4/2
	(2) Wary ambivalence/ Tentative acceptance	4/6	/4	2/4	2/4	
	(1) Unresponsive non-acceptance		/4	/2		
	Mean average:	**2.0**	**1.8**	**2.0**	**2.4**	**3.4**

Scale II: Musical Communicativeness	(4) Musical awareness awakening. Intermittent musical perception and intentionality manifesting					2
	(3) Evoked responses (ii): more sustained and musically related	1	2		1	1
	(2) Evoked responses (i): fragmentary, fleeting	7	5	8	6	7
	(1) No musically communicative responses	2	3	2	3	
	Mean average:	**1.7**	**1.9**	**1.8**	**1.8**	**2.5**

CASE STUDY: BRYONY CONTINUED

As the weeks progressed, eye contact increased in response to musical matching and attunement to Bryony's movements and sounds. She also began to smell Emma's hair. In week five she engaged in a two-chord song structure, making more eye contact, touching Emma, waving in the 'Goodbye' song and inserting an approximation of 'bye'.

Reaching level four of the scale felt like a great achievement for Bryony, who was often difficult to engage in reciprocal relationships. In relation to the progress she made towards level four, developing a 'musical *activity relationship* to the therapist', is described as a 'recurring positive response to the therapy situation; at times there is communicative and sustained eye contact' (Nordoff and Robbins 2007, p.378). Some of the other descriptors in this level also corresponded to the music therapy aims and could be used to describe the extent of Bryony's progress. 'Shows pleasure in being active with the therapist' responded to the aim of developing interactions with an adult. 'Begins to sustain' responded to the aim of 'maintaining shared attention'. However, turn-taking, or 'give-and-take' (p.379) is a feature of the next level and could be considered, within this framework, as an ongoing aim of the work with Bryony. Here the rating scales provide a clear numerical indicator and, where descriptors match the narrative of the clinical journey, may respond to a basic level of measurement required by other agencies.

The next case study shows a contrasting example of using the Nordoff Robbins Scales. When Claire worked with David, she felt that he began in the musical relationship (Scale I) at level four, as, whilst David was difficult to connect with in the early sessions, he appeared to be communicating with intent. The aims she communicated with the team reflect her hopes to build on David's the fleeting connections with David and develop the relationship further.

CASE STUDY: DAVID

Claire's clinical aims for David were:

- to increase his levels of engagement

- to make him less fragmented both verbally and musically

- to develop a more equal musical relationship where David tolerates others and is less controlling.

David's verbal fragmentation usually began when Claire collected him from the classroom. As they walked to the music therapy room he repeated words that appeared unconnected, such as 'beach', 'Robin Hood' and 'Bob the Builder'. Claire would sometimes match music to these words in an attempt to make more connection. In session nine after the familiar 'Hello' song, David said 'chase' twice. Claire responded by playing a tense, rapid melody in a minor key in the right hand with punctuated staccato chords in the left, which echoed a musical-style cartoon chase scene. She gradually eased the paced by playing quavers in a descending pattern and ended with a perfect cadence in C major providing a sense of change in musical direction.

Claire then offered David the xylophone and handed him a beater. David asked what it was and Claire answered 'a beater'.

He replied very defiantly that it was a 'stick'. However, he accepted the offer and began to play in a similar style to the chase, using a quick succession of ascending and descending glissandi on the white notes of the xylophone. Claire matched and mirrored this on the white notes of the piano to provide a sense of grounding in this style for David. As the connection grew, this developed further, turning into a turn-taking and anticipation activity where David would take control in the music, saying, 'Ready, Steady, … Go', for each continued play of glissandi, indicating whose turn it was to go.

David started to vocalise and sing in the key of C major within which the playing had settled. As Claire was providing vamping chords, David spoke and said, 'a 1, a 2, a 1,2,3,4', leading her, which she answered with an improvisation based around a blues idiom. David picked up with a scat-like vocalisation and started initiating triplets into the improvisation. A real sense of joint enthusiasm and increased creativity had developed.

For Scale I, Claire's observations indicate progress in the relationship in this piece of work to level seven, with David demonstrating 'stability and confidence in the musical relationship', as per the aims. At this level, the scale describes, 'through identification with the therapists' expectations, [David] resists own regressive tendencies' (Nordoff and Robbins 2007, pp.375–381), which was particularly noticeable during his improvisation on the xylophone. Here David's ability to sustain a steady pulse and then initiate a *ritardando* leading to a *glissandi* anacrusis and then back into tempo was felt to demonstrate his confidence in their musical play.

Claire's rating for Scale II shows that David achieved high levels of communication through both instrumental and vocal improvisation. He was thought to demonstrate both 'enthusiastic musical competence and creative vocal initiative' (level seven). He was able to show that he was capable of participation, self-expression and musical competence. When reflecting on this, it was clear that David had progressed from the early sessions of evoked responses (level three) to engaging and communicating.

Reflecting the music-centred and humanistic approach, these details can provide the multi-disciplinary team with an outline of clear progression in both numerical and descriptive formats as required. There are helpful and detailed descriptions regarding changes in interpersonal relationships and communication. However, for the emotional regulation or self-management of behaviours, it appears more appropriate to look towards a developmental scale, such as the Assessment of the Quality of Relationship Scale (Schumacher and Calvet 2007).

Assessment of the Quality of Relationship (AQR) (Schumacher and Calvet 2007)

The AQR scales were designed by a music therapist and a developmental psychologist underpinned by the concept of self (Stern 2001) and theories of emotional regulation (Sroufe 1996). They enable the practitioner to review relationship to self, other and instruments through four scales looking at areas of physical/emotional, vocal pre-speech, instrumental qualities and the therapeutic relationship. The following case study shows a developing relationship in music therapy with a five-year-old boy with an autistic spectrum condition, which is then considered within the framework of the AQR scales.

CASE STUDY: FREDDIE

Freddie appeared to be making some contact with Emma, but this was often fleeting and difficult to interpret. For example, he would often raise his head upwards, which appeared to be a communicative gesture but one for which there was not yet a shared understanding. He moved quickly around the music therapy room. Whilst Emma was able to attune to his gestures and vocalisations and make his movements audible through music, he did not yet seem to be aware that he was the focus of this. In contrast he appeared to have a great interest in the guitar. He would choose this repeatedly and, when played, would show recognition of familiar songs and respond to changes in speed and volume. This relationship appeared to be with the instrument rather than the person playing it as he would pass it between Emma and the classroom assistant in the room.

Looking at the fourth scale, therapeutic quality of relationship, it is clear that Freddie is at level one, which is about perception. Schumacher and Calvet (2007, p.87) write: 'the child moves (mostly stereotyped) around the room and notices the therapist's intervention for a short time. His movements become audible by an appropriate musical improvisation. The therapist feels mobilised by the short positive reaction of the child.'

The language reflects current thinking about repetitive behaviours in children with autistic spectrum conditions. As the description continues, the references to Stern's (2010, 2001) concept of affect attunement are recognisable. Freddie's aims were set, following a short assessment, as 'extending focus and attention' and 'increasing awareness of others in musical play, including joint attention, starting and stopping and turn-taking'. The language of the AQR in level one, 'noticing' the therapist, who responds to his movements, gestures and use of instruments into musical play, and the impact of the 'positive reaction', can demonstrate what the therapist feels they have to do to achieve these aims.

CASE STUDY: FREDDIE CONTINUED

As the sessions progressed, I slowly introduced more structure, which appeared to provide the right level of containment for Freddie. Picture symbols were used, in line with Speech and Language Therapy goals, as something to exchange for his favourite songs. Whilst these were sometimes used in a sensory manner, he would often move quickly between songs in a similar way to which he had previously moved around the room. Freddie began to show increased awareness of me in the music, making eye contact more frequently, remaining focused for longer periods, although he maintained a controlling aspect. He began to initiate more intentional communicative gestures including moving his head upwards in gaps provided in the 'Goodbye' song with much more purpose to indicate 'continue' or to request a familiar nursery rhyme again.

As the work with Freddie continued, the relationship appeared to progress to level two, which showed the continuing role of affect attunement in establishing a relationship. Schumacher and Calvet (2007, p.87) describe this level as: 'the therapist attempts to find attunement with the child and to form him by physical, musical, or verbal means. The therapist puts himself thereby totally at the service of this problem and therefore feels functionalised in this respect.'

Considering the level at which the therapist was working in the relationship with Freddie enabled Emma to also suggest other musical activities that could be used in the classroom to work towards the same interpersonal aims. Here using the framework of the AQR can provide assurance for other agencies.

The AQR and the Nordoff Robbins rating scales both outline frameworks with ordinal measurements, which reflect values, which, whilst not constant, are in a logical order. They are based on a clear theoretical underpinning and relate to a specific music therapy approach. In these examples, they provided some guidance in measuring outcomes, describing progress and sharing aims. Nordoff and Robbins write of their scales: 'to the beginning therapist, moving into the unknown of therapy practice, they can provide a source of clinical security' (p.370). In clinical practice however, music therapists, as described in our introduction, are often informed by more than one approach. Keeping this in mind, what other methods are available for describing aims in relation to more measurable outcomes?

Increasing objectivity: counting occurrences through video analysis

Video analysis can provide a more objective perspective by counting things that happen. Scales using this type of method provide clarity on what to measure. In the work described earlier with Bryony, Emma also used the Microanalysis of Interaction in Music Therapy (MIMT) scale (Scholtz, Voigt and Wosch 2007), which counts musical and non-musical interactive behaviours. Emma selected two five-minute sections, from week one and week five of the music therapy, where she felt there was a lot happening in the relationship. She then counted Bryony's gaze towards an object, the therapist or miscellaneous, and her use of instruments in five-second segments of each clip. The findings for each of these can be seen in the two tables below.

Table 8.2: Results for Bryony's gaze from video analysis

Gaze	Bryony	
	Week 1	Week 5
Toward object	Predominant (90%) Predominant (92%)	Predominant (83%) Average (40%)
Toward therapist	Seldom (5%) Seldom (2%)	Seldom (17%) Average (42%)
Toward miscellaneous	Seldom (2%) Seldom (7%)	Seldom (5%)

Table 8.3: Microanalysis of Interaction in Music
Therapy (MIMT) scale (Scholtz, Voigt and Wosch 2007):
Results from weeks one and five for Bryony

Use of Instruments	Bryony		Therapist	
	Week 1	Week 5	Week 1	Week 5
Use of instruments within a musical context	Predominant (78%) Average (62%)	Average (40%) Average (37%)	Predominant (92%) Predominant (87%)	Predominant (100%) Predominant (100%)
Use of instruments without musical context	Seldom (12%) Seldom (17%)	Average (37%)	Seldom (1%)	

Methods such as MIMT, whilst resource heavy, create objective measurements that may be more suited to Individualised Educational Plans, which often require measurable targets, such as 'Susie will look at the therapist three times'. It becomes clear in discussion of findings that both qualitative data and a therapist's awareness of the current evidence base have a role to support these numbers. For example, looking at results for Bryony, the predominant gaze toward an object at the beginning of therapy clearly linked with the information that Bryony's mother provided in the checklist when she said that Bryony *always* avoided contact with others, showing preoccupation with body parts/objects. This finding can also be linked to music therapy research, which suggests that for a child with an autistic spectrum condition an obsessive focus on objects could be expected and could decrease as a child becomes more engaged in a therapeutic relationship based in music (Oldfield 2006a). The results from the MIMT scale showed that Bryony's use of instruments decreased over time, whilst her gaze towards the therapist increased, clearly indicating measured progress towards the first aim: to continue to develop her interactions with an adult. However, the behaviours that are counted in this scale are limited and may not support more individualised aims. Pethybridge (2010, p.63) suggests that 'if video analysis was to be used more frequently ...categories of observation should have clear, measurable definitions relevant to the child's needs that reflect up-to-date clinical practice'.

Keeping in mind Karkou's (2010) comments that psychological therapies in educational settings are predominantly linked to cognitive outcomes, what happens if we look towards the psychology of music, music education and musical development for guidelines?

Making aims more measurable: models developed in collaboration with music education

The Sounds of Intent Framework (Ockelford 2000, 2008, 2013) is a curriculum framework for making music with children and young people, including those with learning difficulties or autism. The framework examines three areas of ability: reactive – listening and responding; proactive – causing, creating and controlling; and interactive – music making with others. Ockelford's team was interested in finding out if 'there were certain things that children had to learn before they could move on to achieve others' (2013, p.114). Developed from reviewing practice in music education and music therapy, the framework supposes that musical structure is learnt through imitation. It scores musical development from encountering sound, through imitation, reaching at its peak communicating through expressive music making, or what they label 'mature musicianship' (p.130). It is suggested that a music therapy or a music education approach might be used to reach the targets in the scale. Wetherick (2009) notes in his review of this framework that 'music education appears to be least effective in achieving progress in the interactive domain – the domain where music therapists would usually focus their attention' (p.46).

Tillotson (2015) demonstrated parity between the Nordoff and Robbins scales and the Sounds of Intent Framework. She identified that both measure the levels of participation and communication and how music can help to develop self-confidence, engagement and musical creativity. Using the Sounds of Intent framework to review David's work, she was able to describe him as 'responding to groups of musical sounds and the relationships between them' (reactive four), 'creating short and simple pieces of music, potentially of growing length and complexity: increasingly "in time" and where relevant, "in tune" and interactive' (proactive five) and 'producing musical motifs in the expectation that they will stimulate a coherent response' (interactive four A) (Ockelford 2013, pp.167–168).

There has been ongoing debate about the relationship between music therapy and music education (Ockelford 2000; Robertson 2000; Warwick 1995). In our experience, teachers and other educational professionals are open to the fact that music therapy does not usually fulfil educational aims but rather supports, them. This is demonstrated in the following case study in which Claire responds to a school inspection about the alignment of music therapy with educational aims.

CASE STUDY: SUPPORTING EDUCATIONAL AIMS IN MUSIC THERAPY

In Claire's early years as a practising music therapist, during an OFSTED Inspection an inspector asked her what her educational aims were. She answered, 'I don't have any. However, I am fully aware of the educational aims of these children and my role is to support them in music therapy by working on engagement, communication and social interaction.'

Using a framework such as Sounds of Intent across a school for music teaching and music therapy may support more integrated ways of working where the difference in approaches are clearly understood.

In this chapter so far, we have tried to identify how making aims and objectives in individually tailored music therapy approaches more measurable may provide increased accountability for music therapy within the multi-disciplinary team. Alison Barrington

(2008), exploring integrated team-working, wrote that the unique service of music therapy should be promoted within collaborative situations. She cites Connie Isenberg-Grezda (1988) in suggesting that 'the creation of assessment procedures specific to music therapy practice is vital in providing opportunities for effective collaborative partnerships' (p.212). Communicating aims and outcomes clearly in written and oral feedback should be central to multi-disciplinary working, but might measurable targets also reduce spontaneity where improvisation is often central to the approach? Can understanding be developed much further in the 'doing' of transdisciplinary approaches? Beyond communicating measurable aims, is the role of the music therapist also to demystify an approach? How do music therapists respond to each child's movements, vocalisations and use of instruments through music? How do music therapists build shared musical moments with children on the autistic spectrum and contribute to developing increased reciprocity? This kind of communication through experiential opportunities and fully integrated collaborations (Twyford and Watson 2008, p.25) will be the focus of the second half of our chapter.

Transdisciplinary working: communicating and developing collaborative aims in more integrated approaches

Experiential sessions

Experiential sessions are often more accessible when a team is in the earlier stages of establishing itself. These may involve staff taking part in group or individual sessions over a period of weeks as an active participant or observer. The following case study is taken from a DVD which included interviews with teaching staff who had participated in music therapy group work.

CASE STUDY: PARTNERSHIPS WITH TEACHING STAFF

Emma, right from the start, made it very clear that I was part of the group as well and that I was to take a turn, and then just gradually the children just realised that I would be there and I've been able to adapt some of the strategies that I've seen Emma use with the children as well… I think the children have been very participative in the whole situation. I do see that's had the same effect within the classroom as well, that they're much more aware of taking turns, much more aware of wait time, much more aware of actually somebody interacting with them and I think they've had great fun with music therapy. (East Lothian Council et al. 2007)

Experiential groups facilitated or led by a music therapist provide an opportunity to guide another person involved in working with the child through the process of music therapy. This may offer another perspective and provide opportunities for the development of more indirect work: interactive music making without the music therapist. As time elapses and services become more integrated within settings, staff naturally begin to follow up ideas that they see the music therapist modelling, supporting both within and outside each session. For example, a Support for Learning staff member comments, 'I have been coming in here and letting him explore the piano. Just like you do in therapy I sit at the other piano, copy what he is doing and wait.'

It can be seen, therefore, that this kind of collaborative experience may help teaching staff to think across modalities and about a 'move from sessions based only on familiar songs to something more enjoyable and meaningful based on communication through music' (Pethybridge 2013, p.31). This may be completely new and a challenging concept, or something that staff naturally engage with quickly. This kind of sharing can increase an understanding of music therapy for others working with the child. However, more integrated collaborations may increase understanding across the different professionals in the team.

More integrated work with educational staff

Beyond groups which are led by the music therapist and provide an opportunity for others to learn through active participation, integrating ideas and approaches further with teachers and learning assistants can bring other benefits. Planning the aims and methods of delivery together can allow for particular difficulties from an Individualised Educational Plan (IEP) to be addressed through the music. For example, alongside other, more traditional music therapy aims, anxiety that one child showed towards a CD player in the classroom was addressed by recording a song that had become familiar through the live interaction in a music therapy group and slowly introducing the CD player and then other recorded songs as part of the session (Pethybridge 2013). In collaborative work, playful improvisation can create new songs, which can be developed and grow into another format with another role in the classroom once the music therapist is no longer there. Appendix 1 includes advice given to a teacher following observation of a group music making session in the classroom with aims clearly outlined for current and suggested activities. It is through this sharing of aims, processes and learning about each other's expectations where the shifts in practice that collaborative work brings can be seen.

More integrated work with Speech and Language Therapists

It becomes clear when trying to unpick what is unique about individual therapies in educational settings with children with an autistic spectrum condition that the professions have as many commonalities as differences. For individuals with severe and complex needs including children with autistic spectrum conditions, who are at an early stage of communication development (pre-verbal fundamentals of communication), music therapy and Speech and Language Therapy share many common goals and approaches. Ockelford (2013, p.186) writes that 'music and speech are closely linked products of the human psyche, which share the same early development journey, and continue to enjoy a special relationship throughout life in songs and chants'.

Peggie and Pethybridge (2009) explored transdisciplinary working between music therapy and Speech and Language Therapy with children with severe communication difficulties, which included Peter.

CASE STUDY: PETER

Peter is 14 years old and is on the autistic spectrum. He is a non-verbal communicator, using mainly gestures, body movement and facial expression to communicate. He can be difficult to engage in a group, often showing limited awareness of his peers. However, he is very motivated by music. He becomes part of a group which is led by Speech and Language Therapist, Laura, and music therapist, Emma. A member of Support for Learning is also present. She is learning transferable skills from both approaches, but also providing invaluable feedback on interactions during the rest of the week with the children in the group.

When the group begins, Laura signs 'hello' to everyone. Peter is not always aware of this to begin with and shows little awareness of his peers. He is given a cymbal and a beater to explore with a 'Hello' song used flexibly to match each beat that he makes. As the song continues, the connections in the music grow and he glances towards the piano. 'Hello' is signed again as he finishes, and he is given a choice between two picture symbols from which to choose his next instrument. At other times Peter uses a repetitive phrase, 'Anusa', and stamps his feet rhythmically. These communications are mirrored by Laura or the Support for Learning Assistant whilst Emma improvises a musical accompaniment to match and encourage further development to this communication.

Differentiating between structured and non-structured approaches has been discussed by others working in partnership with Speech and Language Therapists (Twyford and Parkhouse 2008). Similar to their work, this collaboration explored using spontaneous musical improvisation to respond to vocalisations, movements and use of musical instruments. Laura (Speech and Language Therapist) commented on how this experience increased her awareness of the impact of emotional wellbeing on other communicative behaviours. The participation of a member of support staff in this group created opportunities for transferable skills including increased understanding and use of intensive interaction principles including using eye contact, facial expressions, gestures, vocalisations and body movements in communicative exchanges.

The use of more structured approaches, including visual supports and other augmented communication strategies, can increase an understanding of the structure of therapy sessions for the child with an autistic spectrum condition. A visual timetable might be used to outline the structure of the session and PECS (Picture Exchange Communication System) used in choice activities. Pre-composed play songs may also provide structure and predictability allowing for directed turn-taking and creating anticipation.

Claire's work with Billy demonstrates how similar structures from Speech and Language Therapy, which can provide safe boundaries, predictability and referential communication at a more accessible level, were integrated into her approach.

CASE STUDY: BILLY

Billy was having difficulties with communication sessions with three other children from his class. He presented as a confident child who found turn-taking a challenge and was not keen to pass on or share instruments with the others in the group. He had been attending music therapy with Claire for a term. Everything had to be on Billy's terms. He always wanted to go first, didn't want me to play the piano with him during piano improvisations and found it a challenge listening to the others when it wasn't his turn.

During a Therapy Think Tank it transpired that Billy also had difficulty sharing toys and equipment in class and at home with his younger brother. It was decided that as a team everyone would try to put some communication aids in place to prepare Billy for what was going to happen. The Speech and Language Therapist suggested a 'now and then' board to help Billy with transition from the classroom to the music therapy room and, once in the therapy room, a list of the activities we were going to do as a group. Each activity would be crossed off as they were completed:

- the 'Hello' song

- pass the shaker round

- playing the piano

- choosing an instrument (using PECS)

- the 'Goodbye' song.

This collaborative approach was expanded further to include Billy's mother who was keen to implement strategies from both therapies at home. She was invited to a 'Stay and Play' session a few weeks later with the music therapist and the Speech and Language Therapist.

Working with parents/carers

'Music can help to create a secure environment between the child and the parent and playing simple instruments can remind parents of their own childhood which can bring parents and child closer together' (Oldfield 1993, p.54). The 'Stay and Play' session involves an informal chat over coffee with the parents and carers, outlining the role of therapies within the school, including an overview of music therapy. Parents are encouraged to ask questions and discuss thoughts and queries, often providing support for each other. Claire explains how a group music therapy session is structured and then invites the parents to join in with their children for a one-off experience.

CASE STUDY: BILLY CONTINUED

Billy thought that this was really exciting, seeing his mother in the session, and initially wanted to 'show Mum what he could do'. The Speech and Language Therapist showed Billy the board timetable and he sat down next to his mother. When it came to Billy's turn to choose an instrument, another child had already chosen the guitar, which was Billy's favourite. This led to Billy crying and a small tantrum emerging, but with gentle encouragement he chose the wind chimes. Once everyone had chosen, a symbol card which read 'good waiting' encouraged him to listen to the others. When it was his turn to play, he shared the wind chimes with Mum and a shared sense of space was established. A lovely interaction developed between them as he smiled and 'allowed' Mum to play with him. Claire supported this with improvisation on the piano, mirroring Billy's playing but also trying to support what Mum was doing. A turn-taking game was slowly established between them, with Billy playing and leaving space for Mum to answer. The integration of structured and non-structured therapeutic approaches was seen to have contributed to Billy tolerating increased turn-taking. By illustrating this to his mother, it became something she wanted to continue at home.

At the end of the session, the children were taken back to their classroom and the therapists facilitated discussion with the parents. In the weeks that followed, building on these techniques in school and at home, Billy started to tolerate turn-taking and was less anxious if he didn't get to go first. There was positive feedback from the class teacher regarding his behaviour and his relationships with peers, staff and at home.

Working with parents can offer opportunities to observe relationship patterns between child and parent, looking at how the parent tunes in and responds to the infant (Davies and Richards 2002; Stern 2001, 2010). They can also provide a place to model therapeutic approaches. Music therapy can be seen to provide a 'facilitating environment' (Winnicott 1965). With gentle support and scaffolding from therapists, parents may then experience how musical activities might be adapted in response to their child. Parent feedback suggests that skills learnt in a one-off session can include:

- trying to use music to respond to a child's behaviour

- listening to the children's sounds, responding to actions and letting them lead

- using other songs/tunes to sing what a child is doing

- changing songs to interact

- discovering that you can sing anything to music

- incorporating noises/cries.

Inviting parents to discuss what happened is an important part of the process which encourages more thinking about evaluating progress and looking forwards.

Conclusion

Time is often an issue when demand exceeds resources, yet closer collaborations of a transdisciplinary nature can be essential in communicating aims and approaches and adapting practice in accordance with the team. Experiences which place the child at the centre and build up an understanding of the unique skillset of each profession can build on individual knowledge and begin to generate more integrated approaches. A multi-disciplinary team that communicates well will recognise the unique contribution that each professional has to offer to children with an autistic spectrum condition. This will have many benefits, not least ensuring that referrals and expectations are appropriate so that time is used effectively. Being able to describe aims clearly and accurately in collaborative approaches often relies on practical issues, such as regularity of meetings, time for discussion and clear reporting systems, as well as an understanding of each other's disciplines. Illustrating key moments in therapy and generating clear aims can help to build this understanding in teams. Using measurement tools that accurately account for changes in the process of therapy may increase trust and understanding and have a role to play in detailing the approaches that are being used. Some tools may also enable different professionals to work towards shared aims as well as reflect on when unique skill sets bring a different perspective.

Collaborative working can be considered through the notion of universal, targeted and specialist roles (Scottish Government 2010b). In sharing what is unique about music therapy, specialist roles may be nurtured, understood and given time and space in teams. It may be recognised how music therapy is essential in supporting children with an autistic spectrum condition with social interaction, communication and reciprocal relationships, and this may be recorded in educational documents. By using more targeted approaches, music therapists may be able to advise, train and resource others to carry out indirect approaches informed by music therapy following a period of direct work. Finally considering health promotion and prevention, as part of a universal approach – that is, accessible for everyone – it would appear that the more that people understand and experience the unique properties of music therapy, the more integrated services will become, with different levels of engagement requested at the right time and for the right reasons.

References

BAMT (2017) *Music Therapy in Education*. London: BAMT. Accessed on 27 July 2017 at https://www.bamt.org/british-association-for-music-therapy-resources/bamt-information-leaflets.html.

Barrington, A. (2008) 'Collaboration: The Bigger Picture.' In K. Twyford and T. Watson (eds) *Integrated Team Working: Music Therapy as part of Transdisciplinary and Collaborative Approaches*. London: Jessica Kingsley Publishers.

Davies, A. and Richards, E. (eds) (2002) *Music Therapy and Group Work: Sound Company*. London: Jessica Kingsley Publishers.

East Lothian Council, NHS Lothian and Scottish Arts Council Youth Music Initiative (eds) (2007) *Music Therapy: Working with Groups*. East Lothian: Cormorant Films [DVD].

Geretsegger, M., Elefant, C., Mossler, K.A. and Gold, C. (2014) 'Music therapy for people with autism spectrum disorder.' *Cochrane Database of Systematic Reviews* 6, CD004381. DOI: 10.1002/14651858.CD004381.pub3.

Geretsegger, M., Holck, U., Carpente, J.,A., Elefant, C., Kim, J. and Gold, C. (2015) 'Common characteristics of improvisational approaches in music therapy for children with autism spectrum disorder: Developing treatment guidelines.' *Journal of Music Therapy, 50*, 2, 258–281.

Gold, C., Wigram, T. and Elefant, C. (2006) 'Music therapy for autistic spectrum disorder.' *Cochrane Database of Systematic Reviews 2*, CD004381. DOI: 10.1002/14651858.CD004381.pub2.

Huse, M.H. (2017) 'Caregivers' Dual Role in Music Therapy to Manage Neuropsychiatric Symptoms of Dementia.' In J. Strange, H. Odell-Miller and E. Richards (eds) *Collaboration and Assistance in Music Therapy Practice*. London: Jessica Kingsley Publishers.

Karkou, V. (ed.) (2010) *Arts Therapies in Schools: Research and Practice*. London: Jessica Kingsley Publishers.

Lawes, M. (2012) 'Reporting on outcomes: An adaptation of the 'AQR-instrument' used to evaluate music therapy in autism.' *Approaches: Music Therapy and Special Music Education 4*, 2, 110–120.

Munro, H. (2017) 'Music Therapists' Experiences of Working with Staff in Sessions.' In J. Strange, H. Odell-Miller and E. Richards (eds) *Collaboration and Assistance in Music Therapy Practice*. London: Jessica Kingsley Publishers.

Nind, M. and Hewett, D. (2001) *A Practical Guide to Intensive Interaction*. Kidderminster: British Institute of Learning Disabilities.

Nordoff, P. and Robbins, C. (2007) *Creative Music Therapy: A Guide to Fostering Clinical Musicianship* (2nd edition: Revised and expanded). Gilsum, NH: Barcelona Publishers.

Ockelford, A. (2000) 'Music in the education of children with severe or profound learning difficulties: Issues in current U.K. provision, a new conceptual framework, and proposals for research.' *Psychology of Music 28*, 197–217.

Ockelford, A. (2008) *Music for Children and Young People with Complex Needs*. Oxford and New York: Oxford University Press.

Ockelford, A. (2013) *Music, Language and Autism: Exceptional Strategies for Exceptional Minds*. London: Jessica Kingsley Publishers.

Oldfield, A., (1993) 'Music Therapy with Families.' In M. Heal and T. Wigram (eds) *Music Therapy in Health and Education*. London: Jessica Kingsley Publishers.

Oldfield, A. (2006a) *Interactive Music Therapy – A Positive Approach: Music Therapy at a Child Development Centre*. London: Jessica Kingsley Publishers.

Oldfield, A., (2006b) *Interactive Music Therapy in Child and Family Psychiatry: Clinical Practice, Research and Teaching*. London: Jessica Kingsley Publishers.

Peggie, L. and Pethybridge, E. (2009) 'Joint working: Music Therapy and Speech and Language Therapy with children with severe communication difficulties.' Unpublished presentation. Edinburgh: Scottish Music Therapy Trust

Pethybridge, E. (2010) 'Evaluating rating scales and other measurement tools used in music therapy. A detailed study of methods used to measure changes in children with severe and complex needs.' Unpublished Masters Dissertation. Cambridge: Anglia Ruskin University.

Pethybridge, E. (2013) '"That's the joy of music!" An evaluation of partnership working with a teacher in planning and delivering a music therapy group for three children with autistic spectrum conditions.' *British Journal of Music Therapy 27*, 2, 24–39.

Robertson, J. (2000) 'An educational model for music therapy: The case for a continuum.' *British Journal of Music Therapy 14*, 1, 41–46.

Rogers, C. (2003) *Client-Centred Psychotherapy: Its Current Practice, Implications and Theory*. London: Constable (Original work published 1951.)

Sandall, S., Hemmeter, M.L, Smith, B. and McLean, M.E. (2005) *DEC Recommended Practices: A Comprehensive Guide for Practical Application in Early Intervention/Early Childhood Special Education*. Longmont, CO: Sporis West.

Scholtz, J., Voigt, M. and Wosch, T. (2007) 'Microanalysis of Interaction in Music Therapy (MIMT) with Children with Developmental Disorders.' In T. Wosch and T. Wigram (eds) *Microanalysis in Music Therapy*. London: Jessica Kingsley Publishers.

Schumacher, K. and Calvet, C. (2007) 'The 'AQR-instrument' (Assessment of the Quality of a Relationship). In T. Wosch, and T. Wigram (eds) *Microanalysis in Music Therapy*. London: Jessica Kingsley Publishers.

Scottish Government (2010a) *Statutory Guidance relating to the Education (Additional Support for Learning) (Scotland) Act 2004 as amended*. Edinburgh: GOV.SCOT.

Scottish Government (2010b) *Guidance on partnership working between allied health professionals and education*. Edinburgh: GOV.SCOT.

Sroufe, L.A. (1996) *Emotional Development: The Organization of Emotional Life in the Early Years*. Cambridge: Cambridge University Press.

Stern, D. (2001) *The Interpersonal World of the Infant: A View from Psychoanalysis and Developmental Psychology*. New York, NY: Karnac Books.

Stern, D.N. (2010) *Forms of Vitality: Exploring Dynamic Experience in Psychology, the Arts, Psychotherapy, and Development*. Oxford: Oxford University Press.

Tillotson, C. (2015) 'What is the impact of transdisciplinary working in an ASD setting?' Unpublished Masters Dissertation. Bristol: University of the West.

Tustin, F. (1990). *The Protective Shell in Children and Adults*. London: Karnac Books.

Twyford, K. (2008) 'Collaborative and Transdisciplinary Approaches with Children.' In K. Twyford and T. Watson (eds) *Integrated Team Working: Music Therapy as Part of Transdisciplinary and Collaborative Approaches*. London: Jessica Kingsley Publishers.

Twyford, K. and Parkhouse, K. (2008) 'Transdisciplinary Assessments with Children with Complex Needs.' In K. Twyford and T. Watson (eds) *Integrated Team Working: Music Therapy as Part of Transdisciplinary and Collaborative Approaches*. London: Jessica Kingsley Publishers.

Twyford, K. and Watson, T. (2008) 'Introduction.' In K. Twyford and T. Watson (eds) *Integrated Team Working: Music Therapy as Part of Transdisciplinary and Collaborative Approaches.* London: Jessica Kingsley Publishers.

UK Government (2014) *Children with special educational needs and difficulties (SEND)* London: GOV.UK.

Vaac, N. and Ritter, S. (1995) *Assessment of Pre-school Children.* Greensboro NC: ERIC Clearinghouse on Counseling and Student Services. Accessed on 27 July 2017 at www.ericdigests.org/1996-3/preschool.htm.

Warwick, A. (1995) 'Music Therapy in the Education Service: Research with Autistic Children and Their Mothers. In T. Wigram, B. Saperston and R. West (eds) *The Art and Science of Music Therapy.* England: Harwood Academic Publishers.

Watson, T. (2017) 'Supporting the Unplanned Journey: Music Therapy as a Developmental Resource with People with Profound and Multiple Learning Disabilities and Their Carers and Staff. In J. Strange, H. Odell-Miller and E. Richards (eds) *Collaboration and Assistance in Music Therapy Practice.* London: Jessica Kingsley Publishers.

Wilson, B. and Smith, D. (2000) 'Music therapy assessment in school settings: A preliminary investigation.' *Journal of Music Therapy 37,* 2, 95–117.

Winnicott, D. (1965) *The Family and Individual Development.* London: Tavistock.

Wetherick, D. (2009) 'Book Review *Music for Children and Young People with Severe and Complex Needs* (Ockelford 2008)'. *British Journal of Music Therapy 23,* 1, 46–47.

CHAPTER 9

Finding a Place: Context-Based Music Therapy in a Transitional Centre for Children with Autistic Spectrum Conditions

KATE FAWCETT

Introduction

This chapter seeks to describe how my work with children with autistic spectrum conditions has developed according to the particular conditions of the setting in which our encounters occur. Two main aspects of context have informed my thinking about the work: first, the explicitly transitional nature of the setting, which emphasises the transitional nature of the therapeutic process; second, uncertainty surrounding the physical space available for sessions, which has encouraged me to consider the value of holding conceptual space as a reliable site in which therapeutic work can happen.

Most therapeutic relationships are in some way transitional, with therapy proposed as a way of helping a client to negotiate particular challenges and move forward with strategies that encourage an increased capacity for independence and freedom. The very concept of therapeutic process implies a journey through time, with constantly evolving aims and outcomes. The notion of psychological development is often mirrored by outward momentum in some aspect of the client's life, towards material or behavioural change, recovery or release from specific external circumstances, which may or may not be, partly or wholly, contingent on the therapeutic journey itself. Etymologically, *therapy* is derived from the Ancient Greek verb *therapeutic,* meaning literally to 'attend', 'do service' and 'take care of'. As therapists, we seek to accompany our clients as they travel. In music therapy specifically, this sense of accompanying is peculiarly acute, as the relationship is often established principally through joint improvisation, in which we play alongside clients, actively sharing the audible plane of the journey.

I have found Kenny's initial articulation of her 'field of play' theory (1989) to be a useful starting point when thinking about how to describe and locate these journeys. Jonathan Miller explains the importance, in his work as a stage director interested in improvisational processes, of simply allowing space and trusting in the spontaneous creation of meaning: 'you bootstrap it up from nothingness, and create a contingent somethingness' (Miller 1990, p.235). Similarly, in the context of music therapy, Ansdell and Pavlicevic (2005) highlight 'the pleasure of improvising intimacy', quoting a client exclaiming 'we're good at making something out of nothing, aren't we?' (p.197). By exploring how different children in this setting have used the space and time that has been available for us to share, I describe how each new therapeutic relationship configures and occupies its own 'field of play', in which we improvise ways of approaching each other.

The feeling of sharing a journey which creates its own sense of space may also resonate for the therapist in ways which prompt reflection beyond the clinical content of the session, as is the case in the setting upon which this chapter is based. My clients here are explicitly journeying to find a place, in the concrete sense of a permanent school place. I hold a parallel awareness of trying to find a place for music therapy here, both physically and conceptually, and, further, of trying to find a place in terms of where I might situate my emerging practice and understanding of my identity as a therapist.

The setting

The work discussed takes place in a transitional day centre for children who have been diagnosed with an autistic spectrum condition and are currently without permanent educational provision. In addition to their diagnosed condition: most children attending the centre also face other challenges: they may carry a secondary diagnosis of attention deficit hyperactive disorder or attachment disorder; they may be in foster care, or have experienced domestic violence, sexual abuse or mental health issues. Verbal ability ranges from highly articulate to completely non-verbal. A typical trajectory might begin with exclusion from a previous school setting (most often mainstream, but which may also have been special educational provision or a pupil referral unit) due to behavioural crisis, leading to an indefinite period of unstructured time at home. Following referral to the team, several weeks may then be spent building a relationship with a visiting keyworker, who remains with them when they begin attending the centre, providing crucial stability as they come to terms with returning to an explicitly educational environment. The aim now is first and foremost to help the child to become school-ready, by increasing their academic confidence and social tolerance. The centre acts as a crucial stepping stone from where a suitable permanent school place can be identified. This process is often fraught with setbacks, but staff work hard to ensure that the child feels safely held until the right opportunity to move on presents itself. The relationships that are formed here are necessarily transitional, and whilst being ready to move on once a suitable school place has been found is a positive step, it is also a step into the unknown. My task is to negotiate and hold a safe, effective and realistic place for music therapy in this context.

A place for music therapy?

There are a variety of challenges in terms of maintaining what might be seen as the ideal practical arrangements for providing a therapy service here. Children often arrive as an emergency placement and, with space and staffing resources stretched, room allocation is shuffled to best accommodate them, meaning that therapy sessions may be moved without prior notice to a number of different spaces, depending on availability. All parents are asked to consent to their child spending individual time with me and the child is then given the choice each week of having a session. The timetable for the day is agreed in discussion with pupils and staff when I arrive in the morning, which both gives children a sense of agency and allows me to make the best use of my time, given that pupil attendance can be unpredictable.

Circumstances dictate that the tangible stability suggested by a consistent room and time for therapy sessions is difficult to achieve in this setting. This was a cause of significant concern to me when I began working here. How could I be sure that what I was providing was, in Winnicott's terms, 'good-enough' (1953, p.94), if the logistical boundaries around the work were so mutable? Other therapists in this volume have written about the importance of how the music therapy experience is framed, including reference to the boundaries of time and space. Kenny (2006, p.107) states:

> Even before the onset of therapy it is very important to attend to comfort of the setting. Both the room and the therapist must indicate a safe and inviting environment for the client. Some factors to be considered are lighting, temperature, acoustics, privacy.

In this setting, all of these things can vary on a session-by-session basis. As the authors of the recent (2014–2017) TIME-A randomised control trial into the effectiveness of improvisational music therapy for children with autistic spectrum conditions assert from the outset, the client's sense of being provided with 'a secure environment' is crucial (Geretsegger *et al.* 2015, p.266). However, the final treatment fidelity guidelines for the trial recognise that essentially this rests not in the room but rather with the therapist; 'does the therapist exert strategies to convey security, reliability, and predictability?' (p.266). Where the physical consistency of a designated therapeutic space is lacking, the onus is more than ever on the therapist to offer security of presence. In addition to ensuring that every child is aware that I am in the building and explicitly involving them in negotiations about if they would like to attend a session that day, I also aim to counter the unpredictability of the space in which the therapy takes place with the predictability that I will collect them from their classroom. As we travel, I explain to them which room we are heading for, allowing them to lead the way, so that they can own a sense of agency. I match the rhythms of their footfalls with my own, singing us down the stairs. I check, verbally, how their week has been. All this, along with ensuring that the same instruments are provided wherever we are and that they are laid out in a familiar formation when we enter, re-establishes a context before the session begins and provides an element of ritual which can be relied upon.

Playgrounds

Kim, Wigram and Gold identify social-affective difficulties as a 'core deficit in children with autism' (2009, p.389), reporting that 'studies of early interaction between infants or young children with autism and their parents do not demonstrate the patterns of the affective reciprocal communication that is widespread in typically developing infants and young children'. Winnicott locates the early development of these communication patterns in 'a potential space between mother and baby', stating that 'I call this a playground because play starts here' (1971, p.47). Children with autism often struggle to use this space effectively. Pavlicevic (1997) specifically translates Winnicott's notion of a playground into a music therapy context, explaining that 'the improvisation becomes the "playground". This playground provides a space within which the therapist and client can "play", can test boundaries between the "self" and the "world", conveyed and portrayed here through and by the music' (p.153). Kenny's 'field of play' framework offers a similar metaphor, identifying clinical improvisation as 'a field of being and acting in sound' (2006, p.78). In the absence of a consistent physical working space, holding such ideas of conceptual space in mind has felt important in sessions here – the playground that the client and I co-create and occupy through improvisation is the real location of the therapy.

It is perhaps no coincidence that the actual playground at the centre offers invaluable opportunity for informal observation of the children. I spend time there each week, just watching them play. Even those who might appear to choose entirely autonomous activities often engage, on closer inspection, in some degree of tacit negotiation with their peers in terms of available space and play equipment. However, most do in fact seek social collaboration on an active level. Unexpected alliances are forged and, regardless of verbal competence, a range of assertive communicative strategies are often apparent. Sharing, turn-taking, anticipating, leading, following, matching, inviting, collaborating, negotiating and helping are all in evidence, alongside teasing, goading and arguing. Whilst teaching staff are present, sometimes co-opted into the children's play and intervening as necessary in any altercations, there is a clear understanding (as in any playground) that this space is the children's, to use as they see fit. Watching them as a group can feel like listening to a complicated orchestral score, with different elements intertwining to form the whole picture. As Kenny explains, 'the concept of "the field" allows us to focus and appreciate that which is in the field, and the conditions and relationships among the participants contained within this space' (2006, p.98). The field of the playground serves as a powerful reminder of the myriad ways in which relationships can be formed and of the fact that, whatever their perceived social impairments, the children here are all capable of sharing space and making connections.

Creating patterns, creating relationship

In the playground of clinical improvisation, relationships are formed through musical interaction. Put simply, 'the sounds we make can represent us, and that improvised music can provide the framework for an interpersonal relationship between a therapist and client(s)' (Wigram 2004, p.19). Middleton (1990) goes further in explaining the mechanism behind the relational potential of music: 'music, considered as a structural-semantic system, offers a means of thinking relationships… Musical patterns are saying: as this note is to that note, as tonic is to dominant, as ascent is to descent, as accent is to weak beat (and so on), so X is to Y' (p.223). In the therapy room, amid infinite and constantly shifting Xs and Ys, I am the Y to the client's X. The particular combinations of sounds and silences that pass between us are where relationship begins.

Common behavioural features of children with a diagnosis of autism include 'repetitive, rigid and somewhat unchanging patterns' (Wigram and Gold 2006, p.536). When these patterns are manifest in sound, the opportunities for interacting with them are manifold. The starting point is often mirroring and matching, offering a clear signal to the child that there is someone else in the room who is attending to them and 'their response to this approach [Improvisational Music Therapy] emerges when they realize that the therapist's music is reflecting something to do with them', (p.536). This realisation can occur on a variety of different levels. Some children understand immediately that I have responded to their sound and are quick to articulate this, uttering 'you're copying me!' in delight, bewilderment or consternation.

One child found this particularly problematic. In his first session, he noticed my mirroring instantly and asked why I was doing it. I explained that it was an easy way to begin to make music that fitted together. 'You don't need to worry about that,' he said, 'you just play, and I will fit.' He was indeed able to fit easily into the pulse and rhythms I supplied. We could share extended improvisations successfully as long as I was careful not to crowd him with responses that were too close to his own gestures. In a subsequent session, he requested that we play music from a favourite computer game. When I was unable to recreate it to his satisfaction, he became disgruntled. Trying to distract him, I suggested that it might not really matter, as we could just make our own music together, 'you and me'. No sooner did these words leave my lips than he shot up out of his chair, saying 'I'm outta here' and refusing to be dissuaded. My instinct was that the problem lay specifically in the fact that I had verbalised our sharing of space. Normally chatty when I visited his classroom, he refused to talk to me for the rest of the day. I wrote an apology before I left, asking his teacher to pass it on. The following week, he politely declined the offer of a session. He was persuaded to return the week after that when I enlisted his help in introducing a new and wary client to the instruments. Appealing to his sense of expertise and taking the focus away from my relationship with him and the fact we were occupying the same space was enough to get him back into the room. Thereafter, he was keen to attend sessions again. The therapy entered a different phase in which he seemed specifically to need to explore the boundaries between us and his own sense of control. This was enacted in physical ways, including games of musical chairs, in which I was the only participant and he controlled the music: attempts to trick me into closing my eyes so he could crash a cymbal or blow a whistle in close proximity to hurt my ears; making himself into a one-man band by attaching as many instruments as possible to himself. My participation was on his terms – after I initiated a song about a one-man band, I was expressly forbidden from 'making up songs about what [he was] doing'. He, however, often talked about what he was engaged in or about to do. Our shared instrumental improvisations, in which mutual attunement felt strong, were the only aspect of our time together that he didn't describe verbally. Several weeks later, I slipped up in making brief reference to 'our music'. He froze instantly and again declared 'I'm outta here'. But this time, gentle verbal persuasion, during which I continued to strum the guitar lightly, enabled him to stay in the room. He moved to the keyboard, taking a variety of other instruments with him, and our improvisation continued. After a couple of minutes, he paused and confidently ventured the opinion that he was 'much more creative' than me. 'You're only playing one instrument and I've got loads.' I agreed but said that I was enjoying playing just one. 'And what you're playing doesn't fit with what I'm doing AT ALL!' he went on to announce, gleefully. I pointed out that he had previously instructed me not to try to fit with him. He denied ever having said this and our improvisation continued, with me moving towards matching him more closely than I had yet dared. The negotiation and acknowledgement of shared space was a delicate issue for this client, but one which music eventually helped to afford.

Other children, whether verbal or not, may use eye contact or facial expression to acknowledge initial matching, before inviting continuation by offering a further sound gesture, often followed by a pause to allow me to take my turn. This may quickly become a game, in which they try to catch me out by offering increasingly complex patterns. Some take longer to engage in shared patterning. Some simply do not want, or perhaps do not yet feel safe, to enter into a dialogue. Or they may not consider the gesture they have made to be about sound at all. The primary motivation to hit a drum, for example, may not be the sound it creates. It offers multiple sensory impacts, not just on hearing, so the child may not at first even recognise that my response on an auditory plane is relevant to them. Adding concomitant visual matching, sometimes in a consciously exaggerated way – perhaps larger, or slower, movements, with accompanying facial expressions – can help the child to begin to recognise the opportunity for interpersonal connections to be made in non-verbal ways.

Consciously incorporating a visual element also enhances the potential for foregrounding cause and effect. I am often warned, when I begin working with a new client here, that the child 'doesn't like loud noises'. My experience has generally been that if the child feels in control of the noise themselves, loud is fine. In addition, most sounds which can be predicted, because the physical gestures that will generate them have been made clearly visible, are also well-tolerated. In turn, explicitly engaging on a visual as well as an aural plane makes it possible for me to meet the client's sound gestures simultaneously, as I can likewise predict when his or her falling hand will hit the drum or strike the piano keys. As the child realises this, their play often begins to incorporate an element of anticipation, waiting for me to raise my hand to mirror theirs so we can release the sound together.

Stern's concept of vitality affects, which describe 'the amodal, dynamic, kinetic quality of our experiences' (Pavlicevic 1997, p.106), is crucial in these interactions. The quality of energy with which a drum is struck is equally visible in the movement made and audible in the sound produced. Attempting to match that quality, on a similar or different instrument, simultaneously or in turn, is a compelling and instinctive way to demonstrate a willingness to find a way to meet somebody. It is this very sharing of gestures within musical parameters 'such as tempo, rhythm, intensity, shape, crescendo, and decrescendo' (Dimitriades and Smeijsters 2011, p.115) that allows relationship to develop. Pavlicevic situates the resultant sense of co-created narrative within 'Dynamic Form', claiming that this (1997, p.137), 'crystallises why music makes therapeutic sense', because:

> The creation of sound form for emotional intent is neither a wholly musical nor a wholly emotional event. Rather the quality of the form is a consequence of its psychological function: to communicate, to explore, to express and receive all of these from and with another. (p.154)

In addition to seeking to meet the client by mirroring and matching to encourage dialogue, the development of a musical relationship can also be nurtured by using holding techniques. Establishing an explicitly musical space in the room, especially if the room is a different one to where the last session was held, often feels like a good way to begin. Verbal or non-verbal clues about how the client is feeling as we travel to the session or their behaviour and gestures when we get there may imply a particular mood, so that I can make an initial attempt to play what is in the room by matching musical affect to perceived energy. I will often do this on guitar or piano, which lend themselves easily to looped harmonic patterns that can suggest a background over which the client may begin to play or vocalise. Playing the piano, however, renders my physical position in the room static, and whilst I can move around with the guitar, this feels cumbersome. I also use the violin regularly, which allows me to be much more mobile, whilst still affording harmonic possibilities and offering an instant variety of texture and timbre, such as bowing, pizzicato or double stopping. I can shift quickly from a harmonic to a melodic role, offering the child a greater variety of role possibilities too. Oldfield highlights 'the importance of being able to move around the room while playing', pointing out that 'being mobile enables the music therapist to be playful' (2006, p.168) in terms of allowing games which explore closeness and distance in relationship on a physical plane, alternately approaching and stepping back from the client.

Case studies

Using music to establish relationship is the fundamental premise of music therapy, as Alvin (1978) clearly expresses: 'the techniques aimed at creating all kinds of relationships between me and the child – between the child and the sounds – between the sounds of musical instruments and of his own voice' (p.xi). The parallel planes of audible, visible and physical layers in musical play offer three meshed fields of potential interaction, which together suggest the scope of the playground available in the therapy space. The developing relationship may be played out predominantly in one or another, or move flexibly between all three, according to the client's needs and preferences. In order to illustrate my experience of some of the ways in which clients have explored and configured the territory of the therapeutic relationship, I would like to present three fictionalised case studies. All features of the therapeutic process are drawn from actual interventions undertaken in this setting, but in order to protect the anonymity of clients who lack capacity to give consent, aspects of several cases have been combined and all identifying details changed or removed. I offer three composite portraits, which highlight notable interactions in each of three broad client categories: non-verbal, emergently verbal and fluently verbal. All three are boys, all in the upper-primary age range, representing the dominant demographic in the setting. The imagined time-frame of the therapeutic intervention is a period of roughly two terms (15–20 sessions) in each case.

CASE STUDY: NOAH – MAKING SPACE FOR FEELINGS

Noah's ability to express himself verbally was extremely limited, consisting of about a dozen active words, which he tended only to use when prompted. However, he was proactively vocal, often chattering excitedly in a language of his own. In this, he displayed a fascination with the way in which sound patterns and rhythms can be passed between people, independently of referential semantic content, in quasi-conversational exchange. The concept of communicative musicality (Malloch 1999) highlights the importance of such exchanges in the mother–infant dyad as a pre-linguistic means of 'sharing the sense of time in the mind' (Trevarthen and Malloch 2002, p.10) and how this enables relationships to be nurtured and sustained. By mirroring Noah's vocal gestures with my own voice, we were able to co-create reciprocal patterns. I also frequently used the flute to match his high-pitched chatter with flutter-tonguing and by vocalising into the instrument. Sometimes his urgent chatter would suddenly cease and his energy would seem to drop to a more reflective mood, which I was able to meet with slower melodic lines at a lower tessitura.

Noah also exhibited echolalia, with snippets of sentences from the television featuring alongside more immediate repetition of those around him. Some of this was drawn from his classroom experiences of being encouraged to use language to communicate: 'Can you say…?' Yet he also seemed to recognise that his unsolicited echoing of something I had said was a way to indicate his willingness to enter into a shared pattern of sound and rhythm and begin an exchange. His desire to connect was strongly evident in other ways too; he consistently offered and sought eye contact and was naturally tactile, grabbing my hand as we left the classroom and choosing to sit close to me during sessions.

His favourite instrument was the keyboard, at which he would happily remain for the entire session. He had four distinct ways of playing it, often switching without warning between them. Hammered clusters of notes, played with his entire hand or arm, were accompanied by theatrical screaming and a contorted facial expression. This contrasted sharply with conjunct sequences of single notes played carefully with his right index finger, which he hummed simultaneously at pitch, his facial muscles calm and relaxed, as he progressed from the bottom to the upper reaches of the keyboard, able to pitch-match with unerring accuracy from one end to the other. At other times, he would pull an exaggeratedly sad face, playing single notes in a more laboured manner and a more erratic pattern. He might then segue into what seemed to be the retelling of a frenzied narrative, possibly of a chase scene, with high-pitched chatter interspersed with film quotes in an adult male American accent, alongside rapidly accelerating clusters, before he slumped over the keyboard. His extensive use of exaggerated facial expressions often reminded me of a mime artist, in this case providing his own soundtrack.

Noah seemed to be using the keyboard as a means of exploring the extremes of emotional affect, enjoying matching sound effects to the different feeling states his facial expressions implied. His readiness to audibly and gesturally explore emotional states in a highly playful manner revealed his innate understanding of the possibility that 'the common fabric between music and our feeling life is synthesised' in dynamic form (Pavlicevic 1997, p.154). As Smeijsters (2005) explains, 'when it is possible to describe the musical and psychological processes by means of the same dynamic terms, the analogies between musical forms and forms of feeling are apparent' (p.70). My own role when Noah was at the keyboard was generally one of being alongside. He seemed entirely comfortable with me joining him in any of his modes of playing, whether that be by mirroring and matching, or accompanying and holding. However, although there was often an element of shared response, insofar as I could initiate a change of mood and he would reliably follow, I never felt that his fundamental desire to experiment with music and emotional expression was contingent upon my participation.

Noah increasingly invited opportunities for more collaborative music making. Moving away from the keyboard, he was most often drawn to a pair of one-octave glockenspiels. He was keen to share these, offering me one so that I might join him in a duet. He often tried to pick out known melodies (e.g. 'Baa, Baa Black Sheep') and was able to copy my playing with sufficient accuracy that he could reproduce them. He also initiated anticipation games, holding the beater aloft and teasing me in pretending to bring it down to play but pulling back at the last minute. The preparatory gesture of hands held aloft also featured when we shared the djembe – he would wait expectantly, eyebrows raised, until I copied his position, before initiating a pulse in unison, which then diversified into rhythmic call and response. He also developed an elaborate 'Goodbye' ritual, involving pointedly ignoring my suggestion that it was time to end, continuing to play silent clusters on the keyboard even when he knew it had been switched off, and then initiating not one but several shared countdowns to 'blast off!' on the djembe. Moving through a process which felt playfully teasing before this final collaboration seemed to enable him to leave the room on his own terms.

Once when I went to collect him, Noah was in considerable distress and had been excluded from the classroom as he had been overturning furniture. He was still in a highly volatile state as we entered the therapy room and another chair went flying. He jabbered agitatedly between huge sobs. We sat side by side on the sofa and I met him with a chord sequence on the guitar that I had often used to accompany his miming of a sad state, joining his vocalising and placing a glockenspiel next to him, which he soon reached for and began to play. The strikes he made were isolated and ponderous at first, with no clear pulse. Previous sessions had represented a fun exploration of the potential connections between sound gesture and feeling state, with Noah demonstrating that he knew music could be used to represent an emotional affect that he had playfully chosen. In this instance, the process was turned on its head, as the mood he seemed to be unhappily at the mercy of was something that we could between us acknowledge and make safely audible in music. Gradually, his disconnected strikes moved towards a regular pattern of beats and we negotiated a shared pulse. His muscles began to relax and his tears ceased. Within the music, and with my support, he was able to self-regulate his emotional response. By the end of the session, having engaged in several extended improvisations, which moved through a range of moods, he had regained his emotional equilibrium. The musical experiences we had shared in earlier sessions had given us a safe place in which to meet, which he was able to access even from a state of high emotion.

CASE STUDY: THEO – THE SPACE THAT MUSIC MAKES

Theo was just beginning to use verbal language at the point that his sessions began. I knew, from staff reports and from contact with him outside the context of therapy, that he was able to use single words and short sentences, accompanied by clear body language and eye contact, to make himself understood. However, upon crossing the threshold of the therapy room, he seemed to flick a switch into a different mode of being altogether. In his first session, he headed straight to the percussion instruments and began exploring them with considerable dexterity, quickly working out how to manipulate each one in order to achieve different sounds. All this was done with his back firmly to me. As he moved around the room, any time there was a chance that I would fall into his sightline, he altered his position to preclude eye contact. From a distance, I responded to his exploration of the instruments musically, first by mirroring and matching and then, gradually, by answering in ways that subtly altered his utterances. He responded in turn and a feeling of dialogue was established, through this flexible exchange of motifs: 'repetition and variation are of vital importance in any interaction because they constitute the basic architecture for the experience of sharing existential time' (Gratier and Apter-Danon 2009, p.309). We improvised solidly for 15 minutes in that very first session, incorporating musically sophisticated rhythms which included syncopations and varying sub-divisions, with him moving seamlessly between instruments without rhythmic flow being disrupted, all with no eye contact whatsoever.

This way of relating continued in subsequent sessions. Theo initiated musical dialogue within seconds of entering the room and it flowed near-continuously until I let him know it was time to stop, at which point he would leave calmly. I realised that the only way in which I could reliably elicit eye contact from him was to break our stream of musical conversation by remaining silent when the pattern we had established meant it was my turn to speak, prompting him to shoot me a look. I discovered this by accident in an early session, being slightly too slow to respond during a rapid exchange of musical gestures. In later sessions, it became a tactic I used consciously, albeit occasionally, as a playful challenge when I felt that the intensity of our musical exchange was acquiring a relentless quality. Briefly breaking the flow of sound allowed a sense of breathing space, and the consequent eye contact perhaps acted as a reminder of the potential for forming interpersonal connections beyond music. Over time, it did become increasingly possible to share physical as well as musical space with Theo, as he gradually began to tolerate me moving closer to him, as long as the music continued whilst I did so. Working in closer physical proximity enabled a more detailed and intimate mode of improvising together, including cross-modal matching which related to the precise techniques he was using on particular instruments. The richly responsive nature of Theo's musical gestures suggested that he was listening intently to everything and seemed to expect me to do the same. As Ansdell (2011) states, 'one's own music (played in dialogic improvisation with another person) is itself a probing listening' (p.583). Theo revealed nothing about himself verbally, but the sense of shared meaning in our improvisations offered felt proof of 'the empirical truth that [thinking without words] is possible. We can have shaped, abstract, phrasal experiences prior to language' (Sampson 2011, p.8). Whilst I was aware that his verbal skills were accelerating rapidly outside the therapy room, he remained vocally reticent in sessions. Music seemed to offer him a completely different kind of effortless fluency and the freedom to explore relational expression without the encumbrance of words.

After a few weeks, I was able to persuade him to join me at the keyboard. This was the first time we had shared an instrument. Whilst he had chosen primarily to use untuned percussion in our music making to date, I knew from several forays on the glockenspiel that he had a strong sense of pitch and was well able to incorporate it into his patterns. I set up a four-chord holding sequence at the lower end of the keyboard and he explored tentatively in the upper reaches. Within minutes he had worked out which notes would fit with my ostinato pattern and created a corresponding four-note motif. Over the weeks that followed, he returned again and again to this, transposing it into several different keys, finding the same intervals on the glockenspiel, playing it in different moods and tempi, even creating embryonic divisions, by repeating each note over a slower pulse. As DeNora (2000) explains, 'the client's gestures become traces of his or her identity and, through the therapist's attempts to make sense, musically, of these gestures, the client comes to have, like so-called "normal" people, a fabricated registry of self-identity. The resultant music ratifies the client's presence' (p.70). Theo had created a musical signature.

Whilst Theo's sessions were often characterised by extended shared improvisations, which were musically rich and complex, things didn't always progress so smoothly. Sometimes the patterns he created at the start of a session seemed to be deliberately impenetrable and he remained impervious to any attempt I made to interject. Whilst the musical shape of his initial utterance might on the surface seem very similar to previous beginnings, on these occasions his playing quickly acquired a relentless quality, exhibiting little variation and no breathing space in the music. On these occasions it felt as though he was building a sound wall to block me out. Sometimes this would progress into what felt like an entirely mechanical exploration of sound; he might use a beater to systematically hit everything in the room, or pick up every small instrument he could find and bounce it off the djembe. Sometimes I could persuade him to come and play the keyboard instead and this might enable us to move into more conversational music, but at other times he would suddenly declare 'finish' and leave. After a few sessions of struggling to feel that we were making any kind of satisfactory connection, I turned up to collect him from the classroom and he politely said he didn't want to come that week. For the next few weeks, he was offered a slot as usual and declined, giving full eye contact as he spoke to me. One lunchtime, having declined a session that morning, he asked to come and play with the instruments. Whilst I ate my lunch, he spent ten minutes happily exploring the instruments on the other side of the room, before leaving without comment. Two weeks later, when I arrived in the classroom, he said, beaming at me, 'Can I go to music, please?' I added him to the list for the day. We spent a full half-hour improvising together, his level of creative engagement as complete and subtle as it had ever been. This continued for the duration of our work together.

In his early sessions, Theo's natural understanding of musical patterns seemed to allow him to scope out a playground space in which he could revel in his own fluency and enjoy sharing it with me. I imagine this experience of fluency offered a sense of spaciousness and freedom which contrasted sharply with his painstaking progress towards verbal communication in other contexts. The period in which he chose to step away from engaging in our relationship, first inside the room and then by not coming at all, coincided with him making rapid strides in a verbal arena and I wonder if he struggled to reconcile the two modes, so that his very progression into verbal language somehow disrupted the flow of our sessions. This was also the period in which his transition to a new school was being negotiated, which may have had an impact that he did not know how to express verbally and did not feel it was possible to express musically. For reasons I can only guess at, he made a conscious choice to approach the therapeutic space again, just as he had previously made a conscious choice to leave it.

CASE STUDY: JACK – THE SPACE BETWEEN THESE WALLS

Jack's sessions were unusual in this setting as they took place in the same room at the same time each week. As highly volatile as he was highly articulate, Jack became extremely agitated when around other children and initially spent all his time at the centre in a small room, alone with his keyworker. Although he was regularly invited to join in with communal activities, he chose to accept only rarely and his ability to tolerate any kind of interaction with his peers was invariably short-lived. As a result, he worked, ate and spent all his break times in the same space. Whilst, unlike all the other children I worked with, the physical environment in which his therapy occurred remained consistent, the fact that it was a multi-functional space meant that there was a need to redefine it conceptually. Rather than bringing him into a room with the instruments ready laid out, implicitly suggesting a musical space, the instruments and I arrived each week into what was powerfully his space. After a few weeks, I suggested we might move his sessions into the larger room available; this was the only time I saw true fear in his eyes, as he vehemently refused. Yet he spent a large proportion of his early sessions staging mock escapes from his room, flinging himself at the door and battling to get past the member of staff stationed immediately outside. There was a theatricality in his tendency to test the edges of the space he inhabited, as he could easily have wriggled past his keyworker if he had been determined to, but instead he flailed and hollered and giggled and never made it over the threshold. In time, he found a less physical way to meet his need to confirm this boundary, devising a musical signal (a blast on the duck whistle) to summon his keyworker, only to laugh and tell her to go away as soon as her head appeared around the door. He also displayed a need to test boundaries between me and him, often making as if to attack me with a penny whistle or violin bow, only to make an about-turn at the last minute and feign stabbing himself instead. Once, wheeling around sharply, he accidentally caught my finger and was contrite. After one particularly chaotic session, he turned suddenly and said, in a bewildered tone, 'I thought I was going to hug you just then.' At other times he would spontaneously sit on my lap while we shared an instrument. Despite the fact that he regularly rampaged about the room, he never damaged anything in doing so. He was well aware of the relationship between physical force and effect, and although his behaviour was often wild, he maintained a fine degree of control. One week he insisted on eating jelly in his session, with his fingers. Although he ended up with it all over his hands, his clothes and the wall, not a speck touched any of the instruments scattered around.

Musically, Jack engaged strongly with both me and the instruments from the very beginning, displaying a particular fascination with the violin. He had an instinctive understanding of cross-modal matching and the fact that the violin could be used to 'say' things. He enjoyed it when I mimicked the dynamic form of laughter or screaming and once asked me if I could 'play f*** on the violin', but dismissed my attempts as hilariously unsatisfactory! More than once, he requested 'sad music, like when someone has died', seeming content when I offered gentle melodies in a minor key. He asked me to bring an accordion to one session and, in exploring his responses to different buttons, we discussed that major chords sounded 'happy' and minor ones 'sad'. 'But where are the angry buttons?' he asked. We spent time together finding the angriest sound we could, eventually settling on a minor chord played simultaneously with a major seventh.

Jack had the ability to focus intently when he chose to. We spent most of one session comparing the decay of a singing bowl and a strummed guitar, with him sitting motionless while he listened until the sound had died away completely – several seconds after I could no longer hear it. More often, however, he flitted rapidly from one musical activity to another. This seemed to be prompted by him approaching an emotionally fraught topic. He might begin in a role play from his life, using the instruments to represent everyday objects or to facilitate explicit emotional display, but when difficult events in his narrative were imminent, he would suddenly switch to a fictional story instead. His musical memory was very strong and he paired this with detailed narrative recall, re-enacting scenes from his favourite fantasy films, in which I was instructed to provide the soundtrack and to play all female roles simultaneously.

Free improvisation was a significant feature of Jack's sessions. He was able to use music as a means of non-verbal communication and being together from the outset, co-creating tightly interdependent musical conversations in which he exploited the full range of instruments and possibilities available to him. His hearing was acute and he demonstrated a highly developed sense of both rhythm and pitch. He rejected the violin unless it was perfectly in tune and was easily able to discriminate between two drums pitched almost identically. He was also quick to spot anomalies when I matched his musical gestures in call-and-response games. In later sessions he began to display an interest in musical structures, initiating unprompted experimentation with more abstract exchanges of pattern. He experimented with conducting me and also undertook a spontaneous foray into notation, devising his own graphic system and painstakingly explaining it so that we could play it together. For a child who struggled with, and seemed wary of, any activity involving reading or writing, this felt important. Moving from 'laying a form out through time' (Sampson 2011 p.9) to laying it out on paper, where it takes up physical space and is enduring, revisitable and shareable, perhaps represented, in some small way, his growing sense of creative ownership and a new way to define and claim space – one that was not dependent on him bouncing (quite literally) off the walls and other people.

Sessions tended to finish with Jack hiding as many small instruments as he could grab and chortling while his keyworker and I hunted high and low for them. He often asked if he could keep a harmonica or a penny whistle, and I explained that whilst they were his to use during the session, I needed to take them away with me. Twice he did damage instruments accidentally, though not in his rampaging. Using a penny whistle enthusiastically as a beater, he sliced through a drum skin, and on another occasion snapped a violin bow when focusing intently on the instrument in his other hand. Whilst he wasn't reprimanded significantly for either of these incidents, he was quick to recognise the mild dismay I expressed and he seemed to make a conscious decision to exploit it. In subsequent weeks, he threatened to hit the drum with the penny whistle again, as a means of eliciting a reaction. And in his final session, having tolerated a brief discussion about the fact that he was moving on and our work was therefore ending, he stood in front of me and slowly bent the violin bow, declaring 'I'm going to break this'. He explained that I then wouldn't be able to use it for sessions with anyone else. He didn't break it, but his message was clear. Later on in the session, after a particularly energetic improvisation, he laughingly declared, 'I am the Emperor of Music Therapy!' My clinical notes following our first meeting had reflected on the cell-like quality of the small, bare room in which he spent all his time. I realised now that it was as much kingdom as prison to him and wondered to what extent music, and our time together exploring relationship through it, had enabled his sense of realm to grow. With the support of his keyworker, he was able to acknowledge my 'Goodbye' at the end of this final session. However, later that day, he caught sight of me passing his room and squealed with delight, 'I KNEW I'd see you again!' He invited me in, saying he wanted to give me some of the cakes he had just made. Solemnly, he pulled three large crumbs from a cupcake and placed them in my hand – my leaving present from the Emperor of Music Therapy.

Conclusions

These three clients configured the potential therapeutic space in three very different ways. For Noah, who didn't use words, music was a place to give his emotions audible form, to develop a repertoire which enabled him to express himself in sound and receive audible empathy in return. For Theo, increasingly finding his way with language, music was somewhere to step briefly away from words, where he could experience a fluency in communication and a richness in connection that speech did not yet allow him. Jack was accustomed to seeking confrontation in words and action, pushing against the boundaries provided by others as a means of understanding the shape of his territory of self. For him, music offered a safe and flexible medium for exploring contact that did not have to be about conflict. Unlike physical space, musical space becomes more expansive the more it is shared. Engaging in musical play enabled Jack to break through the walls of the confined space he inhabited, opening up a wider conceptual space in which emotions and relationship could be explored.

The lack of some of the traditional parameters in the therapeutic contract in this setting meant that from the outset I held a heightened awareness of the unknown and the unknowable which exists in any therapeutic relationship. Not being able to be certain from week to week what physical space I would be working in or how long I would be able to work with each client pushed me to recognise and grasp the only things I could be confident of – my presence, the instruments, the possibility of music. In the absence of certain physical space, holding conceptual space for the work in mind has proved crucial for me. The strategy, inspired by Winnicott and Pavlicevic, of seeking to open up a 'playground' space between me and the client, in which we might explore ways to approach each other, has felt key. Kenny's (2006) theory of overlapping fields of relating allows for a flexible understanding of where the potential playground in any particular therapeutic relationship might lie. She describes how her sense of the relevance of field theory to music therapy came directly from observing a colleague: 'I saw so clearly that Rachael [Verney] was creating an environment, a space, a field, which held her young client. Her interaction with him in the music was what I later came to call the musical space' (p.73). Yet she cautions:

> A theory can be a map. But it is not the territory. In order for a music therapist to feel secure, she needs such a map. So, in this sense, the *Field of Play* is the map I have created to feel secure about my work. (p.74).

Kenny's stance implies the existence of concentric circles between the improvisations we co-create with our clients and the understandings we improvise for ourselves when thinking about our work. The express remit of the setting in which my work occurs is to find a place for the children who pass through on their journey to new schools. This awareness underpins my own anxieties about how to find a place for the work, made concrete by a lack of consistent physical space in which to carry it out. Considering therapeutic space in conceptual terms represents a way of improvising meaning which has enabled me to feel more grounded (pun intended) in my work. Fields and playgrounds both suggest open areas of land that are nonetheless safely bordered – spaces defined by what is nurtured in them, not what is kept out. It is in just such spaces that Miller's (1990) meaningful bootstrapping can occur, because 'the only visitable universe is the one within which these improvisations hold sway, and therefore in that sense they are absolute and must be cleaved to, the morality is worth holding to' (p.235).

References

Alvin, J. (1978) *Music Therapy for the Autistic Child*. Oxford: Oxford University Press.

Ansdell, G. (2011) 'Steps Toward an Ecology of Music Therapy: A Guide to Theoretical Wanderings 1989–2011.' In K. Bruscia (ed.) *Readings on Music Therapy Theory*. Gilsum, NH: Barcelona Publishers.

Ansdell, G. and Pavlicevic, M. (2005) 'Musical Companionship, Musical Community. Music Therapy and the Process and Value of Musical Communication.' In D. Miell, R. MacDonald and D. Hargreaves, (eds) *Musical Identities* Oxford: Oxford University Press.

DeNora, T. (2000) *Music in Everyday Life*. Cambridge: Cambridge University Press.

Dimitriades, T. and Smeijsters, H. (2011) 'Autistic spectrum disorder and music therapy: Theory underpinning practice.' *Nordic Journal of Music Therapy 20*, 2, 108–122.

Geretsegger, M., Holck, U., Carpente, J.A., Elefant, C., Kim, J. and Gold, C. (2015). 'Common characteristics of improvisational approaches in music therapy for children with autism spectrum disorder: Developing treatment guidelines.' *Journal of Music Therapy 52*, 2, 258–281.

Gratier, M. and Apter-Danon, G. (2009) 'The Improvised Musicality of Belonging: Repetition and Variation in Mother–Infant Vocal Interaction.' In S. Malloch and C. Trevarthen (eds) *Communicative Musicality: Exploring the Basis of Human Companionship* Oxford: Oxford University Press.

Kenny, C. (1989) *The Field of Play: A Guide for the Theory and Practice of Music Therapy*. Atascadero, CA: Ridgeview Publishing Company.

Kenny, C. (2006) *Music and Life in the Field of Play: An Anthology*. Gilsum, NH: Barcelona Publishers.

Kim, J., Wigram, T. and Gold, C. (2009) 'Emotional, motivational and interpersonal responsiveness of children with autism in improvisational music therapy.' *Autism 13*, 4, 389–409.

Malloch, S. (1999) 'Mothers and infants and communicative musicality.' *Musicae Scientiae, Special Issue 1999–2000, 3*, 29–57.

Middleton, R. (1990) *Studying Popular Music*. Milton Keynes and Philadelphia: Open University Press.

Miller, J. (1990) 'Dr Jonathan Miller.' In R. Dinnage (ed.) *The Ruffian on the Stair: Reflections on Death*. London: Viking.

Oldfield, A. (2006) *Interactive Music Therapy in Child and Family Psychiatry: Clinical Practice, Research and Teaching.* London: Jessica Kingsley Publishers.

Pavlicevic, M. (1997) *Music Therapy in Context: Music, Meaning and Relationship.* London: Jessica Kingsley Publishers.

Sampson, F. (2011) *Music Lessons.* Hexham: Bloodaxe Books.

Smeijsters, H. (2005) *Sounding the Self: Analogy in improvisational Music Therapy.* Gilsum, NH: Barcelona Publishers.

Trevarthen, C. and Malloch, S. (2002) 'Musicality and music before three: Human vitality and invention shared with pride.' *Zero to Three 23,* 1, 10–18.

Wigram, T. (2004). *Improvisation: Methods and Techniques for Music Therapy Clinicians, Educators, and Students.* London: Jessica Kingsley Publishers.

Wigram, T. and Gold, C. (2006) 'Music therapy in the assessment and treatment of autistic spectrum disorder: Clinical application and research evidence.' *Child: Care, Health and Development 32,* 5, 535–542.

Winnicott, D. (1953). 'Transitional objects and transitional phenomena.' *International Journal of Psychoanalysis 34,* 89–97.

Winnicott, D. (1971). *Playing and Reality.* London: Tavistock Publications.

CHAPTER 10

A Team Approach to Supporting Mark's Journey to Increased Social Engagement: Music Therapy Work with a Young Man With Autism

Cindy-Jo Morison

Introduction

Northumberland, Tyne and Wear NHS Foundation Trust is one of the largest mental health and learning disability Trusts in England, working over 60 sites across Northumberland, Newcastle, North Tyneside, Gateshead, South Tyneside and Sunderland. The autism service in Northumberland provides an established inpatient service for adults who are diagnosed with an autistic spectrum condition, who have extremely complex needs and display challenging behaviours to the extent that their needs cannot be met by local assessment and treatment services.

This chapter presents a case study of a man I shall name Mark, not his real name. On referral to the service he was extremely fragile and often communicated through behaviours that were considered a risk. The case study illustrates how music therapy was introduced slowly and incorporated into a collaborative approach that allowed him to slowly build up trust, to tolerate and then begin to engage with different members of the multi-disciplinary team.

Background

Born in 1985 in Scotland, Mark was given the diagnosis of an autistic spectrum condition aged three and half years. He has epilepsy, a severe learning disability and developed extreme anxiety around being touched and bathed. On admission to the autism service, aged 20, he had a developmental age of 20–22 months. Mark has strong family relationships with his parents, brother and grandparents, has little/no speech and does not communicate with other service users. He has preferred members of staff who he communicates better with but on his terms. Prior to admission his physical health was poor.

During his early years Mark lived at home with his parents, where he progressed through special units within mainstream school until the last unit where staff were unable to support him due to challenging behaviours towards himself and others. He therefore became a physical risk to the other vulnerable pupils, prompting the local council to set up a specialised day service for him. This was initially a 1:1 staffing ratio, and then a 2:1 to support increased challenging behaviours, although Mark continued to stay in the family home during this period. This day care service then broke down following a particularly violent episode for which Mark was medicated and detained. Following further hospital admissions Mark was moved to our autism inpatient service aged 20.

Early admission

On admission he presented as a fragile young man. His aggression presented a significant risk to peers and staff and he spent much of each day in his room in a model of care which was effectively seclusion. For this reason he was moved to a flat that allowed him to be on his own with less intrusive observation following a period of increased irritability, agitation and violence. This then offered him the opportunity to self-seclude. Almost immediately, his appetite, mood and behaviour improved and he established a very basic routine programme that included the ability to request staff presence when he needed to, usually by banging on his flat door or shouting.

Future discharge and placement plans are ongoing to return Mark to living near his parents. Nevertheless, whilst he remained within the unit, it was essential that Mark was offered a programme that included opportunities to develop his communication through a wide range of therapeutic activities. A request was made for me to attend a core/multi-disciplinary team meeting to understand how Mark's presentation impacted upon both himself and those staff allocated to work with him.

During Mark's early admission his physical aggression required restraint, and these outbursts could often not be anticipated through triggers (either behavioural or from facial expression) but were frequent, sudden and very forceful. He displayed inappropriate behaviours including sexual frustration and self-isolation in terms of his reluctance to comply with treatment and care plans. His bathing routine was also very problematic as was the very obvious and regular self-harm including rectal poking causing bleeding.

Mark's early admission included an occupational therapy sensory assessment and this suggested he may have a hyper-reactive tactile system. In other words, he would avoid certain types of tactile experiences, preferring to seek vestibular (balance) and proprioceptive (joint position and movement) input for calming. This would include kicking and banging his hand before an activity. A speech and language therapy assessment, completed around the same time, showed that Mark's sensory and communication needs had continued to be a major concern in relation to anxiety levels, communication and behaviours. Recommendations from this assessment were that he should gradually be introduced to objects of reference and intensive interaction to support his engagement with others. The objects of reference were used as a means of communication and could be spoken words/phrases, signing or pictures/symbols. For example, Mark might be told it is 'breakfast time' or shown a Boardmaker picture communication symbol (Mayer-Johnson 2018) of a 'breakfast' consistently at the same time each day. The use of objects of reference was introduced gradually with just one or two being used daily until it was felt that Mark had acknowledged their purpose. Intensive Interaction (Nind and Hewett 2001) was suggested to support Mark to better relate to others and further develop his communication skills.

Additional activities were also being offered through the TEACCH (Treatment and Education of Autistic and Communication related Handicapped Children) programme. This is an evidence-based programme which supports individuals of all ages and skills levels with an autistic spectrum condition. Whilst this programme was developed in America in 1966 and originally set up as a child research project, legislation was passed in 1972 enabling it to become 'the first comprehensive state-wide community based programme of services for children and adults

on the autistic spectrum and other similar developmental disorders'
(National Autistic Society 2017).

There were clearly observable and significant improvements in
Mark's communication and interaction skills as well as his tolerance
levels following the implementation of a basic daily routine
programme, but he was still exhibiting challenging behaviours.

Meeting the team

Following my introduction to this case I was invited to attend a
biopsychosocial formulation meeting. This, I discovered, was a
multi-disciplinary team discussion influenced by an Australian
collaborative approach to clinical formulation (Statewide Behaviour
Intervention Service 2017). It involved the psychiatrist, clinical
psychologist, ward manager, clinical coordinator, registered
nurses, nursing assistants and activities coordinator. In the
meeting the individual had their story told through the five 'p's:
presenting factors (difficult thoughts, emotions and behaviours),
predisposing factors (historical), precipitating factors (triggers for
behaviours), perpetuating factors (what keeps the behaviour going)
and finally the protective factors (what helps/stops the problem
from getting worse). This same multi-disciplinary team would meet
on a regular basis from pre-admission to admission, be involved
in the assessment and treatment process as well as plan for Mark's
future discharge. From the formulation meeting that I was invited
to, the following recommendations were made:

- to find a therapeutic intervention that could offer alternative
  methods of communication to meet the function of current
  challenging behaviours

- to offer more opportunities for positive interactions through
  increased contact and activities.

Planning with the team

Following attendance at this meeting I felt it was important to
separately meet Mark's core team. This was a team made up of two
registered nurses (described as Mark's 'named' nurses and first point
of contact should other staff or his family need them) and nursing

assistants. By placing the patient at the centre of their care, this core team would work directly with Mark on a shift-by-shift basis (where possible) to support these recommendations in terms of offering an approach that would be successful and safe for everyone.

In my mind, I felt it would be helpful to identify different phases of working with Mark, and I divided these into four phases, bearing in mind Stella Compton Dickinson's way of working (Compton Dickinson and Hakvoort 2017). Phases one and two were defined as having the therapeutic aim of increasing Mark's trust in others through activity. Phases three and four would then be identified to look at the therapeutic aim of increasing social interaction. According to his family, Mark had always enjoyed listening to music but would always do this alone. I felt that this phased music therapy approach could support him by offering an outlet for emotional expression through improvisation and shared playing. It could be stimulating and relaxing as well as offering an opportunity to engage with others through a shared musical experience. It could also help the core team to work with him in a different yet still very supportive way, and get to know him through some musical playing.

My work began in September 2009 when, after multi-disciplinary team agreement, I discussed my proposal with his named nurse who was very supportive and helped write the appropriate risk assessments. This involved looking at any risk associated with working with Mark in close proximity, such as his presenting mood prior to a session, the need to prompt him to stay at a safe distance from the exit door, for staff to carry radios/alarms, to consistently have the same number of staff at each session and to acknowledge that if he became agitated or anxious at any point, staff would immediate leave the room.

Music therapy approach

My own approach was informed, in part, by the work of Lawday and Compton Dickinson (2013), particularly in relation to their use of two of the four key Dialectical Behavioural Skills (DBT) within the 'treatment stage': distress tolerance and interpersonal effectiveness attempting to offer these to Mark musically. I was also drawn to Tony Wigram's (2002) assessment process and Amelia Oldfield's (2006) interactive music therapy approach.

During the initial multi-disciplinary team formulation I realised that whilst Mark would be unable to identify his own goal, the Cognitive Analytical Music Therapy (CAMT) approach could further inform the work in terms of considering what needed to happen in order for Mark to achieve these recommendations. Compton Dickinson and Hakvoort (2017) suggest phases of treatment in relation to using a CAMT approach in forensic music therapy. Whilst this could be considered a very different clinical population, Mark was in an autism inpatient service, it was still a secure setting and many of his presenting factors were similar to those of some forensic patients. Whilst I have chosen to use the term 'phases' in my approach, I am not following the CAMT approach, as Mark is non-verbal, but just taking inspiration and guidance from it.

In order to increase Mark's social engagement with others, and for the core team to work effectively together, my approach needed to be fed back to the wider multi-disciplinary team on a regular basis, and for this reason I chose to consider this work in phases. During phase one I paid close attention to the five areas of assessment that Tony Wigram (2002) outlines in his article – communication, social development, emotional needs, cognitive development and areas of therapy specific to autistic spectrum conditions. In my initial observations of Mark these areas went a long way to give me a holistic view of him in terms of how best to present music therapy to him, as well as his abilities and needs in order to best support the recommendations I had been asked to investigate. Using this knowledge, in the primary phase I aimed to build a trusting relationship.

The interactive music therapy approach, documented by Amelia Oldfield (2006), was a way to support Mark once this relationship was established. I was able to offer face-to-face music therapy which allowed for a more directive approach to begin to increase social interaction. This can be important to anyone diagnosed with an autistic spectrum condition in terms of offering predictability and a chance for everyone involved to develop a trusting and safe relationship.

Assessment questions were used to determine if this intervention would contribute to the therapeutic aims. For example, I asked in phase one if Mark's tolerance of and his social engagement with others would increase if music were used. In phase two, I questioned whether using music would result in Mark showing an interest in musical instruments and if he could engage in music making within a weekly activity programme. In phase three, I asked if Mark could routinely use a brief structured music activity within his week and begin to tolerate this activity with members of his core team. Finally, in phase four, I asked if a plan could be devised for introducing new members of staff to Mark using what had been learnt in music therapy.

All these assessment questions would be reviewed in relation to the original therapeutic recommendations of increasing Mark's activity as well as his tolerance of social contact. An appropriate risk assessment was also required at each phase as well as regular meetings with those involved to check they were happy with how the work was progressing. This was important for many reasons including the possibility that:

- Staff may have a tendency to blame the activity or the person for initially increasing negative behaviours, so introducing both carefully is paramount.

- Both social contact and activity will probably increase negative behaviours, so monitoring that each intervention links to the underpinning therapeutic aim is important at each phase before moving to the next.

Building up activities slowly and safely over a longer period seemed likely to, and did, have a greater effect. Rather than just coming up with creative ideas in response to challenging behaviours, it was better to offer the intervention with a clear rationale linked to the overall therapeutic aims; otherwise the work was likely to be thwarted with persistent challenging behaviour.

Music therapy notes review for each phase

Phase one (September 2009 to July 2010) offered the opportunity for me to get to know Mark without entering the flat, which was imperative to the core team in terms of the risk involved.

Initially, I attended the ward every day that it was possible for me to do so in order for Mark to get used to me visiting him. So often, individuals like Mark are picked up and dropped by services and this was why it was so important that Mark knew that I was here to stay and would not be giving up.

In an attempt to observe Mark holistically, I made sure that my visits occurred at different times of the day. The TEACCH programme offered me one such opportunity for observing Mark undertaking an activity. The rationale behind the introduction of this programme was based on Mark being easily distracted by his surroundings and finding it difficult to attend to a task. The evidence for the use of this intervention with Mark was to make his tasks and environment form part of a structure that would promote learning and aim to decrease certain behaviours.

The activity coordinator facilitating this work with Mark was to become one of my consistent colleagues who would support the introduction of music therapy once that time was reached. In terms of how the TEACCH activity worked, Mark was asked to move to the back of his room and sit at the table. The activity coordinator would then set out activity trays on his work table which was near the flat door, thus allowing the activity coordinator a quick exit should Mark become challenging in any way. There was always at least one member of ward staff also present within the corridor throughout the activity. Each activity would be laid out separately and, when completed, Mark would be praised for his achievements. At the end of the activity a favourite DVD would be played for Mark to enjoy. This became another area for which I was asked to advise upon during this initial phase.

A meeting then took place with me, the activity coordinator and a psychological nurse practitioner to discuss ways of moving forward in terms of assessment. The reason these two members of the multi-disciplinary team were chosen to support my work, apart from them volunteering, was two-fold. First, they both knew Mark extremely well as they had been working for the service since his admission. Second, they both worked Monday to Friday and not shifts which therefore offered the additional consistency required to have any chance of the approach being a success. We needed to work together to determine whether music could be used as a face-to-face activity contributing to the therapeutic aim of increasing Mark's interest in an activity and if it could act as a motivator for his engagement with others. Through our discussions there was agreement that music could and should be introduced in a more meaningful and structured way for Mark on a daily basis. Mark at this time had two named nurses allocated to his care and they also agreed that the work could and should move forward with support from two consistent co-workers. As previously mentioned the use of consistent co-workers was very important in terms of Mark developing a trusting relationship with all three of us. This was preferable to being introduced to a new intervention on an ad-hoc basis by different staff facilitating it in perhaps very different ways despite detailed guidelines/risk assessments being in place.

Questions also arose around assessing whether Mark would be interested in musical instruments and, once the work was established, could, and should, this be included within a weekly activity programme? Mark already enjoyed watching DVDs but this didn't support an increase in his tolerance of others and so we wondered how this could be developed. Were CDs the next music-based activity to be introduced and how could this involve staff? This became another area for which I was asked to advise upon during this initial phase. My guidance on this was to suggest that Mark be given a choice of two CDs or DVDs through the window of his locked door. He would be encouraged to point, whether that be through him tapping the window or eye pointing, to offer some choice and the opportunity for him to be in charge of his next activity. Chosen staff members would follow guidelines and risk-assess entering the flat to change the CD or DVD according to Mark's choice. A recording sheet was left for staff to make comments and this appeared to work well. It was evident that Mark appeared to appreciate the opportunity to choose a CD or DVD himself as he clearly engaged with his own choice for longer periods of time than previously when staff had been making the choice for him.

As Mark became familiar with this activity and was engaging well, we decided (myself, the activity coordinator and nurse psychological practitioner with agreement from the core team) to try entering the room with two CDs or DVDs. In line with an updated risk assessment, Mark would have to be sitting at the table at the back of the room, the three of us would approach him and I would offer him two choices at the table. Once Mark had made his choice, we would all withdraw and leave the room. We then stayed and observed Mark's reaction to the CD/DVD chosen and recorded the length of time he engaged. Again it was evident that he continued to enjoy the opportunity to make the choice for himself and would engage with that choice for increasing periods of time.

As the weeks progressed, I decided to include some relaxation CDs into the choice making as Mark was previously only offered pop music, and being a musician I felt he should be given exposure to other genres. I used *Music for Relaxation* by Chapman, Miles and Rhodes (1994) to which Mark appeared accepting as he often chose to listen to this rather than the usual pop music, perhaps for its calming effect.

Another meeting was arranged between the three of us where we talked about the introduction of musical instruments through some direct music therapy work with Mark. We were all positive about this and shared it with the wider core team and then the multi-disciplinary team. Everyone agreed with the activity in principle but required it to be fully risk-assessed beforehand and guidelines written, shared and agreed.

This was done and direct music therapy sessions (phase two) began with Mark in July 2010. The aims for this period of direct music therapy were as follows:

- to increase activity and tolerance of social contact

- to interrupt patterns of isolation

- to facilitate communication

- to decrease challenging behaviours

- to offer an outlet for self-expression.

Following the existing guidelines and risk assessment for entering the flat, Mark was encouraged to sit at his table. The DVD was switched off and Mark would be informed it was time for music therapy. As lead for these sessions, I sang a 'Hello' song to Mark including both the activity coordinator and psychological nurse practitioner within this. I put on some background music that was of a calming and relaxing genre, and offered Mark the large jingling ball. This was a large, see-through ball with bells inside. Bearing in mind we were some distance away from Mark during these initial sessions, the ball had to be rolled towards him. He was encouraged to get up from the table and engage with the ball and pass it back to one of us. To be able to fully feed back to the core team how well these sessions were progressing, it was important to note Mark's motivation to engage with the medium, how long he tolerated us in the room, how many times he would engage with a music-based activity and how the therapeutic relationship was developing. It was evident that Mark was able to tolerate us in the room for increasing periods of time and this is shown as a graph later in this chapter. He was clearly able to indicate if he didn't want to continue and this would be through him either leaving the room and walking into the bathroom at the back of his flat or picking up the ball and appropriately walking towards us with it. During each session Mark responded to his own name through eye contact during the 'Hello' song and demonstrated an awareness of us all in the room as well as an interest in the activity.

Although Mark enjoyed exploring the jingling ball by rolling it in his hands, he seemed unable to roll it back to us, preferring to walk forward and pass it back. We decided after a few sessions to demonstrate our expectation for the activity between the three of us. He appeared to enjoy watching us play together, so after a few rolls of the ball we passed it back to Mark. Again he didn't roll it back but instead passed it to the psychological nurse practitioner, pushing her gently towards the door with the ball as he did this. This was Mark's way of ending the session.

It is important to note here that this did not in any way feel threatening. We all felt the consistent approach and using the same staff was key to the success of this initial introduction to music therapy. Mark was beginning to trust us and was engaging well with the medium. These sessions offered Mark a distant, interactive, yet directive approach.

As we were nearing the end of this second phase of the work, I introduced Mark to a set of boomwhackers. Once again these sessions were facilitated by the three of us adhering to the original guidelines and risk assessment for entering the flat, although now we would be moving towards him and standing at the other side of his table. Mark was encouraged to sit at his table and, when seated, the three of us entered the room. The same 'Hello' song was used and then I demonstrated how the boomwhackers worked by tapping them on the edge of the table, encouraging the activity coordinator and psychological nurse practitioner to join me. Mark appeared interested in these instruments so we offered him two of different lengths. He was able to take turns within our group and smiled, looking at us as he played. Mark was clearly enjoying himself.

At the beginning of phase three (July 2010 to December 2010) it is important to note that whilst Mark was engaging well with music therapy and the instruments, he was still only tolerating this engagement for short periods of time. We wondered if he was just getting bored of the activity and if more music-based opportunities should be made available or whether he still had limited tolerance of others within his space. We also didn't want him to get too comfortable in his ability to disengage when he wanted to, preferring to try to push this a little further (in the safest way) by offering something else to try.

I thought about the use of a floor drum placed halfway between us and Mark's table to increase turn-taking and social engagement. My feeling was that perhaps in time this might even turn into a further opportunity to engage in some shared playing and offer an emotional outlet for Mark. I offered Mark a rhythm on the drum, stepped back and invited him to respond. As with the jingling ball, Mark spent time exploring the drum. He rubbed his hands flat on the skin before lifting it up off the floor and putting it back down. Following my next rhythmic offering Mark picked up the drum, but when he put it down the second time, he tapped the skin with his fingers. He then picked it up again and passed it to the psychological nurse practitioner, indicating the end of that activity. We were, however, able to move on to sharing the boomwhackers with Mark at his table. Mark engaged for a few minutes before gathering all the boomwhackers from each of us together and then passing them back to us. Mark was certainly becoming more able to confidently and appropriately end our shared playing.

As Mark became more confident with the format of music therapy sessions, he introduced a new way of playing the floor drum by using the boomwhackers as beaters. This appeared to amuse him but at the same time was very telling of his ability to engage, be direct and make informed, appropriate and safe choices as well as allowing our presence to gradually increase in time within the flat.

Following further discussions with the core team and wider multi-disciplinary team, phase four (September 2011–January 2012) began with me taking the ukulele into sessions which would continue to increase his exposure to a variety of musical instruments. It had been reported that Mark liked the nursery rhyme 'Old MacDonald' so we used this to offer a potential outlet for increased vocalisations and choice-making. Mark appeared most interested in the ukulele and didn't seem to like my singing, putting his hands over his ears. He did, however, engage with the pictures of farm animals with support. On a few occasions he gestured towards the ukulele and smiled as I handed this to him. He was able to hold it appropriately and strum the strings.

Introducing other members of staff to support music therapy sessions with Mark was the next stage of this final phase of the work. Following the lengthy period prior to 2012, which required the intervention to be offered to Mark slowly and consistently using repeated music-based activities, it was time to introduce other members of the core team into sessions. The multi-disciplinary team met and felt that Mark was tolerating the intervention well and agreed that he was ready. He was displaying less challenging behaviours and allowing staff to work with him in close proximity more openly. Therefore, the intervention would be introduced to other members of staff whom he knew but who hadn't engaged in such an activity with him before. It was also felt that, as with any service, new staff would be employed so the idea of introducing new staff to Mark at this point was, in everyone's opinion, the right thing to do. This would also allow for these activities (particularly the boomwhackers) to be introduced at other times during the week as an extension of the intervention, as well as to continue to work towards the aims set in discussions with the wider multi-disciplinary team.

In terms of supporting Mark's biopsychosocial formulation, and with everyone working as part of a team, these sessions would continue to maintain his strengths which included his positive response to a structured and predictable routine. This empowered him by offering choice and showed his positive response to a directive approach with clear instructions, and his positive response to others encouraging and engaging with his playfulness.

At the point when I was able to step back from sessions Mark was sometimes tolerating up to six members of staff around his table playing with the boomwhackers. Mark did not appear to mind that I was no longer a part of the sessions, clearly enjoying an opportunity to engage and socialise with others in a positive and meaningful way through a shared activity.

Having encouraged and increased Mark's social engagement using this gradual and phased music therapy approach, Mark was also tolerating new activities with other staff including play sessions facilitated by the activity coordinator, who was now enrolled on a play therapy training course. Mark was slowly increasing his ability to engage for longer periods, interrupting the once prolonged periods of self-isolation. He was communicating and expressing his needs appropriately and requesting staff engagement himself by banging on the door or ringing his doorbell.

This engagement has continued to increase to the point where he is no longer locked in but walks freely around the ward with staff, goes off the ward for walks within the hospital grounds, engages with others in activities that are not ward-based and now goes for rides out with his parents in their camper van. A future placement has been identified and it is hoped that Mark will move closer to his family.

Outcomes

As previously stated, it was important to record events during each phase of the intervention and for this purpose I chose three observable elements taken from our Creative Arts Therapies Rating Scale (CAT-SRS) originally formulated by Dr Simon Hackett in 2008. 'The CAT-SRS is based upon goal attainment scales (Hart 1978; Kiresuk and Sherman 1968) which have a long history of use in mental health services to assess a patient's individual goals and whether they have been achieved' (Wadsworth and Hackett 2014, p.64). It was developed further in practice in the service by the arts therapies team and is used with both individuals and groups. It provides a range of 11 descriptors of which any number can be chosen based upon the aims of therapy.

Each of these observable elements has five descriptors and the three chosen aligned closely with Mark's presentation during each session. My ratings were recorded in a table throughout phases two to four of the intervention.

Engagement with Medium					
0	1	2	3	4	5
Not observed/ applicable	No music made	Required encouragement and prompting to attempt music making	Mixed/ ambivalent response to music making	Positive response to music making	Actively focused on music making

Participation					
0	1	2	3	4	5
Not observed/ applicable	Did not participate, even when prompted/ encouraged	Participated in session with prompting/ encouragement	Participated satisfactorily	Motivated attempt to participate	Active participation

Engagement in Therapeutic Relationship					
0	1	2	3	4	5
Not observed/ applicable	Resistant	Reluctantly engaged	Genuine, but guarded	Open	Open and trusting

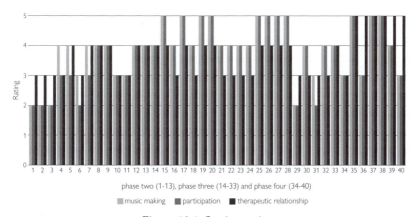

phase two (1-13), phase three (14-33) and phase four (34-40)

■ music making   ■ participation   ■ therapeutic relationship

Figure 10.1: Session ratings

The graph in Figure 10.1 shows my ratings at the end of each session for phases two to four of the work completed with Mark. The ratings suggest an increased confidence in the therapeutic relationship which was observed on a number of occasions through his playful gesturing and sustained eye contact within sessions. Mark demonstrated an interest in the music making and this appeared to support him to make increased appropriate contact with others.

Mark's increased engagement was also shown through the length of time he would tolerate the three of us not just facilitating a session but also being in the room with him. This is shown in the next graph, Figure 10.2. The phases can be split into session numbers as outlined in the previous graph.

During each phase there are dips to Mark's engagement and these appeared to correlate with staff absence or when Mark himself was physically unwell. During discussions with both the activity coordinator and nurse psychological practitioner we wondered if perhaps this demonstrated that Mark was beginning to build positive relationships with key staff members.

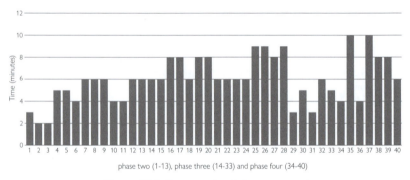

phase two (1-13), phase three (14-33) and phase four (34-40)

Figure 10.2: Increased social engagement

Conclusion

One of the important elements to this work was making sure that all staff were aware of what was going on during each phase. Regular feedback was given which supported the success of the intervention being handed over to staff in order for Mark to access it at other times and more regularly throughout his week. Staff would tend to offer Mark the boomwhackers, as they felt most confident with these instruments, but had also witnessed Mark's enjoyment of them on numerous occasions. They commented on how playful and interactive he was with them. In my opinion, so long as the agreed plan and recommendations were being adhered to, I felt it was acceptable for them to mainly offer boomwhackers and not explore other instruments at this stage, as it was most important that both staff and Mark felt comfortable.

When the initial goals of the work had been attained, the period of my direct involvement ceased. The work was continued by the activity coordinator alongside members of Mark's core team and the report showed the following outcomes had been achieved in working in this way with him:

1. The work, alongside other therapeutic interventions, decreased Mark's periods of isolation. It is now included in his daily routine.

2. The work developed Mark's social skills in terms of tolerance of others in his personal space. This can be seen as the work moved from taking place at the door to inside the room and then to the table.

3. Periods of sustained eye contact increased.

4. The work ran as planned, and was sustainable due to the partnership between myself, the activity coordinator and the nurse psychological practitioner.

5. When the work began, there was no therapy input, but now Mark has a weekly programme of therapeutic work including a dance movement therapist working with him.

6. I am happy to provide ongoing advice and will ensure I am kept informed of Mark's treatment through multi-disciplinary team discussions. Further input from myself and the dance movement therapist will be reviewed, as the dance movement therapist is now able to offer an assessment.

This was a very interesting piece of work but one that required careful thought, planning, implementation and collaborative working with all those involved in Mark's care. The key to the success of this intervention was the team approach. This included regular updates to the wider multi-disciplinary team, meeting with the core team and constantly sharing observations with both the activity coordinator and nurse psychological practitioner following each facilitated session. Sharing our successes with Mark in our small delivery team as the work progressed felt very empowering in terms of not just being one lone voice speaking out. It felt like a very supportive way of working too, particularly when at times feelings of hopelessness began to creep in. Mark clearly benefitted from this collaborative approach. It was certainly a new way of working for me, and one that I have continued to use in my practice whenever the situation showed it was appropriate.

References

Chapman, P., Miles, A. and Rhodes, S. (1994) *Music for Relaxation*. Suffolk: New World Company.

Compton Dickinson, S. and Hakvoort, L. (2017) *The Clinician's Guide to Forensic Music Therapy: Treatment Manuals for Group Cognitive Analytic Music Therapy (G-CAMT) and Music Therapy Anger Management (MTAM)*. London: Jessica Kingsley Publishers.

Kiresuk, T. and Sherman, R. (1968) 'Goal attainment scaling: A general method of evaluating comprehensive mental health programmes.' *Community Mental Health Journal 4*, 6, 443–453.

Lawday, R. and Compton-Dickinson, S. (2013) 'Integrating Models for Integrated Care Pathways: Introducing Group Cognitive Analytic Music Therapy (G-CAMT) to a Women's Enhanced Medium Secure Setting (WEMSS).' In S. Compton Dickinson, H. Odell-Miller and J. Adlam (eds) *Forensic Music Therapy: A Treatment for Men and Women in Secure Hospital Settings*. London: Jessica Kingsley Publishers.

Mayer-Johnson (2018) *Boardmaker software – symbol based software*. Sheffield: Tobii Dynavox UK. Accessed on 21 June 2018 at http://uk.mayer-johnson.com/products/boardmaker.

National Autistic Society (2017) *TEACCH*. London: The National Autistic Society. Accessed on 21 June 2018 at www.autism.org.uk/about/strategies/teacch.aspx.

Nind, M. and Hewett, D. (2001) *A Practical Guide to Intensive Interaction*. Kidderminster: British Institute of Learning Disabilities.

Oldfield, A. (2006) *Interactive Music Therapy: A Positive Approach*. London: Jessica Kingsley Publishers.

Statewide Behaviour Intervention Service (2017) *Clinical Formulation Practice guide: a collaborative approach*. Parramata, Australia: Clinical Innovation and Governance, Ageing, Disability and Home Care, Department of Family and Community Services. Accessed on 21 June 2018 at www.adhc.nsw.gov.au/__data/assets/file/0010/419914/Clinical-Formulation-Practice-Guide-A-collaborative-approach.pdf

Wadsworth, J. and Hackett, S. (2014) 'Dance movement psychotherapy with an adult with autistic spectrum disorder: An observational single case study.' *Body, Movement and Dance in Psychotherapy: An International Journal for Theory, Research and Practice 9*, 2, 59–73.

Wigram, T. (2002) 'Indications in music therapy: Evidence from assessment that can identify the expectations of music therapy as a treatment for autism spectrum disorder; meeting the challenge of evidence based practice.' *British Journal of Music Therapy 16*, 1, 11–28.

PART 3

MUSIC THERAPY APPROACHES CONNECTED WITH AUTISTIC IDENTITY AND CULTURE

CHAPTER 11

Voice and the Autistic Self: An Exploration into How Non-Verbal Voicework in Music Therapy Can Support Intersubjective Relatedness

TINA WARNOCK

Introduction

In this chapter I will be focusing on how use of the non-verbal voice in music therapy can support authentic connection with the self for people with an autistic spectrum condition. Drawing together theories from Stern, Austin and Alvarez, I will be considering how the voice is integral to how we form relationships from birth and how its development relates to our perceptions of self and other.

Having explored in some depth the connection between the voice and the self in previous publications (Warnock 2011, 2012), I will be further developing my model 'Voice and the Self' (Warnock 2011) to incorporate the difficulties that a person with autism may have in relation to vocal communication, developing a sense of self and experiencing relationships. I will look at the trajectory of the voice from a developmental perspective and link this with autistic children's capacity to perceive the emotional experiences of others and share those experiences, otherwise termed implicit relational knowing and affective intersubjectivity (Stern 1985). I will give closest consideration to Stern's theories of intersubjective relatedness – particularly focusing on the sense of the emergent self – and dynamic forms of vitality, which relate most closely to the foundations of our non-verbal vocal experience (Stern 1985, 2010). While the voice has been acknowledged as an important part of the musical relationship in the literature addressing music therapy and autism (Alvin and Warwick 1991; Pavlicevic 1997; Trevarthen *et al.*

1996; Wigram and Cochavit 2009), a deeper focus on the applied use of the non-verbal voice seems to be lacking (Warnock 2012).

I am bringing forward the idea that in music therapy 'the act of vocalising can facilitate self-awareness on its own without the need for verbal interpretation' (Warnock 2011, p.46). This is supported by Stern's description of 'language as a "double edged sword", because as well as dramatically increasing our potential for thought and "being with" another, it also makes some parts of our experience less shareable' (Stern 1985, p.162) and Winnicott's emphasis on 'empathy and attunement rather than interpretation and insight as curative factors in successful treatment' (Holmes 1995, p.12). In his later writing Stern poses the question, 'why was the word, the symbolic, given such a remarkably elevated and protected status?' (Stern 2010, p.119).

Many of the autistic children I have worked with have presented with vocalisations, whether verbal or non-verbal, in which the affect behind the voice has been absent, mismatched or hard to grasp, and I have had to consider carefully how to respond. How much should I use my voice? Does my voice carry authenticity, and does it feel welcome in the room? Should I vocalise only in response to the child's voice, or should I perhaps model uses of my voice so that they feel more inclined to explore their own? In the section 'The music therapist's voice and approach' I will be considering these and other questions with reference to Austin's theories on the voice and the self (Austin 2008). Two case studies (supported by video extracts) will demonstrate how my approach is put into practice. Both these cases involve children diagnosed with autism, severe learning disabilities and other complex needs, whom I have had the privilege to work with for several years in a special school setting. With this client group there seems to be less to grasp in terms of unconscious processes and the work is more about 'the basic processes and structures of interpersonal exchange…forms of dynamic flow' (Stern 2010, p110).

My interest in the non-verbal voice is the result of my own relationship with my voice as well as my own experience in clinical practice. Having come to singing in my late teens, my focus in the beginning was on how others perceived my voice from an external point of view rather than allowing myself to listen from within. This was reflective of myself at the time, and the difficulty I had giving attention to my inner responses, feelings and opinions. However, there was something very intriguing and alluring about singing with others, so I persevered and began writing and performing songs within friendships which evolved to reflect the interpersonal connections we felt within the music. When I later decided to train my voice, the daily vocal exercises drew my focus inwards and I began to notice an increased sense of wellness and emotional integration; my voice was becoming stronger in volume, fuller and richer in tone and my breath deeper and more controlled. In parallel I felt a stronger connection with my identity and a greater confidence to make decisions and pursue personal goals. I also felt more secure with my interpersonal relationships and an ability to challenge and question without fear of falling apart. Allowing myself to listen without judgment was the key to these changes; hearing my non-verbal voice and how it varied in tone and timbre from day to day according to my emotional state allowed me to become more attuned to my feelings which I grew to accept and respect. This personal journey as a singer and songwriter, combined with my BA in Social Psychology and work as a teaching assistant in a special school, solidified my determination to train as a music therapist.

Over the past 18 years of professional practice, my work has included seven years for the NHS (Child and Adolescent Mental Health Service and Child Development Centre) and 14 years in a school for children and young people with severe learning disabilities, autism and complex needs. In each of these settings, the majority of referrals have notably been linked with an autistic spectrum condition which is severely impacting on the individual's capacity to build or sustain healthy relationships with others. My work has been short-, medium- and long-term, the shortest being six weeks and the longest 12 years, with individuals, groups and parent/child dyads. The intellectual capacity of the children and young people and their use of language has varied enormously; some TEACCH non-verbal at the developmental stage of an infant, others non-verbal but with a higher level of receptive language skills. Others have had a good grasp of the definition and pronunciation of words but difficulty understanding the non-verbal context around them or how to express personal experiences. Some have been verbal but emotionally 'cut off' with limited awareness of what it means to be in a relationship, and others emotionally aware but frustrated at their own inability to understand the social context. Despite all this variety, the question that has been very present in all this work is: how can I support and enable these children to build meaningful and positive connections with themselves and others?

The model: voice and the autistic self

In my model 'Voice and the Self' presented in the *British Journal for Music Therapy* (Warnock 2011) I explored the links between the voice, the self and the mother–infant (therapeutic) relationship. Here I will be extending and adapting the model in response to theories about the autistic experience and further observations from my clinical practice.

One fundamental issue that seems to be central to the experience of people with autism is that differences in brain development affect the integration of senses, and the ability for key systems to talk to each other (Berger 2002; Hannaford 2005; Lawson 2011; Trevarthen *et al.* 1996). The autistic brain has a tendency to focus on one sense at a time (Lawson 2011) and this poses many obstacles to forming relationships due to the need for amodal perception (Stern 2010). My model recognises this significant relationship between sensory processing difficulties and an individual's capacity to develop a sense of self and other (Lane *et al.* 2010; Berger 2002) by placing it in a symbolically central position.

With the physical experience being so essential to the foundations of communication and emotional regulation (Hannaford 2005; Trevarthen *et al.* 1996), a focus on the voice feels particularly relevant as it is 'intimately connected to one's breath, body, the feelings and sensations within and one's overall sense of identity' (Austin 2008, p.125). Our voices respond directly to our physical and emotional states and work on the voice can therefore have a direct impact on the self (Austin 2008; Warnock 2011).

Vocal communication: a developmental approach

Austin writes, 'our contact with the outside world is largely a function of our voices, whether we are sighing, groaning, yawning, laughing, crying, shouting, speaking or singing' (2008 p.23). But how does the voice become this sophisticated tool for communication that we take so much for granted? The process is complex and nuanced and requires the formation of complex neural pathways (Hannaford 2005; Norton 2016; Stern 2010). I will now describe the trajectory of the voice as it evolves from birth.

Basic calls/cries

Vocalisations and calls were used to communicate intention and emotion, and to warn of danger in early human communities long before the development of language (Berger 2002; Norton 2016). The six basic human calls and their variations continue to exist today in all human cultures: laughing, sobbing, screaming, groaning, sighing, crying with pain. Although they come in many forms and are rich in meaning, human calls are a lot less diverse than the range of calls in other animal species, perhaps due to the development of language in humans, which circumvented the need for more calls – this is where cognition began to dominate instinctive communication (Berger 2002).

All babies are born with an innate predisposition to use these calls, produced in response to needs identified by our central nervous system which are key to survival such as hunger, tiredness, fear, pain (Berger 2002; Stern 2010). All people, regardless of illness or ability, are capable of using their voices in this way unless there is some physical damage to the vocal apparatus (Berger 2002; Norton 2016).

The inflected/prosaic voice

As well as making these basic vocal sounds, babies also hear other voices around them, starting with their mother's voice in the womb (De Casper and Fifer 1980). Provided their hearing is intact, they begin to internalise what has been called the dynamic form, present in all human activity from birth (Pavlicevic 1997; Stern 2010). Stern describes the dynamic forms of vitality as the five key qualities of movement, time, force, space and intention. For example, 'the force, speed and flow of a vocalisation or gesture, the shift and flight of a gaze, the way one breaks into or out of a smile' (Stern 2010, p.6).

Vocalisations, like all forms of expression, involve movement in the body and the dynamic forms within vocal expressions such as tone, timbre, rhythm and form carry much emotional weight on a sophisticated and often unconscious level (Austin 2008; Berger 2002; Stern 1985). The quality of the flow of air, the muscles that control it, the force the sound is expelled with, the intention behind it and space within it are all part of the dynamic form and can be described with words such as fluttering, gliding, disappearing (Stern 2010). When these actions become organised and internalised, babies begin to experiment with their own voices in the form of babbling and the prosaic voice begins to form (Berger 2002; Pavlicevic 1997). This is when we learn to push and pull our vocal mechanism to express a wider range of experiences and emotions – anticipation, excitement, surprise, joy, affection, hesitation, disappointment, sorrow, fear – all of which are detectable in the non-verbal voice independently of language and contribute to an individual's capacity for intimacy from a young age (Austin 2008; Stern 1985; Wigram and Cochavit 2009).

The development of our prosaic voice seems reliant on our perception of vitality form, ability to regulate and integrate the senses, and capacity to organise actions (Pavlicevic 1997; Stern 2010; Trevarthen *et al.* 1996). It is also dependent on our ability to discriminate between frequencies, timbre and phonetics in a voice (Berger 2002; Trevarthen *et al.* 1996). People with an autistic spectrum condition have been found to experience difficulties in auditory discrimination (Berger 2002) and perceiving the subtler forms of vitality in everyday actions (Di Cesare *et al.* 2017). The implications here are that children with autism have difficulty detecting the more subtle inflections of vocal communication which carry so much of the intention and meaning (Norton 2016; Stern 2010; Trevarthen *et al.* 1996), and they are therefore less able to internalise and use it in their own voice.

The melodic/singing voice

Healthy infants progress naturally towards using their voices in a more musical way, putting two or more notes together to form a melody (Wigram and Cochavit 2009). The brain is able to store heard melodies after a certain amount of repetition, sing them back and later create new ones (Berger 2002). Melodies and well-balanced songs can be used to engage the whole person and encourage a child to be open, communicative, and ready to engage (Wigram and Cochavit 2009). They can also encourage a child to attempt their first phonetic sounds which gradually increase in clarity and become recognisable words as the vocal mechanism develops (Oldfield 2006; Pavlicevic 1997).

Children with an autistic spectrum condition, as with all children beyond the age of six to eight months, seem to have the ability to anticipate and predict forthcoming notes in a melody. This can act as a natural motivator and has implications for the value of using improvised and precomposed songs with children with autism, to draw them into a relationship (Berger 2002; Lawson 2011; Trevarthen *et al.* 1996; Warnock 2012).

Symbolic/verbal voice

Verbal communication can take place only when there is sufficient communication between the brain and the vocal mechanism. As I have touched on throughout this section, deficits commonly associated with autism may cause significant interruptions in the development of vocal and hence verbal communication (Berger 2002; Pavlicevic 1997; Stern 2010). Children with an autistic spectrum condition commonly experience a discrepancy between receptive and expressive language, and this can cause a sense of frustration when attempting to share complex experiences verbally (Oldfield 2006). Those who are verbal may present with an exaggerated, over-animated or monotonous/rigid quality to their speech, unusually fast or slow with incongruent use of phrasing and dynamics. They may be echolalic, where they are able to produce the words physically but have no meaningful connection with the content and may not identify with their voice as coming from themselves (Berger 2002; Oldfield 2006; Trevarthen *et al.* 1996; Warnock 2012).

While language is generally seen as a positive skill necessary for complex relationships to form and learning to take place, it feels important to advocate the central message of this chapter that language is not needed for the sharing of affective states and the experiencing of the self; indeed, it can sometimes create a barrier to authentic connection (Austin 2008; Stern 1985; Warnock 2011). Stern emphasises that 'infants have too much to learn about the basic processes and structures of interpersonal exchange...the forms of dynamic flow that carry social behaviours...before language arrives to mess it all up' (Stern 2010, p.110). Figure 11.1 illustrates the trajectory of the voice and prevalent autistic features which may be present in people with an autistic spectrum condition.

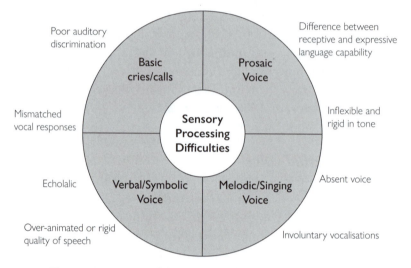

Figure 11.1: Voice and the autistic self – vocal communication

Developing a sense of self

The four senses of self, described by Stern in his theory of intersubjective relatedness, are not phases to be passed through but rather layers to be built upon, and the process depends on a shared framework of meaning which cannot be assumed in children with autistic spectrum conditions (Trevarthen *et al.* 1996; Stern 1985). The sense of an emergent self is the foundation layer, within which 'an overarching sense of self is not yet achieved...but it is coming into being' (Stern 1985, p.38), when affective and cognitive processes cannot be separated, and experience of life is predominantly through the senses (Stern 1985). The fluctuating affects and physical tensions driven by our basic needs (such as breathing, hunger, sleep, elimination) bring a wealth of opportunities for social interaction, and these contribute to the infant's ability to organise their sensory experiences. Internal representations of individuals need to be formed which can be recognised in all of the different senses so that cross-modal matching, otherwise termed amodal perception, can enable us to interact socially; this in combination with our perception of forms of vitality (Stern 1985, 2010).

It is beyond the remit of this chapter to describe dynamic forms of vitality in detail, but I will attempt to summarise the key elements below. It is important to bear in mind that this concept addresses *how* a movement takes place in terms of style, as opposed to *what* or *why* – it is 'separate and distinct from the domains of emotion, sensation and cognition. It stands on its own' (Stern 2010, p.149).

The forms of feeling that result from the vital processes of life are expressed in the continuous movement of the body and mind. The quality of these movements constantly informs how we 'evaluate people's emotions, states of mind, their authenticity, what they are likely to do next, their health and illness' (Stern 2010, p.3). Our natural predisposition to perceive how actions are performed, to store, recall and piece together this information into a whole representation of a person or a social interaction, allows us to build a picture of how relationships work in the unconscious before the arrival of symbolic language in the form of implicit relational knowing (Stern 1985).

However, if there is a constitutional deficit such as autism, this natural predisposition may be lacking; the senses are less integrated, perceptions more fragmented and the self may consequently feel under attack from outside and within, going into fight or flight mode (Alvarez 2012; Lawson 2011; Stern 2010).

The core, subjective and verbal layers rely so heavily on the emergent sense of self and perception of vitality forms that even if an individual with autism appears to be functioning at the more sophisticated levels, there may be essential elements missing from the foundations at the essential local level (Stern 2010; Trevarthen *et al.* 1996). The impact of those missing links affects a person's capacity for playful interaction, identified as fundamental to the development of the self (Schumacher 2014; Winnicott 1971). Alvarez writes about autistic individuals being undrawn or unintegrated where the internal objects are empty:

> The severely autistic, sensory being who is unable to form internal objects suffers from a deficit of the self; there is no mystery or sense of wonder about things and he expects nothing beyond the functional to emerge. For play to occur, the emphasis must

change from 'What does this object do?' to 'What can I do with this object?' and you need a concept of 'I' to achieve this sense of curiosity. (Alvarez 2012, p.152)

Figure 11.2 illustrates Stern's theory of the self and the related features of autistic spectrum condition, which affect its progression.

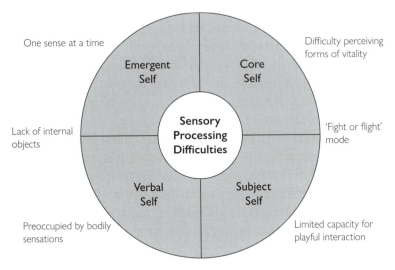

Figure 11.2: Voice and the autistic self – the sense of self

Experiencing relationships (caregiver–infant/therapeutic relationships)

Although there is a lot of common ground between developing a sense of self and experiencing relationships, I have kept them separate in this model to identify the distinct differences that the caregiver–infant therapeutic relationship and vocal development can have on the formation of the self. It is not my aim here to explain the theoretical foundations for healthy relationships but rather to highlight how autism can impact on this.

Aside from the physical presence of the caregiver, much of her emotional availability in the first few months is communicated through the musicality in her voice (Marwick and Murray 2009; Pavlicevic 1997). Through changes in intonation, volume and intensity she is able to communicate complex emotional expressions and responses which enable the infant to form the beginnings of implicit relational knowing (Stern 1985). The capacity in the caregiver to adjust her voice to the infant's developmental stage is reflected in the infant's vocal development and typically the vocal interplay evolves alongside the infant's cognitive capacity (Trevarthen *et al.* 1996).

However, this quality of care depends not only on the caregiver's ability to provide a holding environment (Winnicott 1971) but also on the infant's ability to perceive and receive it (Stern 1985; Winnicott 1971), and where there is an autistic spectrum condition, both sides of the relationship can be severely affected (Trevarthen *et al.* 1996). Alvarez describes the 'whole orchestra of instruments' involved in internalizing the mother's identity and existence – eye gaze, emotional engagement, attention and interest, bodily gestures, vocalisations – which are used expressively and communicatively by the infant within a nurturing relationship. (Alvarez 2012, p.165). An autistic infant may be so consumed by his bodily sensations that he cannot experience joint attention and therefore be drawn into a shared space (Alvarez 2012; Hannaford 2005). He may not recognise his caregiver's voice at birth, due to difficulties perceiving forms of vitality (Di Cesare *et al.* 2017) and the importance of amodal perception in recognising a familiar voice (Sidtis and Kreiman 2012). He may not turn towards her when she coos, preoccupied by another sense and not so able or inclined to filter and prioritise the voice over other curiosities (Berger 2002; Lawson 2011). He may feel so overwhelmed by the barrage of information landing on his senses, which he is unable to filter, that he cries much of the time (Trevarthen *et al.* 1996).

In response to this rather unexpected and unsatisfying behaviour in the infant, a carer may feel de-skilled with lowered expectations of what the relationship may bring (Trevarthen *et al.* 1996). She may feel a sense of loss when she cannot feel the reciprocal warmth and love that she had been anticipating on becoming a parent and consequently develop a sense of inadequacy or disappointment, accompanied by low mood (Alvarez and Reid 1999). As the caregiver's voice begins to reflect these emotional responses, changes will occur in the musicality of her voice and hence her ability to provide the nurturing vocal presence that the infant needs, and a cycle begins which can influence the carer and autistic infant's opportunities for affective intersubjectivity (Marwick and Murray 2009; Stern 1985).

Figure 11.3 represents the caregiver–infant relationship as secure or insecure and the potential obstacles to this relationship forming caused by autistic spectrum condition.

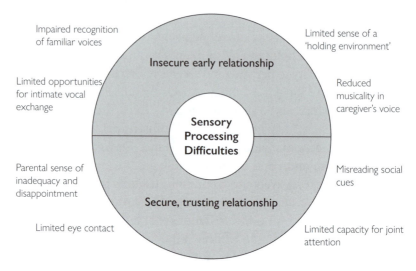

Figure 11.3: Voice and the autistic self – experiencing relationships

In this model I have attempted to define the essential elements which contribute to the development of the voice and the self and how they are affected by features commonly associated with autistic spectrum conditions. The four areas of vocal development can be compared with Stern's four senses of self, and in normal development the parallels are striking. In children with autism, it is possible for vocal communication to progress to the prosaic, melodic and even verbal stages before the individual has built a complete sense of an emergent self and a capacity to perceive vitality form. With this knowledge, music therapists can address difficulties with these earliest forms of intersubjective relatedness by working with the non-verbal voice in music therapy. While this is not the first time the vocal process has been linked with the development of the self (Austin 2008; Moses 1954), this model explores it in more depth within the context of an intimate relationship. The three figures can be overlapped to illustrate an individual's position at different stages in the therapeutic relationship and hence summarise changes in the process, as can be seen in Figures 11.4 and 11.5.

The music therapist's voice and approach

How a music therapist uses their voice in their work depends on their own vocal strength, flexibility and awareness of its potential as a therapeutic tool, as well as on their theoretical approach. The voice holds all the elements needed for affective intersubjectivity and the decisions are with the therapist as to how and when these elements can be used for clinical effect. As a means of attracting and holding attention which can so often be anywhere but in the relationship, or helping the child become unstuck from repetitive actions which form a barrier to communication, providing a holding environment within which he can express his distress and anxiety without becoming overwhelmed, the voice can be used to flexibly respond to an individual's needs (Alvarez 2012; Berger 2002; Stern 1985; Winnicott 1971).

My focus in this section will be on my work with the non-verbal voice with non-verbal children. However, I also use the non-verbal voice with verbal children for many of the reasons outlined above.

Referring to the vocal communication section in my model (Figure 11.1), the therapist needs to be informed about the stages in vocal development so that she can notice and respond to changes in prosody or new vocal sounds appropriately. Responding to changes in the flow and timbre of a melodic line (as well as the pitch) or the tiny inflections in the production of a vocal sound can signal a change in the relationship (see case study 'Jolie' in Warnock 2011).

Authenticity in the voice

Sinason (2017) emphasises the importance of authenticity and the need for a therapist's knowledge of psychological theory to sit behind her in the therapy room, not in front of her as a defence. Quoting a former patient at a recent conference, she said: 'when your theory is in front of you like a shield you are being defensive. It only works when it lives inside you.' As an extension of this, I suggest it is equally important for a music therapist's vocal technique to sit behind her authentic voice when singing so that her emotional openness and availability comes across to the client. Technical training which gives the music therapist control over the tone, timbre and flexibility in her range is certainly a useful tool and maximises the potential for vocal exploration with the client, but a voice which is stylised or technically perfect masks the identity of the singer and can project a sense of otherness, creating distance and perhaps even intimidating the client.

An awareness of qualities in her voice, such as fullness of tone, steadiness and length of breath or tightness in the throat, will inform the therapist of her own emotional state and allow authentic engagement with her feelings. She may ask herself whether her vocal timbre reflects how she feels inside at that moment; does her voice sound soft and relaxed when inside she feels irritated or anxious? Or does her voice have a hard edge to it when inside she feels open and compassionate? Has her voice become unusually animated when inside she feels flat and empty? If there is a mismatch, the inauthenticity within the therapist's voice may be detectable by the client consciously or unconsciously, and may hinder the therapeutic process. Alternatively, a sense of inauthenticity in the therapist's voice can also be a countertransference response to a client who is disconnected from their feelings (Austin 2008). A music therapist must learn to listen to her own voice as closely as she listens to her client's, detecting changes in timbre, tone and pitch which might inform her of her emotional state and countertransference responses (Austin 2008; Warnock 2011).

Austin writes about layers of listening, about how she gathers information when clients talk, move, play or are silent, their body language and other non-verbal communication. She listens to her thoughts and feelings in response to this information and to the physical sensations within her body, as well as to the musical or verbal content in their voices. Only then will she form a musical or verbal response. In close resemblance to Stern's writing on vitality form she describes *how* something was said as opposed to *what* or *why*; for example, 'she spoke in a barely audible voice and sped through her sentences as if someone was chasing her' (Austin 2008 p.23). Stern emphasises the importance of an awareness of vitality form in the therapy room alongside psychodynamic processes such as transference and countertransference: 'the therapist should stay with dynamic events such as movements in time, space and intentionality...pour themselves (empathically) as far as is possible and clinically useful into the lived-movement-evoked experience of the patient' (Stern 2010, p.138).

Clinically appropriate use of the voice

The amount that I use my voice in music therapy sessions changes case by case in response to the contribution it is making to the therapeutic relationship. Many children show an immediate interest in my voice and one or both of our voices are present from the outset (see case study 'Caleb'). Some show little interest in my voice – this may be due to a lack of general curiosity (Alvarez 2012) or difficulty distinguishing it from other sounds in the room (Lawson 2011) or recognising how it relates to their experience (Trevarthen *et al.* 1996). Others may retreat as soon as I sing 'Hello', perhaps signalling they cannot tolerate the sense of intimacy that it evokes. Interpreting the client's response is not always easy and this is why it is so important to be open to countertransference responses and the forms of vitality being expressed (Austin 2008; Stern 2010).

In the case of Carly below, it was some time before my voice felt meaningful to her; at first it felt as unimportant as the other objects in the room to which she paid no attention – perhaps because she expected nothing of interest to emerge (Alvarez 2012). The following case study will describe how both mine and Carly's voices manifested themselves alongside her emerging sense of self (Trevarthan *et al.* 1996) and became integral to the therapeutic process.

CASE STUDY: CARLY

Carly is 14 years old at the time of writing and was referred at the age of six by her grandmother who was hopeful that she would be able to use the non-verbal medium to build a therapeutic relationship. Carly has a diagnosis of autism and a severe learning disability with additional complex needs, was born at 25 weeks' gestation and has a non-specific hearing impairment. At the time of referral eight years ago Carly lived with her grandmother who had been diagnosed with terminal cancer and knew that she would not be able to care for her long-term.

In my paper 'Vocal Connections' (Warnock 2012), I explained 'it was [Carly's] voice that enabled me to feel the impact of her emotional experience' (p.89) and 'her non-verbal voice allowed her to experience a sense of identity and the opportunity to build on this through a creative process' (p.91). The connection between the voice and the body was identified as essential due to her strong sensory focus and experience of physical and emotional trauma in her early years. I would like to follow up this paper with some further insights about Carly, whom I saw intermittently for the first five years and more consistently for the past three years. I will use two videos to support the descriptions of our work together, the first from our early sessions and the second seven years later. Both extracts are available to downloaded from www.jkp.com/voucher using the code MTLIFESPAN. More detail about Carly's background can be found in the paper described above (Warnock 2012).

Figure 11.4a illustrates Carly's position in the first few weeks; our relationship was insecure, she vocalised only with basic cries and presented as being in the sense of the emergent self. Her sensory processing difficulties seem central to her experience.

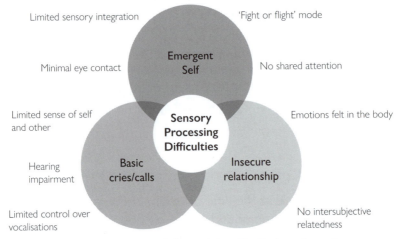

Figure 11.4a: Voice and the autistic self – Carly early sessions

In the video extract documenting an early session we can see Carly's awareness move from an isolated position where she is almost entirely preoccupied by the senses to one of being with (Winnicott 1971) and moving towards a sense of the core self (Stern 1985). At first, she spends her time crying, or pacing up and down with no apparent sense of awareness or attachment. At this point, my voice does not feel helpful to the relationship as Carly does not show any response to it during the 'Hello' song; I therefore use it minimally and only in response to her vocalisations. She begins to notice my body mirroring hers and seeks contact by reaching out to hold my hand, giving a sideways glance and a smile; for a few moments we are in a relationship with joint attention which feels full of vitality and shared affect. A few minutes later I am following Carly's pacing with a drum when she pauses and then lets out a cry in protest – a dynamic vocal communication which signals a new level of intersubjectivity in our relationship, confirming to me that she is aware and interested in my presence, even if she does not want it at that moment. From there I am able to use my voice to build connections cross-modally using the piano and we can see increasing levels of attachment and intimacy as Carly comes physically closer to me. She is able to experience alert inactivity (Stern 1985; Wolff 1966), moments of calm during which she can internalise external events such as me playing the piano in a way that attunes to her vocal sounds; her emotions are contained and she is able to perceive my reflections of her dynamic form, internalising my presence (Stern 1985). The extract closes with Carly sitting on my lap at the piano, gently vocalising with intention and control. Her emotional engagement is strong and she is beginning to play with the length and tone of her voice, taking turns with me and leaving pauses to allow space for my voice to be heard. The cooing and laughing at the end is a rare moment which reveals Carly's more flexible and integrated self, so often concealed by her autism. This feels like a healthy mother–infant interaction, with my voice taking on more animated qualities as she is more open to being nurtured (Trevarthen 1996).

Eight years later I am privileged to still be working with Carly. She is now in a stable and secure foster placement and is comfortable with her routines at school and at home. She is more settled in her body and less emotionally distressed although she still suffers from frequent ear infections which cause her pain and discomfort and can be a significant distraction to her participation in therapy sessions. She continues to seek constant sensory stimulation which she achieves through chewing paper or tapping her teeth. Both these actions result in vibrations through her skull and a require a repetitive muscle movement which seems to calm her down through the vestibular sense. In our sessions, she allows me to take her paper away if I quickly replace it with a resonant instrument which, together with my voice, draws her into a shared space, as shown in the video extract documenting one of Carly's later sessions.

This later extract shows a typical session with Carly at the age of 14. Our relationship is secure, and she has clear expectations of what the sessions will entail, sitting down to face me from the beginning. Initiating vocal communication is still very challenging for Carly; here I am able to use the resonance in my voice and the darbuka (small aluminium drum) together to catch and elicit her attention (Alvarez 2012) and hold her in a shared space where she gives meaningful eye contact, listens attentively and demonstrates a high level of emotional engagement. This leads to quiet but tuneful vocalisations TEACCH from Carly which feel authentic and connected to the self. I use long open vowel sounds to add a harmonic resonance to the instruments, changing the shape of my mouth to keep a sense of vitality and movement in the sound and thus maintain her focus. Carly's autism creates a constant push and pull between our relationship and her senses – her hearing impairment is an additional barrier – and the body of the drum acts as a useful amplifier for my voice.

Carly's complex needs and difficult start in life mean that her cognitive delay is severe and lasting. However, her self-concept has progressed from a position of complete isolation to one where she is able to form attachments and expectations of others. The work continues to feel alive and meaningful.

Figure 11.4b illustrates my current assessment which is that Carly now has a secure sense of a core self and, in her most healthy moments, moves towards a sense of the subjective self where she is able to share an affective state with another. Her sensory needs are still very present but less dominant than in the early sessions and she seems better able to regulate her emotional responses.

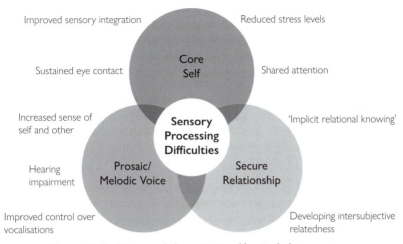

Improved sensory integration

Reduced stress levels

Sustained eye contact

Core
Self

Shared attention

Increased sense of
self and other

Sensory
Processing
Difficulties

'Implicit relational knowing'

Hearing
impairment

Prosaic/
Melodic Voice

Secure
Relationship

Improved control over
vocalisations

Developing intersubjective
relatedness

Figure 11.4b: Voice and the autistic self – Carly later sessions

Responding to autistic and non-autistic parts of the voice

Austin states that different parts of the voice represent different parts of the self, linking these to Jungian concepts such as the hopeful, the wounded and the critical selves. We can learn to use these in the therapeutic process (Austin 2008). With autistic children, we have the added consideration of the autistic self, and it is important that we learn to recognise which sounds are authentic and communicative, and those which are ritualistic and emotionally detached. Responding to the autistic parts of the voice can have the effect of transforming them into a shared and intersubjective experience (see case study 'Jolie' in Warnock 2011); it can also serve to reinforce the sense of disassociation and enhance the empty affect between therapist and child – in these cases, letting the autistic voice take a step back in our attention and waiting for an authentic sound or movement can be more productive (Warnock 2011).

The following case study describes my work with Caleb whose initial vocalisations were plentiful and inflected but with an affect that did not seem to match his other expressions of vitality. It shows how working with different parts of the non-verbal voice can facilitate authentic connection and improve potential for intersubjective relatedness (Austin 2008; Stern 1985).

CASE STUDY: CALEB

Caleb, a ten-year-old boy at the time of writing, was referred to me when he was five years old by his class teacher in a special school setting. The teacher was following up on a request for music therapy by his parents as he had previously responded very positively to music therapy at Great Ormond Street and within a hospice setting. Caleb's difficulties first became apparent at three or four weeks old when his parents noticed he was not responding to visual clues. By four months he had been diagnosed blind with hydrocephalus and osteoporosis and later that year had a bone marrow transplant. His diagnosis of autism came later when he was four years old.

In a recent meeting to support my contribution to this book, Caleb's parents described with emotion how he 'came to life' in his first music therapy session and was able to use music to interact with others. His mother explained how one or both of his parents, or a grandparent, had been with Caleb continuously in hospital and that music, both live and recorded, had had an integral presence in his life from the outset. Although he seemed to be emotionally detached for much of the time, it was music and song that brought his attention to the existence of others and enabled him to build relationships with his family members and carers.

My first sessions with Caleb at five years old took place shortly after he had been given a diagnosis of autism, which the parents had found helpful in understanding his continuous need for fixed routines, repetitive movements, and vocalisations, and his emotional isolation. At this point Caleb frequently vocalised to himself with open vowel sounds but interestingly his expressions felt empty of meaning. My interpretation was that he had been able to learn what to do with his voice by listening to others, but the vitality forms had been hard to grasp due to his blindness and autism. His mood was changeable, his voice transforming quickly from contented cooing and babbling to sudden crying and distress, the cause of which was hard to determine.

Figure 11.5a illustrates the early relationship with Caleb when he seemed to have a sense of a core self, able to briefly acknowledge my voice and musical presence but preoccupied by his senses, including the sound of his own voice in his body.

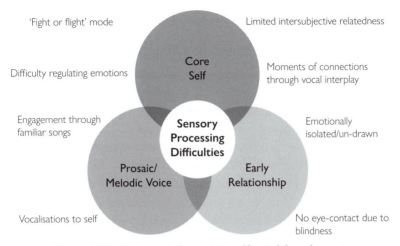

Figure 11.5a: Voice and the autistic self – Caleb early sessions

Caleb: a musical sense of self

A video extract following Caleb's music therapy sessions over a period of five years can be downloaded from www.jkp.com/voucher using the code MTLIFESPAN. It begins with him lying on his back on the floor and rocking his body from side to side. My approach is to merge my music and voice with his physical movements and vocal sounds, whether gentle and smooth or lively and rhythmic, joining and matching him as closely as possible until he notices my presence. Since Caleb cannot see me, my voice plays an essential role in providing a holding environment (Winnicott 1971). After a few weeks he begins to play with me by pausing his rolls or pushing more vigorously, seeming to delight in me as a separate person. He laughs out loud with an animated melodic chuckle, demonstrating his sense of humour, and there is a definite sense of playful interaction.

Three years later our musical relationship is well established, and we can see how Caleb is able to sit securely and use his body and voice to engage in playful interaction. He is listening attentively, noticing my vocal and musical responses and attuning his in return. Caleb is vocalising with intention, demonstrating a complex sense of rhythm and pitch, and using phrases with pauses which allows for turn-taking and a musical dialogue. This transitional space (Winnicott 1971) between us is allowing Caleb to extend his sense of self through our shared affective state and the pleasure he is getting from our vocal exchanges (Pavlicevic 1997; Stern 1985).

In the final part of the extract when he was nine years old, we can see Caleb acknowledging my presence as we settle down to begin with our 'Hello' song. He shows awareness of social norms as he greets me with a hand gesture and smile. He is able to make verbal requests and active choices based on past experience. He also shows a sense of anticipation and follows my musical lead when I respond to his request for the 'shaker shake'. Caleb's curiosity in the instruments, and motivation to discover what he can do with them, demonstrates a significant shift in the way he engages with his environment. He is amused by my whistling, which I use as an alternative to the voice when his attention wanes, and although he is still distracted by his autistic behaviours at times, this is short-lived during the sessions and he notices when my music stops, keen to reconnect. Towards the end of the session Caleb allows a moment of alert inactivity which enables him to internalise our musical dialogue and consequent affective intersubjectivity (Stern 2010). He then acknowledges the ending with another physical gesture and smile, demonstrating the sense of meaning and positive connection he experiences with me during our sessions.

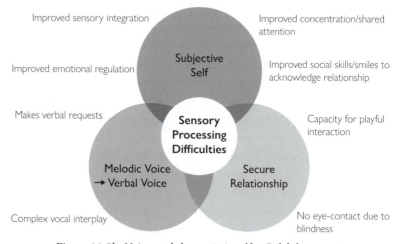

Figure 11.5b: Voice and the autistic self – Caleb later sessions

It is my opinion that the non-verbal vocal relationship I have with Caleb within the music therapy context has contributed significantly to his growing sense of self. By reflecting his forms of vitality through prosaic, melodic, rhythmic and timbral variations in my voice, I can support his capacity to receive and recognise them as his own expressions, enhancing his communication at the most local level and strengthening his foundation layer. This development has been strongly supported by the musical and vocal/verbal relationships he has or has had with other therapists, teachers, family members and carers. Now at the beginning of his verbal self, he is able to say simple sentences such as 'I want to play the egg shaker' and express some feelings verbally such as 'he's sad' in the third person. However, there is still an element of echolalia in his speech and he seems more authentically connected with his non-verbal voice.

Conclusion

This chapter has focused on the importance of non-verbal communication in the development of the self with specific reference to Stern's theories of intersubjective relatedness and forms of vitality. My model 'Voice and the Autistic Self' has offered a means of considering the interrelationship between the self, the voice and the caregiver–infant relationship in the context of the autistic experience. The therapist's relationship with their own voice, and the impact that it has on the therapeutic process, has been explored, drawing on Austin's methods within vocal psychotherapy (Austin 2008) alongside important considerations about voice work that a music therapist should hold in mind when they are working with children with autistic spectrum conditions.

These perspectives from developmental and psychoanalytic theory have been drawn together to support my view that non-verbal singing in music therapy can enable children with autistic spectrum disorders to build positive and meaningful connections with themselves and others. Due to its position within the body, the uniqueness of every individual's voice and the limitless subtle layers of expression that can be created by this most complex of instruments, the non-verbal voice is uniquely placed to enable people with autism to develop the capacity for intersubjective relatedness, even in the most isolated of cases.

References

Alvarez, A. and Reid, S. (1999) *Autism and Personality: Findings from the Tavistock Autism Workshop*. London: Routledge.

Alvarez, A. (2012) *The Thinking Heart*. London: Routledge.

Alvin, J. and Warwick, A. (1991) *Music Therapy for the Autistic Child*. New York, NY: Oxford University Press.

Austin, D. (2008) *The Theory and Practice of Vocal Psychotherapy*. London: Jessica Kingsley Publishers.

Berger, D. (2002) *Music Therapy, Sensory Integration and the Autistic Child*. London: Jessica Kingsley Publishers.

De Casper, A.J. and Fifer, W.P. (1980) 'Of human bonding: Newborns prefer their mother's voices.' *Science 208*, 4448, 1174–1176.

Di Cesare, G., Sparace, L., Pelosi, A., Mazzone, L. (2017) 'Differences in action style recognition in children with autistic spectrum disorders.' *Frontiers in Psychology 8*, 1456, 1–11.

Hannaford, C. (2005) *Smart Moves: Why Learning Is Not All in Your Head*. Salt Lake City, UT: Great River Books.

Hart, R.R. (1978) 'Therapeutic effectiveness of setting and monitoring goals.' *Journal of Consulting and Clinical Psychology 46*, 6, 1242–1245.

Holmes, J. (1995) *Introduction to Psychoanalysis: Contemporary Theory and Practice*. Florence, KY: Routledge.

Lane, A., Young, R., Baker, A. and Angley, M. (2010) 'Sensory processing subtypes in autism.' *Journal of Autism and Developmental Disorders 40*, 1, 112–122.

Lawson, W. (2011) *The Passionate Mind: How People with Autism Learn*. London: Jessica Kingsley Publishers.

Marwick, H. and Murray, L. (2009) 'The Effects of Maternal Deprivation on the "Musicality" of Infant-Directed Speech and Conversational Engagement.' In C. Trevarthan and S. Malloch (eds) *Communicative Musicality*. New York, NY: Oxford University Press.

Moses, P.J. (1954) *The Voice of Neurosis*. New York, NY: Grune & Stratton

Norton, K. (2016). *Singing and Wellbeing*. New York, NY: Routledge.

Oldfield, A. (2006). *Interactive Music Therapy – A Positive Approach*. London: Jessica Kingsley Publishers.

Pavlicevic, M. (1997) *Music Therapy in Context*. London: Jessica Kingsley Publishers.

Schumacher, K. (2014) 'Music Therapy for Pervasive Developmental Disorder, Especially Autism: A Case Study with a Theoretical Foundation and an Evaluation Tool.' In J. De Backer and J. Sutton (eds) *The Music in Music Therapy*. London: Jessica Kingsley Publishers.

Sidtis, D. and Kreiman, J. (2012) 'In the beginning was the familiar voice: Personally familiar voices in the evolutionary and contemporary biology of communication.' *Integrative Psychological and Behavioural Science 46*, 2, 146–159.

Sinason, V. (2017) 'My Most Remarkable Session.' Unpublished Paper, Confer Conference, 14 January 2017.

Stern, D. (1985) *The Interpersonal World of the Infant*. London: Routledge.

Stern, D. (2010). *Forms of Vitality. Exploring Dynamic Experience in Psychology, the Arts, Psychotherapy, and Development*. Oxford: Oxford University Press.

Trevarthen, C., Aitken, K., Papoudi, D. and Robarts, J. (1996) *Children with Autism*. London: Jessica Kingsley Publishers.

Warnock, T. (2011) 'Voice and the self in improvised music therapy.' *British Journal for Music Therapy 25*, 2, 32–47.

Warnock, T. (2012) 'Vocal connections: How voice work in music therapy helped a young girl with severe learning disabilities, autism and complex needs to engage in her learning.' *Approaches: Music Therapy and Special Music Education 4*, 2, 85–92

Wigram, T. and Cochavit, E. (2009) 'Therapeutic Dialogues in Music.' In S. Malloch and C. Trevarthen (eds) *Communicative Musicality*. New York, NY: Oxford University Press.

Winnicott, D. (1971) *Playing and Reality*. London: Tavistock Publications.

Wolff, P.H. (1966) *The Causes, Controls and Organization of Behaviour in the Neonate*. New York, NY: International Universities Press.

CHAPTER 12

Valuing Neurodiversity: A Humanistic, Non-Normative Model of Music Therapy Exploring Rogers' Person-Centred Approach with Young Adults with Autism Spectrum Conditions

Beth Pickard

Introduction

This chapter presents and reflects upon a non-normative approach to music therapy with two individuals who have autism spectrum conditions and profound learning disabilities over a period of six months, at a newly founded post-compulsory educational unit. The music therapy practice was informed by a person-centred approach (Rogers 1959, 2004; Cooper *et al.* 2013), a non-directive attitude (Raskin 1948, 2005; Levitt 2005), engagement with the techniques of pre-therapy (Prouty 2002b) and a belief in a non-normative, social model of disability (Oliver 1990, 2013; Barnes 2014). These concepts will be defined and explored further, before being applied to the clinical practice.

These perspectives are potentially under-represented in music therapy literature (Straus 2014; Gross 2018) and the broader autism discourse (Goodley 2016; Woods 2017) in contrast with other established, behaviourist interventions (Keenan *et al.* 2006; Kalyva 2011) or more directive music therapy practices (Pasiali 2004; Thaut and Hoemberg 2016). While it is recognised that such interventions may generate more measurable and generalisable outcomes, this chapter will consider whether framing the practice and its potential impact from an increasingly humanistic perspective can contribute to the social construction of disability (Rapley 2010), incorporating a narrative of both neurodiversity (Silberman 2015) and 'able identity' through music (Magee 2002, p.191).

Both young people were aged 16 at the time of the clinical work, and were attending the newly established setting, affiliated with a local special school. The setting's focus was on developing functional, vocational and social skills to encourage independence in the transition to adult life, primarily through a behaviourist-informed model, as well as exploring literacy and numeracy in applied contexts. This included developing simple culinary skills, exploring horticulture and campcraft, and developing familiarity and confidence on public transport. This focus on independence and social skills is prominent in the literature discussing the experiences of young people with autism spectrum conditions transitioning from education to adult life, and the numerous challenges they may face (Hume *et al.* 2014). While Wehmeyer 2015, p.21) advocates that promoting self-determination in young adults with and without disabilities is critical for successful school, post-school and transition-related outcomes, in summarising the experiences of young people with autism spectrum conditions transitioning to adulthood, Wehman *et al.* (2014, p.31) state that 'these findings indicate that in general individuals with [autism spectrum conditions] do not experience the autonomy or independence expected of youth transitioning to adulthood'.

It was hoped that the newly integrated music therapy intervention at the setting would complement the social and educational provision, providing an increasingly expressive outlet to the young people and a richer, interdisciplinary approach overall in their holistic progression to adulthood. The referral criterion for the centre is a primary diagnosis of autism spectrum conditions, and the referral to music therapy was often for the young people who communicated through non-verbal mediums and thus may have benefitted from accessing an expressive, creative intervention. The aforementioned focus in the literature on autonomy as a key indicator of successful transition to adult life (Hendricks and Wehman 2009; Wehmeyer 2015) was also an influence on the potential referral and trajectory of music therapy.

The first young person will be named Aleksander. He moved to the area from Poland several years ago, and had engaged with consistent support staff in his previous and current educational placements with whom he had an established, reciprocal relationship. Aleksander, full of energy and enthusiasm and very tall in stature, regularly jumped from his seat in perceived excitement and animation. He appeared to take enjoyment from several repetitive behaviours, including bouncing on the spot and waving his straightened fingers in front of his eyes. Aleksander could be affectionate and sensitive, developing his engagement with the therapeutic relationship significantly during the work. He also had a concurrent diagnosis of Beckwith-Wiedmann syndrome, and communicated through his body language, eye contact, gesture and behaviour.

The second young person will be named Martin. Martin had more recently joined the setting and didn't have the same established relationships or familiarity with the staff team. His transition to the setting had been more challenging and he still appeared unsettled, relying heavily on the iPad which appeared to operate as a transitional object (Winnicott 2005; Levigne 2015) or perhaps an autistic object (Tustin 1980) in its omnipresence. Martin communicated through touch, eye contact, body language and occasional sign or gesture, expressing his experience of initial music therapy sessions in his desire to physically leave the room. Martin enjoyed spending time lying down and appeared comforted at times by familiar nursery rhymes. He could be affectionate when he was in a calm mood, but when distressed his movements could become bolder, faster-paced and increasingly agitated.

The focus in this chapter on young adults with autism spectrum conditions who also have profound learning disabilities and communicate non-verbally represents an important demographic in terms of music therapy and autism spectrum conditions across the lifespan, as Howlin and Taylor (2015, p.771) describe the life experiences of adults with autism spectrum conditions as 'woefully under-researched', within and beyond music therapy. Despite the assertion that 'arguably it is the client group [autism spectrum conditions] with which music therapy has the highest reputation' (Dimitriadis and Smeijsters 2011, p.108), it appears that not all age groups or demographics of those who have autism spectrum conditions are equally represented in the literature. This was striking when searching for research to inform and develop the clinical work. The lack of literature around working with clients with autism spectrum conditions of this age and stage of development was equally limited from the perspective of the non-directive, person-centred approach (Peters 1999a, 1999b; Pörtner 2000).

As such, the work was informed by literature around music therapy and autism spectrum conditions exploring joint attention and joint engagement as precursors to social interaction (Kim, Wigram and Gold 2009; Vaiouli, Grimmet and Ruich 2015); the person-centred and non-directive approach beyond music therapy (Rogers 1985; Prouty 2005; Levitt 2005); person-centred care and person-centred planning (Department of Health 2007, 2009, 2010); and the transition from education to adult life for young people with autism spectrum conditions, also beyond music therapy (Henninger and Taylor 2014; Wehmeyer 2015; Welsh Assembly Government 2016).

Approach to the clinical work
Social model of disability

I approached this work with a belief in a social model of disability (Oliver 1990, 2013; Barnes 2014). This paradigm advocates an understanding that 'a person's disability can be located within their experience of social relations and the ways in which difference and diversity are accommodated and thought about within society' (Thomas 2013 cited in Conn 2016, p.11), and recognises a clear distinction between an impairment which may be physical or cognitive and a disability which can be perceived as socially constructed (Goodley 2011). This contrasts with a medicalised, deficit-based interpretation of disability, or autism, as Conn (2016, p.43) describes below:

> The Medical Model…puts forward the idea that autism is an impairment within the individual that results in a 'deficit of skill' and a 'failure' to develop in ways that reflect a normal developmental pathway. The focus of a medicalised view of autism is fully on the individual, who is seen as requiring the support of interventions in order to develop the skills they are lacking.

A social model interpretation of autism, often expressed in relation to the construct of neurodiversity (Kapp et al. 2013), is offered by

Silberman (2015, p.18), suggesting that in place of the individual developing what may be perceived as 'lacking' skills or deficiencies: 'the cure for the most disabling aspects of autism will never be found in a pill, but in supportive communities'. As Davis (1995, p.24 cited in Cooper 2013, p.136) asserts: '[T]he "problem" is not the person with disabilities; the problem is the way that normalcy is constructed to create the "problem" of the disabled person'.

In line with this ethos, I didn't endeavour to ameliorate perceived deficiencies or 'failures' in development or alleviate 'autistic' behaviours (Collins 2016), but rather to nurture personal, psychological growth through an approach that values neurodiversity as 'an equally valid pathway within human diversity' (Kapp *et al.* 2013, p.59). The ongoing transparency and sharing of the approach within the setting contributed to a systemic awareness of a social model interpretation of disability, and the potential for a social construction of disability to contribute to organisational and societal understanding. While acceptance of such perspectives may take a long time, an awareness of their potential may be a constructive starting point for a paradigm shift towards a non-normative model of engagement, interaction and therapy (Goodley 2016; Woods 2017).

Person-centred approach, pre-therapy and non-directive facilitation

Against the backdrop of this belief in the social model of disability, I held the necessary and sufficient conditions of Rogers' person-centred approach as core values of my non-directive clinical practice (Mearns and Thorne 2013). Rogers proposed that through the presence of the following definable and measurable conditions, growth would occur: psychological contact between therapist and client; incongruence of the client and congruence of the therapist; communication of empathic understanding and unconditional positive regard, from therapist to client (Rogers 1959, p.213).

In relating the necessary and sufficient conditions to the notion of working non-directively, Moon (2005, p.262) concisely asserts that 'the client-centred therapist, when busily engrossed in the task of empathically and non-judgmentally receiving the client, has no agenda other than the agenda of the client, and, as a consequence, is working non-directively.' In recognising that the first condition, psychological contact, can present challenges when working with clients with specific experiences, Prouty (1990) developed an approach entitled pre-therapy to facilitate and develop psychological contact and thus in turn enable psychological growth through the promotion of the necessary and sufficient conditions (Rogers 1957; Prouty 2005). Pre-therapy is typically explored when there is not deemed to be sufficient psychological contact between the client and therapist to initiate or maintain an empathic communication, or if the therapist lacks an empathic understanding of the client's frame of reference to engage with the necessary and sufficient conditions of the person-centred approach (Sommerbeck 2003). The framing of the empathic understanding as the therapist's responsibility feels important in light of a social model interpretation of autism, 'shifting the imbalanced burden of adapting away from autistic individuals' (Woods 2017, p.1094). This preparatory work towards engaging in person-centred, improvisational music therapy felt like a highly relevant framework to explore in relation to the specific needs and experiences of the young people at this setting.

While there is very little literature which uses Rogerian non-directive terminology in discussing music therapy practice, these sentiments felt representative of the music therapist's approach in the way music and the therapeutic relationship was explored to engage with the young people. It is proposed that there is potential for a close alignment between Rogers' person-centred approach, Prouty's pre-therapy and the social model of disability, in that Rogers was 'dismissive of psychological diagnosis of clients' and '[was] concerned to remove obstacles to the organismic valuing process' to enable 'constructive personality change' (Merry 2002, p.51), therefore focusing on the individual's potential and not their diagnosis.

These sentiments reinforce Oliver and Barnes' (2012) views that disability resides within barriers to opportunities and experiences posed by society rather than deficiencies within the individual, and that by removing these obstacles, we can enable meaningful participation in society. Both theoretical perspectives, as well as the therapist's orientation, firmly advocate an inclusive response to neurodiversity as well as maintaining a belief in the individual's innate potential. In integrating these theoretical perspectives, the clinical aims didn't intend to '[change] a problematic or unwanted behaviour...which should be improved or stopped by the end of the intervention' (Kalyva 2011, p.2), but rather to enable and empower growth in the young people, from a non-normative perspective (Straus 2014; Goodley 2016), which celebrates neurodiversity and inclusion: 'clear[ing] a fertile space where the client is trusted to thrive according to his nature, values and choices' (Moon 2005, p.262).

Moon (2005, p.261) continues to position Rogers' approaches in relation to ontology and epistemology in a way that aligns with the aforementioned paradigm shift away from a deficit-based, medical model interpretation of autism spectrum conditions:

> The trajectory of Rogers' theory is phenomenological in nature and forces client-centred therapy and the person-centred approach out of an objectivist, positivist Medical Model, and into a philosophical paradigm. (Rogers 1946; Rogers 1951, p.532; Rogers 1959, p.251)

Grant's (1990, p.83) sentiment on Raskin's (1948) perspective on the non-directive attitude, as 'being humbled before the mystery of others and wishing only to acknowledge and respect them...an almost aesthetic appreciation of the uniqueness and otherness of the client', eloquently resonates with this person-centred, social model ethos, and exemplifies Goodley's (2016) reference to celebrating neurological diversity and both recognising and valuing embodied difference. A further focus of this chapter will be to celebrate the potential of a non-verbal intervention, which moves away from a hierarchical view of verbal communication being more valid or accepted than other mediums of expression (Goodley 2016).

The clinical work

At the outset of the clinical work a four-week assessment period was allocated, dedicated to establishing a therapeutic relationship and enabling clinical aims to emerge with the necessary and sufficient conditions of the person-centred approach in mind. An initial challenge to the music therapist was to reliably determine to what extent the first necessary and sufficient condition, psychological contact, was possible. It is recognised that this challenge may be, in part, due to the music therapist's lack of familiarity with the young people's communicative methods, and thus time was taken to get to know and understand these valid, expressive behaviours. As Hodge (2013, p.114) suggests, 'the client is a guide into a different way of being that the [therapist] may not yet be able to imagine'.

This suggestion, that the communicative inadequacy was that of the therapist, challenges Prouty's medical-model assertion that it is the client who is 'contact impaired' and needs to move towards the therapist's way of communicating (Prouty 2002a, 2002b). Here the framework of pre-therapy is recognised and applied but its positioning is challenged in order to be meaningfully integrated into a non-directive model of music therapy within a social model context: 'This turning of the gaze back on to the oppressor and the oppressor's conception of the human is a hugely important shift' (Goodley 2016, p.148).

In recognising the importance of establishing the necessary and sufficient conditions, namely psychological contact, as the 'ingredients of the psychologically facilitative climate which promotes therapeutic change' (Thorne and Sanders 2013, p.36), the next section will discuss in detail how Prouty's (2002a, 2002b, 2005) model of pre-therapy was engaged with, in recognition of the potential that the young people were not ready to engage with person-centred, improvised music therapy until this initial climate had been established.

Preparing to engage in non-directive music therapy: pre-therapy (Prouty 2005)

It is proposed that during the initial assessment sessions with Aleksander and Martin, establishing perceptible psychological contact was an important milestone. Without verbal language to articulate potential connection or engagement, and with highly individualised communication methods as outlined in the clinical studies, determining reliable psychological contact felt like an important precursor to any relational work.

To develop psychological contact through pre-therapy, Prouty (2005) describes five categories of contact reflections which can facilitate what Rogers describes in psychological contact as 'the therapist and the client each making a perceived difference in the experiential field of the other' (Rogers 1957, cited in Levitt 2005, p.29).

While much of the literature about pre-therapy relates to clients with schizophrenia (Prouty 1990, 2003; Prouty and Kubiak 1998), dementia (Van Werde and Morton 1999) or psychosis (Prouty and Pietrzak 1998; Sommerbeck 2003), it could be argued that, in relation to the experiences of individuals with autism spectrum conditions, including challenges in social interaction (Roth 2010; Coleman and Gillberg 2012) and joint engagement (Vaiouli *et al.* 2015), there may be difficulties for the therapist in recognising psychological contact with clients with autistic spectrum conditions too. This builds on the limited use of pre-therapy techniques in person-centred counselling with clients with learning disabilities (Peters 1999a, 1999b; Pörtner 2000; Krietemeyer and Prouty 2003).

It is proposed that the theory and practice of pre-therapy (Prouty 2005) can be meaningfully applied to the context of working in improvised music therapy with individuals with autism spectrum conditions, as demonstrated in the following clinical case studies, and subsequently that each of the contact reflections (Prouty 2005) can be meaningfully achieved through music therapy techniques, enabling psychological contact and in turn psychological growth to become a possibility when it is not immediately accessible.

Engaging in contact reflections using music therapy techniques

The first of Prouty's (2005, p.29) contact reflections, situational reflections – defined as 'facilitate[ing] reality contact for the client… concretely reflecting what is present in the client's environment' – can be directly related to the music therapy practice of Situation Songs (Kolar-Borsky 2013; Kolar-Borsky and Holck 2014) where the therapist sings improvised lyrics to an improvised melody, expressing themselves musically and verbally: '[Situation songs are] directly related to the actual therapeutic occurrence…invented spontaneously by the therapist for the child, together with the child or by the child themself within the situation' (Plahl and Koch-Temming 2008, p.108).

Kolar-Borsky and Holck (2014) suggest that using the vehicle of a song can be a valuable way of securing the therapeutic space and maintaining the therapeutic attitude in music therapy, as well as bringing to the client's attention the concrete occurrences of the therapeutic work. The first case study shows the therapist using a Situation Song (Kolar-Borsky 2013) or Improvised Song approach (Oldfield and Franke 2005; Turry 2009) to provide situational reflections to the client (Prouty 2005), who appears slightly agitated in his first experience of the music therapy space.

CASE STUDY: MARTIN

Martin appears to explore the perimeter of the room, occasionally reaching for and subsequently pushing away the hand of the teaching assistant who is supporting him during the session. Martin hasn't yet communicated an awareness of the music therapist's presence. The music therapist sits at the piano as Martin explores the space, and uses her voice to sing a simple melodic narrative about Martin's presence in the room. A metallophone crosses Martin's path and he tentatively explores it, producing a muted tone on some of the bars. The music therapist again sings to Martin that he is playing music in the room with the music therapist, naming the instrument, the music therapist, the teaching assistant and Martin himself. The pitches played on the instrument, as well as their inflection and articulation, are matched by the music therapist in the simple, improvised Situation Song. Martin doesn't appear to noticeably relate to the song, but the narrative follows his journey around the perimeter of the room and both acknowledges and values his contributions.

The second contact reflection in pre-therapy defined by Prouty (2005) is facial reflections, where engagement with and recognition of facial expressions develop the client's affective contact. There is a close parallel to situational reflections, but this time the reality contact (Prouty 2005) narrated in the reflection is to focus on the client's facial expression rather than their engagement with their environment. While this is a way of bringing the client's affective experience into the verbal domain through articulation in language, and examples are seen in the therapist's use of Situation Songs (Kolar-Borsky 2013), affect attunement can also be achieved non-verbally or cross-modally through vitality affects (Stern 2010) and communicative musicality (Malloch and Trevarthen 2009).

This may further emphasise the distinction between the medical-model position of working with clients with physical or mental health conditions who are perceived to be unwell and working towards recovery and reintegration into verbal narratives (Chinna 2004; Prouty 2005), and the non-normative model of working non-verbally with clients with autism spectrum conditions who validly communicate in other modalities, and are developing psychological contact through mediums other than verbal language. There are also further perspectives, such as a recovery model (McCaffrey, Edwards and Fannon 2011), which consider that transition from illness to wellness can be effectively facilitated through non-verbal mediums, emphasising the importance of music therapy as a non-verbal therapeutic medium.

To achieve Prouty's (2005) facial reflection, I mirrored and matched Aleksander's facial expression and body language through a range of cross-modal responses to bring him into affective contact, as is described in the second case study. Brief motifs are mirrored and developed, to achieve a 'biological mirror' (Papousek and Papousek 1979) or an 'amplifying mirror' (Schore 1994).

CASE STUDY: ALEKSANDER

Aleksander sways rhythmically in his chair and his attention appears to be drawn to the bright window. Suddenly, his eyes open wide and his eyebrows raise, with an expression akin to surprise or shock. Following Aleksander's gaze, the music therapist plays a searching seventh on the piano keyboard and mirrors Aleksander's facial expression in her own. Aleksander makes eye contact with the music therapist and blinks heavily before repeating the expression. The music therapist mirrors his expression again in repeating the interval on the piano. Aleksander appears to attend to her as she plays and gradually his expression neutralises. This change is reflected in gentle, open chords on the piano, with a much softer articulation and eventually a grounding bass note. Aleksander's body language appears to relax, and his swaying slows in tempo as he and the music therapist emotionally and musically attune. As a smile creeps to his lips, the intensity of the music increases and the music therapist's body language vivifies to match the intensity of Aleksander's facial expression. Aleksander begins to clap in apparent excitement which is further mirrored in the music therapist's articulation and gradually more percussive and enlivened piano playing.

The third contact reflection is entitled 'Word for Word Reflections', a method which particularly aligns with the non-normative, non-directive ethos of the practice. Here, social language is reflected back 'just as it occurs, word for word' even if 'it makes no conventional sense'. It is suggested that the direct reflections of vocal sounds may give the experience of being received as 'a human communicator', a potentially therapeutic experience in itself (Prouty 2005, p.30).

Wigram's (2004) writing about therapeutic improvisatory methods in music therapy, where sounds are mirrored and matched to meet the client at their level in an attempt to achieve synchronicity, aligns closely with this contact reflection. The intentionality of musical mirroring aligns closely with Prouty's (2005) word-for-word reflections: 'Mirroring: Doing exactly what the client is doing musically, expressively and through language at the same time as the client is doing it. The client will then see his or her behaviour in the therapist's behaviour' (Wigram 2004, p.82).

Again, music therapy has the potential to be increasingly inclusive in this context, since all modalities of expression are accepted, mirrored and valued, thus moving away from a hierarchy of verbal language over less socially prevalent or accepted behaviours and communications. If the client is to be received as a 'human communicator' (Prouty 2005, p.30) and their preferred or sole medium of interacting with the world is non-verbal, then this should be nurtured, from an inclusive, social model perspective (Nind and Hewett 2001). Again, the challenge here is for services, institutions and society to adapt and learn augmentative methods of communication to enable authentic and meaningful participation in society (Gernsbacher 2006), rather than focusing upon normalisation of young people with autism spectrum conditions.

Figure 12.1 shows the therapist engaging in what could potentially be framed as a dialogue with Martin, where his vocal sounds are mirrored as exactly as possible to support him in 'perceiving the therapist making a difference in his field' (Rogers 1957 cited in Levitt 2005, p.29), thus achieving psychological contact.

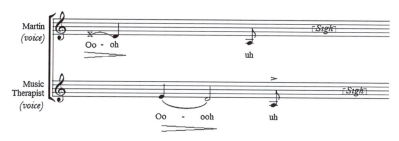

Figure 12.1: An extract of potential dialogue
between Martin and the music therapist

Increasingly inclusive and multi-modal communication is referred to in the contact reflection entitled body reflections (Prouty 2005). Prouty recognises that 'bodily symptoms…are a form of "being-in-the-world" and, as such, express a person's existence' (Prouty 2005, p.30), and advocates reflecting bodily expressions verbally as in situational and facial reflections, or by physically mirroring the behaviour, as discussed by Wigram (2004).

There may again be a significantly distinct context when reflecting upon the bodily expressions of those with autism spectrum conditions in contrast with the echopraxia and catatonia that Prouty and Kubiak (1998) discuss in clients with schizophrenia. Bodily expressions of individuals with autism spectrum conditions can be examples of non-verbal communication or stimming behaviours (Roth 2010) or evidence of valid sensory processing methods (Berger 2002). There are contrasting perspectives in the literature on musically mirroring, matching and bringing into focus these potentially unconscious or sensory-orientated behaviours and interpreting them as intentional or communicative.

In line with Rogers' person-centred approach (Rogers 2004) and Prouty's pre-therapy approach (Prouty 1990), bodily reflections could be interpreted as a vehicle for establishing psychological contact as one of the necessary and sufficient conditions for psychological growth, which is indeed very distinct from bringing these bodily expressions into focus for any 'curative' intention (Kirkham 2017).

The fourth case study shows the music therapist using Wigram's 'Basic Therapeutic Methods' (2004) to engage in body reflections to establish further psychological contact with Martin. Here the auditory dimension of musical movements further embodies the experiences of communicative partners.

CASE STUDY: MARTIN CONTINUED

Martin reaches out and places first his flat palm, and soon after his forehead, on the cold metal cymbal. The music therapist reaches her flat palm to the skin of a nearby djembe and reaches out to appreciate its texture and temperature. Martin doesn't appear to pay significant attention to this gesture. Martin raises his flat hand suddenly to the air, as though he might strike the cymbal with it, but keeps it raised upright. The music therapist also raises her right hand with a similar intensity and poise. The movement in Martin's field of vision appears to capture his attention. Martin returns his hand slowly to the cymbal. The music therapist returns her hand slowly to the djembe.

[Later in the session]… Martin very lightly taps the tip of his right index finger on the cymbal, barely making a sound. The music therapist [facing Martin by this time] gently rests her index finger on the opposite side of the cymbal rim, in Martin's field of vision. The music therapist mirrors Martin's movement and he appears to fix his gaze on her finger. Briefly he raises his gaze to sustain eye contact, before removing his hand from the cymbal.

The final contact reflection advocated by Prouty (2005) to initiate psychological contact is termed reiterative reflections. While a specific technique isn't outlined here, this is the suggestion of 're-contact', whereby any contact reflection which produces a response should be repeated (Prouty 2005). Such reiterative reflection could either be short-term, in relation to an expression repeated within the session; or long-term, in relation to expressions across multiple sessions during the therapy (Prouty 2005).

Contact reflections (Prouty 2005): summary

By engaging in Prouty's contact reflections for pre-therapy, psychological contact was explored and more confidently established with Aleksander and Martin, as demonstrated in the clinical case studies, enabling a therapeutic relationship to develop and a 'fertile space' to be cleared (Moon 2005, p.262) upon which both young people could begin to develop their autonomy and sense of self through the therapeutic relationship, in accordance with their own values and communication styles.

While the notions of using imitation in typical development (Ammaniti and Ferrari 2013; Stern 1985, 2010; Winnicott 1967) or using imitation to engage and develop social skills in individuals with autism spectrum conditions (Field *et al.* 2001; Gernsbacher 2006; Wigram 2004) aren't new concepts, the careful and informed application of contact reflections and their music therapy equivalents, in the framework of a therapeutic engagement to nurture authentic communication strategies, as opposed to development of 'non-autistic communication' (Gernsbacher 2006; Stone 2003), is much less widely explored.

Focus of the subsequent clinical work: developing autonomy

Following establishment of psychological contact through pre-therapy contact reflections (Prouty 2005) utilising music therapy methods, further clinical aims emerged for the remainder of the non-directive, improvisatory music therapy. The clinical aims that were developed, guided by the young people's experiences, included exploring musical improvisation as an opportunity for joint attention and shared engagement; exploring use of initiative and autonomy through music; and developing expression of emotions in a constructive way through musical experiences. These aims were explored through an improvised music therapy approach, with the necessary and sufficient conditions and inherent non-directive attitude maintained (Levitt 2005).

A shared aim for both Aleksander and Martin was the development of autonomy in their music making, with potential for meaningful transfer to broader communication and life skills. This aim was developed having microanalysed extracts of clinical work and noticing Aleksander and Martin's tendency to align with the 'Dependent' and 'Follower' roles in Bruscia's 'Improvisational Assessment Profile' for Autonomy, and the potential for this to limit their own capacity and potential for autonomous, initiated self-expression (Bruscia 1987; Wosch and Wigram 2007). It feels important to clarify that these aims were not developed as recognition of deficiencies or 'failures' in development, as Conn explained the medical interpretation of autism spectrum conditions to be (Conn 2016, p.43), but as opportunities for growth to emerge through a non-directive therapeutic relationship.

In maintaining an evidence-based practice, published research around working with young people with autism spectrum conditions was consulted, and while autonomy was seen as an attribute that could further empower Aleksander's and Martin's psychological growth by 'remov[ing] obstacles to the organismic valuing process' (Merry 2002, p.51), autonomy was equally mirrored as a core attribute in successful transition to adult life and to accessing educational and wider community inclusion outcomes for those with autism spectrum conditions (Hobson 2010; Wehmeyer and Palmer 2003; Wehmeyer et al. 2012; Wehmeyer and Abery 2013; Wehmeyer 2015).

The fifth case study shows how non-directive person-centred music therapy practice empowered Aleksander to develop his use of initiative and autonomy in the 16th session, leading to autonomous selection of instruments, pacing of the session and direction of therapeutic engagement.

CASE STUDY: ALEKSANDER CONTINUED

There is a moment of silence. The music therapist mirrors Aleksander's posture and his relaxed gaze to the bright window. Gradually, Aleksander begins to rock his body gently. The music therapist gently nods her head in time with his body movement and slowly transitions to an oscillating open fifth on the piano to share this motif. Aleksander gradually becomes still again. The silence returns.

Aleksander quite suddenly gets to his feet and quickly reaches for the metallophone beaters, potentially expressing his desire to play the instrument. The music therapist moves her chair so as not to disrupt Aleksander's access to the metallophone. Aleksander sits back in his chair with intensity in his swaying body movement this time. He looks to the music therapist, and before she responds, he reaches out of his chair with the beater to make a bright tone on the metallophone. While the initiative to move the instrument closer isn't instinctive, a clear decision and intent was communicated in reaching for the beater and initiating a fresh musical motif. The music therapist moves the metallophone within reach and Aleksander begins to play a familiar phrase of approximate octaves followed by a melodic descending motif. The music therapist reflects the grounding octave on the piano as an accompaniment and a playful dialogue emerges with the melodic motif, signalling a new chapter in the music making of this session.

Outcomes of the clinical work

The outcomes of the clinical work at the setting were multifaceted. There had been notable development for the young people in relation to the aims established from the therapeutic relationship and the holistic engagement with their ways of being, developed from a belief in 'the innate capacity of each person to reach towards full potential if given a safe, person-centred environment for growth' (Rogers 2013, p.240).

Aleksander developed increased autonomy in his interactions with his environment, his peers and his tutors, documented in the sessions by increased engagement with the role of 'Partner' and 'Leader' as exemplified by Bruscia's Autonomy Profile (Bruscia 1987) and in anecdotal evidence from the school setting and Aleksander's parents. It was apparent in the therapy room as well as the broader school context and at home that he had begun to use his initiative more confidently to make choices and initiate interactions.

The progress for Martin was more subtle but no less significant. He steadily developed joint attention and joint engagement, and began to tolerate, explore and potentially enjoy reciprocal social interaction, as is reflected upon in the sixth case study.

CASE STUDY: MARTIN CONTINUED

[Martin and the music therapist are both attending to the cymbal with their body language and gently begin to explore a vocal dialogue]… The music therapist softly sings, in a lullaby timbre, a Situation Song about Martin's posture attending to the cymbal. Martin appears to recognise his name being sung and turns to engage in eye contact with the music therapist. Martin reaches out his flat right hand to the music therapist who holds his hand in hers as she sings. Martin sustains eye contact and appears to listen to the song. Almost inaudibly at first, Martin offers a vocalisation in the pause between the improvised phrases of the song. The music therapist smiles and mirrors the inflection of Martin's vocalisation in the key and pace of the song. Martin sings this time a pitched phrase with more sustain and looks almost questioningly to the music therapist. The music therapist smiles again and repeats Martin's phrase with slight elaboration at the end of the phrase. Martin smiles broadly and continues to offer another vocalisation and becomes a partner in the Situation Song.

Martin's engagement became increasingly sustained during the sessions and his use of verbal as well as non-verbal communication increased. While the musical content of the interactions remained tolerable to him at only a very simple level, this felt like important developmental work. Both clients' autism was as present and prevalent as at the outset, but person-centred, non-directive therapy and the human relationships this afforded provided opportunities for psychological growth: 'For Rogers, the key is how people are treated. If they were responded to in fundamentally positive, respectful and empathic ways…Rogers observed that individuals grew in a positive, prosocial direction' (Bohart 2013, p.94).

Central to this work was an understanding of autism, advocated by the Neurodiversity Movement, as 'a harmless neurological difference rather than a pathology' (Kirkham 2017, p.107). As such, addressing autism spectrum conditions was never the intention of the work, but rather enabling growth and for meaningful therapeutic relationships to develop.

Implications of a person-centred, social model of autism spectrum conditions in music therapy

It is proposed that engaging with a person-centred approach to music therapy celebrates neurodiversity (Silberman 2015): engaging clients with an inherent respect for their unique qualities (Grant 1990; Rogers 2013) and their role as expert in their own experience (Woods 2017) rather than a focus on pathology or diagnoses (Kirkham 2017). This chapter seeks to demonstrate that music therapy is a particularly inclusive vehicle for engaging with Rogers' person-centred values, enabling clients with increasingly diverse communication styles and learning needs to engage in psychological growth through a discourse that values, accepts and nurtures their individual ways of being. This celebration of the individual aligns with the social model of disability (Oliver 1990, 2013), as the responsibility or 'burden' of adjustment is placed upon society, or in this case the music therapist, rather than the individual (Woods 2017).

While the demonstrable clinical outcomes have been briefly discussed, it is further proposed that by working from the perspective of the social model of disability as opposed to the medical model of disability, arguably the dominant discourse in autism studies (Graby 2016; Goodley 2016; Kirkham 2017; Woods 2017), there is a potentially significant impact on the client's experience of the therapy and of broader society. Inherent in this proposition is the inclusion of person-centred values (Rogers 2004) and recognition of language's contribution to the social construction of disability in society (Kapp et al. 2013; Kenny et al. 2016). Woods (2017, p.1092) asserts: 'The primary social barrier to be removed is the negative language and discourse of the autism label, such as deficit and disorder.' In light of these theories, it is suggested that by working in a way that removes the hierarchy of the therapist as expert (Wood 2008) and the hierarchy of verbal language as a primary medium of communication (Hehir 2002), there is opportunity for clients to take ownership of a neurodiverse identity and feel valued as a human communicator (Prouty 2005). There is a profound ethical and philosophical connotation to working with clients as human beings as opposed to as patients, diagnoses or pathologies, and further research is needed to explore the potential measurable impact of this way of working (Entwistle and Watt 2013).

While Rogers recognised the transferability of his approach in suggesting that it was not exclusive to therapy and could indeed be applied to any relationship (Rogers 1959, 2004), Prouty (2005) has further demonstrated how the approach can be adapted and developed for working with clients who may not verbally communicate their engagement with the necessary and sufficient conditions.

Natalie Rogers (2013) has demonstrated how the necessary and sufficient conditions can be explored through creative modalities other than verbal therapy, and many community music and community arts practitioners have demonstrated how therapeutic theory as well as social model thinking can be translated to arts in health and arts for wellbeing practices (Clements, Hughes and Stiller 2015; Gross 2018; Shiloh and Lagasse 2014; Williams 2013).

It is hoped that a paradigm shift towards this discourse of neurodiversity may challenge the perpetuation of ableism and internalised ableism in the education system, therapy practice and in broader society (Bolt 2016; Campbell 2008; Hadley 2014; Milton, Martin and Melham 2016) and enable wider engagement with an informed, person-centred model of music therapy practice with those with autism spectrum conditions, providing a 'growth-promoting environment through active and empathic listening with unconditional positive regard' (Kim 2010, p.94) as opposed to curative aims (Kirkham 2017).

Critical engagement with the person-centred, social model of autism spectrum conditions in music therapy

Many of the theories and approaches that I draw from in this chapter pose inherent challenges and occasional contradictions, which feel important to address here. While an exhaustive discussion is beyond the scope of this chapter, some key critical points will be further explored.

Is the assumption of client incongruence commensurate with a deficit-based model?

Having clearly allied with a social model of disability both broadly (Oliver 1990, 2013) and in specific relation to autism spectrum conditions (Woods 2017), the necessary and sufficient condition that the client is in a state of incongruence (Rogers 1957) may appear contradictory. While this is recognised and reflected upon, there may well be instances of client incongruence, not necessarily allied with the diagnosis of autism spectrum conditions, which are to be addressed through therapy.

For Martin, a lack of engagement with staff and provision at the setting, as well as instances of potentially self-injurious behaviour were firmly communicated as areas of concern, and potential incongruence, at the point of referral. These experiences may or may not have been associated with Martin's diagnosis of autism spectrum conditions; however, the focus of the therapeutic work was on developing congruence for Martin, not on removing or challenging any of his experiences of autism spectrum conditions. The consideration of whether these experiences can be separated out is one for further study.

How integral is insight or cognitive ability to the person-centred approach?

Rogers' writing discusses work with clients who communicate verbally (Rogers 1959, 1985, 2004) and he is said to have stated that he wasn't working with clients with learning disabilities or communicative challenges (Prouty 2002b). There is very limited literature on application of the Rogerian approach to working with clients with autism spectrum conditions and/or learning disabilities who may have limited engagement with verbal interaction (Flitton and Buckroyd 2002; Hawkins 2002), with increased focus in psychoanalytic (Wilson 2003) or psychodynamic approaches (Cottis 2009), as well as disagreement in the broader counselling literature about the potential of psychotherapeutic interventions for those with learning disabilities (Beail 2003; Hurley 2005; King 2005; Sturmey 2006; Willner 2005; Wilson 2003) and autism spectrum conditions (Koenig and Levine 2011; Volkmar 2011). Raffensperger (2009, p.498) writes:

> Low cognitive ability has frequently been cited as a factor which reduces one's ability to benefit from counselling (Benson 2004, p.353) and such clients 'are rarely offered the full range of psychotherapeutic options' (Mohr 2007, p.13). However, 'over the past decade this assumption has been increasingly challenged' (Willner and Hatton 2006, p.1) both explicitly and implicitly.

It could be argued that Rogers' approach is inherently inclusive in that its necessary and sufficient conditions for the client are psychological contact and 'that the client perceives, at least to a minimal degree...the unconditional positive regard of the therapist for him, and the empathic understanding of the therapist' (Rogers 1959, p.214). The extent to which the latter can be reliably measured is unclear; however, the specificity of a 'minimal degree' potentially makes this approach accessible to those with profound learning disabilities and challenges in relating to the environment and other people.

Foley-Nicpon and Lee (2012) note that within their 20-year content analysis of five counselling psychology journals, only 1–2.7 per cent of content related to disability research. Their call for increased empirical investigation of disability in the field of counselling and psychotherapy as an important aspect of diversity is a valid and important one.

Critique of Rogers' person-centred approach

Rogers' work is widely and frequently critiqued for its rigour and effectiveness (Thorne and Sanders 2013), as is the potential and plausibility of working wholly non-directively (Brodley 2005). While it is vital to continue to explore and develop person-centred, non-directive practice to determine its potential and rigour, it is likely that it is the under-developed evidence base that contributes to the lack of acceptance of this work over more empirical and positivist interventions such as Applied Behaviour Analysis (ABA) which generate measurable scientific validation (Keenan *et al.* 2006; Kirkham 2017; Odom *et al.* 2010).

There is perhaps a methodological discussion to be had around whether it is possible to empirically measure the outcomes of person-centred work, and what the potentially observable outcomes may be. Further, there may be an ongoing debate around the hierarchy of evidence, and how subtle, sensitive, therapeutic work fits this model (Aigen 2015). Aigen's writing has long reflected the tension in the music therapy profession between empirical, scientific research and the often individual, relational nature of improvised music therapy practice:

This study was based upon the documented schism in the field that showed an incompatibility between research and clinical practice. The study demonstrated that music therapy research methodologists operated from a view of science congruent with the received view and that the philosophical assumptions of this view conflicted with the premises of creative and improvisational approaches to music therapy. (Aigen 2015, p.13)

There is a need for an ethical discussion around the application of positivist, curative aims to working with those who cannot give informed consent to participation. While Kirkham (2017) references the perspectives of some autistic self-advocates on the use of ABA, the ethical and philosophical connotations of 'curing' or negating 'autistic behaviours' (Kalyva 2011) needs further discussion (Runswick-Cole, Mallett and Timimi 2016; Woods 2017).

Johnson (2011) provides an insightful discussion into the person-centred approach as 'disabled people's favored approach to counselling' (Reeve 2006; Swain, Griffiths and Heyman 2003) while taking a critical stance about how 'conditions of worth can silence disabled people from talking about their experiences' (Johnson 2011, p.260). Hodge (2013) further critically discusses ableism inherent in counselling and psychotherapeutic practices which may perpetuate deficit-based narratives and discourses; it is hoped that this chapter provides an alternative position in relation to the potential of therapeutic practice for both therapists and individuals with autism spectrum conditions.

Social model of disability as potentially reductionist or inapplicable to autism spectrum conditions

There is well-documented critique of the social model of disability since its inception (Owens 2015). In a recent piece entitled 'The social model of disability: Thirty years on', Oliver (2013, p.1024) recognises the limitations of the model: 'At no point did I suggest that the individual model should be abandoned, and neither did I claim that the social model was an all-encompassing framework within which everything that happens to disabled people could be understood or explained.'

The two main criticisms are that it (a) doesn't engage with embodied experiences and (b) fails to take account of individual differences (Owens 2015; Thomas 2010). While there are many articles which debate these issues with rigour and passion (Anastasiou and Kauffman 2013; Coleman-Fountain and McLaughlin 2013; Corker 1999; Meekosha and Shuttleworth 2009), Oliver (2013) reminds us, in a contemporary context, how destructive returning to a solely medical model could be, and the personal and political implications of abandoning the progress made since the social model was initially proposed, despite its limitations. Woods (2017) further demonstrates the relevance of the application of social model thinking, particularly in relation to autism spectrum conditions in a contemporary context:

> The social model [of disability] should be shifting the burden of making adjustments away from autistic people onto Predominant Neurotype institutions. This can be done by changing the law or fully implementing existing legislation, such as local authorities' and NHS Trusts' obligations to The Autism Act 2009, along with institutions enacting reasonable adjustments under The Equality Act 2010, and also changing the autism discourse to take on positive connotations of autism by moving away from toxic words and debates like 'disorder' and 'deficit'. By doing this, Predominant Neurotype society will finally treat autistic individuals as equal to themselves, leading to full autism emancipation. (p.1094)

With an openness and awareness of the contrasting Nordic and other relational models (Mallett and Runswick-Cole 2014; Runswick-Cole *et al.* 2016; Kristiansen and Transtadóttir 2004), and recognition of challenges to the original conception of the social model (Levitt 2017; Owens 2015), Woods (2017) makes a passionate and informed case for the continued relevance and integration of complementary models of disability in the specific contemporary context of autism spectrum conditions.

Conclusion and recommendations

This chapter proposes that through working from the perspectives of the social model of disability (Oliver 1990, 2013), person-centred approach (Rogers 2004) and a non-normative model of music therapy (Gross 2018; Straus 2014), psychological growth can be nurtured in individuals with autism spectrum conditions, in a way that is congruent with and respectful of '[their] own nature, values and choices' (Moon 2005, p.262). Pre-therapy (Prouty 2005) has been demonstrated to be a potentially valuable transitional framework for clients not yet ready to fully engage in person-centred, improvised music therapy. Honisch (2014) rightly states that 'such a move requires engaging in a different set of critical concerns, beginning not with medical or clinical diagnoses, but rather with reflexivity, digging at the methodological foundations of both scholarly research, and the philosophical assumptions of therapeutic practice'. It is proposed that this paradigm shift from medical or clinical diagnoses to increasingly humanistic considerations was explored in the engagement with this clinical work, and that the implications for the psychological growth of the young people demonstrates the potential of this perspective.

Gernsbacher (2006, p.142) asserts that the perceived deficiencies of individuals with autism spectrum conditions needs to be turned on its head: '[W]hat was needed was greater social and emotional reciprocity – social and emotional reciprocity *by* the teachers and the researchers *toward* the autistic child.' Movement away from the accepted deficit-based paradigm (Goodley 2016; Kapp *et al.* 2013) could create opportunities for meaningful engagement and participation in society, achieved by 'taking the focus away from individual impairment and shifting the gaze towards societal structures' (Woods 2017, p.1094). In response to this assertion, the provision and attitudes of services towards these young people could further enable them to more meaningfully integrate into and participate within their communities and society. As Sinclair (1993, p.5) eloquently summarises:

> Approach respectfully, without preconceptions, and with openness to learning new things, and you'll find a world you could never have imagined. Yes, that takes more work than relating to a non-autistic person. But it can be done – unless non-autistic people are far more limited than we [autistic people] are in their capacity to relate. We spend our entire lives doing it.

References

Aigen, K. (2015) 'A critique of evidence-based practice in music therapy.' *Music Therapy Perspectives* 33, 1, 12–24.

Ammaniti, M. and Ferrari, P. (2013) 'Vitality affects in Daniel Stern's thinking – a psychological and neurobiological perspective.' *Infant Mental Health Journal* 34, 5, 367–375.

Anastasiou, D. and Kauffman, J.M. (2013) 'The social model of disability: Dichotomy between impairment and disability.' *Journal of Medicine and Philosophy* 38, 4, 441–459.

Axline, V. (1947) *Play Therapy*. Boston, MA: Houghton-Mifflin.

Barnes, C. (2014) 'Understanding the Social Model of Disability: Past, Present and Future.' In N. Watson (ed.) *Routledge Handbook of Disability Studies*. Oxon: Routledge.

Beail, N. (2003) 'What works for people with mental retardation? Critical commentary on cognitive-behavioral and psychodynamic psychotherapy research.' *Mental Retardation* 41, 6, 468–472.

Berger, D. (2002) *Music Therapy, Sensory Integration and the Autistic Child*. London: Jessica Kingsley Publishers.

Bohart, A.C. (2013) 'The Actualizing Person.' In M. Cooper, M. O'Hara, P.F., Schmid and A.C. Bohart (eds) *The Handbook of Person-Centre Psychotherapy and Counselling* (2nd edition), Basingstoke: Palgrave Macmillan.

Bolt, D. (ed.) (2016) *Changing Social Attitudes Toward Disability: Perspectives from Historical, Cultural and Educational Studies*. Oxon: Routledge.

Brodley, B.T. (2005) 'About the Non-Directive Attitude.' In B. Levitt (ed.) (2005) *Embracing Non-Directivity: Reassessing Person-Centered Theory and Practice in the 21st Century*. Ross-On-Wye: PCCS Books.

Bruscia, K. (1987) *Improvisational Models of Music Therapy*. Springfield, IL: Charles C. Thomas.

Campbell, F. (2008) 'Exploring internalized ableism using critical race theory.' *Disability and Society* 23, 2, 151–162.

Chinna, C. (2004) 'Music therapy and psychosocial rehabilitation: Towards a person-centred music therapy model.' *Canadian Journal of Music Therapy* 11, 1, 8–30.

Clements, N., Hughes, R. and Stiller, K. (2015) *Person-Centred Creativity*. Bridgend: Valley and Vale Community Arts.

Coleman, M. and Gillberg, C. (2012) *The Autisms* (4th edition). New York, NY: Oxford University Press.

Coleman-Fountain, E. and McLaughlin, J. (2013) 'The interactions of disability and impairment.' *Social Theory and Health* 11, 2, 133–150.

Collins, G. (2016) 'Does a Diagnosis of ASD Help Us to Help a Person with Intellectual Disabilities?' In K. Runswick-Cole, R., Mallet and S. Timimi (eds) *Re-Thinking Autism: Diagnosis, Identity and Equality*. London: Jessica Kingsley Publishers.

Conn, C. (2016) *Observation, Assessment and Planning in Inclusive Autism Education: Supporting Learning and Development*. Oxon: Routledge.

Cooper, H. (2013) 'The Oppressive Power of Normalcy in the Lives of Disabled Children: Deploying History to Denaturalize the Notion of the 'Normal Child.' In T. Curran and K. Runswick-Cole (eds) *Disabled Children's Childhood Studies: Critical Approaches in a Global Context*. Basingstoke: Palgrave Macmillan.

Cooper, M., O'Hara, M., Schmid, P.F. and Bohart, A.C. (2013) *The Handbook of Person-Centre Psychotherapy and Counselling* (2nd edition), Basingstoke: Palgrave Macmillan.

Corker, M. (1999) 'Differences, conflations and foundations: The limits to accurate theoretical representation of disabled people's experience.' *Disability and Society* 14, 5, 627–642.

Cottis, T. (2009) *Intellectual Disability, Trauma and Psychotherapy*. London: Routledge.

Department of Health (2007) *Services for People with Learning Disabilities and Challenging Behaviour or Mental Health Needs*. London: DoH.

Department of Health (2009) *'A Better Future': A Consultation on a Future Strategy for Adults with Autistic Spectrum Conditions*. Accessed on 10 April 2015 at https://webarchive.nationalarchives.gov.uk/20130124045946/http://www.dh.gov.uk/prod_consum_dh/groups/dh_digitalassets/documents/digitalasset/dh_098604.pdf.

Department of Health (2010) *Person-centred Planning: Advice for Providers*. London: DoH.

Dimitriadis, T. and Smeijsters, H. (2011) 'Autistic spectrum disorder and music therapy: Theory underpinning practice.' *Nordic Journal of Music Therapy 20*, 2, 108–122.

Entwistle, V.A. and Watt, I.S. (2013) 'Treating patients as persons: A capabilities approach to support delivery of person-centered care.' *American Journal of Bioethics 13*, 8, 29–39.

Field, T., Field, T., Sanders, C. and Nadel, J. (2001) 'Children with autism display more social behaviors after repeated imitation sessions.' *Autism 5*, 3, 317–323.

Flitton, B. and Buckroyd, J. (2002) 'Exploring the effects of a 14 week person-centred counselling intervention with learning disabled children.' *Emotional and Behavioural Difficulties 7*, 3, 164–177.

Foley-Nicpon, M. and Lee, S. (2012), 'Disability research in counselling psychology journals: A 20 year content analysis.' *Journal of Counselling Psychology 59*, 3, 392–398.

Gernsbacher, M.A. (2006), 'Toward a behavior of reciprocity.' *Journal of Developmental Processes 1*, 1, 139–152.

Goodley, D. (2016) 'Autism and the Human.' In K. Runswick-Cole, R. Mallett and S. Timimi (eds) *Re-Thinking Autism: Diagnosis, Identity and Equality*. London: Jessica Kingsley Publishers.

Goodley, D. (2011) *Disability Studies: An Interdisciplinary Introduction*. London: SAGE

Graby, S. (2016), 'Unworkable Conditions: Work, Benefits and Disabled People's Resistance to Capitalism.' Paper presented to Association for Social and Political Philosophy Conference, London, 29 June 2016, Accessed on 8 April 2017 at www.academia.edu/28495623/Unworkable_Conditions_work_benefits_and_disabled_peoples_resistance_to_capitalism_2016.

Grant, B. (1990), 'Principled and Instrumental Non-Directiveness in Person-Centred and Client-Centred Therapy.' In D.J. Cain (ed.) (2002) *Classics in Person-Centred Approach* Ross-on-Wye: PCCS Books.

Gross, R. (2018) 'The social model of disability and music therapy: Practical suggestions for the emerging clinical practitioner.' *Voices: A World Forum for Music Therapy 18*, 1. Accessed on 16 March 2018 at https://voices.no/index.php/voices/article/view/958/843.

Hadley, S. (2014) 'Shifting frames: Are we really embracing human diversities?' *Voices: A World Forum for Music Therapy 14*, 3. Accessed on 24 July 2017 at www.voices. no/index.php/voices/article/view/801/666.

Hawkins, J. (2002) *Voices of the Voiceless: Person-Centred Approaches and People with Learning Difficulties.* Ross-on-Wye: PCCS Books.

Hehir, T. (2002) 'Eliminating ableism in education.' *Harvard Educational Review 72*, 1, 1–32.

Hendricks, D.R. and Wehman, P. (2009) 'Transition from school to adulthood for youth with autism spectrum disorders: Review and recommendations.' *Focus on Autism and Other Developmental Disabilities 24*, 2, 77–88.

Henninger, N.A. and Taylor, J.L. (2014) 'Family perspectives on a successful transition to adulthood for individuals with disabilities.' *Intellectual and Developmental Disabilities 52*, 2, 98–111.

Hobson, R.P. (2010) 'Explaining autism: Ten reasons to focus on developing self.' *Autism 14*, 5, 391–407.

Hodge, N. (2013) 'Counselling, autism and the problem of empathy.' *British Journal of Guidance and Counselling 41*, 2, 105–116.

Honisch, S. (2014) 'Music…to cure or disable: Therapy for whom?' *Voices: A World Forum for Music Therapy,* Accessed on 31 July 2017 at https://voices.no/index. php/voices/article/view/793/658.

Howlin, P. and Taylor, J.L. (2015) 'Addressing the need for high quality research on autism in adulthood.' *Autism 19*, 7, 771–773.

Hume, K., Boyd, B.A., Hamm, J.V. and Kucharczyk, S. (2014) 'Supporting independence in adolescents on the autistic spectrum.' *Remedial and Special Education 35*, 2, 102–113.

Hurley, A.D. (2005) 'Psychotherapy is an essential tool in the treatment of psychiatric disorders for people with mental retardation.' *Mental Retardation 43*, 6, 445–448.

Kalyva, E. (2011) *Autism: Educational and Therapeutic Approaches.* Los Angeles, CA: SAGE.

Johnson, C. (2011) 'Disabling barriers in the person-centered counseling relationship.' *Person-Centered and Experiential Psychotherapies 10*, 4, 260–273.

Kapp, S.K., Gillespie-Lynch, K., Sherman, L.E. and Hutman, T. (2013), 'Deficit, difference, or both? Autism and neurodiversity. *Developmental Psychology 49*, 1, 59–71.

Keenan, M., Henderson, M., Kerr, K.P. and Dillenburger, K. (2006) *Applied Behaviour Analysis and Autism: Building a Future Together.* London: Jessica Kingsley Publishers.

Kenny, L., Hattersley, C. Molins, B., Buckley, C., Povey, C. and Pellicano, E. (2016) 'Which terms should be used to describe autism? Perspectives from the UK autism community.' *Autism: The International Journal of Research and Practice 20*, 4, 442–462.

Kim, S. (2010) 'A story of a healing relationship: The person-centered approach in expressive arts therapy.' *Journal of Creativity in Mental Health 5*, 1, 93–98.

Kim, J., Wigram, T. and Gold, C. (2009) 'Emotional, motivational and interpersonal responsiveness of children with autism in improvisational music therapy.' *Autism 13*, 4, 389–409.

King, R. (2005) 'Proceeding with compassion while awaiting the evidence: Psychotherapy and individuals with mental retardation.' *Mental Retardation 43*, 6, 448–450.

Kirkham, P. (2017) 'The line between intervention and abuse: Autism and applied behaviour analysis.' *History of the Human Sciences 30*, 2, 107–126.

Koenig, K. and Levine, M. (2011) 'Psychotherapy for individuals with autism spectrum disorders.' *Journal of Contemporary Psychotherapy 41*, 1, 29–36.

Kolar-Borsky, A. (2013) 'Singing About You and Me: Situation Songs and Their Use in Paediatric Music Therapy.' Unpublished Masters Thesis: Aalborg University, Aalborg, Denmark. Accessed on 20 April 2017 at http://projekter.aau.dk/projekter/da/studentthesis/singing-about-you-and-me%28d6129d78-2da0-4d84-8f74-2290964bb5d4%29.html.

Kolar-Borsky, A. and Holck, U. (2014) 'Situation Songs: Therapeutic intentions and use in music therapy with children.' *Voices: A World Forum For Music Therapy 14*, 2. Accessed on 20th July 2017 at https://voices.no/index.php/voices/article/view/744/646.

Krietemeyer, B. and Prouty, G. (2003) 'The art of psychological contact: The psychotherapy of a mentally retarded psychotic client.' *Person-Centred and Experiential Therapies 2*, 3, 151–161.

Kristiansen, K. and Traustadóttir, R. (eds) (2004) *Gender and Disability Research in the Nordic Countries*. Lund, Sweden: Studentlitteratur.

Levigne, A. (2015) *The Music of Being: Music Therapy, Winnicott and the School of Object Relations*. London: Jessica Kingsley Publishers.

Levitt, B. (ed.) (2005) *Embracing Non-Directivity: Reassessing Person-Centered Theory and Practice in the 21st Century*. Ross-on-Wye: PCCS Books.

Levitt, J. (2017) 'Exploring how the social model of disability can be re-invigorated: In response to Mike Oliver.' *Disability and Society 32*, 4, 589–594.

McCaffrey, T., Edwards, J. and Fannon, D. (2011) 'Is there a role for music therapy in the recovery approach in mental health?' *The Arts in Psychotherapy 38*, 3, 185–189.

Magee, W. (2002) 'Disability and Identity in Music Therapy.' In R. Macdonald, D. Hargreaves, D. and D. Miell, (eds) *Musical Identities*. Oxford: Oxford University Press.

Mallett, R., and Runswick-Cole, K. (2014) *Approaching Disability: Critical Issues and Perspectives* London: Routledge.

Mallett, R. and Runswick-Cole, K. (2016) 'The Commodification of Autism: What's at Stake?' In K. Runswick-Cole, R., Mallett and S. Timimi (eds) *Re-Thinking Autism: Diagnosis, Identity and Equality*. London: Jessica Kingsley Publishers.

Malloch, S. and Trevarthen, C. (2009) *Communicative Musicality: Exploring the Basis of Human Companionship*. New York, NY: Oxford University Press.

Mearns, D. and Thorne, B. (2013) *Person-Centred Counselling in Action* (4th edition). London and Thousand Oaks, CA: SAGE.

Meekosha, H. and Shuttleworth, R. (2009) 'What's so critical about critical disability studies?' *Australian Journal of Human Rights 15*, 1, 47–76.

Merry, D. (2002) *Learning and Being in Person-Centred Counselling* (2nd edition). Ross-on-Wye: PCCS Books.

Milton, D., Martin, M. and Melham, P. (2016) 'Beyond reasonable Adjustment: Autistic-Friendly Spaces and Universal Design.' In D. Milton and N. Martin (eds) *Autism and Intellectual Disabilities in Adults* (Vol. 1). Hove: Pavilion.

Moon, K.A. (2005) 'Non-Directive Therapist Congruence in Theory and Practice.' In B. Levitt. (ed.) *Embracing Non-Directivity: Reassessing Person-Centered Theory and Practice in the 21st Century*. Ross-on-Wye: PCCS Books.

Nind, M. and Hewett, D. (2001) *A Practical Guide to Intensive Interaction*. Kidderminster: BILD Publications.

Odom, S.L., Boyd, B.A., Hall, L.J. and Hume, K. (2010) 'Evaluation of comprehensive treatment models for individuals with autism spectrum disorders.' *Journal of Autism and Developmental Disorders 40*, 4, 425–436.

Oldfield, A. and Franke, C. (2005) 'Improvised Songs and Stories in Music Therapy Diagnostic Assessments at a Unit for Child and Family Psychiatry: A Music Therapist's and a Psychotherapist's Perspective.' In F. Baker and T. Wigram (eds) *Songwriting: Methods, Techniques and Clinical Applications for Music Therapy Clinicians, Educators and Young People*. London: Jessica Kingsley Publishers.

Oliver, M. (1990) *The Politics of Disablement*. London: Macmillan.

Oliver, M. (1996) *Understanding Disability: From Theory to Practice*. Chatham: Mackays.

Oliver, M. (2013) 'The social model of disability: Thirty years on' *Disability and Society 28*, 7, 1024–1026.

Oliver, M. and Barnes, C. (2012) *The New Politics of Disablement*. Basingstoke: Palgrave.

Owens, J. (2015) 'Exploring the critiques of the social model of disability: The transformative possibility of Arendt's notion of power.' *Sociology of Health and Illness 37*, 3, 385–403.

Papousek, H. and Papousek, M. (1979) 'Early Ontogeny of Human Social Interaction: Its Biological Roots and Social Dimensions.' In M. Von-Cranach, K. Foppa, W. Lepenies, and D. Ploog (eds) *Human Ethology: Claims and Limits of a New Discipline*. Cambridge: Cambridge University Press.

Pasiali, V. (2004) 'The use of prescriptive therapeutic songs in a home-based environment to promote social skills acquisition by children with autism: Three case studies.' *Music Therapy Perspectives 22*, 1, 11–20.

Peters, H. (1999a) 'Pre-therapy: A client-centered/experiential approach to mentally handicapped people.' *Journal of Humanistic Psychology 39*, 4, 8–29.

Peters, H. (1999b) 'Client-centered therapy in the care of mentally handicapped.' *The Person-Centered Journal 6*, 164–178.

Plahl, C. and Koch-Temming, H. (2008) *Musiktherapie mit Kindern: Grundlagen, Methoden, Praxisfelder* (2nd edition). Bern: Hans Huber.

Pörtner, M. (2000) *Trust and Understanding: The Person-centred Approach to Everyday Care for People with Special Needs*. Ross-on-Wye: PCCS Books.

Pörtner, M. (2002) 'Concluding Thoughts – Pre-Therapy in the Context of the Person-Centred Approach.' In G. Prouty, D. Van Werde, and M. Pörtner (eds) *Pre-Therapy: Reaching Contact Impaired Clients*. Ross-On-Wye: PCCS Books.

Prouty, G. (1990) 'Pre-therapy: A Theoretical Evolution in the Person-Centred/Experiential Psychotherapy of Schizophrenia and Retardation.' In G. Lietaer, J. Rombauts, and R. Van Balen (eds) *Client-Centered and Experiential Therapy in the Nineties*. Leuven, Belgium: Leuven University Press.

Prouty, G. (1994) *Theoretical Evolutions in Person-Centred/Experiential Therapy: Applications to Schizophrenic and Retarded Psychoses*. Westport, CT: Praeger-Greenwood.

Prouty, G. (2002a) 'Pre-Therapy as a Theoretical System.' In G. Wyatt and P. Sanders (eds) *Rogers' Therapeutic Conditions: Evolution, Theory and Practice, Volume 4. Contact and Perception*. Ross-on-Wye: PCCS Books.

Prouty, G. (2002b) 'The Theory of Pre-Therapy.' In G. Prouty, D. Van Werde, and M. Pörtner (eds) *Pre-Therapy: Reaching Contact Impaired Clients*. Ross-on-Wye: PCCS Books.

Prouty, G. (2003) 'Pre-therapy: A newer development on the psychotherapy of schizophrenia.' *The Journal of American Academy of Psychoanalysis and Dynamic Psychiatry 31*, 59–73.

Prouty, G. (2005) 'Forms of Non-Directive Psychotherapy: The Non-Directive Tradition.' In B. Levitt (ed.) *Embracing Non-Directivity: Reassessing Person-Centered Theory and Practice in the 21st Century*. Ross-on-Wye: PCCS Books.

Prouty, G. and Kubiak, M. (1998) 'The development of communicative contact with a catatonic schizophrenic.' *Journal of Communication Therapy 4*, 1, 13–20.

Prouty, G. and Pietrzak, S. (1998) 'The pre-therapy method applied to persons experiencing hallucinatory images.' *Person-Centred Review 3*, 4, 426–441.

Prouty, G. Van Werde, D. and Pörtner, M. (2002) *Pre-Therapy: Reaching Contact-Impaired Clients*. Ross-on-Wye: PCCS Books.

Raffensperger, M.K. (2009) 'Factors that influence outcomes for clients with an intellectual disability.' *British Journal of Guidance and Counselling 37*, 4, 495–509.

Rapley, M. (2010) *The Social Construction of Intellectual Disability*. Cambridge: Cambridge University Press.

Raskin, N.J. (1948) 'The development of non-directive therapy.' *Journal of Consulting Psychology 12*, 2, 92–110.

Raskin, N.J. (2005) 'The Non-Directive Attitude.' In B. Levitt (ed.) *Embracing Non-Directivity: Reassessing Person-Centered Theory and Practice in the 21st Century*. Ross-on-Wye: PCCS Books

Reeve, D. (2006) 'Towards a Psychology of Disability: The Emotional Effects of Living in a Disabling Society.' In D. Goodley and R. Lawthom (eds) *Disability and Psychology*. Basingstoke: Palgrave Macmillan.

Rogers, C. (1946) 'Significant aspects of client-centered therapy.' *American Psychologist 1*, 10, 415–422.

Rogers, C. (1951) *Client Centred Therapy*. Boston, MA: Houghton-Mifflin.

Rogers, C. (1957) 'The necessary and sufficient conditions of personality change.' *Journal of Consulting Psychology 21*, 2, 95–103.

Rogers, C. (1959) 'A Theory of Therapy, Personality and Interpersonal Relationships. As Developed in the Client-Centered Framework.' In S. Koch (ed.) *Psychology: A Study of a Science Volume 3. Formulations of the Person and the Social Context*. New York, NY: McGraw Hill.

Rogers, C. (1985) 'Toward a more human science of the person.' *Journal of Humanistic Psychology25*, 4, 7–24.

Rogers, C. (2004) *On Becoming a Person: A Therapist's View of Psychotherapy* London: Constable. (Original work published 1961.)

Rogers, N. (2013) 'Person-Centred Expressive Arts Therapy: Connecting Body, Mind and Spirit.' In M. Cooper, M. O'Hara, P.F. Schmid and A.C. Bohart (eds) *The Handbook of Person-Centre Psychotherapy and Counselling* (2nd edition). Basingstoke: Palgrave Macmillan.

Roth, I. (2010) *The Autism Spectrum in the 21st Century: Exploring Psychology, Biology and Practice*. London: Jessica Kingsley Publishers.

Runswick-Cole, K., Mallett, R. and Timimi, S. (eds) (2016) *Re-Thinking Autism: Diagnosis, Identity and Equality*. London: Jessica Kingsley Publishers.

Schore, A.N. (1994) *Affect Regulation and the Origin of the Self: The Neurobiology of Emotional Development*. Mahwah, NJ: Erlbaum.

Shiloh, C.J. and Lagasse, A.B. (2014) 'Sensory friendly concerts: A community music therapy initiative to promote neurodiversity.' *International Journal of Community Music 7*, 1, 113–128.

Silberman, S. (2015) *Neurotribes: The Legacy of Autism and How to Think Smarter About People Who Think Differently*. London: Allen & Unwin.

Sinclair J. (1993) 'Don't mourn for us.' *Our Voice 1*, 3, 5–6.

Sommerbeck, L. (2003) *The Client-Centred Therapist in Psychiatric Contexts: A Therapist's Guide to Psychiatric Landscape and its Inhabitants*. Ross-on-Wye: PCCS Books.

Steen Moller, A., Odell-Miller, H. and Wigram, T. (2002) 'Indications in music therapy: evidence from assessment that can identify the expectations of music therapy as a treatment for autistic spectrum disorder (ASD): Meeting the challenge of evidence based practice.' *British Journal of Music Therapy 16*, 1, 11–28.

Stern, D. (1985) *The Interpersonal World of the Infant*. New York, NY: Basic Books.

Stern, D. (2010) 'The issue of vitality.' *Nordic Journal of Music Therapy 19*, 2, 88–102.

Stern, D. (2010) *Forms of Vitality: Exploring Dynamic Experience in Psychology, the Arts, Psychotherapy, and Development*. Oxford: Oxford University Press.

Stone, F. (2003) *Autism – The Eighth Colour of the Rainbow: Learn to Speak Autistic* London: Jessica Kingsley Publishers.

Straus, J. (2014) 'Music therapy and autism: A view from disability studies.' *Voices: A World Forum for Music Therapy, 14*, 3. Accessed on 20 July 2017 at https://voices.no/index.php/voices/article/view/785/656.

Sturmey, P. (2006) 'Against psychotherapy with people who have mental retardation: In response to the responses.' *Mental Retardation 44*, 1, 71–74.

Swain, J., Griffiths, C., and Heyman, B. (2003) 'Towards a social model approach to counselling disabled clients.' *British Journal of Guidance and Counselling 31*, 1, 137–152.

Thaut, M. and Hoemberg, V. (2016) *Handbook of Neurologic Music Therapy* (2nd edition). New York, NY: Oxford University Press.

Thomas, C. (2010) 'Medical Sociology and Disability Theory.' In G. Scambler and S. Scambler (eds) *New Directions in the Sociology of Chronic and Disabling Conditions: Assaults on the Lifeworld*. London, New York: Palgrave Macmillan.

Thorne, B. and Sanders, P. (2013) *Carl Rogers: Key Figures in Counselling and Psychotherapy Series* (3rd edition). London: SAGE.

Turry, A. (2009) 'Integrating musical and psychological thinking: The relationship between music and words in clinically improvised songs.' *Music and Medicine 1*, 2, 106–116.

Tustin, F. (1980) 'Autistic objects.' *International Review of Psycho-Analysis 7*, 1, 27–39.

Vaiouli, P., Grimmet, K. and Ruich, L.J. (2015) "Bill is now singing': Joint engagement and the emergence of social communication in three young children with autism.' *Autism 19*, 1, 73–83.

Van Werde, D. and Morton, I. (1999) 'The Relevance of Prouty's Pre-Therapy to Dementia Care.' In I. Morton (ed.) *Person-Centred Approaches to Dementia Care*. Oxon: Winslow Press.

Volkmar, F.R. (2011) 'Asperger's disorder: Implications for psychoanalysis.' *Psychoanalytic Inquiry 31*, 3, 334–344.

Von Cranach, M., Foppa, K., Lepenies, and Ploog, D. (eds) *Human Ethology: Claims and Limits of a New Discipline*. New York, NY: Cambridge University Press.

Wehman, P., Schall, C., Carr, S., Targett, P., West, M. and Cifu, G. (2014) 'Transition from school to adulthood for youth with autism spectrum disorder: What we know and what we need to know.' *Journal of Disability Policy Studies 25*, 1, 30–40.

Wehmeyer M.L. (2015) 'Framing the future: Self-determination.' *Remedial and Special Education 36*, 1, 20–23.

Wehmeyer, M.L. and Abery, B.H. (2013) 'Self-determination and choice'. *Intellectual and Developmental Disabilities 51*, 5, 399–411.

Wehmeyer, M.L. and Palmer, S.B. (2003) 'Adult outcomes for young people with cognitive disabilities three years after high school: The impact of self-determination.' *Education and Training in Developmental Disabilities 38*, 2, 131–144.

Wehmeyer, M.L., Palmer, S.B., Shogren, K., Williams-Diehm, K. and Soukup, J. (2012) 'Establishing a causal relationship between interventions to promote self-determination and enhanced student self-determination.' *Journal of Special Education 46*, 4, 195–210.

Welsh Assembly Government (2016) *Special Educational Needs Transition from School to Further Learning: Final Report*. Accessed on 25 March 2017 at http://gov.wales/topics/educationandskills/publications/wagreviews/sen-transition/?lang=en.

Welsh Assembly Government (2016) *Refreshed Autistic Spectrum Disorder Strategic Action Plan*. Accessed on 25 March 2018 at http://gov.wales/topics/health/socialcare/asd/?lang=en.

Wigram, T. (2004) *Improvisation: Methods and Techniques for Music Therapy Clinicians, Educators and Young People*. London: Jessica Kingsley Publishers.

Williams, J.Q. (2013) *Music and the Social Model: An Occupational Therapist's Approach to Music with People Labelled as Having Learning Disabilities*. London: Jessica Kingsley Publishers.

Willner, P. (2005) 'The effectiveness of psychotherapeutic interventions for people with learning disabilities: A critical overview.' *Journal of Intellectual Disability Research 49*, 1, 73–85.

Wilson, S. (2003) *Disability, Counselling and Psychotherapy: Challenges and Opportunities*. Basingstoke: Palgrave Macmillan.

Winnicott, D.W. (1967) 'Mirror-Role of Mother and Family in Child Development.' In P. Lomas (ed.) *The Predicament of the Family: A Psychoanalytical Symposium*. London: Hogarth Press and the Institute of Psychoanalysis.

Winnicott, D.W. (2005) *Playing and Reality*. London, New York, NY: Routledge.

Wood, J.K. (2008) *Carl Rogers' Person-Centered Approach: Toward an Understanding of its Implications*. Herefordshire: PCCS Books.

Woods, R. (2017) 'Exploring how the social model of disability can be re-invigorated for autism: In response to Jonathan Levitt.' *Disability and Society 32*, 7, 1090–1095.

Wosch, T. and Wigram, T. (2007) *Microanalysis in Music Therapy: Methods, Techniques and Applications for Clinicians, Researchers, Educators and Students*. London: Jessica Kingsley Publishers.

CHAPTER 13

Self-Realisation in Music Therapy: Developing Insight into the Young Autistic Person's Sense of Self in the Quest for Wholeness Through a Synthesis of Music Therapy, Psychosynthesis and a Developing Sense of Self

PETER WHELAN

Introduction

Music therapy, identity and the young person with an autistic spectrum condition are the focus of this chapter, through the lens of psychosynthesis. After a brief review of the music therapy literature, the introduction to psychosynthesis theory will provide a more detailed description of psychosynthesis and its relationship to music therapy. I will illustrate the theoretical discussion with a case study of a young person with an autistic spectrum condition, whom I will call John. The case study will exemplify how a young person's sense of Self can emerge in music therapy with an increasing awareness of different parts of Self as they emerge into consciousness through musical improvisation.

As we gain new experiences, and as our awareness of different parts of the psyche and their relationship to one another expands, the sense of Self is constantly evolving. These parts form and transform into personal identity in music therapy, and through consciousness may develop a greater capacity for Self-realisation. In the psychosynthesis section, I will introduce the work of the pioneer Assagioli (1965) who refers to two levels of therapy work: first, the level of the personal self, working through feelings and thoughts that were formed in early childhood and manifesting in lives today; second, therapy work engaging creative potentials and unrealised gifts and talents at the level of the transpersonal (Assagioli 1965; Firman and Gila 2002). Self, with a capital S, includes both of these levels holding the emerging personal traits as they manifest in music therapy, alongside the transpersonal qualities and forces emerging through musical improvisation that heal, transform and vitalise authentic identity and personality. In this chapter, I will discuss how music therapy, as a synthesis of many elements, sub-parts and theories, releases our potential and allows us to attain inner authority through I-Self relationship, a key concept in psychosynthesis inherent for Self-realisation.

Music therapy: a brief literature review

Over the past 20 years or more, music therapy gained much of its public recognition in the United Kingdom from working with the development of relational skills so often impaired or disordered in young people with autistic spectrum conditions (Alvin and Warwick 1991/1978). Through the pioneering work of Juliette Alvin, who set up the first music therapy training course in the United Kingdom, and Nordoff and Robbins who developed their own creative music therapy approach, we see the first links between music therapy, autism and special education in the UK (Bunt and Sloboda 2018). Music therapy became recognised as an effective intervention to develop interaction, communication and social skills. Increased understanding of the early infant's awareness of Self (Stern 1985) and how musical interaction underpins non-verbal interaction and communication (Trevarthen *et al.* 1998) furthered the theoretical underpinning of how music therapy can help to develop communication and relationships with children with autistic spectrum conditions.

As theory became more established, research followed. Edgerton's (1994) study showed that creative music therapy increased the communication in six- to nine-year-old clients with autistic spectrum conditions, demonstrating the parallels between non-verbal communication and musical communication. This view was consolidated by Geretsegger *et al.*'s (2014) Cochrane report exemplifying music therapy as an effective medium for developing social interaction, verbal communication, initiating behaviours and social emotional reciprocity in young people with autistic spectrum conditions. In this report, Self is not mentioned explicitly, although perhaps inferred through the process of gaining communication and relating skills through musical exchanges.

My question is how this approach to clinical work relates to or promotes a deeper sense of Self. Can focusing on the micro-musical interactions that increase non-musical interaction and communication increase awareness of macro-musical relationship of the higher Self manifesting I-Self musical improvisation; a context and purpose of therapy for Self-realisation? Should the emerging higher Self in music therapy be given space to realise its fullest creative potential, 'more than' measuring the capacity to interact and communicate?

Coming closer to theories of the all-encompassing higher Self, Alvin and Warwick (1991/1978) emphasise music therapy as an integrative force employing musical techniques that provide structures physically, emotionally, psychologically and socially at the child's personal level of functioning. They highlight how engaging mothers in the therapeutic process musically with their child can increase communication, bonding, relationship and belonging in the world. Other authors working with children and families look at influencing how parents respond, interact and relate with their children, increasing parental bonds and relationships (Oldfield 1993; Oldfield and Bunce 2001; Woodward 2003, 2004). The holistic nature of musical improvisation makes speaking to the many levels within the multiplicity of the individual with an autistic spectrum condition a therapeutic possibility. As such, music can be a matrix of many parts, elements and potential energies, which may include musical styles and culture and be informed by a wide range of theories. They are the matrix in which the person with an autistic spectrum condition finds himself. Using these in therapy can facilitate interaction with a child on multiple levels developing communication, interaction and social relating (Robarts 1998).

Nordoff and Robbins (1977, 1992) wrote of the 'music child' as an innate entity within us all that is allowed to flourish through creative music making. Their 'music child' links with Assagioli's (1965) theory considering the 'personalities', different ages and our inner child the essence of our creativity. Assagioli suggests that within each of us there is a collection of parts or subpersonalities alongside our inner child with a core Self that regulates the relationship between these parts, including the personal self, the ego and the higher Self. Discovering these parts and their relationship to one another is a psychosynthetic venture, much like Brown's views of the therapeutic relationship as an unfolding moment-to-moment organic process (Brown 2002). Implicit in this chapter is the role of 'I' in staying with, guiding and witnessing the unfolding musical story of the client. I would propose that the therapist's capacity to be led by the I-Self unfolding in music therapy is related to the client's capacity to stay with their own I-Self connection.

Psychoanalytical music therapy uses creative musical improvisation to connect with the unconscious parts of Self embodied in the music (Priestley 1994). This creative use of musical improvisation draws on the innate and spontaneous imagination of the client manifesting unconscious feelings and thoughts in music. It focuses on repressed material that may be in some way sabotaging the client's life. Unlocking the repressed material by expressing it musically can release the client from subservience to the unconscious. Psychosynthesis theory proposes a slightly different view: that the client's symptoms are Self seeking connection and expression. These symptoms are not to be repressed or denied but transformed into internal systems through listening and responding to the symptom as a portal to the higher Self.

There are many psychological theories exploring the autistic spectrum condition from different levels including aetiology as a different brain configuration (Lawson 2001), deficits in the theory of mind influencing the capacity to read the other person (Baron-Cohen 1992) and the triad of impairments: language, social relating and imagination (Wing and Gould 1978). Music therapy attempts to include and address these areas of autistic spectrum conditions by increasing interaction, communication and play skills. An explicit inclusion of the potential higher Self is not often considered.

Kim, Wigram and Gold's (2009) study looks at the emotional, motivational and interpersonal responses of children with autism in music therapy, successfully encouraging engagement and relationship through musical improvisation. Through synthesis of theory and music therapy practice, they merge Stern's concepts of attunement and inter-affectivity within musical improvisation into 'musical-attunement', a synthesis of parts of the mother–child relationship (Kim *et al.* 2009; Stern 1985). Trevarthen (1980, 1993) uses the term intersubjectivity to describe the sharing of states that include feelings and thoughts, proposing that human beings are born social creatures and that mother–infant interaction does not just meet physical needs of the body. Stern posits that the baby craves social contact for contact's sake alone, sharing feelings and thoughts at their level of development (1985). Stern (2010) explores the musicality of these connections and makes links to the role of non-verbal therapies, in particular music therapy, looking in detail at some of the techniques described by Wigram (2004). I would also suggest a link between this process and transferential phenomena; the inner world of a client can be transferred through musical improvisation and communicated to the music therapist unconsciously.

Few writings refer directly to young people with autistic spectrum conditions in terms of spirituality and music therapy. It seems to me, however, that there is a call to explore this and the search for meaning and transcendence. McClean, Bunt and Daykin (2012) researched and wrote about music therapy and cancer patients in residential care through spiritual transcendence (rising above everyday experience); connectedness; the search for meaning; and faith and hope as overarching themes that shift and evolve in time. Priestley (1994) points to the spiritual aspects of music therapy in different cultures and music's healing role in communities where music has specific functions. Marom (2004) and Alvin (1975) cite the importance of music to the ancient Greeks and Romans spanning the history of modern mankind. More recently, music therapy and spirituality is an emerging voice in palliative care (Aldridge 2003; Amir 2002a, 2002b; Chase 2002; Highfield 1992; Rollins 2008). Tsiris (2017) published an international review of music therapists' perceptions around spirituality and music therapy, suggesting perhaps an opening into viewing therapy as a spiritual endeavour for all people, a shared cultural understanding of music and spirituality. However, the only writing I discovered linking spirituality to autism was Bogdashina (2013) discussing Self and Soul from a number of Western and Eastern psychological viewpoints. She defines the characteristics as continuity, unity, anchored in the body, in charge and having a capacity for reflection.

This section highlights gaps in the literature in relation to the transpersonal: the higher Self, the archetypal whole being that is seeking to emerge in all of us. This led me to explore psychosynthesis, which I will define and explore in terms of music therapy before illustrating these ideas through a case study which explores the question: what does mean for this young person John with an autistic spectrum condition?

Psychosynthesis

Roberto Assagioli, an Italian psychotherapist and a contemporary of Freud and Jung, engaged in a quest for wholeness through Self-realisation: becoming more aware and conscious of our true potential and the hidden capacities which remain unconscious for a myriad of reasons. Much of his insights into Eastern philosophy and psychospiritual teaching focus on our connection with the Higher Self, that transpersonal aspect of us which is seeking to emerge in our personal lives. Psychosynthesis, as a therapeutic experience, allows us to flourish to become more whole through self-awareness and consciousness: Self-Realisation. Assagioli (1965) believed that all energy could be refined, transmuted and transformed in therapy, taking our defensive and survival systems into service of I-Self authenticity. He gave us the 'egg diagram' (Figure 13.1) as a psycho-spiritual map to reflect on our experiences and our internal world describing a psychological theory alongside the psychospiritual dimension to Self: our whole being.

At the centre of Figure 13.1 at point (5) is the 'I' – pure consciousness, which becomes filled with our history, feelings, emotions and thoughts. The 'I' as conductor of our internal world where the parts of the orchestra are subservient to the conductor just as our internal parts, sub-personalities, must be under direction of the personal self 'I', lest they take over the system. The lower unconscious (1) contains all the material which we repress and/or suppress to avoid pain and suffering or at least confusion. Our ego defences are employed to limit confusion and maintain the status quo to allow us to operate with optimum efficiency and minimal effort or loss of energy (Masterson 1990). The danger is that those defences and patterns of behaviour that allowed us to cope in the face of confusion and/or suffering become a prison of protection and prevent us from adapting, assimilating and transforming our experiences in service of Self (Kalsched and Sieff 2008).

This 'I', the spark of higher Self in matter, dwells in the middle unconscious (2), where we are aware of the world around us and half-aware of the preconscious material that is just under our attention. A concept heralded by Assagioli and psychosynthesis is the 'superconscious' (3) where all our potentials, creative qualities and unfulfilled talents and gifts dwell awaiting formation. The superconscious, and all its aspirational, creative qualities, is linked to the lower unconscious containing all our fears, pain and suffering; what you do to one so do you to the other. Hence, awakening to the unconscious realm awakens the corresponding unconscious realm in the field of consciousness. For me, the act of engaging in creative musical improvisation releases our superconscious creative aspects of Self and the repressed material of the lower unconscious into music, where we can experience all levels of our Being in sound and music. Through an unfolding process of musical and emotional expression, music can bypass the defences and give life to the repressed parts of the young person with an autistic spectrum condition, transforming stereotypical music into authentic musical repetition, musical defences into musical structures and musical avoidance into mutual freedom of expression.

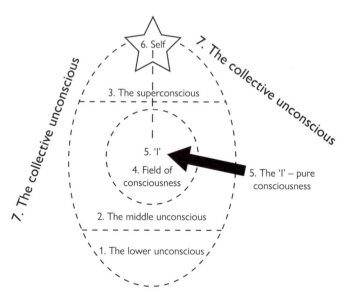

Figure 13.1: Egg Diagram (Assagioli 1965)

As Self emerges in therapy, we discover our many parts, repressed feelings and unconscious subpersonalities that make up our identity hidden in the shadows. In psychosynthesis therapy we are exploring the many subpersonalities of Self and the relationship between each part. For example, the devoted Fan, the Rock-Star and the musical improviser. This process may raise awareness and consciousness of our many identities within the whole Self from the psychodynamic process of engaging with repressed difficult feelings (Priestley 1994) to the absolute music therapy approaches which evoke the creative Self (Nordoff and Robbins 1992), or what Nordoff and Robbins referred to as the 'music-child'. As such, we are influenced by these systemic forces, mindsets and worldviews, and as therapists we must become conscious and aware of our own music therapy culture that we have become identified with unconsciously or consciously.

> We are dominated by everything with which our self is identified. We can dominate and control from which we disidentify ourselves. The normal mistake we all make is to identify ourselves with some content of consciousness itself. Some people get their identity from the feelings, others from their thoughts, other from their social roles. But this identification with a part of the personality destroys the freedom which comes from the experience of pure 'I'. (Assagioli and Keen 1974, p.6)

Psychosynthesis is a 'will and love' psychology allowing our higher Self to manifest in our lives through awareness and consciousness (Assagioli and Keen 1974, p.5). In psychosynthesis theory, will is the closest expression of Self preventing us from becoming stuck in identifications or defences when we encounter intense energies or feelings. 'I' is the spark of higher 'Self' in a body, coordinating and conducting our orchestra of inner parts through identification, disidentification and choice. Pure consciousness of 'I' allows the internal system to include the survival mechanisms and subpersonalities formed to preserve aspects of the higher Self (Assagioli 1975). Our 'I' has no content of its own and it is the personal self that operates in the world in pursuit of connection to our higher Self. Authenticity is achieved through I-Self relationship as we engage with our aspirations and potentials beyond our ego defences which have become redundant, ineffectual or overbearing. These ego defences served us in childhood, but have become over-identified imprisoning us in maintaining cycles that no longer serve us (Kalsched and Sieff 2008). The number of ego defences in the young person with an autistic spectrum condition in this chapter may be less in quantity but they operate on a level of survival and protection in a direct way, using engagement and disengagement as a form of defence. Part of therapy involves transforming defences so they serve the individual and are not driving our lives but serving us. This is where forms of engagement and shutting down are the main mechanisms for managing unknowns. Musical interaction and improvisation can replace these defences, becoming the structure and form of personal expression as the mechanism for articulating Self. Learning about love and will in psychosynthesis drew my attention to how music therapy is nurturing and nourishing whilst balancing the force of will with loving reflection, compassion and holding. Love and will in therapy allows us to include our ego defences in service of I-Self and I hope to show how this is conveyed through musical improvisation.

In our early lives, we form subpersonalities which preserve the qualities of Self that were repressed to survive in the changing world and now in our current lives we have become too dependent on them to the point they imprison us in familiar defences (Kalsched and Sieff, 2008). The process of psychosynthesis therapy is about one becoming more in touch with I-Self connection where our true feelings, emotions and thoughts are manifesting in each subpersonality. This is achieved through a process of identification and disidentification with the sensation, feelings and thoughts. Music, I believe, has an inherent capacity to facilitate this through sound as we play with music and reflect on the sounds and music we are making together. Musical identification and musical disidentification coincide in musical improvisation as we make moment-to-moment decisions about what music we sound together.

Evans's (2002, 2007) triphasic model maps out the pre-personal, personal and transpersonal realms of consciousness, conveying how Self is manifesting in these three levels. With soul having the capacity to transcend the three levels, music therapy, like psychosynthesis, engages the 'I' at the level of soul to bring the transpersonal and the personal into consciousness. Assagioli (1965) also spoke of three realms of consciousness: the lower unconscious, where we repress our intense unmanageable feelings; the middle unconscious, where our personal self the 'I' manages daily life by regulating our inner and outer world; and the superconscious where our transpersonal qualities dwell, emerging through the higher Self. He believed that therapy was on at least two levels, the personal and the transpersonal. In therapy we unpack in the 'here and now' the personal feelings and repressed material of the lower unconscious by allowing the emerging qualities of the superconscious to manifest and be assimilated (Ferruchi 2004; Firman and Gila 1997).

Music therapy and psychosynthesis

Through the lens of psychosynthesis the music therapy relationship can include the qualities of the Higher Self through creative music therapy improvisation, establishing a context for I-Self relationship. Our unknown creative abilities are brought into musical consciousness as music connects the lower unconscious and the superconscious and releases the archetypal energies of the higher Self. Defences which can be seen to preserve our 'inner child' by managing chaos through ritual routine and order exist in all human beings, from a psychosynthesis perspective. How I use my unconscious skills to navigate and bring on board all the aspects of Self depends on my own capacity for I-Self relationship which includes embracing the many disparate, diverse and paradoxical parts. An autistic spectrum condition may be seen as one of these parts.

The autistic self is an essential aspect of personal experience that provides clarity, organisation and perspective at the level of ego, I and Self. Kalsched and Sieff (2008) talk of an autistic response to the world as the early infant discovers difference, separateness and unpredictability in his immediate relationships to mother in the world. Whelan (2010) wrote of the dilemma that faces a mother when her empathic holding and relating is not registered by her autistic child. Her attempts at synchronous connection may be missed or misinterpreted by the child with an autistic spectrum condition whose executive functioning either shuts down or is impaired from birth. Perhaps the experience becomes confused or frightening.

The formation of a healthy, malleable ego is vital in transgressing the gaps in our experience, our failures and achievements, and internalising the good-enough mother (Winnicott 1971). If the young person with an autistic spectrum condition cannot form an I–Ego–Self relationship that regulates these gaps and the anxieties they evoke, then his development may be different. Self may become identified with his sensations (Id) and experiences from his own perspective, with little capacity to empathise with others. Self may be identified with personal self, and his experience of the world may be very frightening when that world behaves in a way that is outside his identified experience. The music therapy relationship allows the young person to be in the centre of their world. Even when it moves in different tempos, rhythms and melodies, the textures, and tonalities, the central focus remains that the young person can experience themselves within the organically changing music.

Music therapy can explore the archetypal personalities becoming conscious in the young person's life. The musical relationship includes the defences, understands and acknowledges their validity and allows them to expand and grow through improvisation into healthy parts assimilated by the ego into I-Self. It has the capacity for many levels of multiplicity, allowing a unique experience of Self, in all its levels, much like different characters in an opera hold melodies for conflicting emotional states or roles such as the hero, the anti-hero and the higher Self in the form of a magical nymph.

The art of singing, sounding instruments or directing the music therapist's improvisations through physical gestures and responses in this relationship is the act of musical consciousness. Self is being expressed in music as 'I' chooses sounds spontaneously reflecting the internal world. I-Self relating includes our natural ego defences, including natural autistic states and behaviours but are not driven by them; instead, 'I' considers and reflects on what is taking place in our responses and reaches beyond the survival mechanisms and subpersonality structures in our soul's journey for wholeness. Defensive music making where one musical partner blocks the other's music out, or reacts defensively, avoiding or distracting the musical relationship away from authentic spontaneous expression, may reflect an I-it relationship. This relationship stops being subjective and becomes a defence against the emerging Higher-Self.

In music therapy, I believe that 'I' is the conscious musical improviser choosing his sounds and rhythms to express feelings and emotions, to connect with the music therapist, and to explore the internal and external world through sounds and music. The unfolding process of musical improvisation is a manifestation of the 'I-Self' relationship, a process where Self is becoming more known to itself through authentic awareness and consciousness of all aspects of Self.

Firman and Gila (2002) write that the Higher Self is experienced at all levels due to its immanent and transcendent nature. It can take us to the deepest unconscious parts of our difficult encounters in the lower unconscious and also the shining, perhaps intimidating, heights of our creativity in the Superconscious. It has the capacity to mediate the levels of pre-personal, personal and transpersonal, connecting the levels in a matrices of Self-realisation. Hence, psychosynthesis is a soul-making therapy, expanding Self to include the Light and Dark. Likewise, connecting with the music-child can be a soulful experience that transcends and includes all the aspects of Self both in Light and Shadow: the transcendent-immanent Higher Self.

Welwood (1992) argues the importance of living all aspects of life, warning that the mystic who transcends life and suffering is avoiding Self Realisation – a subtle defence against the process of transformation. We live an ordinary life with our feet firmly on the ground, looking upwards towards our aspirational Self and bringing Self into our daily lives in ordinary ways (Welwood 1992). Just as the 'I' is Self in matter as the spark of all we are yet to become in the world, so the 'Will' is the closest expression of Higher Self (Evans 2002; Ferruchi 2004; Firman and Gila 2002). Psychosynthesis is a psychology of 'love' and 'will' in action, embodied in the purest form of conscious, the 'I' (Assagioli and Keen 1974, p.5). Together Love and Will form the creation of I-Self in action. Love binds, expressed in our attachments and the impulse to connect with Self and with Other: Maternal Love. Will promotes growth and development towards higher self and becoming all we truly meant to be. In music therapy, connection in sound is loving and accepting, with the music therapist mirroring musically the sounds and presence of the young person with an autistic spectrum condition. Love supports growth and development, and by musically holding and containing someone in therapy, his capacity for I-Self connection in music is allowed to flourish. As he feels accepted musically, confidence grows, and his musical meaning comes from the therapist reflecting congruently the inner world of the young person. Music as sound in motion, has all the qualities of will in action, as each musical idea or fragment is becoming musically more authentic through a process or sounds and responses acknowledging and affirming the young person with an autistic spectrum condition.

Music therapy is holding the 'I' in musical improvisation within and alongside the greater music of twoness: musicking (Small 1998). Spontaneous creative musicking calls out the 'I' through the act of engaging our music-child which is closely connected to our soul-child: improvising at the level of soul.

CASE STUDY: JOHN

Musical subpersonalities, the young person with an autistic spectrum condition, and a developing sense of Self

John came to our school from a pupil referral unit. He lived with his mother and siblings, with no contact with his father. A strong and powerful character, John found it difficult to manage his frustration and anger at times. He was referred to music therapy to help him regulate his challenging behaviour and help him with the transition into this new special school. His mother hoped music therapy might channel his behaviour into something productive in service of his wellbeing. She felt he was very musical and very motivated by music. The music therapy assessment showed that John followed the music therapist very closely in musical improvisation, struggling to maintain his role at times. He also expressed a lot of energy, including anger, in his music in sporadic moments of heightened musicality. He had some language, mainly short sentences, and presented with word-finding difficulties which improved during our work by learning to improvise vocally with song words. He used a mixture of words, short phrases and unclear sounds that followed the flow of his sentences, suggesting his intentionality in communication, which now is considerably better, clear and distinct communication. John had lots of strong will, and a keen sense of what he wanted, often controlling his environment through his challenging behaviour.

My initial impressions were that his I-Self connection was overwhelmed by sensory stimulation as he struggled to regulate polarised intense emotions. With an inconsistent personal self 'I', he was subservient to his thoughts, feelings and emotions, moving quickly from excitement to anger or sadness to becoming shut-off. He leaned heavily on an adult to support him when his environment triggered him to a point of having no control. I felt that music therapy might help him to assert control over his behaviour, in essence gaining a sense of Self in regulation and realisation.

Echo – The musical Fan (sessions 1–25)

In the first stage of our music therapy work together, John followed me very closely in musical improvisation. He repeated everything I sang and played, mirroring me exactly, clinging to my music. He appeared unable to create music independently. He stopped and started with me, mirrored my rhythms and melodies, and anxiously looked to me to make more music so that he could join in and pick up my apparent energy and music in the improvisation. He appeared unable to maintain an improvisation, overcoming this gap in his interaction skills by physically prompting me or shout 'Go!' when he wanted more of something. He seemed to need an Other to provide music that he could feed off, resourcing himself as I improvised on his mood, smiles, physical excitement and innate responsive vocalisations. His musical Self was clear and apparent in the way he picked up my melodies and rhythms, responding to my rubato, tempo and changing dynamics: musical-attunement (Kim, Wigram and Gold 2009). I recognised a latent musical Self behind his interaction and communication skills which had adopted the role of active listener and responder. I was the cause and he was the effect, indicating a clear early level of communication which I hoped we might build on. This we certainly did over time.

In my countertransference (Priestley 1994), I noticed that I was also anxious. I wondered what this was about, in my role of producing music that I felt met his need to be mirrored and carried by an Other. I had images of a young child on the shoulders of his father and I noticed an emerging Will: energy to ask him to stand up and become more of a partner in the musical improvisation. Was this my projection as I wanted therapy to work? I stayed away from judgments too soon, but I noticed that I was 'performing' more with songs and melodies which sometimes left me feeling unable to fulfil his demands. He appeared to adore the musical attention and the happiness it gave him led me to delivering mini-concerts in music therapy that could be heard around the school.

I began to notice that he managed our interaction through engaging and disengaging with the music (Kalsched and Sieff 2008). It felt like he was using an early ego defence to manage the world between us (Masterson 1990), stopping and starting his responses to music which evolved into him conducting me musically through this behaviour. He had my undivided attention and this seemed important to him. The role of the devoted Fan subpersonality kept him in the relationship, but also outside of it as he withheld his own music and directed mine.

Over time, I took the risk to not fulfil all of his musical needs, thereby creating a demand for him to engage as a partner in the music. By disidentifying from my countertransference, John had the space to assume the role of performer. I wondered if I had modelled something to him about how to be in music. On reflection, it seems he had a natural flare for performing that he might have manipulated me into during the early stage of the work. The 'Rock-Star' had qualities he needed for nourishment and resourcing in music therapy. His I-Improviser began to emerge with him responding and interacting musically and quickly developing an enthusiastic drumming style as we followed each other closely on the drums.

The Rock-Star (sessions 25 – 47)

This emerging subpersonality that emerged in stage two of music therapy, the Rock-Star was expressed on the electric guitar or the drum kit. It felt like the Rock-Star subpersonality emerged from the 'superconscious' with a desire to be seen and heard rejoicing in being alive and the immediacy of these grown-up instruments. The characteristics of the instruments came into play as John demonstrated an awareness of how they could be used in Western culture. Initially, his chords on the guitar were approximations of harmonic rhythms of familiar chart songs with a basic harmonic structure. Over time, he founds his own way to discern the chords patterns of I-IV-V-I and when we improvised in different keys he found the chords perfectly within a few minutes. He managed his own version of the finger shapes and adapted his skills spontaneously as we improvised each week. In a sense, he appeared to grow into the music therapy improvisation model, discover his I-Improviser and begin to embrace another way of being through music.

Through the countertransference, I wondered if the Rock-Star wanted to be adored, allowing his healthy narcissistic needs to be fulfilled, whilst keeping another eye on what was emerging from the lower unconscious. Having found his musical improvisation style, he dominated the musical space and there was now little room for anyone else. He wanted to lead without knowing where he was going and as his therapist I was to be his backing vocals, his band member and his audience. Somehow, I became the Fan who told him each week how amazing he was, which wasn't a difficult task, as his music was so energetic and joyful approaching a congruent musical experience each week.

I became frustrated with my earlier desire for him to sing out and play with exuberance and now I felt the desire for some space, constantly feeling at this stage that I must keep up with his marathon of rock music. As the Rock-Star became established in the music therapy relationship, I became aware of the significance of the vivacious, joyful music played in Rock rhythms and pulse. We are carried by the triumphant joy of rhythmic, syncopated Rock improvisations which contained feelings in a steady pulse growing organically through the obvious familiar musical style and a shared musical context. Allowing him to lead and witnessing his music, I began to wonder what Rock-Star held for him and how this served his Self? I felt this subpersonality held the energy of confidence and joy that feeds the soul, nourishing Self, and expressed his musicality. In bifocal vision and multi-listening, I wanted to know who else was seeking to emerge. My keeping up with his need and surviving his demands allowed him to test me in a musical way that was more sophisticated than him engaging and disengaging. It felt like the Rock-Star was honouring his talent whilst protecting his more vulnerable nature which was afraid to fail or angry when he could not make himself understood.

Once he found this role in music therapy, it appeared as if he found it difficult to let go and embrace more vulnerable parts and feelings. He expressed anger if I suggested musically exploring the music in the shadows: quieter, softer sounds, songs and music. When offered, these were quickly turned into excited, happy music.

He had learned to feed his narcissistic need to be seen and heard and he was not ready to let go and move to a deeper place.

The quiet Mouse and the roaring Lion (sessions 48 – 61)

Over time, I began to notice the quiet mouse emerging from the lower unconscious, repressed, silent and fearful. This took the form of high-pitched notes on the electric guitar, as he laughed saying 'mousey'. I took this opportunity to mirror quieter music on the shape of the squeaking Mouse motif and he used the motif throughout our improvisations over some weeks. What began as a humorous mimicking became an exchange between us that was softer and more reflective musically. As the Mouse became more present musically, vulnerable feelings appeared to emerge and the purpose of the Rock-Star became more visible: to protect the vulnerable quiet Self. His capacity to be vulnerable was tentative and fleeting; he preferred to retreat into the bravado of the Rock-Star and avoid any feelings of vulnerability that might come from fear, anxiety and confusion. As quietness and vulnerability was allowed into the music, the Rock-Star transformed into a reflective musical Self and then into a musically confident leader, who improvised with the tonality of songs following modulations and initiating key changes with new verses of music. The quality of his listening changed and his musical improviser role was more inclusive of Other as he became musically aware and musically reflective.

The quieter vulnerable part seemed less frightened and less reluctant to emerge. The music of the quiet vulnerable parts evolved slowly over time and we discovered that underneath this part, this quiet Mouse masked a roaring Lion who was so angry that only silence and quiet music could keep the roars under control. Allowing the Lion into the therapy space meant that the 'I' began to tame the Lion and share the energy of the Rock-Star so that these parts of Self were no longer hiding or fighting for leadership, but playfully and co-consciously sounding music together in I-Self musical relationship. Control became free expression and 'I' was allowed to be quiet, roaring, joyful and exuberant by coming into relationship with the unconscious parts musically.

Discussion
I-Self relating and the musical improviser

The autistic desire for order, ritual and routine may have temporarily alleviated John's difficult feelings linked with vulnerability. We are not in therapy to remove defences or, indeed, autistic systems for being in the world. We worked to support those systems to serve Self more successfully by not taking over the 'I-Self' relationship; rather enhancing and developing Self-awareness and Self-realisation. By listening to the quiet, vulnerable part within John's confident, exuberant Rock-Star, a relationship between confidence and vulnerability was heard, responded to and transformed within the therapeutic relationship. Music therapy allowed his autistic qualities to come under the direction of 'I-Self', drawing on the strengths of the rituals and routines in his life by transforming them into musical relating. This I-improviser playfully engaged with the Rock-Star, the Mouse, the Lion, as the organiser took over the role of engaging the lower unconscious.

Making friends with his subpersonalities, taming the Lion and engaging in service of Self, can be seen to be a spiritually healing aspect of music therapy. This young autistic person used music to connect with archetypal energies and feelings that he might have ritualistically repressed previously. The archetypal warrior was expressed as the Rock-Star: energetic, heroic music that said, 'I am here, listen to me.' This called out the archetypal mother energy of being adored by the Fan and transformed into the Lioness protecting her vulnerable cubs, roaring and nurturing her space and her vulnerabilities. The autistic qualities transformed into organising musical catalyst around which the relationships between the parts emerged; instead of keeping subpersonalities compartmentalised, they were brought together musically. Assessing a sense of Self involves listening to the presenting sub-personality and understanding its role within the internal system. Every part is living in a dyadic pair, and by allowing that to be expressed, other layers of Self emerge. Over time, the 'I' gained inner authority and the sub-personalities were no longer running the whole system but became in service of Self. This holistic capacity to be with the one and the many, the aspects of Self expressed through subpersonality, ego defences and the inner child work all belong to Self-Realisation.

As a music therapist, I believe psychosynthesis offers us a lens to process our experience of music therapy. Much like psychosynthesis, at the core of music therapy is a synthesis of physical matter, sensation and sensory experience, intuition and imagination, leading to awareness of our higher Self and sense of Self.

Musical improvisation included John's obsessive ritualistic behaviour, exploring its meaning and purpose for the client in a gentle, light way to reduce his anxiety and make his experiences 'ordinary in the world'. The music was his tonality, pulse, texture and tone, all of which conveyed his personality, his needs and the potential transformation lying in the potential of the higher Self being realised through musical relationship. The music therapist encouraged the music of each part to express its needs and form a relationship with the other parts; his collective sounds of Self could then be seen to be the music of the soul.

Self became embodied in the musical composition and musical improvisation through authentic emotional expression including John and his relationship to the unspoken parts of him in music. The sound of 'I' allowed the 'song of the soul' (our wholeness) to emerge as the young person made their 'music-child' heard and experienced in music therapy. Musical mirroring and musical exploration of personality forged John's identity and an authentic I-Self relationship. Each part, or subpersonality, held an aspect of his higher Self, protecting and preserving that part. Calling out to the 'I' through musical improvisation facilitated the journey from Rock-Star to Lioness to I-Self relating. Putting the young person in the centre of their musical improvisation, capturing their sounds, mood, behaviour, personality through the musical relationship, created a platform for 'I' to emerge as the centre of pure consciousness. Music therapy evoked John's Will.

The music and the music therapy relationship contained his intense feelings repressed in the lower unconscious, allowing them to be expressed in sound through improvisation. In turn, his aspirational creative qualities of the higher Self, hidden in the superconscious, were also sounded, heard and exchanged between therapist and client. Drawing him into relationship with the parts he feared and his creative Self musically created a system of interpersonal musical transformation. Considering attunement and intersubjectivity in musical terms helped me to discern more successfully the content of transferential exchanges, distinguishing between feelings, emotions and states or levels of Being.

The field of consciousness from a psychosynthesis perspective is the space between client and therapist where an exchange of energy happens unconsciously. Looking inwards to my feelings, thoughts and states allowed me to connect to the field of consciousness between us, and the exchange of musical-attunement and musical-intersubjectivity was possible. As we became aware of the music of each of his many inner parts (i.e. subpersonalities), we changed each one by giving it a musical voice. This transformed his sense of Self by helping him relate to each part musically. Through the field of consciousness and the transferential phenomena we exchanged roles, parts and states in an improvisation constructed from musical attunement and musical intersubjectivity. I felt that music therapy shared the psychosynthesis context of working at the levels of pre-personal (ego), personal (I) and transpersonal (Self) through a synthesis of different psychologies and theories for Self-Realisation.

In this chapter references to music therapy theory, psychosynthesis theory and music therapy theory unfold my understanding of the young person's emerging sense of Self in context. I particularly focused on how the transpersonal world of the young person with an autistic spectrum condition can manifest and be fulfilled in music therapy. Musical-attunement leading to musical-intersubjectivity helped me discern more successfully the content of transferential exchanges distinguishing between feelings, emotions and states or levels of being. Multi-tasking and negotiating these different aspects of our system is a musical endeavour and, in music therapy, improvisation helped John gain a sense of control and confidence when processing conflicting energy, skills and communication. The case study showed that through musical improvisation, John's personal expression was transformed by connecting him to his Higher Self which created ease in his relationship to the many other parts of himself that were sometimes difficult to navigate in the past. As the work in the case study came to a close, he no longer overused the Rock-Star subpersonality; he appeared to become more Self-reflective and present in his relationships.

References

Aldridge, D. (2003) 'Music therapy and spirituality: A transcendental understanding of suffering.' *Music Therapy Today 4*, 1, 1–28 Accessed on 28 April 2017 at https://issuu.com/presidentwfmt/docs/mtt_4_1_-4_3__2003.

Alvin, J. (1975) *Music Therapy.* New York, NY: Basic Books.

Alvin, J. and Warwick A. (1991) *Music Therapy for the Autistic Child* (2nd edition). Oxford: Oxford University Press. (First published 1978.)

Amir, D. (2002a) 'Spirituality in music therapy.' [blog] *Voices: A World Forum for Music Therapy.* Accessed on 1 June 2017 at: https://voices.no/community/?q=content/spirituality-music-therapy.

Amir, D. (2002b) 'Spiritual music therapy: Opening ourselves to the mysterious qualities of music therapy.' *Voices: A World Forum for Music Therapy.* Accessed on 3 September 2017 at: http://testvoices.uib.no/community/?q=fortnightly-columns/2002-spiritual-music-therapy-opening-ourselves-mysterious-qualities-music-therap.

Assagioli, R. (1965) *Psychosynthesis: A Manual of Principles and Techniques.* Oxford: Hobbs, Dorman & Co.

Assagioli, R. and Keen, S. (1974) 'The golden mean of Roberto Assagioli.' *Psychology Today.* Accessed on 27 April 2018 at two.not2.org/psychosynthesis/articles/GoldenMean.pdf.

Assagioli, R. (1975) *Psychosynthesis: A Collection of Basic Writings.* London: Turnstone Books.

Baron-Cohen, S. (1992). *Autism: The Facts.* Oxford: Oxford University Press.

Bogdashina, O. (2013) *Autism and Spirituality.* London and Philadelphia: Jessica Kingsley Publishers.

Brown, S. (2002) 'Hullo Object! I Destroyed You.' In L. Bunt and S. Hoskyns (eds) *The Handbook of Music Therapy.* East Sussex: Brunner-Routledge.

Bunt, L. and Sloboda, A. (2018). 'Encounters with three music therapy pioneers: Juliette Alvin; Mary Priestley and Maggie Picket.' Paper presented at the BAMT Music Therapy Conference Music, Diversity and Wholeness 2018, The Barbican Centre, London.

Chase, K.M. (2002) 'Spirituality in music therapy.' [moderated discussion] *Voices: A World Forum for Music Therapy.* Accessed on 1 June 2017 at https://voices.no/community/?q=content/spirituality-music-therapy.

Edgerton, C.L. (1994) 'The effect of improvisational music therapy on the communicative behaviours of autistic children.' *Journal of Music Therapy 31*, 1, 31–62.

Evans, J. (2002) *Core Principles in Psychosynthesis Volume I and II.* London: Institute of Psychosynthesis.

Evans, J. (2007) *Soul Making at Work (Spiritual Praxis and Basic Counselling Skills).* London: Anamcāra Press.

Ferruchi, P. (2004) *What We May Be: Techniques for Psychological and Spiritual Growth Through Psychosynthesis* (2nd edition). New York, NY: Tarcher/Penguin.

Firman, J. and Gila, A. (1997) *The Primal Wound.* Albany, NY: State University of New York Press.

Firman, J. and Gila, A. (2002) *Psychosynthesis: A Psychology of the Spirit.* Albany, NY: State University of New York Press.

Geretsegger, M., Elefant, C., Mössler, K.A. and Gold, C. (2014) 'Music therapy for people with autism spectrum disorder.' *Cochrane Database of Systematic Reviews 2014, 6*, CD004381. DOI: 10.1002/14651858.CD004381.pub3.

Highfield, M. (1992) 'Spiritual health of oncology patients: Nurse and patient perspectives.' *Cancer Nursing 15*, 1, 1–8.

Kalsched, D. and Sieff, D. (2008) *Unlocking the Secrets of the Wounded Psyche: The Miraculous Survival System That is Also a Prison*. Accessed on 8 March 2017 at http://www.danielasieff.com/wp-content/uploads/2014/09/Unlocking-the-Secrets-of-the-Wounded-Psyche-2008-JN-b..pdf.

Kim, J., Wigram, T. and Gold, C. (2009) 'Emotional, motivational and interpersonal responsiveness of children with autism in improvisational music therapy.' *Autism 13*, 4, 389–409.

Lawson, W. (2001) *Understanding and Working with the Spectrum of Autism: An Insider's View*. London: Jessica Kingsley Publishers.

Marom, M. (2004) 'Spiritual Moments in Music Therapy: A Qualitative Study of the Music Therapist's Experience.' In B. Abrams (ed) *Qualitative Inquiries in Music Therapy. Monograph Series, Volume 1*. Gilsum, NH: Barcelona Publishers.

Masterson, J. (1990) *The Search for the Real Self*. New York, NY: The Free Press.

McClean, S., Bunt, L. and Daykin, N. (2012) 'The healing and spiritual properties of music therapy at a cancer care centre.' *Journal of Alternative and Complementary Medicine 18*, 4, 402–407.

Nordoff, P. and Robbins, C. (1977) *Creative Music Therapy: Individualised Treatment for the Handicapped Child*. Gilsum, NH: Barcelona Publishers.

Nordoff, P. and Robbins, C., (1992) *Therapy in Music for Handicapped Children*. London: Victor Gollancz.

Oldfield, A. (1993) 'Music Therapy with Families.' In M. Heal and T. Wigram (eds) *Music Therapy in Health and Education*. London: Jessica Kingsley Publishers.

Oldfield, A. and Bunce, L. (2001) 'Mummy can play too... short-term music therapy with mothers and young children.' *British Journal of Music Therapy 15*, 1, 27–36.

Priestley, M. (1994) *Essays on Analytical Music Therapy*. Gilsum NH: Barcelona Publishers.

Robarts, J. (1998) 'Music Therapy and Children with Autism.' In C. Trevarthen, K. Aitken, D. Papoudi and J. Robarts (eds) *Children with Autism: Diagnosis and Interventions to Meet Their Needs* (Revised 2nd edition). London: Jessica Kingsley Publishers.

Rollins, W. L. (2008) 'Re: spirituality in music therapy' [moderated discussion]. *Voices: A World Forum for Music Therapy*. Accessed on 1 June 2017 at https://voices.no/community/?q=content/spirituality-music-therapy-.

Small, C. (1998) *Musicking The Meanings of Performing and Listening*. Middletown, CT: Wesleyan University Press.

Stern, D. (1985) *The Interpersonal World of the Infant*. New York, NY: Basic Books.

Stern, D.N. (2010) *Forms of Vitality: Exploring Dynamic Experience in Psychology, the Arts, Psychotherapy and Development*. Oxford: Oxford University Press.

Trevarthen, C. (1980). 'The Foundations of Intersubjectivity: Development of Interpersonal and Cooperative Understanding of Infants.' In D. Olson (ed.) *The Social Foundations of Language and Thought: Essays in Honor of J. S. Bruner*. New York, NY: W. W. Norton.

Trevarthen, C. (1993) 'The Self Born in Intersubjectivity: The Psychology of an Infant Communicating.' In U. Neisser (ed.) *The Perceived Self: Ecological and Interpersonal Sources of Self-Knowledge.* New York, NY: Cambridge University Press.

Trevarthen, C., Aitken, K., Papoudi, D. and Robarts, J. (1998) *Children with Autism Diagnosis and Interventions to Meet Their Needs.* London: Jessica Kingsley Publishers.

Tsiris, G. (2017) 'Music therapy and spirituality: An international survey of music therapists' perceptions.' *Nordic Journal of Music Therapy 26,* 4, 293–319.

Welwood, J. (1992) *Ordinary Magic, Everyday Life as Spiritual Path.* Boston, MA: Shambhala.

Whelan, P. (2010) 'Music therapy and the young autistic person: The use of music therapy with an autistic client approaching young adult life.' Unpublished MA thesis (Philosophy). University of West of England and Bristol Music Space.

Wigram, T. (2004) *Improvisation: Methods and Techniques for Music Therapy Clinicians, Educators and Students.* London: Jessica Kingsley Publishers.

Wing, L. and Gould, J. (1978) 'Systematic recording of behaviours and skills of retarded and psychotic children.' *Journal of Autism and Childhood Schizophrenia 8,* 1, 79–97.

Winnicott, D.W. (1971) *Playing and Reality.* London and New York, NY: Routledge.

Woodward, A., (2003) 'Three's company: Brief music therapy intervention for an autistic child and her mother.' *Community, Relationship and Spirit. Continuing the dialogue and debate.* Papers from the BSMT/APMT Annual Conference. BSMT Publications.

Woodward, A., (2004) 'Music therapy for autistic children and their families: A creative spectrum.' *British Journal of Music Therapy 18,* 1, 8–14.

Postlude: Music Therapy and Autism Across the Lifespan

ELIZABETH COOMBES AND EMMA MACLEAN

Introduction

This final chapter serves as a summary of the book as a whole and aims to make a final reflection on how the contributions reflect current trends in music therapy. This sits alongside contemporary perspectives on culture and identity for therapeutic work with people with autistic spectrum conditions across the lifespan in the UK. It will consider how relationships between research and practice are presented, the rich diversity of approaches and the apparent role of different contexts when music therapists describe their work and collaborate with others. Finally, it will reflect on how we might expect music therapy practice in the UK to continue moving forwards.

Collating the sections and chapters of the book has been an exciting process. We have had the privilege of watching the music therapists who have written so compellingly about their practice explore and develop their thinking while writing their contributions. This has in turn inspired us not just in our own clinical work but also when compiling the final text in order to ensure we do justice to the range of ideas and practices current in the UK.

Each author has shared a window into their everyday practice, which brings with it a richness and diversity that we believe will enable debate and further development of music therapy. Much as the book itself offers a spectrum of approaches for those with autistic spectrum conditions, so the text itself contributes to the body of literature that has gone before. Alvin (1978) and Nordoff and Robbins (1971, 1977) wrote pioneering texts which in some ways laid the groundwork for the growth and explorations that followed. Jackie Robarts' writing was seminal, as it appeared in a publication not about music therapy, but about children with autism (Trevarthen *et al.* 1998). In this she wove together theory and music-centred work in an innovative way that still has a contemporary feel over 20 years later. What followed was a development in international 'gold-standard' research, including the first Cochrane review in 2006, updated in 2014 (Geretsegger *et al.* 2014), which highlighted evidence for improved social interaction and communication as well as improved quality of parent–child relationships. Alongside this development in the evidence base, thinking about autistic spectrum conditions began to shift from a 'disorder' towards 'condition'. The subheading of Silberman's (2015) text 'Neurotribes' was pivotal in challenging everyone 'how to think smarter about people who think differently'. Music therapy publications in the 21st century began to outline newer approaches, which built on what had been pioneered so many years previous and considered contemporary practice with people with autistic spectrum conditions using an interactive approach (Oldfield 2006a, 2006b), behavioural approaches (Kern and Humpal 2012), working in school settings (McTier 2012), working with adults with learning disabilities (Saville 2007) and measuring the quality of relationships in work with children (Schumacher 2014). This publication was born out of this context; to bring the voices of contemporary practitioners in the UK together to consider, beyond research, what practice-based evidence can add to our knowledge of how, why and when we practice music therapy in a variety of settings across the lifespan. We will begin this journey with a brief reflection on the UK context.

The UK context

This book very much locates its practice within the UK. The work of each practitioner may occur within different settings such as schools, private practice, day centres or NHS facilities. Acting almost as a second skin containing these diverse areas of work is the music therapist's professional registration with the Health and Care Professions Council (HCPC), as well as the profession-specific body, the British Association for Music Therapy (BAMT). Although the Association of Professional Music Therapists (APMT) was first formed in 1976, merging with the British Society for Music Therapy (BSMT) to become BAMT in 2011, it was not until 1999 that the arts therapies professions of music therapy, art therapy and dramatherapy became state registered under the umbrella of the HCPC (Watson 2015).

As Robin Bates states in his chapter in this book, the HCPC is an organisation that provides Standards of Proficiency (HCPC 2013) for all the professions it regulates. It also sets out profession-specific requirements. For music therapists, these revolve around:

- the ability to recognise the importance of different approaches to music therapy in different cultures

- adapting the practice of music therapy to each setting

- an understanding of the importance of musical improvisation in the music therapy work, emphasising the relational process and psychological significance of this

- knowing a broad range of genres and musical styles, and having a high degree of musical proficiency in at least one instrument, plus accompanying and vocal skills.

At a time when continuation of this regulatory function is under scrutiny, it seems important to remember that these standards have been and continue to be devised and revised through consultation with the relevant professions, stakeholders and service users. The voice of the service user is considered to be of the utmost importance by the HCPC. Registration and regulation may instil confidence in service users that those practising music therapy are accountable at a high level for the work they do. In addition to regulating music therapists and their practice, there also exist standards governing the Masters level courses offered by educational institutions in the UK to enable musicians to become music therapists, and ensure and fitness for practice at entry level and beyond (HCPC 2013).

While to those unaccustomed to this level of professional regulation it may seem, perhaps, that this level of scrutiny could feel intrusive and overbearing, the writings of those in this book seem to show the opposite. In Chapter 3 Robin Bates demonstrates that in fact the boundaries set out by the HCPC enable music therapy work to thrive and develop safely. The contents of this book seem to bear witness to the fact that music therapists have a professional commitment and requirement to continuously develop and refine practice in line with these latest developments. This second skin, mooted as an analogy for the HCPC above, appears to provide a support that is strong and flexible. Rather like skin itself, it is a semi-permeable membrane which allows for the to-ing and fro-ing of fresh ideas. Practice developments occur as the therapist receives stimulation from outside sources including supervision (Robertson, Chapter 6) and further training (Gravestock, Chapter 2; Whelan, Chapter 13), in turn enriching their practice and that of others. The professional and ethical boundaries delineated by the HCPC would then seem to support and enhance practice.

The standards also outline the importance of practitioners engaging in evidence-based practice, but what constitutes evidence? As Daphne Rickson and her colleagues suggest:

> Many music therapists have turned away from the medical model which fosters hierarchical relationships and power imbalances between therapist and client, and ignores culture and context. Instead they look towards approaches that recognise health and wellbeing as a process, involve patients in their care process and take account of their cultural and social contexts. (Rickson *et al.* 2016, p.121)

Once again the central role of the service-user voice is highlighted. Here we purposefully quote a music therapist based in New Zealand to reflect the larger, international stage within which the evidence base continues to grow. The following section will consider the ways in which contributors to this book presented both evidence-based practice and practice-based evidence.

Evidence-based practice

The chapters by Oldfield *et al.* (Chapter 1) and Maclean and Tillotson (Chapter 8) both refer to recent increased demands for outcome measures in music therapy. The former reflects on UK participation in a large international randomised control trial (Crawford *et al.* 2017; Geretsegger, Holck and Gold 2012) whereas the latter explores using outcome measures to satisfy a more local requirement from within school settings for measurable aims or progress. Oldfield *et al.* (Chapter 1) pose the question: will staff and parents, having seen the quantitative data, which indicated no significant changes in contrast to the qualitative data, become discouraged and no longer seek this intervention? They outline, through case studies, individual changes not captured by the measurement tools used. Wimpory and Gwilym (Chapter 4) ask, in response to this same data, whether a shift to focusing on a social timing perspective, central to the Musical Interaction Therapy Approach, rather than symptomatology, may be appropriate. Both questions highlight the benefits and tensions of positivist research methods, which require standardised approaches and adherence to a specific hypothesis which may not always be relevant to such a heterogeneous population.

Tillotson and Maclean (Chapter 8) offer a different perspective. Whilst echoing Oldfield et al.'s (Chapter 1) position, that measurement tools which accurately account for positive changes may create increased trust and understanding, they also ask: might there be other ways to do this? They advocate for clear communication and increased collaborative approaches as teams become more established. This focus on collaborative approaches has merited a number of recent publications in Music Therapy (Twyford and Watson 2008; Strange, Odell Miller and Richards 2017) and may be relative to a maturing of the profession. Writing from the perspective of working in New Zealand, Molyneux et al. (2012) demonstrate that collaboration with parents, carers and other professionals is key to setting individualised goals. They explore the dichotomy between outcomes that are based on 'success' and approaches where therapists are 'working in a psychodynamically informed, client centred way, where all behaviour is accepted as communication' (p.16). This dichotomy is reflected clearly in the individually tailored approaches that are described with so much thought and attention to each relationship that is created, developed and given space to grow in the case studies presented in this publication.

Aigen (2014, p.218) outlines the difference between a 'scientific vision', where theory can 'provide explanatory models and help develop a dynamic understanding of cause and effect relationships for phenomena under observation', and the 'more artistic, music-based view of music therapy'. It is within this second 'artistic vision' that this book mainly orients itself where treatment is 'guided by exemplars' and that theory provides 'post-hoc rationales, an overall worldview and value system, and guidelines for the types of skills that are necessary for the successful education of music therapists'. To illustrate this more clearly, Table 14.1 outlines the content of each chapter in terms of the clients, the type of intervention and approach, suggested benefits and therapist skills highlighted.

Table 14.1: Benefits of music therapy across the lifespan

Chapter	Age of clients	Type of intervention and approach	Suggested benefits	Specific therapist skills highlighted
Warwick	Children and young people	Psychodynamic	Confidence to face individual problems through the medium of music and words and to cope	Non-judgemental attitude, ability to use music to connect with each client and give them an experience of a relationship based on trust and respect with clear boundaries
Oldfield, Blauth, Finnemann and Casey	Children aged 4–7	Individual improvisational music therapy low intensity (once a week) or high intensity (three times a week) and three parent counselling sessions in accordance with improvisational music therapy (Geretsegger 2015)	Quantative data showed no significant improvements to social affect or parental social responsiveness Qualitative data showed improvements in social communication skills and emotional wellbeing, increased focus and attention, reduced sensory-stimulating or attention-seeking behaviour, reduced stress and increased ability to tolerate new experiences	Specifics outlined in Oldfield's (2006) approach: motivating aspect of music therapy sessions; the structure inherent in the sessions and in music making; the balance between following and initiating; the basic non-verbal exchanges; the fact that children can be in control in a constructive way; movement combined with music; playfulness and drama in music and working jointly with parents

Gravestock	Children with high-functioning autism	Individual longer-term work using a psychoanalytic and relational approach	Being and becoming in the presence of a therapist	Additional training in relational approach, trauma and attachment theory Considering diagnosis and co-morbidities as well as complex familial and social circumstances Free improvisation and the use of toys and art materials
Bates	An adolescent	Individual work using a graduated approach	Meaningful connections Increased interactions	An ethical rudder Awareness of the school of Object Relations, transference/countertransference and the potential of musical quickening (Ansdell 1995) A solid therapeutic frame/holding environment to create a 'potential space' (Winnicott 2005/1971)
Wimpory and Gwilym	Pre- and primary school aged children	Musical Interaction Therapy (MIT) programme used with carer and individual child	Positive changes in temporal synchrony and social communicative development Emergence of teasing, empathy, symbolic play and manifestations of attachment Improved relational synchrony or reciprocity between carer and child	Microanalysis of both visual and auditory aspects of early interaction, sensitivity and attunement to encourage move from pre-intentional to more intentional communication Awareness of theories of interpersonal synchrony (Stern 1985) Using improvised music to foster social timing and temporal synchrony between carer and child, making social experiences more accessible and predictable

cont.

Chapter	Age of clients	Type of intervention and approach	Suggested benefits	Specific therapist skills highlighted
White	Adolescents	Groupwork using a music-centred approach within psychodynamic frameworks	Improved social interaction and 'togetherness' with peers An opportunity to explore identity and increase self-esteem Sensory regulation and increased awareness of physical and emotional selves	Careful planning of frameworks: inner (instruments, staff, flexibility) and outer (consistent space and time) Awareness of early relationship theories (Trevarthen and Malloch 2000) Creating a 'potential space' (Winnicott 1971) A focus on the therapeutic significance of musical events and specific techniques: grounding; matching; single-line melodic improvisation
Robertson	Adult inpatient – NHS treatment and assessment ward for adults with a learning disability	Individual and group work using a music-centred model but also considering group psychotherapeutic processes (Yalom 1995) and use of other art forms	Increased meaningful connections, engagement, measured flow of communication and hope Increased awareness of individuality and identity Reduced frustration	A listening stance, alertness to unspoken communications across modalities, i.e. in music, art and movement Openness to creative processes connecting with authenticity, beyond the use of 'autistic objects' (Tustin 1992/1981) Awareness of group processes and attachment theory, including the secure base (Bowlby 2005/1979) Paying attention to the dialogue between therapist and carer, which can mirror and support the client's journey and build a communication enhancing environment

| Nugent | Children with their families in their own homes | A relational approach to build relationships between therapist, child and family members | Growth in interpersonal relationships expanding interactive experiences and active participation and focus and attention Improved self-regulation Reduced fragmentation | Requires creativity, holding and flexibility Awareness of psychodynamic (Winnicott 1971, Alvarez 1992 and Tustin cited in Spensley 1995) theories and music-centred techniques |
| Maclean and Tillotson | Children in educational settings | Individual and group work using music-centred (Nordoff and Robbins 2007), humanistic or client-centred (Rogers 2003/1951), interactive (Oldfield 2006a; 2006b) and relational (Stern 2010) approaches | Increased social interaction Improved communication Improved reciprocity, shared attention/ engagement Self-confidence Reduced anxiety towards a specific event Improved emotional wellbeing and subsequent impact on other behaviours | Multi-disciplinary and transdisciplinary approaches with professionals and families Universal, targeted and specialist roles Measurement tools that account for changes and detail approaches |

cont.

Chapter	Age of clients	Type of intervention and approach	Suggested benefits	Specific therapist skills highlighted
Fawcett	Children and young people in a transitional day centre, who are currently without permanent educational provision	Three individuals – upper primary ages	Increased emotional expression in a therapeutic relationship Exploring different and meaningful connections Increased communication	To negotiate a safe, effective and realistic place, frame or potential playground in a place where space, time and length of contact is often unknown, using Kenny's (2006) theories of overlapping fields of relating and Winnicott's (1971) 'potential space' Awareness of vitality affects (Stern cited in Pavlicevic 1997) and the concept of 'communicative musicality' (Malloch 1999) to consider the therapeutic relationship through musical dialogues
Morison	Adult autism inpatient service	Individual	Increased social interactions Improved communication, i.e. eye contact Increased engagement in music making, participation and acceptance of therapeutic input	A gradual and phased collaborative team approach, including skill sharing and a clear assessment approach (Wigram 2002) Focus on 'distress tolerance' and 'interpersonal effectiveness' used in Cognitive Analytical Music Therapy (Compton Dickenson 2017) and interactive music therapy (Oldfield 2006a) Use of Creative Arts Therapies Rating Scale (CAT-SRS) to monitor individual goals

Warnock	Children	Individual	Positive and meaningful connections with self and others	Use of non-verbal voice
				Intersubjectivity (Stern 1985, 2010)
			Improved intersubjective relatedness	Vocal Psychotherapy (Austin 2008)
Pickard	Young adults in a post-compulsory educational unit	Two individuals	Psychological growth congruent with personal choices	A paradigm shift towards the discourse of neurodiversity
			Meaningful connections, integration and participation	A person-centred approach (Rogers 1959; 2004; Cooper *et al.* 2013)
				A non-directive attitude (Raskin 1948, 2005; Levitt 2005)
				Engagement with the techniques of pre-therapy (Prouty 2002)
				Belief in a non-normative, social model of disability (Oliver 1990, 2013; Barnes 2014)
Whelan	Young person in a special school setting	Individual	Self-realisation: increased awareness of authentic self and identity	Integration of the principles of psychosynthesis into music therapy theory and practice
			Interpersonal musical transformation	

The table clearly shows that improvements in social interaction, communication, or meaningful connections, and participation are the most common benefits highlighted by contributors, which align with the Cochrane Review (Geretsegger *et al.* 2014). Others can also be aligned with contemporary research; for example, increased focus and attention (Chapter 1, Oldfield *et al.*) was the focus of Kim, Wigram and Gold's 2009 study. Further outcomes described, such as exploring identity and self-esteem (White, Chapter 5), hope and self-awareness (Robertson, Chapter 6), reduced fragmentation (Nugent, Chapter 7), and increased emotional expression (Fawcett, Chapter 9) are considered harder to measure in positivist terms. However, if we were to try to bring together some of the more qualitative benefits described by clinicians currently working with people with autistic spectrum conditions in the UK, we could summarise that all contributions demonstrate that working with each individual in a range of different and yet similar improvisational music therapy approaches can gradually increase connections with a person's inner musicality or inner world, and draw them towards what might be considered a positive change.

As Bates (Chapter 3) outlines, this process may require the therapist to recognise his or her own values and orientation; whether the condition is considered a deficit or a neurodiversity appears to be central to the way benefits or 'outcomes' are considered. Pickard (Chapter 12) advocates for a paradigm shift towards neurodiversity in which therapy provides an environment where growth can occur rather than curative aims. The benefits she outlines in psychological growth chime with what Gravestock (Chapter 2) writes about 'becoming and being a person' in the presence of a therapist, and Whelan's exploration of self-realisation through music therapy (Chapter 13). In contrast, Wimpory and Gwilym, in Chapter 4, write about specific changes to temporal synchrony, which they indicate can be measured by microanalysis and specific developmental changes, such as the emergence of teasing, empathy and symbolic play. Of course, at the root of this is how each therapist trained originally, and further training that may have influenced their approaches, which we will now explore further.

Approaches

When soliciting chapters for the book, it was interesting to note the wide variety of approaches used by music therapists. However, whilst this final publication showcases a number of different models, it is very much centred in a UK perspective and all of the approaches included are mainly improvisational. This way of working contrasts with some of the models presented by Aigen (2014) and Kern and Humpal (2012) as current in the USA. However, as the profession builds on pioneering work in the UK (Alvin 1978; Nordoff and Robbins 1971, 1977), therapists appear to be developing and evolving approaches and models that combine personal preference (Bates, Chapter 3) and skills and orientations of the academic programme in which they trained (Gravestock,

Chapter 2; Maclean and Tillotson, Chapter 8), and adapt to the context within which they are working (Morison, Chapter 10; Nugent, Chapter 7). This, we believe, showcases music therapy as an increasingly sophisticated profession in which music therapists draw on a wealth of experience and training, and continually strive to improve and develop the services they offer to their clients.

Examples of the scope of work described in the book include diverse approaches. There is MIT (Chapter 4), a way of working in which the therapy is delivered by a music therapist, in this text Elise Gwylim, but which utilises theory very much born of psychology, in this case the work of Dawn Wimpory. Beth Pickard (Chapter 12) examines Rogers' person-centred approach alongside Prouty's model of pre-therapy with non-verbal young people with an autistic spectrum condition, proposing a humanistic, non-normative approach. Amelia Oldfield writes, together with Laura Blauth, Johanna Finnemann and Órla Casey (Chapter 1), of employing her interactive model of music therapy within a research project, while others, such as Becky White (Chapter 5), adopt a more music-centred approach. Psychodynamic (Fawcett, Chapter 9), psychoanalytic (Gravestock, Chapter 2), psychosynthesis (Whelan, Chapter 13) and relational models (Nugent, Chapter 7) also have their place in this rich collection of work, as does the concept of deriving inspiration from art therapy in order to develop ways of working with older clients, as Alastair Robertson describes in Chapter 6. Whilst many authors consider the role of intersubjectivity, and in particular Daniel Stern's writing about the ways in which non-verbal therapies can work more directly with what is implicit in relationships, Tina Warnock's contribution (Chapter 11) outlines how voice-work in particular can support this.

It seems clear, then, when taking an overview of the approaches used by music therapists in this book, that what shines through is the importance of theory explaining practice rather than theory dictating it. This pragmatic approach, which prioritises service to clients over fidelity to agendas dictated by abstract conceptual systems, is one that appears to have allowed the work to develop somewhat organically. Music therapy practice, then, has responded to need. The music therapists in this book appear to be committed to working in a way that is deeply rooted in the belief of music therapy as a service profession. Considering each individual person with an autistic spectrum condition at the centre of our practice draws us into considering cultural aspects in more depth and how they might wish to be seen or conceptualise themselves in our society.

Considering cultural and social contexts

As Warwick states in the prelude, the 'amount published by people with the condition...has been far more valuable than any research paper'. Whilst no service users have authored chapters in this book, case studies throughout have served to highlight the ways in which clinicians feel that they offer individually tailored approaches, and many different voices have come through the case studies: Donald's use of books, fleeting moments of connection and desire to work on the periphery of a group (Robertson, Chapter 6); the parts which belonged to John's 'devoted Fan', 'Rock-Star' and 'musical improviser' and how they could be experienced and brought together in music therapy (Whelan, Chapter 13); and Carly's cries, and how, through relationship, these transformed to more flexible coos and laughter (Warnock, Chapter 11). These voices in turn informed each therapist, and many were challenged to re-think their practice and to seek further training to help them to explore further with their clients what might be useful about music therapy. In turn, editing this book, and, we hope, reading it, enables all of us to reframe our own clinical lenses and think about how the people, contexts and environments with which we work continue to inform and shape our thinking.

Warwick, in her opening prelude, eloquently writes about the children and young people she worked with over many years within a school context and what each music therapy relationship taught her about 'being with' and making connections within a secure environment. She reflects on the changing context for the profession of music therapy, in which she observes a reduction in the need to be so prescriptive alongside the development of a stronger identity. What is clear from her writing is how each individual child informed her practice. What is also clear is her alignment with the traditional model of allied health care, which adheres to a medical model when she writes: 'if our clients are to survive in the neurotypical world, they need support through what means are available to them in learning how to cope' (see p.30).

Many of the chapters in this book echo this premise in describing a range of approaches to and accounts of therapeutic work that offers psychological development or change for the individual. However, as mentioned earlier in this summary, Pickard (Chapter 12) turns the normative model on its head, considering instead a social model interpretation and demonstrating how practitioners can move towards valuing neurodiversity. She asks if perhaps attitudes and services also need to grow and change in order to 'create opportunities for meaningful engagement and participation in society' (see p.321). Strong arguments could be made for both and it is clear here that the many different contexts in which therapists are working play a part in shaping the work. Current strategic thinking in the UK, however, certainly reflects a similar shift as professionals are being encouraged to use increasingly universal interventions focusing on integrated support and self-management as well as the more traditional clinical or specialist approaches (Scottish Government 2017). What might this look like for music therapists?

Whilst the profession could be considered to be in a mature stage of development, it is only recently that guidelines for specific approaches with specific clinical populations have been created. Geretsegger *et al.* (2015) looked at common characteristics to develop the first international guidelines for improvisational music therapy for children with autistic spectrum conditions. They outline the essential principles to be 'facilitating musical and emotional attunement, musically scaffolding the flow of interaction, and tapping into the shared history of musical interaction between child and therapist', many of which have been brought to life in the case studies in this book. White's chapter (Chapter 5) in particular discusses the musical techniques of grounding, matching and single-line improvisations, which could be seen to scaffold the flow of interaction between the adolescents she works with to explore 'togetherness' and develop self-identity. In the current political climate in the UK, where formal systems, such as the evidence base and diagnosis, may be closely linked to commissioning processes and funding outcomes (Oldfield *et al.* Chapter 1; Gravestock, Chapter 2), guidelines such as these may fulfil an important role of bringing together key features of the growing profession of music therapy. In turn, these could be used to develop research protocols and promote further recognition of the profession in public health documents such as the National Institute for Health and Care Excellence (2014) and Scottish Intercollegiate Guidelines Network (2016) guidelines. However, they are not able to consider individuals and groups in context as each contribution to this book has done. Guidelines may form a basic structure for practice but do not consider the learning that each individual presents to the therapist who is ready to listen, motivate and support. With political shift to focus on the voice of the service-user perhaps now is the time for books such as this to bring our awareness and focused listening to different cultures and identities through music therapy to the forefront.

Final thoughts

This book captures a period of the music therapy profession in the UK working with people with autistic spectrum conditions across the lifespan. Contributions explore the therapeutic journeys shared between clinicians and service users in everyday practice. Together these provide a rich resource, which demonstrates how the profession continues to grow within changing contexts across health, education and social care.

During the editing process the question continued to arise about the relationship between describing therapeutic processes, evaluating theoretical underpinnings, and demonstrating an up-to-date awareness of what is considered evidence by whom. The range of skills required by professionals to respond to this balancing act should continue to be an area of debate amongst service users, practitioners, educators and regulators. In a recent event for Allied Health Professionals working with children and young people in Scotland, Smith and Walker (2018) suggested that the five main skills required by professionals to achieve meaningful outcomes for children and young people are 'motivation, listening, support, expertise and outcomes'. It is our opinion that balancing these different skills in this context requires collaboration and learning amongst people with autistic spectrum conditions and their families, music therapists, teachers, clinicians, lecturers, policy makers and researchers. We hope that this book offers a window into some of these collaborations and identifies some of the contexts and cultures within which music therapists currently practise. Most of all we hope that it makes you, the reader, consider and re-evaluate your own perspective on music therapy practice with people with autistic spectrum conditions across the lifespan.

References

Aigen, K. (2014) *The Study of Music Therapy: Current Issues and Concepts*. New York, NY, and Abingdon: Routledge

Alvin, J. (1978) *Music Therapy for the Autistic Child*. Oxford: Oxford University Press.

Crawford, M.J., Gold, C., Odell-Miller, H., Thana, L., Faber, S. and Assmus, J. (2017) 'International multicentre randomised controlled trial of improvisational music therapy for children with autism spectrum disorder: Time-A study.' *Health Technology Assessment 21*, 59, 1–40.

Geretsegger, M., Holck, U. and Gold, C. (2012) 'Randomised controlled trial of music therapy's effectiveness for children with autism spectrum disorders (TIME-A): Study protocol.' *BMC Pediatrics 12*, 2 doi:10.1186/1471-2431-12-2.

Geretsegger, M., Elefant, C., Mössler, K.A. and Gold, C. (2014) 'Music therapy for people with autism spectrum disorder.' *Cochrane Database of Systematic Reviews 6*, CD004381. DOI: 10.1002/14651858.CD004381.pub3.

Geretsegger, M., Holck, U., Carpente, J.A., Elefant, C., Kim, J. and Gold, C. (2015) 'Common characteristics of improvisational approaches in music therapy for children with autism spectrum disorder: Developing treatment guidelines.' *Journal of Music Therapy 52*, 2, 258–81.

HCPC (2013) *Standards of Proficiency for Arts Therapists*. London: HCPC. Accessed on 30 March 2018 at www.hpc-uk.org/publications/standards/index.asp?id=39.

Kenny, C. (2006) *Music and Life in the Field of Play: An Anthology*. Gilsum, NH: Barcelona Publishers.

Kern, P. and Humpal, M. (eds) (2012) *Early Childhood Music Therapy and Autism Spectrum Disorders: Developing Potential in Young Children and Their Families*. London: Jessica Kingsley Publishers.

Kim, J., Wigram, T. and Gold, C. (2009). 'Emotional, motivational and interpersonal responsiveness of children with autism in improvisational music therapy.' *Autism 13*, 4, 389–409.

McTier, I. (2012) 'Music Therapy in a Special School for Children with Autistic Spectrum Disorder, Focusing Particularly on the Use of the Double Bass.' In J. Tomlinson, P. Derrington and A. Oldfield (eds) *Music Therapy in Schools: Working with Children of All Ages in Mainstream and Special Education*. London and Philadelphia: Jessica Kingsley Publishers.

Molyneux, C., Koo, Na-H., Piggot-Irvine, E., Talmage, A., Travaglia, R. and Willis, M. (2012) 'Drawing it together: Collaborative research on goal-setting and review in a music therapy centre.' *New Zealand Journal of Music Therapy 10*, 6–38.

National Institute for Health and Care Excellence (2014) *Autism. Quality Standard* [QS51] Accessed on 30 June 2018 at www.nice.org.uk/guidance/qs51.

Nordoff, P. and Robbins, C. (1971) *Therapy in Music for Handicapped Children*. London: Victor Gollancz.

Nordoff, P. and Robbins, C. (1977) *Creative Music Therapy*. New York, NY: John Day.

Oldfield, A., (2006a) *Interactive Music Therapy – A Positive Approach: Music Therapy at a Child Development Centre*. London: Jessica Kingsley Publishers.

Oldfield, A., (2006b) *Interactive Music Therapy in Child and Family Psychiatry. Clinical Practice, Research and Teaching*. London: Jessica Kingsley Publishers.

Rickson, D.J., Castelino, A., Molyneux, C., Ridley, H. and Upjohn-Beatson, E. (2016) 'What evidence? Designing a mixed methods study to investigate music therapy with children who have autistic spectrum disorder (ASD) in New Zealand contexts.' *The Arts in Psychotherapy 50*, 119–125

Saville (2007) 'Music Therapy and Autistic Spectrum Disorder.' In T. Watson (ed.) *Music Therapy with Adults with Learning Disabilities*. Hove: Routledge.

Schumacher, K. (2014), 'Music Therapy for Pervasive Developmental Disorders, Especially Autism: A Case Study with a Theoretical Foundation and an Evaluation Tool.' In J. De Backer and J. Sutton (eds) *The Music in Music Therapy. Psychodynamic Music Therapy in Europe: Clinical, Theoretical and Research Approaches*. London and Philadelphia: Jessica Kingsley Publishers.

Scottish Government (2017) *Allied Health Professions Co-creating Wellbeing with the People of Scotland: The Active and Independent Living Programme in Scotland*. Edinburgh: The Scottish Government.

Scottish Intercollegiate Guidelines Network (2016) *SIGN 145. Assessment, Diagnosis and Interventions for Autism Spectrum Disorders: A National Clinical Guideline*. Edinburgh: Healthcare Improvement Scotland. Accessed on 30 June 2018 at http://sign.ac.uk/assets/sign145.pdf.

Silberman, S. (2015) Neurotribes: *The Legacy of Autism and How to Think Differently about People Who Think Differently*. London: Allen & Unwin

Smith, S. and Walker, E. (2018) 'Connor goes swimming – achieving meaningful outcomes for children and young people.' Presentation at Children and Adolescents Health and Wellbeing in Action Plan and Allied Health Professionals in CYP Event, Relationships and Collaboration for CYP Outcomes. Stirling: The Scottish Government and the Active and Independent Living Programme (AILP)

Strange, J., Odell-Miller, H. and Richards, E., (2017) (eds) *Collaboration and Assistance in Music Therapy Practice*. London: Jessica Kingsley Publishers.

Trevarthen, C., Aitken, K., Papoudi, D. and Robarts, J. (1998) *Children with Autism: Diagnosis and Interventions to Meet Their Needs*. London: Jessica Kingsley Publishers.

Twyford, K. and Watson, T. (eds) (2008) *Integrated Team Working: Music Therapy as Part of Transdisciplinary and Collaborative Approaches*. London: Jessica Kingsley Publishers.

Watson, T. (2015) 'United Kingdom: Country report on professional recognition of music therapy.' *Approaches: Music Therapy and Special Music Education, Special Issue 7*, 1, 187–188.

Appendix 1: An example of integrating ideas from music therapy into classroom music making

Aims	Ideas	Suggested Activities
Sharing an instrument: The group can share an instrument with the recorded song, 'Shall we bang the drum together?' Each child puts his hands on the drum at different times. Teaching staff maintain a regular beat. Some children reflect the melody of the song.	Exploring leading and following: Choose one adult leader first to exaggerate beating on the drum with large arm movements, other teaching staff model and support following a leader. Choose a child to lead and follow exactly what they do (even if it is nothing).	Developing a joint pulse: Without the recording, allow the song to develop a pulse from following any drum beats that happen. Stopping and starting. Modelling anticipation and joint timing. Anticipation before the word 'bang' every time and exaggerated arm movements.
Play together on similar instruments: The group can play tambourines at the same time with a recorded song, 'Let's play the tambourine' (slow and fast verses).	Variation: Stand-up and dance with the tambourine in the fast section to increase contrasts.	Taking turns on one shared instrument: Using only one tambourine the leader can hold this and invite each child to play one at a time. When the music is fast the leader moves quickly between the children, when it is slow, slowly with exaggerated flying motion to encourage the children to track and anticipate where it might go next.

cont.

Aims	Ideas	Suggested Activities
Playing with a sound track: Each child can choose a big or little shaker using the PECS. The group can play big or little shakers with recorded music.	Recorded excerpts, start and stop. CD of favourite music from home.	Play-along with chosen instrument. Increase choice – introduce new instruments made in class (string, wind, percussion).
Movement in music: Each child can choose a movement using the picture board for the song Blues in Action. Copying an adult or a peer. Leading new movements.	Moving together – leading and following. Stamping feet, clapping hands – exaggerate movements for children to copy. Copy movements initiated by the children subconsciously – increasing awareness.	Music therapist to record a version of the song without words to increase variations of movements to be used.
Singing together: Some of the children can hum familiar melodies which are simple, repetitive and catchy usually after the song has finished. The children can locate their own prop or photo from an appropriate number of choices. The children can locate peers passing an instrument or prop at the end of a song. The children can follow instructions in a song, such as putting an elephant prop underneath their chairs on at a time when each turn is finished.	Themed songs: Pause occasionally and encourage children to use words or vocal sounds in gaps, hum the melody or make a movement to continue. Continue the song as soon as a sound or movement is made. Use counting songs or songs based on classroom topics/themes.	The music therapist can compose songs related to classroom topics on request in a simple and repetitive style to encourage participation.

Having a conversation in music: Give one instrument to a child and one to an adult. Using intensive interaction principles the adult should follow the child's lead; imitating and reflecting what the child is playing. Number of sounds (2/3, is it the same?). Volume of sound (loud/quiet). Type of sound (hitting/scraping).	Variations: Copy and exaggerate movements or vocalisations.	
Emotions: To recognise 'sad' and 'happy' supported in a song. Take turns.	'Happy' and 'sad' song. Anticipation of the word 'sad' or 'happy' according to the music and symbols used.	'Sad and happy' with symbols?

Contributors to the Book

Robin Bates, *Music Therapist and Supervisor, Cornwall Music Therapy Trust*

Robin qualified in 2004 at the Royal Welsh College of Music and Drama, completed a two-year course in psychodynamic and psychoanalytic supervision in Bristol in 2017 and led a team of 12 music therapists until 2018 when he decided to pinch back more time for thinking, writing and composition. He works mainly with children and teenagers with autistic spectrum conditions. Born in Birmingham, he has lived on the Lizard Peninsula, Cornwall, since 1978.

Laura Blauth, *Freelance Music Therapist*

Laura Blauth has worked as a music therapist with children and their families in various settings, including mainstream and special schools, and a child development centre. She is currently doing a PhD at Anglia Ruskin University, Cambridge, looking into the effects of music therapy and parent counselling on resilience in young children with autism.

Órla Casey, *Head of Music Therapy at Cambridgeshire Music, Cambridgeshire County Council*

Órla has worked with a range of clients across the lifespan in a range of settings including clinics, throughout Cambridgeshire and Peterborough. She has a keen interest in the use of music therapy with autism, including children experiencing family breakdown and attachment difficulties. She has presented and lectured widely. She has also contributed to the national discussion on evidence-based policies for the profession.

Elizabeth Coombes, *Course Leader, University of South Wales MA Music Therapy and Freelance Music Therapist and Supervisor*

Elizabeth qualified in music therapy in 2000 from the Royal Welsh College of Music and Drama and is psychodynamically orientated in her practice. During her career she has worked with a wide range of client groups including children and young people in education and psychiatric inpatient care. She has an ongoing involvement with therapeutic music skill-sharing in a variety of settings at home and abroad. She is a fully qualified GIM practitioner. She has published and presented widely.

Henry Dunn, *Music Psychotherapist, Arts Therapies Service, Devon Partnership NHS Trust*

Henry Dunn qualified from University of Surrey, Roehampton, in 2002. Since then he has spent 16 years working for Devon Partnership NHS Trust in their Arts Therapies Service, addressing the needs of adults accessing this department. He has also worked in special education with children on the autistic spectrum, the visually impaired, those who have suffered trauma, and those with profound and multiple learning disabilities. He set up, and continues to coordinate, the Autistic Spectrum Conditions network for the British Association for Music Therapy.

Kate Fawcett, *Freelance Music Therapist and Musician*

Kate Fawcett read English and French at Oxford University, before undertaking postgraduate study in performance at Birmingham Conservatoire and, later, Music Therapy at the University of the West of England. Her portfolio career currently combines music therapy with children with autistic spectrum conditions and older adults, performance as a period-instrument specialist on violin and viola, and teaching in a variety of contexts, including at Royal Birmingham Conservatoire.

Johanna Finnemann, *Cognitive Neuroscientist*

Johanna Finnemann is a cognitive neuroscientist studying sensory processing and motor control in autism. While her research concerns more basic aspects of neurophysiology, she is a strong supporter of integrating the arts and the sciences.

Joy Gravestock, *Freelance Music Therapist*

Joy is a freelance music therapist in the East Midlands. She has an MA in Psychoanalytic Music Therapy and is a PhD candidate at Sheffield University researching relational repair from trauma effects occurring via micro-moments of attunement within an embodied musical therapeutic relationship. Her forthcoming book (also with Jessica Kingsley Publishers) explores psychoanalytic, attachment-based, relational music therapy for adoptees (with trauma experience) and their families.

Elise Gwilym, *Freelance Music Therapist*

As a music therapist Elise has been doing Musical Interaction Therapy since 2003 and has worked at Tŷ Gobaith Children's Hospice in North Wales since 2006. She was always drawn to working developmentally with children or young adults and now works in education, using the skills she learnt from MIT, and at a children's hospice working particularly with children with special needs.

Emma Maclean (née Pethybridge), *Lead Music Therapist, NHS Lothian, Lecturer in Music Therapy, Queen Margaret University, Scotland*

It was the enjoyment Emma gained in volunteering with children with autistic spectrum conditions, whilst studying Music and Hispanic Studies in Birmingham, that first sparked her interest in training to be a music therapist. Since qualifying in 2004 she has worked in a range of pre-school and educational settings with children with ASCs and has several publications in this area of practice. Emma also works in adult and older people's mental health, and teaches and supervises on the MSc in Music Therapy at Queen Margaret University, Scotland.

Cindy-Jo Morison, *Senior Music Psychotherapist, Northumberland, Tyne and Wear NHS Foundation Trust*

Cindy-Jo Morison is NMT (neurologic music therapy) and ADOS trained and supervises members of the team. She has experience of working with children, young people and adults who have intellectual and developmental disabilities and complex and challenging needs. Outside of the Trust she regularly supports Rett UK in an advisory role, attending regional days and clinics. She is also a member of the UK Working Group for Rett Disorders and is keen to promote her work within the arts therapies team and has presented at a number of UK and European conferences.

Helen Mottram, *Music Therapist*

Helen qualified as a music therapist in 2009. She has worked with children with learning disabilities and autism as well as with adopted children and adolescents. She currently works at a children's hospice, in a special care baby unit, and in an NHS inpatient setting with women with severe postnatal depression and their babies. She has been a guest lecturer on the MA Music Therapy training at Anglia Ruskin University and taught on India's first music therapy training course.

Josie Nugent, *Music Therapist for Foyle Down Syndrome Trust, Derry, Northern Ireland, and Freelance Music Therapist*

As well as being a music therapist for Foyle Down Syndrome Trust, Josie also works in a freelance capacity in the fields of autism, brain injury, dementia and cross-community music projects in Northern Ireland. She has been a guest lecturer on the MA Music Therapy Training Course, University of Limerick, and at Marino College of Education, Dublin, since 2015. She trained in music therapy at Anglia Ruskin University (2010), previously working as a post doctoral virologist (1997–2008) for the Animal Health Trust, Suffolk, UK. She has published in various peer-reviewed journals, and is a peer reviewer for selected veterinary journals.

Adam Ockelford, *Professor of Music, and Director of the Applied Music Research Centre, University of Roehampton, London*

Adam Ockelford has worked in the field of music and special needs/abilities for the last 40 years, as a composer, teacher, researcher, writer and lecturer. His work with people on the autism spectrum is internationally recognised, and he has a TED talk with his protégé, the musical savant Derek Paravicini, available at: www.ted.com/talks/derek_paravicini_and_adam_ockelford_in_the_key_of_genius

Amelia Oldfield, *Music Therapist, NHS*

Dr Amelia Oldfield has worked as a music therapist with young children with autism and their families for nearly 40 years. She has researched, written and taught extensively about this subject, and has recently made a full-length documentary film, following up families who received treatment 16 years previously.

Beth Pickard, *Senior Lecturer, University of South Wales, Wales, and Freelance Music Therapist*

Beth Pickard studied music therapy at the University of the West of England and is also a neurologic music therapist. Beth has completed an MSc in Applied Psychology of Intellectual Disabilities and a PGCert in Developing Professional Practice in Higher Education at the University of South Wales. Beth is a trustee of the Birmingham-based charity 'Melody' which promotes instrumental tuition and musical opportunities for children and young people who have learning disabilities. She is a passionate advocate of inclusive and social model practice within music therapy, music education and higher education.

Alastair Robertson, *Music Therapist in the NHS and Voluntary Sector, Scotland*

Alastair Robertson originally trained as a nurse in learning disabilities and following this worked in the voluntary sector in both day and residential care. Since training as a music therapist in 2004, he has worked in the NHS and voluntary sector with adults with a learning disability doing community music and music therapy.

Claire Tillotson, *Freelance Music Therapist*

Claire is a qualified music teacher and freelance music therapist specialising in autism. Until 2001 Claire worked as a music teacher in a secondary school. She then studied music therapy at the Nordoff Robbins Music Therapy Centre in London and gained a PGDip. Subsequently she gained her MA at the University of the West of England and is now a freelance music therapist working primarily with children and young adults with autism in and around the London Borough of Bromley.

Tina Warnock, *Freelance Music Therapist, Director for Belltree Music Therapy CIC and Vocal Psychotherapy UK*

Tina Warnock has been practicing as a music therapist since 2000 following a Social Psychology degree and several years performing as a singer/songwriter. Her experience includes seven years in the NHS for a Child and Adolescent Mental Health Service and a Child Development Centre, and 15 years at a special school, alongside running Belltree Music Therapy CIC which she set up in 2009. She is a registered supervisor and visiting lecturer on the MA Music Therapy course at Roehampton University.

Auriel Warwick, *Retired Music Therapist*

Auriel has been a music therapist since the 1970s and co-authored *Music Therapy and the Autistic Child* in 1978 with Juliette Alvin, one of the pioneers of music therapy.

Peter Whelan, *Senior Music Therapist, Whitefield Schools*

Peter has worked as a music therapist for over 20 years in special education with a range of special educational needs and Disabilities including autism. He recently retrained as a Psychosynthesis Psychotherapist working verbally with people who have experienced trauma, abuse and dissociation.

Becky White, *Associate Lecturer, University of the West of England, and Freelance Music Therapist*

Having gained a music degree at the University of Wales, Cardiff, Becky obtained her music therapy qualification at the Guildhall, London. She is currently an associate lecturer at the University of the West of England and the University of South Wales, teaching on their MA Music Therapy courses. She also has a music therapy practice in schools. Becky is currently working towards a PhD, researching flow experiences connected to the learning of improvised music.

Dawn Wimpory, *Consultant Clinical Psychologist – Lead for ASD (NHS) and Lecturer (Bangor University, joint appointment)*

Dawn's career in autism began as a nanny to a four-year-old with an autistic spectrum condition, an experience which has always had a strong influence on her professional role. Following training in Child Clinical Psychology, she has held a joint clinical and research post for three decades. Her interest focuses on preverbal interaction as the context for developing symbolic functioning; how children with autistic spectrum conditions may be helped by what we can learn from typically developing children, particularly in relation to social timing-related developments such as teasing, pretence and empathy.

Subject Index

adolescent music groups
  and autism 138–40
  bass guitar in 146–7
  Becky White's experience
    of 137–8
  case studies 142–6
  grounding in 148–9
  group work in 140–1
  matching 150–1
  melodic improvisation in 149–50
  setting for 151–2
Alvin, Juliette 19
Assessment of the Quality of
  Relationship (AQR) 210, 212
Attention Autism activity 188
autism
  in adolescents 138–40
  and arts therapies 156
  confusion about 173
  music therapy with 40–1, 198
  relational music therapy in 71–2
  social timing-based
    model of 97–8
Autism Diagnostic Observation
  Schedule (ADOS)
  in Musical Interaction
    Therapy 122
  in TIME-A project s36, 37–8,
    42, 43, 46, 49, 50–2

Blauth, Laura 38, 44–50
British Association for Music
  Therapy (BAMT) 356

case studies
  adolescent music groups 142–6
  Community Music Therapy
    model 158–67
  family-based music
    therapy 185–92
  Musical Interaction
    Therapy 122–5
  person-centred approach
    306–8, 310, 312–14
  relational music therapy
    60–1, 63
  school collaboration 201–5,
    207–12, 215–17, 219–22
  Self-realisation 343–7
  in TIME-A project 44–54
  transitional day centres 236–46
  voice 285–8, 290–3
  Warwick Auriel's work 26–7
Casey, Órla 36–7, 38
Chinnor Autistic Units 18–19
Coates, Stella 18–19
Cognitive Analytical Music
  Therapy (CAMT) 256
Community Music Therapy model
  barriers to 157–8
  case studies 158–67
  move towards 156–7
  shifting boundaries in 167–8
  supervision in 171
  and support workers 169–70
contact reflections 305–7, 308–11
Creative Arts Therapies Rating
  Scale (CAT-SRS) 264

Detection of Autism by Infant
    Sociability Interview
    (DAISI) 122
Dialectical Behavioural
    Skills (DBT) 255
Dyadic Communication Measure
    for Autism (DCMA) 126

Education Act (Handicapped
    Children) (1970) 16
encouragement
    countertransference in 90–3
    ethical basis for 77–8, 81–5
    graduated approach to 85–8
    incident described 78–81
    perfect fifth for 88–90
Episodes of Social Engagement
    (ESE) 127
ethics
    of encouragement 77–8, 81–5
    Ethical Thinking in Music
        Therapy (Dileo) 78
evaluations
    of Musical Interaction
        Therapy 126–8
    in school collaborations
        205–7, 210, 212–15
    of social engagement 264–8
    of TIME-A project of 37,
        42–3, 46–7, 49–54

family-based music therapy
    Auriel Warwick on 22–3
    case studies 185–92
    development of 179–80
    in home setting 180–4
Finnemann, Johanna 38

grounding 148–9
Gwilym, Elise
    on Musical Interaction
        Therapy 112–23

Health and Care Professions
    Council (HCPC) 356–7

Improvised Song approach 306
Interactive Music Therapy 179

language development
    role of music in 66–7
    and social timing-based
        model of 98–102

matching 150–1
Mental Health Ethics – The
    Human Context (Barker) 78
Microanalysis of Interaction
    of Music Therapy
    (MIMT) 212, 213, 214
Mueller, Pierrette 22, 23
Music for Relaxation (Chapman,
    Miles & Rhodes) 260
music therapy
    benefits across lifespan 360–6
    for children with autism
        40–1, 198
    cultural and social
        contexts for 368–70
    different approaches to 366–8
    as evidence-based
        practice 358–66
    ideas for schools 373–5
    and language development 66–7
    literature review 332–6
    music as defence against
        intimacy 67–9

and Musical Interaction
  Therapy 112–14
and psychosynthesis 340–3
and social engagement 251–68
in the UK 356–8
Musical Interaction Therapy (MIT)
  adult participation in 120–2
  approach of 106–7
  case studies 122–5
  Elise Gwilym on 112–23
  evaluations of 126–8
  instruments in 120–1
  leading in 118–19
  negotiating timing in 116–17
  and Nordoff-Robbins
    approach 112–13
  pacing in 117–18
  pausing in 117–18
  phases of social timing 114
  relation to music therapy 112–14
  research evidence for 126–8
  role of music in 110–11
  selective attunement 116–17
  sharing in 114–16
  strategies used in 107–10
  temporal synchrony in 119–20

Nobody Nowhere (Williams) 26
Nordoff-Robbins approach
  112–13, 155, 205–7, 215, 332

Oldfield, Amelia 36–7

parents
  collaboration with in
    schools 221–3
  and mother/child/therapist
    interaction 22–3 see also
    family-based music therapy

person-centred approach
  case studies 306–8, 310, 312–14
  client incongruence in 316–17
  and cognitive ability 317–18
  contact reflections in
    305–7, 308–11
  critiques of 318–20
  developing autonomy in 311–13
  outcomes of 313–14
  and music therapy 297–8
  pre-therapy 301–3, 304–5
  and social model of disability
    300–1, 314–16, 319–20
  work with clients 298–300
Principles of Biomedical Ethics
  (Beauchamp & Childress) 78
Pre-School Autism Communication
  Trial (PACT) 126, 130
Principles of Health Care
  Ethics (Gillon) 78
psychosynthesis
  description of 336–40
  and music therapy 340–3

relational music therapy
  approach to 58–9, 64–6, 72–3
  autistic experience in 71–2
  being and presence in 69
  case studies 60–1, 63
  children in study 59–60
  holding facility of music 70–1
  musical connections in 73–4
  psychoanalytic thinking in 70
  referral and consultation
    processes 63–4
  sense-making in 58–9
  settings for 61–2
  theoretical framework for 63
Richer, John 19, 27
Richer, Sheila 19

schools
case studies 201–5, 207–12,
215–17, 219–22
collaborative approaches
with 199–201, 216–23
collaboration with
therapists 197–8, 218
evaluation of 205–7, 210, 212–15
music therapy ideas for 373–5
Nordoff-Robbins
approach in 205–7
parental collaborations 221–2
Self-realisation
case studies 343–7
and musical improvisation
348–50
and psychosynthesis 336–43
in therapy work 331–2
Situation Songs approach 305, 306
social engagement
evaluation of 264–8
role of music therapy in 251–68
social model of disability
300–1, 314–16, 319–20
Social Responsiveness Scale (SRS)
in TIME-A project 37–8, 42,
43, 46, 49, 51, 52–3
social timing-based model
and autistic deficits 97–8
gesture and speech
difficulties 104–5
preverbal interactions
98–100, 101–2, 105–6
social timing difficulties 102–4
symbolic functioning
stage 100–1
temporal synchrony in 101–2
Sounds of Intent Framework
214, 215
Standards of Conduct, Performance
and Ethics (HCPC) 77

Supervision in the Helping
Professions (Hawkins
& Shohet) 171

TIME-A project
background to 36–7
Cambridgeshire site in 37–40, 41
case studies in 44–54
description of 35–6, 37
evaluation of 37, 42–3,
46–7, 49–54
improvisation in 41
reflections on 50–4
transitional day centres
case studies 236–46
as place for music
therapy 229–30
pattern-making in 232–6
play in 231–2
relationships in 232–6
setting for study 228–9
therapeutic relationships
as transitional 227–8

voice
appropriate use of voice 285
autistic and non-autistic 289
and autistic self 274–82
authenticity in 283–4
calls and cries 275
case studies 285–8, 290–3
inflected voice 275–6
music therapists voice in 283–93
in music therapy 271–4
and relationships 280–2
and sense of self 278–80
singing/melodic voice 276–7
symbolic voice 277–8
vocal communication 274–5
Voice and the Self model 274, 293

Warwick, Auriel
    case studies 26–7
    evaluation of work 27–8
    growth in understanding
        and perception 21–2
    gut feeling 20–1
    on how to be with
        clients 18–19, 30
    learns dangers of assumptions
        17–18
life skills and socialisation
    teaching 28
and mother/child/therapist
    interaction 22–3
over-consciousness of
    autism 19–20
therapeutic relationship 28–30
work as music therapist 15–30

Author Index

Abery, B.H. 312
Adamson, L. 117
Ahn, E.S. 104
Aigen, K. 83, 318, 319, 359, 366
Aitken, K.J. 98, 99, 104, 156
Aldred, C. 126
Aldridge, D. 335
Allgood, N. 180
Allman, M.J. 104
Als, H. 117
Alvarez, A. 148, 163, 183,
    186, 193, 271, 279–80,
    281, 283, 285, 288, 363
Alvin, J. 141, 156, 180, 181, 182, 236,
    271, 332, 333, 335, 355, 366
American Psychiatric
    Association 104
Amir, D. 335
Ammaniti, M. 311
Amos, P. 104
Anastasiou, D. 320
Ansdell, G. 82, 85, 137, 155, 157,
    168, 171, 228, 241, 361
Apicella, F. 102
Apter-Dano, G. 240
Assagoili, R. 331, 332, 336,
    337, 338, 339, 342
Atkins, S. 69
Alvin, J. 40
Austin, D. 271, 272, 274, 276, 277,
    282, 284, 285, 289, 293, 365

Barker, P. 78
Barnes, C. 297, 300, 302, 365

Baron-Cohen, S. 128, 334
Barrington, A. 215–16
Bates, E. 101
Beail, N. 317
Beauchamp, T.L. 78
Bebko, J.M. 104
Berger, D.S. 113, 121, 148, 274,
    275, 276, 277, 281, 283, 309
Bergmann, T. 184
Berlin, I. 82–3
Bieleninik, L. 35, 41, 52
Bion, W.R. 87
Blastland, M. 92
Blauth, L. 40
Bogdashina, O. 335
Bohart, A.C. 314
Bolt, D. 316
Boucher, J. 104
Bourne, J. 168
Bowlby, J. 163, 167, 362
Bragge, A. 156
British Association for Music
    Therapy (BAMT) 40, 200
Brock, J. 104
Brodley, B.T. 318
Brown, B.B. 138, 143, 144, 151
Brown, M. 173
Brown, S. 87, 334
Brownlow, C. 84
Bruner, J.S. 106, 107, 109
Bruscia, K. 91, 311, 313
Bryan, A. 141
Buckroyd, J. 317
Bull, R. 180
Bunce, L. 333

Bunt, L. 91–2, 332, 335
Burack, J.A. 105

Caldwell, L. 183
Callery, P. 179
Calvet, C. 197, 198, 210, 211
Camaioni, L. 101
Campbell, F. 316
Camus, A. 83
Cariffe, G. 99
Carter, E.W. 140, 151
Casey, O. 39
Chadwick, P. 98
Chapman, P. 260
Chase, K.M. 335
Childress, J.F. 78
Chinna, C. 307
Christie, P. 106, 129
Clements, N. 316
Cochavit, E. 272, 276, 277
Coleman, M. 305
Coleman-Fountain, E. 320
Collins, G. 301
Collins, R. 137, 144, 145
Compton Dickinson, S.
    113, 255, 256, 364
Conn, C. 300, 312
Constantine, E. 139
Constantino, J.N. 37
Cooper, C.M. 145
Cooper, H. 297
Cooper, M. 301
Corker, M. 320
Cottis, T. 317
Courchesne, E. 104, 129
Crawford, M.J. 130
Cross, J. 138, 151

Dabrowska, A. 51
Daniel, S. 66, 103
Davies, A. 222

Davies, E. 40
Davies, G. 188
Daykin, N. 335
De Backer, J. 69
De Casper, A.J. 275
De Marchena, A. 105
Deek, H. 179
DeNora, T. 241–2
Department of Health 300
Derrington, P. 40, 141
DesNoyers Hurley, A. 168
Di Cesare, G. 276
Dileo, C. 78
Dimitriades, T. 235, 299

East Lothian Council 217
Eberhart, H. 69
Edgerton, C.L. 332
Edwards, J. 307
Eidelman, A.I. 106
Eigsti, I. 105
Elefant, C. 198
Entwhistle, V.A. 315
Estes, A. 51
Evans, J. 339, 342

Fannon, D. 307
Fein, D. 104, 129
Feldman, R. 100, 101, 102, 104, 106
Feldstein, S. 99, 105
Fenner, P. 156
Ferrari, P. 311
Ferruchi, P. 340, 342
Fiamenghi, G.A. 99
Fifer, W.P. 275
Finnegan, R. 139
Firman, J. 332, 340, 342
Fitzpatrick, P. 104
Fletcher, K.L. 138, 151
Flitton, B. 317
Flower, C. 179, 180, 192, 193

Foley-Nicpon, M. 318
Franck, L.S. 179
Franke, C. 306
Friel, B. 182

Gattino, G.S. 141
Gattis, M. 101
Geretsegger, M. 35, 41, 141, 198,
    230, 332, 356, 358, 360, 365, 369
Gernsbacher, M.A. 308, 311, 321
Gila, A. 332, 340, 342
Gillberg, C. 305
Gillon, R. 78
Gold, C. 141, 181, 198, 231,
    232, 300, 334, 344, 358
Gold, K. 35, 67, 71
Gomez, L. 86
Goodley, D. 297, 300, 301,
    303, 304, 315, 321
Gordon, P. 59
Gould, J. 334
Graby, S. 315
Grandin, T. 186
Grant, B. 303, 314
Grassi, L. 188–9
Gratier, M. 240
Greeff, A.P. 51
Green, J. 126, 130
Green, L. 139, 144
Greenbaum, C.W. 102
Griffiths, C. 319
Grimmet, K. 300
Grocke, D. 110
Gross, R. 297, 316, 321
Grossberg, S. 104
Gruber, C.P. 37

Hackett, S. 168, 264
Hadley, S. 316
Hakvoort, L. 255, 256

Hall, J. 40
Hamilton, J.T. 81
Hannaford, C. 274, 275, 281
Hargreaves, D.J. 139
Harrist, A.W. 105
Hart, R.R. 264
Hawkins, J. 317
Hawkins, P. 171
Health and Care Professions
    Council (HCPC) 77, 78, 357
Heaton, P. 104, 111
Heerey, E. 128
Hedenbro, M. 105
Hehir, T. 315
Hendricks, D.R. 298
Henninger, N.A. 300
Hesling, I. 105
Hewett, D. 107, 202, 253, 308
Heyman, B. 319
Highfield, M. 335
Hobson, R.P. 101, 104, 129, 312
Hodge, N. 304, 319
Hoemberg, V. 297
Hoika, E. 101
Holck, U. 35, 109, 305, 358
Holmes, J. 83, 272
Honisch, S. 321
Hoskyns, S. 91–2
Howlin, P. 299
Hughes, R. 316
Hume, K. 298
Humpal, M. 356, 366
Hurley, A.D. 317

Isenberg-Grezda, C. 216
Ives, C. 15

Jacobsen, S.L. 179, 182
Jaffe, J. 100, 102, 106
Jao Keehn, R.J. 186

Jasmow, M. 99
Johnson, C. 319
Joyce, A. 183

Kaenampornpan, P. 179
Kalsched, D. 337, 339, 340, 345
Kalyva, E. 297, 303, 319
Kapp, S.K. 300, 301, 315, 321
Karkou, V. 200, 214
Kauffman, J.M. 320
Keen, S. 338, 342
Keenan, M. 297, 318
Kenny, L. 228, 230, 231,
    232, 247, 315, 364
Kern, P. 356, 366
Khanna, R. 51
Kim, J. 141, 231, 300, 316,
    334, 335, 344
King, R. 317
Kinney, D. 138
Kiresuk, T. 264
Kirkham, P. 309, 314, 315,
    316, 318, 319
Klein, M. 86
Klin, A. 104
Koch-Temming, H. 305
Koenig, K. 317
Koffmann, J. 184
Kokkinaki, T. 99
Kolar-Borsky, A. 109, 305, 306
Kreiman, J. 281
Krietemeyer, B. 305
Kristiansen, K. 320
Kubiak, M. 305, 309
Kubicek, L.F. 102
Kuchuck, S. 73
Kuhl, P.K. 104

Lagasse, A.B. 316
Lane, A. 274

Lawday, R. 255
Lawes, M. 69, 204
Lawson, W. 274, 277, 279,
    281, 285, 334
Lee, C. 137
Lee, S. 318
Levinas, E. 69
Levine, M. 317
Levinge, A. 182, 191, 193, 299
Levitt, B. 297, 300, 304,
    308, 311, 320, 365
Lindley, R. 83
Logotheti, K. 101
Loombe, D. 147, 180
Lord, C. 37, 122

MacDonald, R.A.R. 139, 150, 151
Magee, W. 298
Mallarmé, S. 85
Mallett, R. 319, 320
Malloch, S. 99, 112, 137,
    237, 306, 362, 364
Marks-Tarlow, T. 57, 72
Marom, M. 335
Marsh, K. 104
Martin, M. 316
Marwick, H. 280, 281
Masterson, J. 336, 345
Mayer-Johnson 253
McCaffrey, T. 307
McClean, S. 335
McFerran, K. 181, 192
McLaughlin, J. 320
McTier, I. 40, 141, 146, 356
Mearns, D. 301
Meekosha, H. 320
Melham, P. 316
Meltzer, D. 156
Mental Health Foundation 173
Merry, D. 302, 312

Middleton, R. 232
Miell, D. 139
Miles, A. 260
Miller, J. 228
Milton, D. 316
Mitchell, E. 181, 182, 189, 193
Molyneux, C. 359
Monson, I. 145
Moon, K.A. 301, 303, 311, 321
Morris, A.S. 139
Morton, I. 305
Mory, M.S. 138
Moses, P.J. 282
Moshe, M. 100
Mottron, L. 104
Müller, P. 180, 181, 182, 192
Munro, H. 200
Muratori, f. 102
Murray, L. 100, 102, 280, 281
Music, G. 184

Nadel, J. 100, 102
Nall, K. 39
Nash, S. 97, 98, 104, 106, 126, 129
National Autistic Society 140, 254
National Institute for Health
    and Care Excellence 370
Newson, E. 97, 98, 100,
    104, 110, 129
Newson, J. 98, 100
Nicholas, B. 97, 98, 104, 129
Nicholls, T. 141
Nind, M. 107, 130, 202, 253, 308
Ninio, A. 101
Nordoff, P. 40, 83, 98, 112, 113, 119,
    141, 156, 187, 197, 205, 206,
    212, 333, 338, 355, 363, 366
Norton, K. 275
Nugent, N. 179

Ockelford, A. 214, 215, 218
Odell-Miller, H. 141, 359
Odom, S.L. 318
Ogden, T. 72, 166
O'Kelly, L. 184
Oldfield, A. 40, 41, 53, 120, 147, 179,
    192, 197, 214, 221, 236, 255, 256,
    277, 306, 333, 356, 360, 363, 364
Oliver, M. 297, 300, 302, 315,
    316, 319, 320, 365
Owens, J. 319, 320

Palmer, S.B. 312
Panek, R. 186
Papoudi, D. 156
Papousek, H. 307
Papousek, M. 307
Parkhouse, K. 219
Pasiali, V. 297
Pavlicevic, M. 98, 112, 114,
    115–16, 118, 119, 150, 155,
    228, 231, 235, 238, 271, 275,
    276, 277, 280, 291, 364
Peggie, I. 218
Peppe, S. 105
Peters, H. 300, 305
Pethybridge, E. 204, 206,
    214, 217, 218
Piccinnini, J. 146, 149
Pickles, A. 126
Pietrzak, S. 305
Pisula, E. 51
Pizziolo, P. 146
Plahl, C. 305
Plancantonakis, D.G. 104
Pörtner, M. 300, 305
Preston, J. 146
Prevezer, W. 106, 107, 110, 111
Priestley, M. 58, 63, 91,
    334, 335, 338, 344
Prior, M.R. 104

Prouty, G. 297, 300, 302, 304,
    305, 306, 307, 308, 309, 310,
    311, 315, 317, 321, 365
Pyramid Educational
    Consultants 140

Raffensperger, M.K. 317
Rapley, M. 298
Raskin, N.J. 297, 303, 365
Reddy, V. 101, 106
Reeve, D. 319
Reid, S. 163, 281
Rhodes, S. 260
Richards, E. 190, 222, 359
Richards, H. 141
Richdale, A.L. 104
Rickson, D.J. 358
Ritter, S. 198
Robarts, J.Z. 156, 184, 193, 333, 355
Robbins, C. 40, 83, 98, 112, 113,
    119, 141, 156, 187, 197, 205, 206,
    212, 333, 338, 355, 363, 366
Robertson, J. 215
Rogers, C. 197, 297, 300, 301, 302,
    303, 304, 308, 309, 313, 314, 315,
    316, 317, 318, 320, 363, 365
Rogers, N. 316
Rollins, W.L. 335
Ross Williams, R. 164
Rosscornes, C. 40
Roth, I. 305, 309
Rozga, A. 103
Ruich, I.J. 300
Runswick-Cole, K. 319, 320

Saleeba, A. 179
Sampson, F. 241, 245
Sandall, S. 200
Sanders, P. 304, 318
Saville 356
Scholtz, J. 212

Schore, A.N. 307
Schumacher, K. 197, 198,
    210, 211, 279, 356
Schuttleworth, J. 187
Scottish Government 199,
    200, 223, 369
Scottish Intercollegiate
    Guidelines 370
Segawa, M. 104
Seidman, D. 104
Sherman, R. 264
Shiloh, C.J. 316
Shohet, R. 171
Shuttleworth, R. 320
Sidtis, D. 281
Sieff, D. 337, 339, 340, 345
Siegel, D. 72
Sigman, M. 128
Silberman, S. 298, 301, 314, 356
Siller, M. 128
Sills, F. 59
Sinason, V. 157, 170, 283
Sinclair, J. 321
Sletvold, J. 66
Sloboda, A. 332
Small, C. 343
Smeijsters, H. 235, 238, 299
Smith, D. 140
Smith, S. 370
Snow, C.E. 101
Sommerbeck, L. 302, 305
Spensley, S. 183, 363
Sroufe, L.A. 210
Statewide Behaviour
    Intervention Service 254
Steinberg, L. 139
Stern, D. 57, 64–5, 66, 69, 90, 100,
    112, 116, 119, 197, 198, 210, 211,
    222, 271, 272, 274, 275, 276, 277,
    278, 279, 281, 283, 284, 285, 286,
    287, 289, 291, 292, 306, 311,
    332, 335, 361, 363, 364, 365

Stiller, K. 316
Stone, B. 58
Stone, F. 311
Strange, J. 141, 359
Straus, J. 297, 303, 321
Sturmey, P. 317
Suvini, F. 102
Swain, J. 319
Szelag, F. 104

Tarrant, M. 139
Taylor, J.L. 299, 300
Test, D.W. 140
Thaut, M. 297
Thomas, C. 300, 320
Thompson, G. 179, 181, 192
Thoreau, H. 15
Thorne, B. 301, 304, 318
Tillotson, C. 215
Timini, S. 319
Tjus, T. 1–3
Todres, L. 67, 71, 74
Tomlinson, J. 39, 40, 147
Tordjman, S. 104
Totton, N. 63, 72
Transtadóttir, R. 320
Trevarthen, C. 66, 98, 99, 100, 101,
    102, 103, 104, 112, 137, 156, 237,
    271, 274, 277, 278, 279, 281, 285,
    287, 306, 332, 335, 355, 362
Trondalen, G. 58, 63, 64, 65
Tronick, E. 117
Tsiris, G. 335
Turry, A. 306
Tustin, F. 146, 148, 156, 157, 161,
    183, 193, 198, 299, 362, 363
Twyford, K. 199, 200, 216, 219, 359

UK Government 199
UNC School of Medicine 140
Urwin, C. 106, 128, 158, 168, 170

Vaac, N. 199
Vaiouli, P. 300, 305
Van der Kolk, B. 63
Van der Walt, K. 51
Van Werde, D. 305
Verney, R. 247, 248
Voigt, M. 212
Volkmar, F.R. 317
Volterra, V. 101

Wadsworth, J. 264
Walker, T. 370
Walsh-Stewart, R. 141
Warnock, T. 271, 272, 274, 277,
    283, 284, 285, 286, 289
Warren, P. 179
Warwick, A. 40, 140, 141, 156, 180,
    181, 182, 192, 215, 271, 332, 333
Watson, T. 198, 200, 216, 357, 359
Watt, I.S. 315
Wehman, P. 298
Wehmeyer, M.L. 298, 300, 312
Welkowitz, J. 99
Welsh Assembly Government 300
Welsh, J.P. 104
Welwood, J. 342
Wetherick, D. 214
Whelan, P. 340
White, B. 141, 145
Wigram, T. 63, 110, 137, 141, 146,
    147, 148, 150, 198, 231, 232, 255,
    256, 272, 276, 277, 300, 308,
    309, 311, 334, 335, 344, 364
Wilkinson, M. 58, 63
Williams, D. 26
Williams, J.Q. 316, 317
Willner, P. 317
Wilson, B. 199
Wilson, G.B. 150
Wilson, P. 157
Wilson, S. 317

Wimpory, D. 97, 98, 100, 101, 103, 104, 106, 110, 122, 126, 127, 128, 129, 130

Wing, L. 334

Winnicott, D. 66, 69, 70, 85, 92, 113, 137, 146, 149, 156, 183, 184, 188, 193, 222, 230, 279, 281, 283, 286, 291, 299, 311, 341, 361, 362, 363, 364

Wolff, P.H. 287

Woods, R. 297, 301, 302, 314, 315, 316, 319, 320, 321

Woodward, A. 333

Wosch, T. 212, 311

Yalom, I.D. 144, 362

Yirmiya, N. 102